SOURCES

Notable Selections in *Mass Media*

SECOND EDITION

About the Editors

JARICE HANSON is a professor of communication in the Department of Communication at the University of Massachusetts–Amherst. She received her Ph.D. in 1979 from Northwestern University's Department of Radio-TV-Film. She is coeditor, with Alison Alexander, of *Taking Sides: Clashing Views on Controversial Issues in Mass Media and Society* (Dushkin/McGraw-Hill), now in its fifth edition. She has published numerous articles and books, including *Connections: Technologies of Communication* (HarperCollins, 1994) and *New Communication Technologies in Developing Countries,* coauthored with Uma Narula (Lawrence Erlbaum, 1990).

DAVID J. MAXCY received his Ph.D. from the Department of Communication at the University of Massachusetts–Amherst in 1993. He is currently an audiovisual technician and lecturer at the University of Massachusetts–Amherst. His publications focus on issues of popular culture and advertising.

SOURCES

Notable Selections in
Mass Media

SECOND EDITION

Edited by

JARICE HANSON
University of Massachusetts–Amherst

DAVID J. MAXCY
University of Massachusetts–Amherst

Dushkin/McGraw-Hill

A Division of The McGraw-Hill Companies

Manufactured in the United States of America

Second Edition

123456789FGRFGR4321098

Library of Congress Cataloging-in-Publication Data
  Main entry under title:
   Sources: notable selections in mass media/edited by Jarice Hanson and David J.
   Maxcy.—2nd ed.
   Includes bibliographical references and index.
   1. Mass media. I. Hanson, Jarice, *comp.* II. Maxcy, David J., *comp.*

0-07-303182-8

302.23
95-83882

 Printed on Recycled Paper

Preface

*T*he study of mass communication has followed trends similar to those of other social science disciplines, such as sociology, psychology, and anthropology. What makes communication research different—and what makes it a distinct discipline—is that it involves the study of a unique social phenomenon: human communication as an elemental process of human social formation. In the case of mass media, this fundamental process is mediated not only by language and the dynamics of interpersonal interactions but also by the institutions and technologies that distribute messages to broad, often heterogeneous groups of people. Despite the rich variety of conceptual and methodological research perspectives, the 38 selections contained in this book do not simply represent a babble of conflicting opinions concerning the impact of mass media on society. Rather, we have selected key texts that illuminate the development of specific research questions and theoretical perspectives that have animated the field throughout its history. In each case we have chosen the selection because it represents the scope and explanatory power of its particular "brand" of media research. We do not evaluate any of these perspectives; instead, we attempt to show how they have developed internally and how they have responded to each other within the scientific field of mass media scholarship.

As we began our search for the original selections included in this text, we found that, like popular stories and mythology, the retelling of these seminal works has undergone some embellishment, some broad interpretation, and some distortion. Surprisingly, we found that many of the references later writers made to primary works were inadvertently inaccurate, drawing instead on later revisions of the original works. We hope that *Sources* will serve to remind students and teachers of the real evolution in mass media research and how history has played a role in shaping the questions, methods, and interpretations of the studies.

The relatively few women authors in the early years of mass media study is worth noting. In more recent research, we find a greater variety of perspectives discussed by both women and minorities. As a result, the field of research in media and society has broadened, and with it, the number of perspectives has grown.

We hope that these selections help focus students' attention on the growth and development of the field of research in mass media and society and that theories and methodologies will be considered more closely for the way they shape and define a research agenda.

i

Organization of the book.   In each of the 15 chapters of this book, we have attempted to trace the evolution of a research question, perspective, or theory. In some cases, later selections refer to earlier articles, but they often refine some of the original ideas by clarifying the research questions, contextualizing the earlier study, or elaborating on a concept. Chapters 1 through 4 are loosely defined as "effects" research because they deal with attempts to understand how and why people are persuaded to act in certain ways. In each of these chapters the last selection is a current example of research that follows in the footsteps of the earlier sources. Chapters 5 and 6 deal with more formal aspects of the media: in chapter 5, the medium itself is questioned as the prime focus of influence, and in chapter 6, attempts to regulate technology are questioned. Chapters 6 and 7, which are new to this edition, add a dimension to media studies that was missing in the first edition of *Sources.* Chapter 8 examines issues of power and ideology that influence media content, and chapter 9 explores topics that subtly influence the way we look at culture through media artifacts. Chapter 10 takes the perspective that media and culture change as the result of a cultural *process.* Chapter 11 presents viewpoints on criticizing culture. Chapters 12 and 13 explore the images presented to us by media but develop different parameters by which to judge the media. Chapters 14 and 15 look at the internationalization (or globalization) of media and media industries and examine many of the issues that are relevant for international and intercultural study. Each selection is preceded by a short introductory headnote that establishes the relevance of the selection and provides biographical information on the author.

Suggestions for reading the selections.   Students are encouraged to read the introductory headnotes prior to reading the selections. The headnotes will give you a way of thinking about the selections as you read them. Keep in mind that the language used in some early selections is undoubtedly sexist and, in some cases, racist. While we are more sensitive to the impact of certain words today, some of these selections were written at a time in which different values and standards were the norm. Although the selections have been edited for brevity, they have not been altered with regard to the authors' original style and use of speech. Therefore, such usages as the masculine pronoun *he* to refer to everyone may not be acceptable today, but it does reflect a certain sense of history.

On the Internet.   Each part in this book is preceded by an *On the Internet* page. This page provides a list of Internet site addresses that are relevant to the part as well as a description of each site.

A word to the instructor.   An *Instructor's Manual With Test Questions* (multiple-choice and essay) is available through the publisher for instructors using *Sources: Notable Selections in Mass Media* in the classroom.

Sources: Notable Selections in Mass Media is only one title in the Sources series. If you are interested in seeing the table of contents for any of the other titles, please visit the Sources Web site at http://www.dushkin.com/sources/.

Acknowledgments. We would like to extend our appreciation to the many professors who reviewed the first edition of *Sources.* Our thanks go to those who responded with specific suggestions for this edition:

Jeffrey Klenoti
University of New Hampshire

Jeff Shires
Campbellsville University

Diana Papademas
SUNY College at Old Westbury

Phyllis Zrzavy
Franklin Pierce College

This edition of *Sources* would not have been possible without the careful attention by David Dean, list manager for the Sources program, and the excellent work of the Dushkin production staff. In our view, Dushkin remains one of the best publishers in the business.

If readers have any comments or suggestions for other selections to be considered for inclusion in future editions of *Sources,* please write to us in care of SOURCES, Dushkin/McGraw Hill, Sluice Dock, Guilford, CT 06437.

Jarice Hanson
University of Massachusetts–Amherst

David J. Maxcy
University of Massachusetts–Amherst

SOURCES

Contents

"A convenient way to describe an act of communication is to answer the following questions: Who, Says What, In Which Channel, To Whom, With What Effect?"

"It is clear that the mass media reach enormous audiences.... Knowledge of consumption data in the field of mass media remains far from a demonstration of their net effect upon behavior and attitude and outlook."

"The vagaries of research lead us away from a principal concern with the impact of press, radio, television, and magazines, but nothing would seem to have banished our not yet empirically demonstrated beliefs that the mass media are more influential than we would sometimes wish."

"Given the image of the atomized audience which characterized so much of mass media research, the surprising thing is that interpersonal influence attracted the attention of the researchers at all."

"One of the ways people integrate media into their social lives is by establishing symbolic, or parasocial, relationships (PSR) with media characters.... Much research has advanced our understanding of why and how
these relationships develop, but there are mixed results regarding the ways
in which PSR relate to social relationships."

"As a social process, communication is essential to society and to human
survival. Every human society—so-called primitive or modern—depends
on communication to enable its members to live together, to maintain and
modify working arrangements about the social order and social regulation,
and to cope with the environment. Participation in the communication process establishes a person as a social being and as a functioning member of
society."

"The last few years have witnessed something of a revival of direct empirical investigations of audience uses and gratifications, not only in the United
States but also in Britain, Sweden, Finland, Japan, and Israel.... Taken together, they make operational many of the logical steps that were only implicit in the earlier work."

"The objective of the current study is to explore patterns of use of news
media by college students and the relationship among traditional news gratifications functions."

"The 'mainstream' can be thought of as a relative commonality of outlooks
that television tends to cultivate. By 'mainstreaming' we mean the sharing
of that commonality among heavy viewers in those demographic groups
whose light viewers hold divergent views."

"As mass media become more centralized and homogeneous, the cultural
currents become narrower, more standardized, and more sharply defined,
and mass communication becomes a more effective mechanism of social
control."

"While the mass media may have little influence on the direction or intensity of attitudes, it is hypothesized that *the mass media set the agenda for each
political campaign, influencing the salience of attitudes toward the political issues.*"

"Political advertising is now the major means by which candidates for the
presidency communicate their messages to voters."

" 'The medium is the message' means, in terms of the electronic age, that a
totally new environment has been created."

"Television does not extend or amplify literate culture. It attacks it. If television is a continuation of anything, it is of a tradition begun by the telegraph
and photograph in the mid-nineteenth century, not by the printing press in
the fifteenth."

"The homogenized information networks fostered by electronic media offer
individuals a comparatively holistic view of society and a wider field within
which to measure their relative lot."

"In many countries today—including some in Central Europe—information media are passing into the hands of non-residents.... Whole sections of the entertainment industry, traditionally part of national, city, local, regional, or ethnic political and social life and manners, are passing into the control of managements whose outlook is exclusively global."

"What was valuable in the traditional culture was defined, effectively, as anything that did not impede the growth of Western capitalist endeavors; what had to change culturally was anything that interfered with this process."

PART ONE

Media Effects

On the Internet . . .

Sites appropriate to Part One

This large Web site links to a variety of key issues that are relevant to the National Association of Broadcasters. Information may be found on TV parental guidelines, laws and regulations, and employment in the media industries, from entry-level to upper-level positions.

http://www.nab.org/

This Web site of the Broadcast Education Association provides updated information on issues related to broadcast education and research in the area.

http://www.beaweb.org/

The *Journal of Computer-Mediated Communication* is a project of the Annenberg School for Communication at the University of Southern California. This quarterly online journal, published since June 1995, features theme issues and a variety of topics dealing with the impact and effects of media, especially computer-mediated communication.

http://www.ascusc.org/jcmc/

Live Culture, a Netzine from the Institute for Learning Technologies, contains several features, including one video feature per issue. Many articles deal with the influence of media and technology on perceptual processes.

http://www.ilt.columbia.edu/projects/
    live_culture/index.html

CHAPTER 1 The Relationship of Media and Society

1.1 HAROLD D. LASSWELL

The Structure and Function of Communication in Society

Many of the early studies in mass media and society proceeded under the assumption that media provided a stimulus for *direct effects* upon the individuals in the audiences. This concept was later termed the *magic bullet* model of communication. Studies of *propaganda* (defined as any form of persuasive message) led researchers to study how media might influence individuals' attitudes and beliefs. In an effort to understand the growing phenomenon of media and society, several attempts were made to clarify what actually happened in the process of message exchange.

Harold D. Lasswell's influential article "The Structure and Function of Communication in Society," in Lyman Bryson, ed., *The Communication of*

Ideas (Institute for Religious & Social Studies, 1948), from which the following selection has been taken, provides an important refinement to the "magic-bullet" model. In the article's summary, Lasswell states, "The communication process in society performs three functions: (a) *surveillance* of the environment... ; (b) *correlation* of the components of society... ; and (c) *transmission* of the social inheritance." Later, other scholars added the function of "entertainment" to Lasswell's original description. Lasswell's concept of media function compares both individual and society to biological organisms. Just as different types of cells work together in the body, mass media "functions" only when they work smoothly together with other parts, thereby contributing to the integrity of the whole organism, either individual or social. And, as when cells proliferate erratically, causing cancer and the breakdown of an organism, mass media can *dysfunction* if they fail to meet social and individual needs for information, explanation, cultural transmission, and release from drudgery.

Lasswell (1902–1978) continued his propaganda research with the Experimental Division for the Study of War-Time Communications during World War II, where he worked with Paul F. Lazarsfeld, Kurt Lewin, and Wilbur Schramm. All participated in the Rockefeller Communication Seminar, which met monthly from September 1939 to June 1940. In 1948 papers from these meetings were published in *The Communication of Ideas.*

Key Concept: media functions

THE ACT OF COMMUNICATION

A convenient way to describe an act of communication is to answer the following questions:

> Who
> Says What
> In Which Channel
> To Whom
> With What Effect?

The scientific study of the process of communication tends to concentrate upon one or another of these questions. Scholars who study the "who," the communicator, look into the factors that initiate and guide the act of communication. We call this subdivision of the field of research *control analysis.* Specialists who focus upon the "says what" engage in *content analysis.* Those who look primarily at the radio, press, film and other channels of communication are doing *media analysis.* When the principal concern is with the persons reached by the media, we speak of *audience analysis.* If the question is the impact upon audiences, the problem is *effect analysis.*[1]

Whether such distinctions are useful depends entirely upon the degree of refinement which is regarded as appropriate to a given scientific and managerial objective. Often it is simpler to combine audience and effect analysis, for instance, than to keep them apart. On the other hand, we may want to concentrate on the analysis of content, and for this purpose subdivide the field into the study of purport and style, the first referring to the message, and the second to the arrangement of the elements of which the message is composed.

STRUCTURE AND FUNCTION

Enticing as it is to work out these categories in more detail, the present discussion has a different scope. We are less interested in dividing up the act of communication than in viewing the act as a whole in relation to the entire social process. Any process can be examined in two frames of reference, namely, structure and function; and our analysis of communication will deal with the specializations that carry on certain functions, of which the following may be clearly distinguished: (1) The surveillance of the environment; (2) the correlation of the parts of society in responding to the environment; (3) the transmission of the social heritage from one generation to the next.

BIOLOGICAL EQUIVALENCIES

At the risk of calling up false analogies, we can gain perspective on human societies when we note the degree to which communication is a feature of life at every level. A vital entity, whether relatively isolated or in association, has specialized ways of receiving stimuli from the environment. The single-celled organism or the many-membered group tends to maintain an internal equilibrium and to respond to changes in the environment in a way that maintains this equilibrium. The responding process calls for specialized ways of bringing the parts of the whole into harmonious action. Multi-celled animals specialize cells to the function of external contact and internal correlation. Thus, among the primates, specialization is exemplified by organs such as the ear and eye, and the nervous system itself. When the stimuli receiving and disseminating patterns operate smoothly, the several parts of the animal act in concert in reference to the environment ("feeding," "fleeing," "attacking").[2]

In some animal societies certain members perform specialized roles, and survey the environment. Individuals act as "sentinels," standing apart from the herd or flock and creating a disturbance whenever an alarming change occurs in the surroundings. The trumpeting, cackling or shrilling of the sentinel is enough to set the herd in motion. Among the activities engaged in by specialized "leaders" is the internal stimulation of "followers" to adapt in an orderly manner to the circumstances heralded by the sentinels.[3]

Within a single, highly differentiated organism, incoming nervous impulses and outgoing impulses are transmitted along fibers that make synaptic junction with other fibers. The critical points in the process occur at the relay stations, where the arriving impulse may be too weak to reach the threshold which stirs the next link into action. At the higher centers, separate currents modify one another, producing results that differ in many ways from the outcome when each is allowed to continue a separate path. At any relay station there is no conductance, total conductance or intermediate conductance. The same categories apply to what goes on among members of an animal society. The sly fox may approach the barnyard in a way that supplies too meager stimuli for the sentinel to sound the alarm. Or the attacking animal may eliminate the sentinel before he makes more than a feeble outcry. Obviously there is every gradation possible between total conductance and no conductance.

ATTENTION IN WORLD SOCIETY

When we examine the process of communication of any state in the world community, we note three categories of specialists. One group surveys the political environment of the state as a whole, another correlates the response of the whole state to the environment, and the third transmits certain patterns of response from the old to the young. Diplomats, attachés, and foreign correspondents are representative of those who specialize on the environment. Editors, journalists, and speakers are correlators of the internal response. Educators in family and school transmit the social inheritance.

Communications which originate abroad pass through sequences in which various senders and receivers are linked with one another. Subject to modification at each relay point in the chain, messages originating with a diplomat or foreign correspondent may pass through editorial desks and eventually reach large audiences.

If we think of the world attention process as a series of *attention frames*, it is possible to describe the rate at which comparable content is brought to the notice of individuals and groups. We can inquire into the point at which "conductance" no longer occurs; and we can look into the range between "total conductance" and "minimum conductance." The metropolitan and political centers of the world have much in common with the interdependence, differentiation, and activity of the cortical or subcortical centers of an individual organism. Hence the attention frames found in these spots are the most variable, refined, and interactive of all frames in the world community.

At the other extreme are the attention frames of primitive inhabitants of isolated areas. Not that folk cultures are wholly untouched by industrial civilization. Whether we parachute into the interior of New Guinea, or land on the slopes of the Himalayas, we find no tribe wholly out of contact with the world. The long threads of trade, of missionary zeal, of adventurous exploration and scientific field study, and of global war, reach the far distant places. No one is entirely out of this world.

Among primitives the final shape taken by communication is the ballad or tale. Remote happenings in the great world of affairs, happenings that come to the notice of metropolitan audiences, are reflected, however dimly, in the thematic material of ballad singers and reciters. In these creations far away political leaders may be shown supplying land to the peasants or restoring an abundance of game to the hills.[4]

When we push upstream of the flow of communication, we note that the immediate relay function for nomadic and remote tribesmen is sometimes performed by the inhabitants of settled villages with whom they come in occasional contact. The relayer can be the school teacher, doctor, judge, tax collector, policeman, soldier, peddler, salesman, missionary, student; in any case he is an assembly point of news and comment.

MORE DETAILED EQUIVALENCIES

The communication processes of human society, when examined in detail, reveal many equivalencies to the specializations found in the physical organism, and in the lower animal societies. The diplomats, for instance, of a single state are stationed all over the world and send messages to a few focal points. Obviously, these incoming reports move from the many to the few, where they interact upon one another. Later on, the sequence spreads fanwise according to a few to many pattern, as when a foreign secretary gives a speech in public, an article is put out in the press, or a news film is distributed to the theaters. The lines leading from the outer environment of the state are functionally equivalent to the afferent channels that convey incoming nervous impulses to the central nervous system of a single animal, and to the means by which alarm is spread among a flock. Outgoing, or efferent impulses, display corresponding parallels.

The central nervous system of the body is only partly involved in the entire flow of afferent-efferent impulses. There are automatic systems that can act on one another without involving the "higher" centers at all. The stability of the internal environment is maintained principally through the mediation of the vegetive or autonomic specializations of the nervous system. Similarly, most of the messages within any state do not involve the central channels of communication. They take place within families, neighborhoods, shops, field gangs, and other local contexts. Most of the educational process is carried on the same way.

A further set of significant equivalencies is related to the circuits of communication, which are predominantly one-way or two-way, depending upon the degree of reciprocity between communicators and audience. Or, to express it differently, two-way communication occurs when the sending and receiving functions are performed with equal frequency by two or more persons. A conversation is usually assumed to be a pattern of two-way communication (although monologues are hardly unknown). The modern instruments of mass communication give an enormous advantage to the controllers of printing plants, broadcasting equipment, and other forms of fixed and specialized capital. But it should be noted that audiences do "talk back," after some delay; and many controllers of mass media use scientific methods of sampling in order to expedite this closing of the circuit.

Circuits of two-way contact are particularly in evidence among the great metropolitan, political and cultural centers in the world. New York, Moscow, London and Paris, for example, are in intense two-way contact, even when the flow is severely curtailed in volume (as between Moscow and New York). Even insignificant sites become world centers when they are transformed into capital cities (Canberra in Australia, Ankara in Turkey, the District of Columbia, U.S.A.). A cultural center like Vatican City is in intense two-way relationship with the dominant centers throughout the world. Even specialized production centers like Hollywood, despite their preponderance of outgoing material, receive an enormous volume of messages.

A further distinction can be made between message controlling and message handling centers and social formations. The message center in the vast Pentagon Building of the War Department in Washington, D.C., transmits with no more than accidental change incoming messages to addressees. This is the role of the printers and distributors of books; of dispatchers, linemen, and messengers connected with telegraphic communication; of radio engineers, and other technicians associated with broadcasting. Such message handlers may be contrasted with those who affect the content of what is said, which is the function of editors, censors, and propagandists. Speaking of the symbol specialists as a whole, therefore, we separate them into the manipulators (controllers) and the handlers; the first group typically modifies content, while the second does not.

NEEDS AND VALUES

Though we have noted a number of functional and structural equivalencies between communication in human societies and other living entities, it is not implied that we can most fruitfully investigate the process of communication in America or the world by the methods most appropriate to research on the lower animals or on single physical organisms. In comparative psychology when we describe some part of the surroundings of a rat, cat, or monkey as a stimulus (that is, as part of the environment reaching the attention of the animal), we cannot ask the rat; we use other means of inferring perception. When human beings are our objects of investigation, we can interview the great "talking animal." (This is not that we take everything at face value. Sometimes we forecast the opposite of what the person says he intends to do. In this case, we depend on other indications, both verbal and non-verbal.)

In the study of living forms, it is rewarding, as we have said, to look at them as modifiers of the environment in the process of gratifying needs, and hence of maintaining a steady state of internal equilibrium. Food, sex, and other activities which involve the environment can be examined on a comparative basis. Since human beings exhibit speech reactions, we can investigate many more relationships than in the non-human species.[5] Allowing for the data furnished by speech (and other communicative acts), we can investigate human society in terms of values; that is, in reference to categories of relationships that are recognized objects of gratification. In America, for example, it requires no elaborate technique of study to discern that power and respect are values. We can demonstrate this by listening to testimony, and by watching what is done when opportunity is afforded.

It is possible to establish a list of values current in any group chosen for investigation. Further than this, we can discover the rank order in which these values are sought. We can rank the members of the group according to their position in relation to the values. So far as industrial civilization is concerned, we have no hesitation in saying that power, wealth, respect, well being, and enlightenment are among the values. If we stop with this list, which is not exhaustive, we can describe on the basis of available knowledge (fragmentary though it may often be), the social structure of most of the world. Since values are not equally distributed, the social structure reveals more or less concentration of relatively abundant shares of power, wealth and other values in a few hands. In some places this concentration is passed on from generation to generation, forming castes rather than a mobile society.

In every society the values are shaped and distributed according to more or less distinctive patterns (*institutions*). The institutions include communications which are invoked in support of the network as a whole. Such communications are the ideology; and in relation to power we can differentiate the political *doctrine,* the political *formula* and the *miranda.*[6] These are illustrated in the United States by the doctrine of individualism, the paragraphs of the Constitution, which are the formula, and the ceremonies and legends of public life, which comprise the miranda. The ideology is communicated to the rising generation through such specialized agencies as the home and school.

Ideology is only part of the myths of any given society. There may be counter ideologies directed against the dominant doctrine, formula, and miranda. Today the power structure of world politics is deeply affected by ideological conflict, and by the role of two giant powers, the United States and Russia.[7] The ruling elites view one another as potential enemies, not only in the sense that interstate differences may be settled by war, but in the more urgent sense that the ideology of the other may appeal to disaffected elements at home and weaken the internal power position of each ruling class....

EFFICIENT COMMUNICATION

... One task of a rationally organized society is to discover and control any factors that interfere with efficient communication....

But even technical insufficiencies can be overcome by knowledge. In recent years shortwave broadcasting has been interfered with by disturbances which will either be surmounted, or will eventually lead to the abandonment of this mode of broadcasting. During the past few years advances have been made toward providing satisfactory substitutes for defective hearing and seeing. A less dramatic, though no less important, development has been the discovery of how inadequate reading habits can be corrected....

Some of the most serious threats to efficient communication for the community as a whole relate to the values of power, wealth and respect. Perhaps the most striking examples of power distortion occur when the content of communication is deliberately adjusted to fit an ideology or counter ideology. Distortions related to wealth not only arise from attempts to influence the market, for instance, but from rigid conceptions of economic interest. A typical instance of inefficiencies connected with respect (social class) occurs when an upper class person mixes only with persons of his own stratum and forgets to correct his perspective by being exposed to members of other classes. . . .

SUMMARY

The communication process in society performs three functions: (a) *surveillance* of the environment, disclosing threats and opportunities affecting the value position of the community and of the component parts within it; (b) *correlation* of the components of society in making a response to the environment; (c) *transmission* of the social inheritance. In general, biological equivalents can be found in human and animal associations, and within the economy of a single organism.

In society, the communication process reveals special characteristics when the ruling element is afraid of the internal as well as the external environment. In gauging the efficiency of communication in any given context, it is necessary to take into account the values at stake, and the identity of the group whose position is being examined. In democratic societies, rational choices depend on enlightenment, which in turn depends upon communication; and especially upon the equivalence of attention among leaders, experts and rank and file.

NOTES

1. For more detail, consult the introductory matter in Bruce L. Smith, Harold D. Lasswell and Ralph D. Casey, *Propaganda, Communication, and Public Opinion: A Comprehensive Reference Guide,* Princeton University Press, Princeton, 1946.

2. To the extent that behavior patterns are transmitted in the structures inherited by the single animal, a function is performed parallel to the transmission of the "social heritage" by means of education.

3. On animal sociology see: Warder C. Allee, *Animal Aggregations,* University of Chicago Press, Chicago, 1931; *The Social Life of Animals,* Norton, New York, 1935.

4. Excellent examples are given in Robert Redfield's account of *Tepoztlan, A Mexican Village: A Study of Folk Life,* University of Chicago Press, Chicago, 1930.

5. Properly handled, the speech event can be described with as much reliability and validity as many non-speech events which are more conventionally used as data in scientific investigations.

6. These distinctions are derived and adapted from the writings of Charles E. Merriam, Gaetano Mosca, Karl Mannheim, and others. For a systematic exposition see the forthcoming volume by Harold D. Lasswell and Abraham Kaplan.

7. See William T. R. Fox, *The Super-Powers,* Harcourt, Brace, New York. 1944, and Harold D. Lasswell, *World Politics Faces Economics,* McGraw-Hill, New York, 1945.

1.2 PAUL F. LAZARSFELD AND ROBERT K. MERTON

Mass Communication, Popular Taste, and Organized Social Action

The following influential article was authored by Paul F. Lazarsfeld, who was director of the Bureau of Applied Social Research at Columbia University, and his colleague in the Department of Sociology, Robert K. Merton. In writing this article, published in Lyman Bryson's 1948 book *The Communication of Ideas* (Institute for Religious & Social Studies), the authors took the perspective that perhaps media create no social change. Instead, they reasoned, mass media's chief social effect is to enforce existing norms and values.

In the following selection, the authors identify the *status-conferral* power of the media, which suggests that the audience will perceive an issue of importance if the media call attention to it. Similarly, individuals portrayed by the media would have their status legitimized by media coverage. Related to the later concept of *agenda setting,* the status-conferral function helps to explain how audiences view the importance of topics and people covered by the media.

While the authors view media as reaffirming and legitimizing social norms, they also articulate a different perspective in what they term the *narcotizing dysfunction* of media. This idea explains how too much information sometimes makes audience members incapable of critically judging what they see or hear in the media. An effect of the narcotizing dysfunction would be to make people think that because they know about something, they need not take action about it. For example, if a person feels that he or she knows something about the issues in an election, he or she might not feel the need to vote.

Finally, the authors extend their thesis to explain what they believe would be the ultimate effect of a greater use of media. They foretell of lower critical standards, less critical thought, and more widespread mediocrity throughout popular culture.

Lazarsfeld (1901–1976) was known as the father of market research, and he excelled in empiricist methods. Merton (b. 1910) is a theorist who became associated with the Bureau of Applied Research and whose work enhanced many of the studies of the bureau. Both theorists authored or coauthored many influential works in media and society, including the groundbreaking studies on the social impact of radio that can be found in the collection edited by Lazarsfeld et al. called *Radio Research, 1942–1943*, and in Merton's *Mass Persuasion* (Greenwood Press, 1971).

Key Concept: status-conferral and narcotizing dysfunction

THE SOCIAL ROLE OF THE MACHINERY OF MASS MEDIA

What role can be assigned to the mass media by virtue of the fact that they exist? What are the implications of a Hollywood, a Radio City, and a *Time-Life-Fortune* enterprise for our society? . . .

It is clear that the mass media reach enormous audiences. Approximately forty-five million Americans attend the movies every week; our daily newspaper circulation is about fifty-four million, and some forty-six million American homes are equipped with television, and in these homes the average American watches television for about three hours a day. These are formidable figures. But they are merely supply and consumption figures, not figures registering the effect of mass media. They bear only upon what people do, not upon the social and psychological impact of the media. To know the number of hours people keep the radio turned on gives no indication of the effect upon them of what they hear. Knowledge of consumption data in the field of mass media remains far from a demonstration of their net effect upon behavior and attitude and outlook.

[W]e cannot resort to experiment by comparing contemporary American society with and without mass media. But, however tentatively, we can compare their social effect with, say, that of the automobile. It is not unlikely that the invention of the automobile and its development into a mass-owned commodity has had a significantly greater effect upon society than the invention of the radio and its development into a medium of mass communication. Consider the social complexes into which the automobile has entered. Its sheer existence has exerted pressure for vastly improved roads, and, with these, mobility has increased enormously. The shape of metropolitan agglomerations has been significantly affected by the automobile. And, it may be submitted, the inventions which enlarge the radius of movement and action exert a greater influence upon social outlook and daily routines than inventions which provide avenues for ideas—ideas which can be avoided by withdrawal, deflected by resistance, and transformed by assimilation.

Granted, for a moment, that the mass media play a comparatively minor role in shaping our society, why are they the object of so much popular concern and criticism? Why do so many become exercised by the "problems" of the radio and film and press and so few by the problems of, say, the automobile and the airplane? In addition to the sources of this concern which we have noted previously, there is an unwitting psychological basis for concern which derives from a socio-historical context.

Many make the mass media targets for hostile criticism because they feel themselves duped by the turn of events.

The social changes ascribable to "reform movements" may be slow and slight, but they do cumulate. The surface facts are familiar enough. The sixty-hour week has given way to the forty-hour week. Child labor has been progressively curtailed. With all its deficiencies, free universal education has become progressively institutionalized. These and other gains register a series of reform victories. And now, people have more leisure time. They have, ostensibly, greater access to the cultural heritage. And what use do they make of this unmortgaged time so painfully acquired for them? They listen to the radio and go to the movies. These mass media seem somehow to have cheated reformers of the fruits of their victories. . . .

Paul F. Lazarsfeld and Robert K. Merton

SOME SOCIAL FUNCTIONS OF THE MASS MEDIA

In continuing our examination of the social role which can be ascribed to the mass media by virtue of their "sheer existence," we temporarily abstract from the social structure in which the media find their place. We do not, for example, consider the diverse effects of the mass media under varying systems of ownership and control, an important structural factor which will be discussed subsequently.

The mass media undoubtedly serve many social functions which might well become the object of sustained research. Of these functions, we have occasion to notice only three.

The Status-Conferral Function

The mass media *confer* status on public issues, persons, organizations, and social movements.

Common experience as well as research testifies that the social standing of persons or social policies is raised when these command favorable attention in the mass media. In many quarters, for example, the support of a political candidate or a public policy by the *Times* is taken as significant, and this support is regarded as a distinct asset for the candidate or the policy. Why?

For some, the editorial views of the *Times* represent the considered judgment of a group of experts, thus calling for the respect of laymen. But this is only one element in the status-conferral function of the mass media, for enhanced status accrues to those who merely receive attention in the media, quite apart from any editorial support.

The mass media bestow prestige and enhance the authority of individuals and groups by *legitimizing their status.* Recognition by the press or radio or magazines or newsreels testifies that one has arrived, that one is important enough to have been singled out from the large anonymous masses, that one's behavior and opinions are significant enough to require public notice. The operation of this status-conferral function may be witnessed most vividly in the advertising pattern of testimonials to a product by "prominent people." Within wide circles of the population (though not within certain selected social strata), such testimonials not only enhance the prestige of the product but also reflect prestige on the person who provides the testimonials. They give public notice that the large and powerful world of commerce regards him as possessing sufficiently high status for his opinion to count with many people. In a word, his testimonial is a testimonial to his own status. . . .

The Enforcement of Social Norms

Such catch phrases as "the power of the press" (and other mass media) or "the bright glare of publicity" presumably refer to this function. The mass media may initiate organized social action by "exposing" conditions which are at variance with public moralities. But it need not be prematurely assumed that this pattern consists *simply* in making these deviations widely known. . . .

Many social norms prove inconvenient for individuals in the society. They militate against the gratification of wants and impulses. Since many find the norms burdensome, there is some measure of leniency in applying them, both to oneself and to others. Hence, the emergence of deviant behavior and private toleration in these deviations. But this can continue only so long as one is not in a situation where one must take a public stand for or against the norms. Publicity, the enforced acknowledgment by members of the group that these deviations have occurred, requires each individual to take such a stand. He must either range himself with the nonconformists, thus proclaiming his repudiation of the group norms, and thus asserting that he, too, is outside the moral framework or, regardless of his private predilections, he must fall into line by supporting the norm. *Publicity closes the gap between "private attitudes" and "public morality."* Publicity exerts pressure for a single rather than a dual morality by preventing continued evasion of the issue. It calls forth public reaffirmation and (however sporadic) application of the social norm.

In a mass society, this function of public exposure is institutionalized in the mass media of communication. Press, radio, and journals expose fairly well-known deviations to public view and, as a rule, this exposure forces some degree of public action against what has been privately tolerated. The mass media may, for example, introduce severe strains upon "polite ethnic discrimination" by calling public attention to these practices which are at odds with the norms of nondiscrimination. At times, the media may organize exposure activities into a "crusade." . . .

The crusade may affect the public directly. It may focus the attention of a hitherto lethargic citizenry, grown indifferent through familiarity to prevailing corruption, upon a few dramatically simplified issues. As Lawrence Lowell once observed in this general connection, complexities generally inhibit mass action. Public issues must be defined in simple alternatives, in terms of black and white, to permit organized public action. And the presentation of simple alternatives is one of the chief functions of the crusade. The crusade may involve still other mechanisms. If a municipal government is not altogether pure of heart, it is seldom wholly corrupt. Some scrupulous members of the administration and judiciary are generally intermingled with their unprincipled colleagues. The crusade may strengthen the hand of the upright elements in the government, force the hand of the indifferent, and weaken the hand of the corrupt. Finally, it may well be that a successful crusade exemplifies a circular, self-sustaining process, in which the concern of the mass medium with the public interest coincides with its self-interest. The triumphant crusade may enhance the power and prestige of the mass medium, thus making it, in turn, more formidable in later crusades, which, if successful, may further advance its power and prestige.

Whatever the answer to these questions, mass media clearly serve to reaffirm social norms by exposing deviations from these norms to public view. Study of the particular range of norms thus reaffirmed would provide a clear index of the extent to which these media deal with peripheral or central problems of the structure of our society.

The Narcotizing Dysfunction

The functions of status conferral and of reaffirmation of social norms are evidently well recognized by the operators of mass media. Like other social and psychological mechanisms, these functions lend themselves to diverse forms of application. Knowledge of these functions is power, and power may be used for special interests or for the general interest.

A third social consequence of the mass media has gone largely unnoticed. At least, it has received little explicit comment and, apparently, has not been systematically put to use for furthering planned objectives. This may be called the narcotizing dysfunction of the mass media. It is termed *dys*functional rather than functional on the assumption that it is not in the interest of modern complex society to have large masses of the population politically apathetic and inert. How does this unplanned mechanism operate?

Scattered studies have shown that an increasing proportion of the time of Americans is devoted to the products of the mass media. With distinct variations in different regions and among different social strata, the outpourings of the media presumably enable the twentieth-century American to "keep abreast of the world." Yet, it is suggested, this vast supply of communications may elicit only a superficial concern with the problems of society, and this superficiality often cloaks mass apathy.

Exposure to this flood of information may serve to narcotize rather than to energize the average reader or listener. As an increasing meed of time is devoted to reading and listening, a decreasing share is available for organized action. The individual reads accounts of issues and problems and may even discuss alternative lines of action. But this rather intellectualized, rather remote connection with organized social action is not activated. The interested and informed citizen can congratulate himself on his lofty state of interest and information and neglect to see that he has abstained from decision and action. In short, he takes his secondary contact with the world of political reality, his reading and listening and thinking, as a vicarious performance. He comes to

Paul F. Lazarsfeld and Robert K. Merton

mistake *knowing* about problems of the day for *doing* something about them. His social conscience remains spotlessly clean. He *is* concerned. He *is* informed. And he has all sorts of ideas as to what should be done. But, after he has gotten through his dinner and after he has listened to his favored radio programs and after he has read his second newspaper of the day, it is really time for bed.

In this peculiar respect, mass communications may be included among the most respectable and efficient of social narcotics. They may be so fully effective as to keep the addict from recognizing his own malady.

That the mass media have lifted the level of information of large populations is evident. Yet, quite apart from intent, increasing dosages of mass communications may be inadvertently transforming the energies of men from active participation into passive knowledge.

The occurrence of this narcotizing dysfunction can scarcely be doubted, but the extent to which it operates has yet to be determined. Research on this problem remains one of the many tasks still confronting the student of mass communications.

THE STRUCTURE OF OWNERSHIP AND OPERATION

To this point we have considered the mass media quite apart from their incorporation within a particular social and economic structure. But clearly, the social effects of the media will vary as the system of ownership and control varies. Thus to consider the social effects of American mass media is to deal only with the effects of these media as privately owned enterprises under profit-oriented management. It is general knowledge that this circumstance is not inherent in the technological nature of the mass media. In England, for example, to say nothing of Russia, the radio is to all intents and purposes owned, controlled, and operated by government.

The structure of control is altogether different in this country. Its salient characteristic stems from the fact that except for movies and books, it is not the magazine reader nor the radio listener nor, in large part, the reader of newspapers who supports the enterprise, but the advertiser. Big business finances the production and distribution of mass media. And, all intent aside, he who pays the piper generally calls the tune.

SOCIAL CONFORMISM

Since the mass media are supported by great business concerns geared into the current social and economic system, the media contribute to the maintenance of that system. This contribution is not found merely in the effective advertisement of the sponsor's product. It arises, rather, from the typical presence in magazine stories, radio programs, and newspaper columns of some element of confirmation, some element of approval of the present structure of society. And this continuing reaffirmation underscores the duty to accept.

Paul F. Lazarsfeld and Robert K. Merton

To the extent that the media of mass communication have had an influence upon their audiences, it has stemmed not only from what is said, but more significantly from what is not said. For these media not only continue to affirm the status quo but, in the same measure, they fail to raise essential questions about the structure of society. Hence, by leading toward conformism and by providing little basis for a critical appraisal of society, the commercially sponsored mass media indirectly but effectively restrain the cogent development of a genuinely critical outlook.

This is not to ignore the occasionally critical journal article or radio program. But these exceptions are so few that they are lost in the overwhelming flood of conformist materials. . . .

Since our commercially sponsored mass media promote a largely unthinking allegiance to our social structure, they cannot be relied upon to work for changes, even minor changes, in that structure. It is possible to list some developments to the contrary, but upon close inspection they prove illusory. A community group, such as the PTA, may request the producer of a radio serial to inject the theme of tolerant race attitudes into the program. Should the producer feel that this theme is safe, that it will not antagonize any substantial part of his audience, he may agree, but at the first indication that it is a dangerous theme which may alienate potential consumers, he will refuse, or will soon abandon the experiment. Social objectives are consistently surrendered by commercialized media when they clash with economic gains. Minor tokens of "progressive" views are of slight importance since they are included only by the grace of the sponsors and only on the condition that they be sufficiently acceptable as not to alienate any appreciable part of the audience. Economic pressure makes for conformism by omission of sensitive issues.

IMPACT UPON POPULAR TASTE

Since the largest part of our radio, movies, magazines, and a considerable part of our books and newspapers are devoted to "entertainment," this clearly requires us to consider the impact of the mass media upon popular taste.

Were we to ask the average American with some pretension to literary or aesthetic cultivation if mass communications have had any effect upon popular taste, he would doubtlessly answer with a resounding affirmative. And more, citing abundant instances, he would insist that aesthetic and intellectual tastes have been depraved by the flow of trivial formula products from printing presses, radio stations, and movie studios. The columns of criticism abound with these complaints.

In one sense, this requires no further discussion. There can be no doubt that the women who are daily entranced for three or four hours by some twelve consecutive "soap operas," all cut to the same dismal pattern, exhibit an appalling lack of aesthetic judgment. Nor is this impression altered by the contents of pulp and slick magazines, or by the depressing abundance of formula motion pictures replete with hero, heroine, and villain moving through a contrived atmosphere of sex, sin, and success.

Yet unless we locate these patterns in historical and sociological terms, we may find ourselves confusedly engaged in condemning without understanding, in criticism which is sound but largely irrelevant. What is the historical status of this notoriously low level of popular taste? Is it the poor remains of standards which were once significantly higher, a relatively new birth in the world of values, largely unrelated to the higher standards from which it has allegedly fallen, or a poor substitute blocking the way to the development of superior standards and the expression of high aesthetic purpose?

If aesthetic tastes are to be considered in their social setting, we must recognize that the effective audience for the arts has become historically transformed. Some centuries back, this audience was largely confined to a selected aristocratic elite. Relatively few were literate. And very few possessed the means to buy books, attend theaters, and travel to the urban centers of the arts. Not more than a slight fraction, possibly not more than one or two percent, of the population composed the effective audience for the arts. These happy few cultivated their aesthetic tastes, and their selective demand left its mark in the form of relatively high artistic standards.

With the widesweeping spread of popular education and with the emergence of the new technologies of mass communication, there developed an enormously enlarged market for the arts. Some forms of music, drama, and literature now reach virtually everyone in our society. This is why, of course, we speak of *mass* media and of *mass* art. And the great audiences for the mass media, though in the main literate, are not highly cultivated. About half the population, in fact, have halted their formal education upon leaving grammar school.

With the rise of popular education, there has occurred a seeming decline of popular taste. Large numbers of people have acquired what might be termed "formal literacy," that is to say, a capacity to read, to grasp crude and superficial meanings, and a correlative incapacity for full understanding of what they read. There has developed, in short, a marked gap between literacy and comprehension. People read more but understand less. More people read but proportionately fewer critically assimilate what they read.

Our formulation of the problem should now be plain. It is misleading to speak simply of the decline of aesthetic tastes. Mass audiences probably include a larger number of persons with cultivated aesthetic standards, but these are swallowed up by the large masses who constitute the new and untutored audience for the arts. Whereas yesterday the elite constituted virtually the whole of the audience, they are today a minute fraction of the whole. In consequence, the average level of aesthetic standards and tastes of audiences has been depressed, although the tastes of some sectors of the population have undoubtedly been raised and the total number of people exposed to communication contents has been vastly increased....

PROPAGANDA FOR SOCIAL OBJECTIVES

This final question is perhaps of more direct interest to you than the other questions we have discussed. It represents something of a challenge to us since it provides the means of resolving the apparent paradox to which we referred previously: the seeming paradox arising from the assertion that the significance of the sheer existence of the mass media has been exaggerated and the multiple indications that the media do exert influences upon their audiences.

What are the conditions for the effective use of mass media for what might be called "propaganda for social objectives"—the promotion, let us say, of nondiscriminatory race relations, or of educational reforms, or of positive attitudes toward organized labor? Research indicates that, at least, one or more of three conditions must be satisfied if this propaganda is to prove effective. These conditions may be briefly designated as (1) monopolization, (2) canalization rather than change of basic values, and (3) supplementary face-to-face contact. Each of these conditions merits some discussion.

MONOPOLIZATION

This situation obtains when there is little or no opposition in the mass media to the diffusion of values, policies, or public images. That is to say, monopolization of the mass media occurs in the absence of counterpropaganda.

In this restricted sense, monopolization of the mass media is found in diverse circumstances. It is, of course, indigenous to the political structure of authoritarian society, where access to the media of communication is wholly closed to those who oppose the official ideology. The evidence suggests that this monopoly played some part in enabling the Nazis to maintain their control of the German people.

But this same situation is approximated in other social systems. During the war, for example, our government utilized the radio, with some success, to promote and to maintain identification with the war effort. The effectiveness of these morale-building efforts was in large measure due to the virtually complete absence of counterpropaganda....

This general pattern has been described by Kenneth Burke in his *Attitudes toward History*: "businessmen compete with one another by trying to *praise their own commodity* more persuasively than their rivals, whereas politicians compete by slandering the *opposition*. When you add it all up, you get a grand total of absolute praise for business and grand total of absolute slander for politics."

To the extent that opposing political propaganda in the mass media are balanced, the net effect is negligible. The virtual monopolization of the media for given social objectives, however, will produce discernible effects upon audiences.

CANALIZATION

Prevailing beliefs in the enormous power of mass communications appear to stem from successful cases of monopolistic propaganda or from advertising. But the leap from the efficacy of advertising to the assumed efficacy of propaganda aimed at deep-rooted attitudes and ego-involved behavior is as unwarranted as it is dangerous. Advertising is typically directed toward the canalizing of preexisting behavior patterns or attitudes. It seldom seeks to instill new attitudes or to create significantly new behavior patterns. "Advertising pays" because it generally deals with a simple psychological situation. For Americans who have been socialized in the use of a toothbrush, it makes relatively little difference which brand of toothbrush they use. Once the gross pattern of behavior or the generic attitude has been established, it can be canalized in one direction or another. Resistance is slight. But mass propaganda typically meets a more complex situation. It may seek objectives which are at odds with deep-lying attitudes. It may seek to reshape rather than to canalize current systems of values. And the successes of advertising may only highlight the failures of propaganda. Much of the current propaganda which is aimed at abolishing deep-seated ethnic and racial prejudices, for example, seems to have had little effectiveness.

Media of mass communication, then, have been effectively used to canalize basic attitudes, but there is little evidence of their having served to change these attitudes.

SUPPLEMENTATION

Mass propaganda which is neither monopolistic nor canalizing in character may, nonetheless, prove effective if it meets a third condition: supplementation through face-to-face contacts.

A case in point will illustrate the interplay between mass media and face-to-face influences. The seeming propagandistic success achieved some years ago by Father Coughlin [a right-wing radio talk show host from the 1930s] does not appear, upon inspection, to have resulted primarily from the propaganda content of his radio talks. It was, rather, the product of these centralized propaganda talks *and* widespread local organizations which arranged for their members to listen to him, followed by discussions among themselves concerning the social views he had expressed. This combination of a central supply of propaganda (Coughlin's addresses on a nationwide network), the coordinated distribution of newspapers and pamphlets and locally organized face-to-face discussions among relatively small groups—this complex of reciprocal reinforcement by mass media and personal relations proved spectacularly successful.

Students of mass movements have come to repudiate the view that mass propaganda in and of itself creates or maintains the movement. Nazism did not attain its brief moment of hegemony by capturing the mass media of communication. The media played an ancillary role, supplementing the use of organized violence, organized distribution of rewards for conformity, and organized centers of local indoctrination. The Soviet Union has also made large and impressive use of mass media for indoctrinating enormous populations with appropriate ideologies. But the organizers of indoctrination saw to it that the mass media did not operate alone. "Red corners," "reading huts," and "listening stations" comprised meeting places in which groups of citizens were exposed to the mass media in common. The 55,000 reading rooms and clubs which had come into being by 1933 enabled the local ideological elite to talk over with rank-and-file readers the content of what they read. The relative scarcity of radios in private homes again made for group listening and group discussions of what had been heard.

In these instances, the machinery of mass persuasion included face-to-face contact in local organizations as an adjunct to the mass media. The privatized individual response to the materials presented through the channels of mass communication was considered inadequate for transforming exposure to propaganda into effectiveness of propaganda. In a society such as our own, where the pattern of bureaucratization has not yet become so pervasive or, at least, not so clearly crystallized, it has likewise been found that mass media prove most effective in conjunction with local centers of organized face-to-face contact....

Face-to-face contacts with those who have been socialized in our culture serve primarily to reinforce the prevailing culture patterns.

Thus the very conditions which make for the maximum effectiveness of the mass media of communication operate toward the maintenance of the going social and cultural structure rather than toward its change.

Paul F. Lazarsfeld and Robert K. Merton

The Mass Media and Voting

Research on political communication effects has undergone three major shifts. Initially, the mass media were regarded as having considerable power to shape opinion and belief. During the second stage (1945–1960), mass media were regarded primarily as forms that would reinforce existing beliefs, but they were thought to have little effect on initial attitudes or opinion change. The third stage, from 1960 to the present, involves the ways in which media shape the image of candidates and the way voters respond to the images and agendas set forth by the media.

The following selection is from "The Mass Media and Voting," in Eugene Burdick and Arthur J. Brodbeck, eds., *American Voting Behavior* (Free Press, 1959). In it, Kurt Lang and Gladys Engel Lang demonstrate a shift toward limited effects research and thus represent the second stage. The Langs' approach helped later researchers focus on how media contribute to the shaping of political images. As the Langs write in this selection, earlier voting studies tended to show weaknesses in the methodologies that were used rather than evaluating the impact of mass media on voters' beliefs or actions. The Langs discuss, among other key ideas regarding media impact and voting, the importance of audience selectivity in perceiving mediated messages and people's tendency to filter unwanted messages.

At the time this article was written, Kurt Lang was on the staff of the Canadian Broadcasting Corporation, and Gladys Engel Lang had been associated with Carlton University in Ottawa, Ontario. Both eventually moved to the University of Washington, where Kurt was director of the School of Communication and Gladys had a joint appointment in political science and sociology. The Langs have coauthored several research studies, including *Politics and Television* (1968), *Politics and Television Re-Viewed* (1984), and *The Battle for Public Opinion: The President, the Press, and the Polls During Watergate* (1983).

Key Concept: voting and indirect effects of the mass media

*Kurt Lang
and Gladys
Engel Lang*

After each national election students of political behavior comment on how little effect the mass media appear to have had on the outcome. Franklin D. Roosevelt and Harry S. Truman won *in spite of* the press. The personal nature of the Eisenhower victory in 1952 showed that the campaign was so much shouting and tumult; the election was won before the campaign had even begun. Still, all of us—politicians, candidates, public servants, symbol manipulators, members of the Great Audience, and even students of political behavior in our private capacities as interested and partisan citizens—much as we may publicly belittle what the mass media do, act most of the time *as if* we believed in their potency. Republican members of the faculty pay for a newspaper ad supporting their candidate; the Democrats must counter with their own publicity. The vagaries of research lead us away from a principal concern with the impact of press, radio, television, and magazines, but nothing would seem to have banished our not yet empirically demonstrated beliefs that the mass media are more influential than we would sometimes wish. Outcries against certain political television shows during and between campaigns, as well as the enduring and enthusiastic acceptance accorded to George Orwell's [novel] *1984,* indicate vividly that our research may not tell us what our common sense reveals is there to be told.

At first glance recent research on voting behavior appears to go along with this emphasis on *how little* the mass media determine the vote. The reader's attention is called to influences that intervene between the content itself and the individual's voting decision. Emphasis also moves away from a concern with the power once attributed to mass communications to the personal dispositions and group influences that circumscribe it.

None of the three voting studies—Elmira, 1948; Bristol North-East, 1951; the U.S. national survey in 1952[1]—draw any explicit conclusions to the effect that mass communications are *not* an important influence in voting behavior. They all point to their own methodological inadequacies, and in the most recent of the three studies the problem of mass-media impact has actually been avoided.[2] At many points, the importance of the mass media is stressed; nowhere is their role in connection with the vote actually belittled. Yet there may be a difference between the author's own interpretations and more or less popular understandings of what their findings mean.

MASS COMMUNICATIONS
DURING THE CAMPAIGN

Exactly what do we learn about the influence of mass communication on voting behavior by studying its effect within the scope of a single campaign?

Both the Elmira and the Bristol studies reiterate findings of earlier research. In Elmira the group who changed their voting intentions during the campaign, compared with those who followed through, included fewer people who were interested in the election. They were less "exposed" to the mass media, and they arrived at their decision later. Likewise in Bristol, "floaters [those inconsistent either in their intentions or in their vote], no matter what their final party, listened to fewer broadcasts and read fewer national newspapers than the regular voters."[3] These observations are consistent with the most widely accepted finding on mass-media impact: "Media exposure gets out the vote at the same time that it solidifies preferences. It crystallizes and reinforces more than it converts."[4]

Accordingly, then, the election period serves less as a force for change than as a period for reclarification. There are several concrete circumstances in a campaign which severely circumscribe opportunities for observing the influence of mass-media propaganda.

Most obvious in this connection is the observation, confirmed in different contexts and by different methods, that the minds of most voters are closed even before the campaign officially opens. At various places and at different times, this figure has been set at anywhere from 50 to 84 per cent of the voters.[5] But even if a voter arrives at his decision late in the campaign, he is not necessarily in a constant quandary, endlessly pulled in opposite directions by conflicting propaganda. Evidence from panel studies indicates that in most cases where the final decision comes late in the campaign, prior leanings are crystallized into a firm intent. The impregnability of voting intentions as a whole limits drastically the number of people who are, so to speak, potential converts.

Moreover, during a campaign, people cannot help but be aware, however unhappily, that they are the targets of deliberate propaganda. Neither side enjoys a monopoly of available space or time, and so propaganda is almost always exposed as such. Expecting attempts at persuasion, voters come prepared with stereotyped meanings. It is not altogether unusual to hear speeches discounted as so much campaign talk. People, being aware of the intent of the messages, tend to avoid views contrary to their own. They tend to believe their own side and to question the arguments of the other. As long as old loyalties are activated, selective perception will serve as an effective screen....

At any rate, the number of people who have already "made up their minds" before the campaign begins, the overwhelming importance of "filtering" effects resulting from self-selection and selective perception of media content, and the awareness of the intent with which all campaign statements are phrased all work together to make "conversion" through any medium particularly difficult during an election. But, in addition, there is something in the way the problem is approached which may obscure certain ways in which the mass media are effective....

PERSONAL INFLUENCE AND MASS INFLUENCE

The mass media, then, exert some of the influence they do because they are more than a channel through which national party policy is brought before the local electorate. In filtering, structuring, and spotlighting certain public activities, the media content is not confined to conveying what party spokesmen proclaim and what the candidates say. All news that bears on political activity and beliefs—and not only campaign speeches and campaign propaganda—is somehow relevant to the vote. Not only during the campaign but also in the periods between, the mass media provide perspectives, shape images of candidates and parties, help highlight issues around which a campaign will develop, and define the unique atmosphere and areas of sensitivity which mark any particular campaign. Any long-run view, therefore, reveals certain differences among elections which make clear that in each case voters, much as they may respond to traditional allegiances, also respond to a unique historical situation.

The scheme of analysis outlined in *Voting* barely touches upon the role of the mass media in creating a secondhand reality, through which public policy is elaborated and the effects of that policy on the voter clarified and made tangible. The "main concern," we are told, "is with the electorate itself. How many individuals pay *direct* attention to the campaign via the mass media?"[6] In this scheme the mass media act primarily as transmitters of content supplied by the national parties and by their candidates and subsequently consumed, in one way or another, by the electorate. The personal network of communications within the community hooks onto and makes use of the mass media. Opinion leaders usually pay more attention to the mass media than their peers, and they relay relevant information to those less firm in their partisan convictions....

The persons generally designated by social scientists as "opinion leaders" prepare the ground for mass-media impact. They translate the mass-media reality into the experience of local groups. Some persons may enjoy informal status as opinion leaders precisely because they attend to the relevant mass-media content. Or it may be that in order to wield influence a man may have to be especially knowledgeable about what the mass media do and say. In either case, the opinion leaders exhibit greater responsiveness to the mass media, channeling for their peers—to whose dispositions they are particularly sensitive—that which the mass media have already made significant.

Theirs is essentially a transmission function and through them the views and interests of persons not directly exposed to the content of the mass media are involved. Yet these leaders select what they will transmit, and hence such influentials need not act only as a stabilizing influence. An emergent local leadership at odds with the official party may make use of whatever prestige or credibility the mass-media content has per se to subvert older loyalties.

The short-run frame of reference, with its primary concern with the electorate and how it lines up within the course of a single campaign, has perhaps exaggerated the dominant role of personal influences and the effectiveness of "normal" social pressures. For it puts the accent on the type of changer who is most susceptible—perhaps by a sort of default—to such influences, that is, it draws attention almost exclusively to changers who are converted or whose decision crystallizes only *during the campaign*. In the first place, such persons are, quite logically, those with a relatively low interest in politics and for whom political loyalties are not ordinarily salient; second, they are further characterized by low mass-media exposure....

SECONDHAND REALITY AND
THE MASS AUDIENCE

Persons in the mass society are, as we all know, members of many more or less formally organized groups. Some of these memberships are, of course, more politically relevant than others. Trade unionists in the United States tend to vote Democratic; in England they most often side with Labour. Some minority groups "stick together" politically, and some organizations formed to defend "majority" interests have their own characteristic voting patterns. We know a considerable amount about the political perspectives that derive from such memberships and about the cross-pressures exerted by multiple allegiances.

We are also aware that most of what people know about political life comes to them secondhand—or even thirdhand—through the mass media. The media do structure a very real political environment but one which, even in these days of TV, we can only know "at a distance." Because of the way people select from the political content of the mass media and interpret what they select, the political communication system serves to transmit materials peculiarly relevant to persons in various milieus. Beyond this, however, the mass media also structure a larger, nonlocal reality from which it is hard to escape. The content filters through, even though people are not directly exposed to it or do not claim to be paying a great deal of attention.[7] There is something obtrusive about what the mass media present, something that makes their influence cumulative.

The mass media have, then, another function. They not only transmit materials that feed into the political perspectives of relevant groups; they leave an impress of their own. There are political perspectives that rise out of an individual's position as a member of a mass, as the object of direct and indirect stimuli coming from the mass media. The relationships between voting behavior and the perspectives developed by virtue of one's position in the mass have as yet been inadequately investigated, perhaps because of the very real methodological difficulties involved, perhaps because we overestimate the difficulties or fear to risk criticism of our results....

CONCLUSION

... Studies in voting behavior have dealt with both long-run trends and short-run changes. In either case, since voting rates and voting decisions can be determined with a high degree of validity, we seek inferences about antecedent conditions influencing these end products of political activity. Such influences as age differences, regional locations, and traditional political affiliations which may affect voting habits can with relative ease be isolated for examination. When we come to deal with mass-media influences, however, these are much more difficult to single out. They operate among a multitude of other factors and their effects do not always take tangible shape. Consequently, the measures of mass-media exposure are usually crude and the effects looked for are relatively specific and short run.

Quite naturally, campaign studies such as we have been considering, have focused on the short-range influences operating during the period of active electioneering and on how these culminate in a final voting decision. It so happens, as we have tried to point out, that this approach to the problem, with its emphasis on individual conversion during the "official" campaign, minimizes the important cumulative influences of the mass media and emphasizes instead how political communications are transmitted through personal networks and how latent tendencies are activated. In this way, attention has been focused on the limits to mass-media influence.

Where the question for study is "What makes the electorate tick?" research is naturally shaped to fit the problem; the mass media become just one among many concerns. On the other hand, experts in mass communications have not in recent years distinguished themselves by probing the long-range influence of mass media on political life—and more particularly on voting behavior. The cumulative and society-wide effects about which we often talk vaguely as shifts in public moods or drifts in political opinion are hard to demonstrate; yet, if we would further our knowledge of political behavior, such effects are much in need of clarification. And they can only be clarified through research specifically designed to get at them.

In turning attention to the continuous, and not only the intermittent, aspects of mass-media influence, we must deal, first, with the role of *mass* communications as such, focusing not only on the communicator's job as a transmitting agent for party propagandists but on the direct impress the communications have on what individuals in the mass society know of the larger political world. We have to get at the political perspectives that rise out of the individual's remote participation in politics as a member of the mass and at the relationships between voting behavior and these perspectives.

Moreover, we must develop a more apt definition of relevant changes and "changers." In place of turnover during a campaign, changes in party allegiances between one election and the next, together with discrepancies between "fundamental dispositions" and voting decisions, ticket splitting, and the like, are suggested.

A few specific problems for study have been directly outlined or indicated. The imagery made especially relevant by the mass media—the imagery of the "public imagination," of public personalities, of what politics is really like—and the relationship of such imagery to party alignments seem noteworthy. Among other subjects, the specific role of television, its authenticity and the exploitation of that authenticity by public officials and publicity directors, and the impact of such exploitation on voting participation constitute important areas for inquiry.

NOTES

1. B. R. Berelson, P. F. Lazarsfeld, and W. N. McPhee, *Voting* (Chicago: University of Chicago Press, 1954); R. S. Milne and H. C. Mackenzie, *Straight Fight* (London: the Hansard Society, 1954); and Angus Campbell, Gerald Gurin, and W. E. Miller, *The Voter Decides* (Evanston, Ill.: Row, Peterson, 1954).

2. In a separate article, the authors have discussed the role of television but qualify their data in stating that they had "no clear evidence" on how it affected the voting. Cf. Angus Campbell and Others, "Television and the Elections," *Scientific American,* 188 (1953), 46–48.

3. Milne and Mackenzie, *op. cit.,* pp. 96 ff.

4. Berelson, Lazarsfeld, and McPhee, *op. cit.,* p. 248.

5. In Erie County, Ohio (1940), roughly one half were pre-campaign deciders. Cf. P. F. Lazarsfeld, B. R. Berleson, and Hazel Gaudet, *The People's Choice* (2d ed.; New York: Columbia University Press, 1948), p. 53. According to a "Gallup" poll before nomination day, 84 per cent of the British electorate were already decided. Cited by R. B. McCallum and A. Readman, *The British General Election of 1945* (London: Oxford University Press, 1947), p. 201. British figures seem to hover around the 80 per cent mark, with American figures, perhaps because of the more protracted campaign period, on the whole closer to two-thirds.

6. Berelson, Lazarsfeld, and McPhee, *op. cit.* p. 235. Italics supplied.

7. Berelson, Lazarsfeld, and McPhee, *op. cit.,* report this "unexpected" finding: "More people showed signs of exposure than claimed to be paying 'attention.' "

1.4 ELIHU KATZ

The Two-Step Flow of Communication: An Up-to-Date Report on an Hypothesis

Elihu Katz was a member of the Bureau of Applied Social Research at Columbia University. Much of his work there was influenced by prominent market researcher Paul F. Lazarsfeld, coauthor of the marketing study *The People's Choice: How the Voter Makes Up His Mind in a Presidential Campaign.* In commenting on this study's conclusions, Katz wrote, "Of all the ideas in *The People's Choice,* . . . the two-step flow hypothesis is probably the one that was least well documented by empirical data."

In the following excerpt from his article "The Two-Step Flow of Communication: An Up-to-Date Report on an Hypothesis," *Public Opinion Quarterly* (Spring 1957), Katz compares some of the studies that followed *The People's Choice* to analyze interpersonal influence and its impact on voter behavior. Three studies—*The Rovere Study, The Decatur Study,* and *The Elmira Study*—each further examined the role of opinion leaders in influencing attitudes and behaviors. Katz also applies the two-step flow hypothesis to what became known as *The Drug Study* to determine interpersonal influence in diffusion research.

By further exploring the applications of the two-step flow hypothesis, Katz attempted to explain how and under what circumstances ameliorating factors in interpersonal influence might occur. His comparative research on the role of personal influence had a great impact on many subsequent studies.

29

Katz received his Ph.D. from Columbia University. He was an assistant professor at the University of Chicago and a lecturer in sociology at the Hebrew University in Jerusalem. He is now with the Communication Institute at the Hebrew University. He has authored or coauthored many books on the study of media, including *Broadcasting in the Third World: Promise and Performance* (Harvard University Press, 1977), with George Wedell; *The Export of Meaning: Cross-Cultural Readings of Dallas* (Oxford University Press, 1990), with Tamar Liebes; and *Media Events: The Live Broadcasting of History* (Harvard University Press, 1992), with Daniel Dayan.

Key Concept: personal influence and two-step flow

*A*nalysis of the process of decision-making during the course of an election campaign led the authors of *The People's Choice* to suggest that the flow of mass communications may be less direct than was commonly supposed. It may be, they proposed, that influences stemming from the mass media first reach "opinion leaders" who, in turn, pass on what they read and hear to those of their every-day associates for whom they are influential. This hypothesis was called "the two-step flow of communication."[1]

The hypothesis aroused considerable interest. The authors themselves were intrigued by its implications for democratic society. It was a healthy sign, they felt, that people were still most successfully persuaded by give-and-take with other people and that the influence of the mass media was less automatic and less potent than had been assumed. For social theory, and for the design of communications research, the hypothesis suggested that the image of modern urban society needed revision. The image of the audience as a mass of disconnected individuals hooked up to the media but not to each other could not be reconciled with the idea of a two-step flow of communication implying, as it did, networks of interconnected individuals through which mass communications are channeled.

Of all the ideas in *The People's Choice*, however, the two-step flow hypothesis is probably the one that was least well documented by empirical data. And the reason for this is clear: the design of the study did not anticipate the importance which interpersonal relations would assume in the analysis of the data. Given the image of the atomized audience which characterized so much of mass media research, the surprising thing is that interpersonal influence attracted the attention of the researchers at all.[2]

In the almost seventeen years since the voting study was undertaken, several studies at the Bureau of Applied Social Research of Columbia University have attempted to examine the hypothesis and to build upon it. Four such studies will be singled out for review. These are Merton's study of interpersonal influence and communications behavior in Rovere;[3] the Decatur study of decision-making in marketing, fashions, movie-going and public affairs, reported by Katz and Lazarsfeld;[4] the Elmira study of the 1948 election campaign reported by Berelson, Lazarsfeld and McPhee;[5] and, finally, a very recent study by Coleman, Katz and Menzel on the diffusion of a new drug among doctors.[6] ...

DESIGNS OF THREE SUBSEQUENT STUDIES

... 1. *The Rovere Study.* Undertaken just as the 1940 voting study was being completed, the earliest of the three studies was conducted in a small town in New Jersey. It began by asking a sample of 86 respondents to name the people to whom they turned for information and advice regarding a variety of matters. Hundreds of names were mentioned in response, and those who were designated four times or more were considered opinion leaders. These influentials were then sought out and interviewed.[7] ...

2. *The Decatur Study,* carried out in 1945–46, tried to go a step further.[8] Like the voting study, but unlike Rovere, it tried to account for decisions—specific instances in which the effect of various influences could be discerned and assessed. Like Rovere, but unlike the voting study, it provided for interviews with the persons whom individuals in the initial sample had credited as influential in the making of recent decisions (in the realms of marketing, movie-going, and public affairs). The focus of the study this time was not on the opinion leaders alone, but (1) on the relative importance of personal influence and (2) on the person who named the leader as well as the leader—the advisor-advisee dyad....

The authors of *The People's Choice* had said that "asking people to whom they turn and then investigating the interaction between advisers and advisees... would be extremely difficult if not impossible." And, in fact, it proved to be extremely difficult. Many problems were encountered in the field work, the result of which was that not all the "snowball" interviews could be completed.[9] In many parts of the analysis of the data, therefore, it was necessary to revert to comparisons of leaders and non-leaders, imputing greater influence to groups with higher concentrations of self-designated leadership. Yet, in principle, it was demonstrated that a study design taking account of interpersonal relations was both possible and profitable to execute.

But about the time it became evident that this goal was within reach, the goal itself began to change. It began to seem desirable to take account of chains of influence longer than those involved in the dyad; and hence to view the adviser-advisee dyad as one component of a more elaborately structured social group.

These changes came about gradually and for a variety of reasons. First of all, findings from the Decatur study and from the later Elmira study revealed that the opinion leaders themselves often reported that their own decisions were influenced by still other people.[10] It began to seem desirable, therefore, to think in terms of the opinion leaders of opinion leaders.[11] Secondly, it became clear that opinion leadership could not be viewed as a "trait" which some people possess and others do not, although the voting study sometimes implied this view. Instead, it seemed quite apparent that the opinion leader is influential at certain times and with respect to certain substantive areas by virtue of the fact that he is "empowered" to be so by other members of his group. Why certain people are chosen must be accounted for not only in demographic terms (social status, sex, age, etc.) but also in terms of the structure and values of the groups of which both adviser and advisee are members. Thus, the unexpected rise of young men to opinion leadership in traditional groups, when these groups faced the new situations of urbanization and industrialization, can be understood only against the background of old and new patterns of social relations within the group and of old and new patterns of orientation to the world outside the group.[12] Reviewing the literature of small group research hastened the formulation of this conception.[13]

One other factor shaped the direction of the new program as well. Reflecting upon the Decatur study, it became clear that while one could talk about the role of various influences in the making of fashion *decisions by individuals,* the study design was not adequate for the study of fashion in the aggregate— *fashion as a process of diffusion*—as long as it did not take account of either the content of the decision or the time factor involved. The decisions of the "fashion changers" studied in Decatur might have cancelled each other out: while Mrs. X reported a change from Fashion A to Fashion B, Mrs. Y might have been reporting a change from B to A. What is true for fashion is true for any other diffusion phenomenon: to study it, one must trace the flow of some specific item over time. Combining this interest in diffusion with that of studying the role of more elaborate social networks of communication gave birth to a new study which focused on (1) a specific item, (2) diffusion over time, (3) through the social structure of an entire community.

3. *The Drug Study.* This study was conducted to determine the way in which doctors make decisions to adopt new drugs. This time, when it came to designing a study which would take account of the possible role of interpersonal influence among physicians, it became clear that there were so few physicians (less than one and one-half per 1000 population) that it was feasible to interview all members of the medical profession in several cities. If all doctors (or all doctors in specialties concerned with the issue at hand) could be interviewed, then there would be no doubt that all adviser-advisee pairs would fall within the sample. All such pairs could then be located within the context of larger social groupings of doctors, which could be measured by sociometric methods....

In addition to the opportunity of mapping the networks of interpersonal relations, the drug study also provided for the two other factors necessary for a true diffusion study: attention to a specific item in the course of gaining acceptance, and a record of this diffusion over time. This was accomplished by means of an audit of prescriptions on file in the local pharmacies of the cities studied, which made it possible to date each doctor's earliest use of a particular new drug—a drug which had gained widespread acceptance a few months before the study had begun. Each doctor could thus be classified in terms of the promptness of his decision to respond to the innovation, and in terms of other information provided by the prescription audit....

THE IMPACT OF PERSONAL INFLUENCE

Personal and the Mass Media Influence

The 1940 study indicated that personal influence affected voting decisions more than the mass media did, particularly in the case of those who changed their minds during the course of the campaign. The Decatur study went on to explore the relative impact of personal influences and the mass media in three other realms: marketing, fashions and movie-going. Basing its conclusions on the testimony of the decision-makers themselves, and using an instrument for evaluating the relative effectiveness of the various media which entered into the decisions, the Decatur study again found that personal influence figured both more frequently and more effectively than any of the mass media.[14]

In the analysis to date, the drug study has not approached the problem of the relative effectiveness of the various media from the point of view of the doctor's own reconstruction of what went into the making of his decision. Comparing mere frequency of mention of different media, it is clear that colleagues are by no means the most frequently mentioned source. Nevertheless, exploration of the factors related to whether the doctor's decision to adopt the drug came early or late indicates that the factor most strongly associated with the time of adoption of the new drug is the extent of the doctor's integration in the medical community. That is, the more frequently a doctor is named by his colleagues as a friend or a discussion partner, the more likely he is to be an innovator with respect to the new drug. Extent of integration proves to be a more important factor than any background factor (such as age, medical school, or income of patients), or any other source of influence (such as readership of medical journals) that was examined. . . .

THE FLOW OF PERSONAL INFLUENCE

The 1940 voting study found that opinion leaders were not concentrated in the upper brackets of the population but were located in almost equal proportions in every social group and stratum. This finding led to efforts in subsequent studies to establish the extent to which this was true in areas other than election campaigns and also to ascertain what it is that *does* distinguish opinion leaders from those whom they influence.

The first thing that is clear from the series of studies under review is that the subject matter concerning which influence is transmitted has a lot to do with determining who will lead and who follow. Thus, the Rovere study suggests that within the broad sphere of public affairs one set of influentials is occupied with "local" affairs and another with "cosmopolitan" affairs.[15] The Decatur study suggests that in marketing, for example, there is a concentration of opinion leadership among older women with larger families, while in fashions and movie-going it is the young, unmarried girl who has a disproportionate chance of being turned to for advice. There is very little overlap of leadership: a leader in one sphere is not likely to be influential in another unrelated sphere as well.[16]

Yet, even when leadership in one or another sphere is heavily concentrated among the members of a particular group—as was the case with marketing leadership in Decatur—the evidence suggests that people still talk, most of all, to others like themselves. Thus, while the marketing leaders among the older "large-family wives" also influenced other kinds of women, most of their influence was directed to women of their own age with equally large families. In marketing, fashions, and movie-going, furthermore, there was no appreciable concentration of influentials in any of the three socio-economic levels. Only in public affairs was there a concentration of leadership in the highest status, and there was some slight evidence that influence flows from this group to individuals of lower status. The Elmira study also found opinion-leaders in similar proportions on every socio-economic and occupational level and found that conversations concerning the campaign went on, typically, between people of similar age, occupation, and political opinion.

What makes for the concentration of certain kinds of opinion leadership within certain groups? And when influential and influencee are outwardly alike —as they so often seem to be—what, if anything, distinguishes one from the other? Broadly, it appears that influence is related (1) to the *personification of certain values* (who one is); (2) to *competence* (what one knows); and (3) to *strategic social location* (whom one knows). Social location, in turn, divides into whom one knows within a group; and "outside."

Influence is often successfully transmitted because the influencee wants to be as much like the influential as possible.[17] That the young, unmarried girls are fashion leaders can be understood easily in a culture where youth and youthfulness are supreme values. This is an example where "who one is" counts very heavily.

But "what one knows" is no less important.[18] The fact is that older women, by virtue of their greater experience, are looked to as marketing advisers and that specialists in internal medicine—the most "scientific" of the practicing physicians—are the most frequently mentioned opinion leaders among the doctors. The influence of young people in the realm of movie-going can also be understood best in terms of their familiarity with the motion picture world. The Elmira study found slightly greater concentrations of opinion leadership among the more educated people on each socioeconomic level, again implying the importance of competence. Finally, the influence of the "cosmopolitans" in Rovere rested on the presumption that they had large amounts of information.

It is, however, not enough to be a person whom others want to emulate, or to be competent. One must also be accessible. Thus, the Decatur study finds gregariousness—"whom one knows"—related to every kind of leadership. The Rovere study reports that the leadership of the "local" influentials is based on their central location in the web of interpersonal contacts. Similarly, studies of rumor transmission have singled out those who are "socially active" as agents of rumor.[19]

Of course, the importance of whom one knows is not simply a matter of the number of people with whom an opinion leader is in contact. It is also a question of whether the people with whom he is in touch happen to be interested in the area in which his leadership is likely to be sought. For this reason, it is quite clear that the greater interest of opinion leaders in the subjects over which they exert influence is not a sufficient explanation of their influence. While the voting studies as well as the Decatur study show leaders to be more interested, the Decatur study goes on to show that interest alone is not the determining factor.[20] In fashion, for example, a young unmarried girl is considerably more likely to be influential than a matron with an equally great interest in clothes. The reason, it is suggested, is that a girl who is interested in fashion is much more likely than a matron with an equally high interest to know other people who share her preoccupation, and thus is more likely than the matron to have followers who are interested enough to ask for her advice. In other words, it takes two to be a leader—a leader and a follower.

Finally, there is the second aspect of "whom one knows." An individual may be influential not only because people within his group look to him for advice but also because of whom he knows outside his group.[21] Both the Elmira and Decatur studies found that men are more likely than women to be opinion leaders in the realm of public affairs and this, it is suggested, is because they have more of a chance to get outside the home to meet people and talk politics. Similarly, the Elmira study indicated that opinion leaders belonged to more organizations, more often knew workers for the political parties, and so on, than did others. The drug study found that influential doctors could be characterized in terms of such things as their more frequent attendance at out-of-town meetings and the diversity of places with which they maintained contact, particularly far-away places. It is interesting that a study of the farmer-innovators responsible for the diffusion of hybrid seed-corn in Iowa concluded that these leaders also could be characterized in terms of the relative frequency of their trips out of town.[22]

THE OPINION LEADERS AND THE MASS MEDIA

The third aspect of the hypothesis of the two-step flow of communication states that opinion leaders are more exposed to the mass media than are those whom they influence. In *The People's Choice* this is supported by reference to the media behavior of leaders and non-leaders.

The Decatur study corroborated this finding, and went on to explore two additional aspects of the same idea.[23] First of all, it was shown that leaders in a given sphere (fashions, public affairs, etc.) were particularly likely to be exposed to the media appropriate to that sphere. This is essentially a corroboration of the Rovere finding that those who proved influential with regard to "cosmopolitan" matters were more likely to be readers of national news magazines, but that this was not at all the case for those influential with regard to "local" matters. Secondly, the Decatur study shows that at least in the realm of fashions, the leaders are not only more exposed to the mass media, but are also more affected by them in their own decisions. This did not appear to be the case in other realms, where opinion leaders, though more exposed to the media than non-leaders, nevertheless reported personal influence as the major factor in their decisions. This suggests that in some spheres considerably longer chains of person-to-person influence than the dyad may have to be traced back before one encounters any decisive influence by the mass media, even though their contributory influence may be perceived at many points. This was suggested by the Elmira study too. It found that the leaders, though more exposed to the media, also more often reported that they sought information and advice from other persons.[24]

Similarly, the drug study showed that the influential doctors were more likely to be readers of a large number of professional journals and valued them more highly than did doctors of lesser influence. But at the same time, they were as likely as other doctors to say that local colleagues were an important source of information and advice in their reaching particular decisions.

Finally, the drug study demonstrated that the more influential doctors could be characterized by their greater attention not only to medical journals, but to out-of-town meetings and contacts was well. This finding has already been discussed in the previous section treating the *strategic location* of the opinion leader with respect to "the world outside" his group. Considering it again under the present heading suggests that the greater exposure of the opinion leader to the mass media may only be a special case of the more general proposition that opinion leaders serve to relate their groups to relevant parts of the environment through whatever media happen to be appropriate. This more general statement makes clear the similar functions of big city newspapers for the Decatur fashion leader; of national news magazines for the "cosmopolitan" influentials of Rovere; of out-of-town medical meetings for the influential doctor; and of contact with the city for the farmer-innovator in Iowa as well as for the newly-risen, young opinion leaders in underdeveloped areas throughout the world.[25]

CONCLUSIONS

... Opinion leaders and the people whom they influence are very much alike and typically belong to the same primary groups of family, friends and co-workers. While the opinion leader may be more interested in the particular sphere in which he is influential, it is highly unlikely that the persons influenced will be very far behind the leader in their level of interest. Influentials and influencees may exchange roles in different spheres of influence. Most spheres focus the group's attention on some related part of the world outside the group, and it is the opinion leader's function to bring the group into touch with this relevant part of its environment through whatever media are appropriate. In every case, influentials have been found to be more exposed to these points of contact with the outside world. Nevertheless, it is also true that, despite their greater exposure to the media, most opinion leaders are primarily affected not by the communication media but by still other people.

The main emphasis of the two-step flow hypothesis appears to be on only one aspect of interpersonal relations—interpersonal relations as channels of communication. But from the several studies reviewed, it is clear that these very same interpersonal relations influence the making of decisions in at least two additional ways. In addition to serving as networks of communication, interpersonal relations are also sources of pressure to conform to the group's way of thinking and acting, as well as sources of social support. The workings of group pressure are clearly evident in the homogeneity of opinion and action observed among voters and among doctors in situations of unclarity or uncertainty. The social support that comes from being integrated in the medical community may give a doctor the confidence required to carry out a resolution to adopt a new drug. Thus, interpersonal relations are (1) channels of information, (2) sources of social pressure, and (3) sources of social support, and each relates interpersonal relations to decision-making in a somewhat different way.[26]

NOTES

1. Paul F. Lazarsfeld, Bernard Berelson and Hazel Gaudet, *The People's Choice*, New York: Columbia University Press, 1948 (2nd edition), p. 151.

2. For the discussion of the image of the atomized audience and the contravening empirical evidence, see Elihu Katz and Paul F. Lazarsfeld, *Personal Influence: The Part Played by People in the Flow of Mass Communications*, Glencoe, Illinois: The Free Press, 1955, pp. 15–42; Eliot Friedson, "Communications Research and the Concept of the Mass," *American Sociological Review,* Vol. 18, (1953), pp. 313–317; and Morris Janowitz, *The Urban Press in a Community Setting*, Glencoe, Illinois: The Free Press, 1952.

3. Robert K. Merton, "Patterns of Influence: A Study of Interpersonal Influence and Communications Behavior in a Local Community," in Paul F. Lazarsfeld and Frank N. Stanton, eds., *Communications Research, 1948–9,* New York: Harper and Brothers, 1949, pp. 180–219.

4. Elihu Katz and Paul F. Lazarsfeld, *op. cit.,* Part Two.

5. Bernard R. Berelson, Paul F. Lazarsfeld and William N. McPhee, *Voting: A Study of Opinion Formation in a Presidential Campaign,* Chicago: University of Chicago Press, 1954.

6. A report on the pilot phase of this study is to be found in Herbert Menzel and Elihu Katz, "Social Relations and Innovation in the Medical Profession," *Public Opinion Quarterly,* Vol. 19, (1955), pp. 337–52; a volume and various articles on the full study are now in preparation.

7. Merton, *op. cit.,* 184–185.

8. Katz and Lazarsfeld, *op. cit.,* Part Two.

9. Partly this was due to inability to locate the designated people, but partly, too, to the fact that original respondents did not always know the person who had influenced them as is obvious, for example, in the case of a woman copying another woman's hat style, etc. See *Ibid.* pp. 362–363.

10. *Ibid.,* p. 318; Berelson, Lazarsfeld and McPhee, *op. cit.,* p. 110.

11. This was actually tried at one point in the Decatur study. See Katz and Lazarsfeld, *op. cit.* pp. 283–287.

12. See, for example, the articles by Eisenstadt, *op. cit.,* and Glock, *op. cit.;* the Rovere study, too, takes careful account of the structure of social relations and values in which influentials are embedded, and discusses the various avenues to influentiality open to different kinds of people.

13. Reported in Part I of Katz and Lazarsfeld, *op. cit.*

14. Katz and Lazarsfeld, *op. cit.,* pp. 169–186.

15. Merton, *op. cit.,* pp. 187–188.

16. For a summary of the Decatur findings on the flow of interpersonal influence, see Katz and Lazarsfeld, *op. cit.,* pp. 327–334.

17. That leaders are, in a certain sense, the most conformist members of their groups —upholding whatever norms and values are central to the group—is a proposition which further illustrates this point. For an empirical illustration from a highly relevant study, see C. Paul Marsh and A. Lee Coleman, "Farmers' Practice Adoption Rates in Relation to Adoption Rates of Leaders," *Rural Sociology*, Vol. 19 (1954), pp. 180–183.

18. The distinction between "what" and "whom" one knows is used by Merton, *op. cit.*, p. 197.

19. Gordon W. Allport and Leo J. Postman, *The Psychology of Rumor*, New York: Henry Holt, 1943, p. 183.

20. Katz and Lazarsfeld, *op. cit.*, pp. 249–252.

21. It is interesting that a number of studies have found that the most integrated persons within a group are also likely to have more contacts outside the group than others. One might have expected the more marginal members to have more contacts outside. For example, see Blau, *op. cit.*, p. 128.

22. Bryce Ryan and Neal Gross, *Acceptance and Diffusion of Hybrid Seed Corn in Two Iowa Communities*, Ames, Iowa: Iowa State College of Agriculture and Mechanic Arts, Research Bulletin, 372, pp. 706–707. For a general summary, see Ryan and Gross, "The Diffusion of Hybrid Seed Corn in Two Iowa Communities," *Rural Sociology*, Vol. 8 (1942), pp. 15–24. An article, now in preparation, will point out some of the parallels in research design and in findings between this study and the drug study.

23. Katz and Lazarsfeld, *op. cit.*, pp. 309–320.

24. Berelson, Lazarsfeld and McPhee, *op. cit.*, p. 110.

25. See the forthcoming book by Lerner, *et. al* cited above.

26. These different dimensions of interpersonal relations can be further illustrated by reference to studies which represent the "pure type" of each dimension. Studies of rumor flow illustrate the "channels" dimension; see, for example, Jacob L. Moreno, *Who Shall Survive*, Beacon, N.Y.: Beacon House, 1953, pp. 440–450. The study by Leon Festinger, Stanley Schachter and Kurt Back, *Social Pressures in Informal Groups*, New York: Harper and Bros., 1950, illustrates the second dimension. Blau, *op. cit.*, pp. 126–129, illustrates the "social support" dimension.

1.5 JONATHAN COHEN

Parasocial Relations and Romantic Attraction

The following selection is from "Parasocial Relations and Romantic Attraction: Gender and Dating Status Differences," *Journal of Broadcasting and Electronic Media* (vol. 41, 1997). In it, Jonathan Cohen provides an example of effects research informed by years of studying the relationships between forms of media and society. Cohen's study explores how individuals form *parasocial* relationships with television characters and how the attitudes conditioned by this phenomenon influence real interpersonal relationships. Parasocial relationships are imagined relationships with media characters. However, the parasocial relationship is not an imaginary relationship that people form with media characters but one that is grounded in symbolism and attraction. The concept advances researchers' understanding of whom in the media individuals tend to like, admire, or evaluate. Parasocial relationships often result in fanaticism but may exist merely in terms of identification and attraction.

Several features of Cohen's article demonstrate how effects studies have evolved over the years. First, Cohen presupposes that social relationships are complex and subject to a wide range of competing influences. Second, he is able to draw from previous literature, which advanced many of his ideas and assumptions. Third, he attempts to be very specific about the age group he examines. Finally, and most important in the evolution of effects research, he does not attempt to extrapolate his findings to a broad, heterogeneous audience. Instead, his study is constrained by parameters, and, when compared to many earlier studies, Cohen is refreshingly humble in his suggestion of how this study contributes to knowledge of media and social relationships.

Cohen's article shows the complexity between mediated and real interpersonal relationships and draws from literature that analyzes gender differences and attraction in social relationships. Although Cohen used quantitative measurements, the data have been edited here for readability.

Cohen is a lecturer in the Department of Communication at the University of Haifa. This study is based on the author's doctoral dissertation, written at the Annenberg School for Communication at the University of Southern California.

Key Concept: parasocial relationships

One of the ways people integrate media into their social lives is by establishing symbolic, or parasocial, relationships (PSR) with media characters (Horton & Wohl, 1956; Caughey, 1984). Studies have found that PSR are in many ways similar to social relationships (Rubin & McHugh, 1987). Much research has advanced our understanding of why and how these relationships develop, but there are mixed results regarding the ways in which PSR relate to social relationships. Although PSR were originally conceptualized as compensation for lack of social interaction (Horton & Wohl, 1956), Rubin, Perse and Powell (1985) did not find a link between loneliness and PSR. This discrepancy suggests that PSR may be understood and experienced differently by different people. In the current study individual differences in how PSR are perceived by viewers are proposed. These differences are explained as resulting from differences in the content and accessibility of thoughts and feelings about real-life attachment figures, as well as the gender and life position of viewers. It is suggested that while some viewers may experience PSR as symbolic attachments, others may experience PSR as distinct from their social relationships.

The way people understand, feel, and respond to their romantic partners is influenced by their childhood relationships with their primary caregivers (Bowlby, 1969, 1973, 1988; Hazan & Shaver, 1987). The psychological mechanisms that link early experiences with adult feelings, thoughts, and behaviors in relationships comprise an individual's "working model" of attachment. Working models are "cognitive representations of self and others that evolve out of experiences with attachment figures and are concerned with the regulation and fulfillment of attachment needs" (Hazan, Collins, & Clark, 1996, p. 39). The attachment needs of adults consist of a need for intimacy, a secure base and caregiving (Bowlby, 1988), and attachment relationships are those relationships in which we seek to satisfy such needs.

The content of individuals' working models of attachment affects their behavior in attachment relationships.... [A]ttachment researchers have identified three types of attachment styles among adults (Hazan & Shaver, 1987). The secure style is based on positive beliefs about the self and others. People with a secure attachment style are confident and trusting in their relationships with others, and their relationships are characterized by stability, love, security and trust. The avoidant style is based on negative beliefs regarding the outcomes of close relationships. People with an avoidant attachment style tend to avoid romantic involvement, and they prefer to spend time alone. Finally, the anxious attachment style is based on an overriding anxiety about separation and abandonment, and on a preoccupation with being loved by others. People with an anxious attachment style desire extremely intense relationships and develop a 'clingy' relationship orientation (Hazan & Shaver, 1987)....

People with different attachment styles have been shown to differ in the way they think about themselves and their relationships (Bartholomew & Horowitz, 1991), how they interpret and respond to their partner's behaviors (Collins, 1994), how long their relationships tend to last, and how satisfied they are in their relationships (Feeney, Noller, & Callan, 1994). Attachment styles also affect people's attitudes toward their work and the way they use work situations to complement or compensate for their close relationships (Hazan &

Shaver, 1990). While secure adults tend to enjoy their work more and are able to separate their professional and personal lives, avoidants tend to use work as a way to avoid social ties, and anxiously attached adults tend to use work situations as a way to compensate for problems in their relationships (Hazan & Shaver, 1990).

Recently, the attachment perspective has been extended to show that the relationship of the members of fan clubs of stars like Michael Jackson (Steever, 1994), or the felt attachment of religious people with God (Kirpatrick, 1994) are influenced by their attachment models. These studies provide preliminary evidence that people may use their working models of attachment to think about symbolic relationships. . . .

Parasocial Relationships (PSR)

As originally developed by Horton and Wohl in 1956, parasocial relationships are "one-sided interpersonal relationships that television viewers establish with media characters" (Rubin & McHugh, 1987, p. 280.) PSR develop through ongoing interaction between media personae and audience members. From the viewers perspective, PSR increase liking of, and loyalty to, the program, and are positively associated with greater viewing intention, attention, perceived realism, and affinity for TV (Rubin & Perse, 1987).

Several studies suggest that likening PSR to social relationships is more than a useful metaphor. Perse and Rubin (1989) found that length of acquaintance was positively related to strength of relationship in both social and parasocial relationships. Cortez (1992) found that, as in interpersonal relationships, the choice of newscasters with whom viewers formed PSR was predicted by physical and social attraction, shared values, attitudes, background and similarity in communicative style. Thus, parasocial attraction follows many of the patterns identified in interpersonal attraction (Cialdini, 1993).

Moreover, people may use PSR to substitute for lack of social interaction in real life and to prevent themselves from feeling lonely. For example, Yanof (1991) found that compared with light and non-viewers, women who were heavy TV viewers reported stronger parasocial relations but less involvement with their interpersonal relationships. Interestingly, these heavy viewers did not report less satisfaction with their social lives than did light or non-viewers. Thus, it seems that parasocial relations may substitute for diminished interpersonal contact. More generally, in reviewing research on motivations for TV viewing, Rubin (1985) argued that, like interpersonal interaction, TV is often viewed as a way to battle loneliness.

Though TV viewing, and PSR specifically, are often seen as substituting for interpersonal relationships, Rubin, Perse, and Powell (1985) found no correlation between loneliness and the intensity of viewers' PSR. The conflicting findings regarding the use of PSR to alleviate loneliness suggest that PSR may function to broaden the scope of interpersonal relations rather than to compensate for lack of relationships. Another possibility is that there are important situational and individual differences in how people perceive characters and why they develop PSR. Additionally, whereas there is evidence of similarities between PSR and interpersonal relationships, it is unclear whether PSR are similar specifically to attachment relationships or perhaps to friendships, casual acquaintances, or other types of interpersonal relations.

To specify the exact nature of PSR is difficult. Steever (1994) found that some of the members of Michael Jackson's fan club developed very intense PSR that resembled romantic attachments. Analyzing fan mail, she found that many of the fans used terms that indicate attachment relations. However, it is unlikely that such intense fandom is the norm, so it is unreasonable to assume that all people think of PSR as attachment relationships. An attachment perspective may help explain some PSR, but it may be irrelevant to the PSR experienced by others.

PSR and Attachment

... Who, then, is likely to apply working models of attachment to understanding and responding to PSR? In many social situations accessibility has been found to be important in predicting which cognitive structures people will apply (e.g., Fiske & Taylor, 1984; Devine, 1989; Higgins & King, 1981). This suggests that when engaging in PSR, people whose attachment models are more active and accessible are more likely to apply their attachment models to their reactions and feelings.

Because the most salient attachment figures for young adults are their romantic partners (Hazan & Zeifner, 1994), working models of attachments are more likely to be accessible to adults who are involved in romantic relationships than to those who are not. Thus, while relating to TV characters, dating young adults should be more likely than non-dating young adults to activate their attachment models. Therefore, a greater correspondence is expected between the content of dating adults' working models (attachment anxiety, security, and feelings about intimacy), and the intensity of their PSR. ...

While expecting a stronger correlation between attachment and PSR for dating subjects than for single subjects, the direction of such associations remains unclear. One possibility is that viewers develop PSR as a way to compensate for problems in their relationships, because PSR are safe and stable (Cohen & Metzger, 1995). In this case, PSR would be more intense the more anxious a subject is. Another possibility is that viewers will use PSR simply to complement existing attachment relationships, and PSR will be more intense the more secure a subject is about his or her attachment. Why certain viewers use PSR to complement, and others to compensate, for interpersonal relationships may reflect differences in how different viewers think of interpersonal relationships.

Gender Differences

The literature on personal relationships has documented the different ways in which men and women experience relationships. Men, unlike women, have been found to think of their friendships more as goal-oriented than expressive (Fox, Gibbs, & Auerbach, 1983). Reviewing gender differences in close relationships, Acitelli and Young (1996) conclude that men report relationship anxiety more than women, and that women monitor and evaluate their relationships more than men, and think about relationships in a more complex fashion than men (Acitelli & Young, 1996). Men tend to think about close relationships mainly when problems arise, whereas women tend to think about their relationships more spontaneously than men (Burnett, 1987).

Wood (1986) argues that in the romantic relationship domain, men and women think about crises in their relationships differently. Whereas women tend to focus on themselves and talk about problems in relational levels and self-identity, men look outside themselves and tend to define the problem in terms of flaws in their partner and external circumstances. It is logical, then, that men who are anxious about the state of their romantic relationships may turn to PSR for support, whereas insecure women will focus their energy on fixing their romantic relationship rather than depending on PSR.

Whereas men use PSR to deal with attachment anxiety, women may use PSR to seek additional social interaction when relationships are going well. It has been suggested that men often rely only on their partners for emotional support, whereas women maintain other support networks such as family and friends (Helgeson, 1994). Thus men, who may have less social support than women, are more likely to turn to TV for comfort when they are anxious about the future of their relationships. Women, on the other hand, may depend more on family and friends. This suggests that as women are more secure about their relationships they may be more likely than men to develop PSR as additional outlets for relational expression....

METHOD

Participants

209 graduate and undergraduate students from two college campuses in the Los Angeles area completed questionnaires as part of a larger study between March and May 1995....

While not randomly selected, the sample was quite diverse: ethnically 46.4% of the sample was Caucasian, 30.1% was Asian, 13.4% was Hispanic, 2.9% was African-American. 3.8% of the sample reported identifying as part of other ethnic groups and 3.3% did not report their ethnic background. The sample consisted of 120 males and 88 females, who ranged in age from 17 to 48 ($m = 20.7$ years, $SD = 4.5$ years). 81 subjects were dating at the time of the study, 119 were not dating, and 9 did not report their relationship status.

Procedure

Subjects were recruited from a variety of classes in departments including Math, Physics and Economics, as well as from graduate and undergraduate Communication courses. Following initial contact with the author, instructors agreed to allow class time for the completion of questionnaire. Classes ranged in size, but none had less than a dozen subjects. Thus, all questionnaires were completed in large groups. . . .

Subjects completed a questionnaire entitled "The media and you". They were assured of the anonymity of their responses, and were told that their participation was strictly voluntary. Once the survey was completed, all subjects were fully debriefed about the goals of the research and allowed to ask questions.

Measurement

Demographic questions. Subjects were first asked a series of demographic questions including age, gender, ethnicity and year in school. The questionnaire also included questions regarding relationship status. Subjects were asked whether they were currently in a relationship, and if not, if they had ever been involved in a relationship. Several questions assessing satisfaction with, and duration of, both present or past relationships were also included. In the case of past relationships subjects were asked when their last one ended, and how long their past relationships lasted.

Attachment styles. Individual differences in attachment were measured using the Collins and Read (1990) adult Attachment Scale (AAS) as modified by Collins (1994). The AAS consists of statements regarding one's beliefs and feelings about romantic attachments. It includes 18 statements that measure the three dimensions that underlie Working models of attachment: Close, Depend and Anxiety.

As described by Collins (1994), the Close dimension represents " . . . the extent to which a person is comfortable with closeness and intimacy." The Depend subscale measures " . . . the extent to which a person is comfortable depending on others and believes that people can be relied upon when needed." The Anxiety subscale measures " . . . the extent to which a person is worried about being rejected and abandoned by others" (pp. 13–14). Subjects were asked to respond to all statements in terms of close relationships. Responses ranged from 1 (not at all characteristic of me) to 5 (very characteristic of me). . . .

Parasocial relations. To assess the intensity of the parasocial relations viewers developed with characters, each subject was asked to write the name of his or her favorite TV character and the name of the show in which the character appears. Subjects were then asked to respond to the short version of the ParaSocial Interaction scale developed by Rubin, Perse, and Powell (1985). These statements were taken from the original twenty items as described by Rubin and Perse (1987). The scale includes ten statements to which subjects respond on a five-point scale ranging from 1 (strongly disagree) to 5 (strongly agree). Items described behaviors and feelings toward a TV persona, such as "My favorite character makes me feel comfortable, as if I am with friends." . . .

Favorite character choices. No instructions or limitations were specified as to the character choices subjects were to make. Nonetheless, close to 90% of subjects chose fictional characters, 7% chose animated characters and the rest chose real TV personae. 71% chose male characters as their favorite. Women were more likely to choose a favorite male character (74% of women) than men were to choose favorite female character (27% of men). No other gender differences were found in choices of characters. 68% chose characters from comedy series, 31% from drama series, and the rest chose characters from news or reality shows. Dating subjects were more likely to choose opposite sex favorite characters than same sex characters (41 opposite sex vs. 26 same sex), while the reverse was true for non-daters (35 opposite sex vs. 54 same sex).... No other dating status differences were found in character choices. Choice of same-sex or different-sex favorite characters was not related to any of the components of working models of attachment, nor was it related to the intensity of PSR. No differences in any of the 3 attachment dimensions or the intensity of PSR were found among subjects choosing real, fictional, or animated characters or among subjects choosing male and female characters. Thus, it seems that the type of character chosen had little effect on the association between attachment and the intensity of PSR. Rather, it seems that individual differences among viewers account for these associations.

Analysis

The first hypothesis predicted that the correlations between attachment dimensions and levels of PSR would be greater for dating than non-dating subjects. By dividing the sample into two groups based on their dating status, comparisons of the relationships between attachment and PSR for each of the groups separately were made. This comparison revealed that for non-dating subjects, none of the attachment dimensions were significantly related to PSR. Among dating subjects the Depend factor of attachment correlated significantly with PSR..., as predicted. Attachment anxiety was positively related to PSR but this association was not significant... and comfort with intimacy was not related to PSR....

The second hypothesis predicted that the PSR of dating women would be positively related to attachment security. This was based on the assumption that women in secure relationships would be more likely to broaden their relationship networks by engaging in imaginary relationships. PSR for women, therefore, was expected to play a complementary rather than a compensatory role.

This hypothesis was supported. Female subjects' ability to depend on their partner was substantially related to PSR.... Comfort with intimacy, another measure of attachment security, was also marginally related to PSR.... As expected, attachment anxiety was not associated with PSR for women....

The third hypothesis was that men's PSR would be associated with attachment anxiety but not attachment security. Men, it was argued, would be more likely to turn to PSR for relational compensation when they were anxious about their real-life relationships. This prediction was confirmed by findings that among male daters attachment anxiety was positively correlated with PSR.... The ability to depend on one's partner was not related to PSR... nor was one's comfort with intimacy....

In sum, our results show that the use of working models of attachment in PSR was limited to dating subjects, and that their use differed by gender. Women seem to perceive PSR as a way to expand their relational network, and indeed, their attachment security was positively related to the intensity of their PSR. Men, on the other hand, turned to PSR more as they were anxious about the future of their social relationships, and so the intensity of their PSR was positively related to their attachment anxiety.

DISCUSSION

This study set out to explore the way TV viewers understand their symbolic relationships with favorite TV characters. It was hypothesized that viewers would apply their thoughts and feelings about close relationship to TV personae. By applying Attachment Theory, and the concept of working models, differences in how PSR were experienced by different groups defined by their life position and gender were predicted. It was found that working models of attachment were more likely to be activated by dating than non-dating subjects in PSR. Moreover, gender differences in how subjects thought about PSR were consistent with previous research on gender differences in interpersonal relationships.

... This study suggests that the gender differences in PSR are parallel to those in social relationships. Moreover, while the results of this study do not bear directly on how people think of TV viewing as a whole, how they use TV, and what it means in their lives, there is reason to believe that gender differences exist in the general meaning TV takes on in people's lives. From this and other studies, it seems that women experience TV viewing as a more relational activity than men, whereas men are more task-oriented in their understanding and use of TV than are women.

That TV viewing is a more relational experience for women is also supported by their favor for drama and other fiction depicting relationships. On the other hand, the task-oriented nature of TV viewing for men is evident in their favor for non-fictional shows (e.g., Morley, 1986). The higher intensity of PSR developed by women than by men in this study also supports the suggested pattern of gender differences in understanding of TV viewing. Finally, the use of PSR by women in an attempt to complement secure attachments, and by men to deal with fears of being abandoned, also suggests that men turn to TV to solve problems whereas women see TV as a friend or companion....

The nature of symbolic relationships with TV characters varies, it seems, as do other aspects of audience reactions to, and interpretations of, televised texts. Just as viewers' experiences reflect their cultural background (Liebes & Katz, 1990), psychological needs (Conway & Rubin, 1991), and life position (Rubin, 1985), the way they relate to characters reflects their attachment needs and working models. This is consistent with evidence that mediated interactions, more generally, follow patterns of interpersonal interactions rather than a schema all their own (Reeves & Nass, 1996).

That reception differences follow both cultural and personal factors has been part of the canon of media scholarship for some time (Hoijer, 1992), but as Livingstone (1996) has noted, there is a need to specify differences in reception. As in Livingstone's work (Livingstone, 1991), this study demonstrates that by using concepts from social cognition research, as well as from other areas of social-psychological inquiry, it is possible to make advances in understanding how people experience TV. A final implication of this work is the extension of Attachment Theory into media studies. The ability to use Attachment Theory in analyzing audience psychology is further evidence of the theory's usefulness.

Limitations and Future Research

Due to certain limitations, the results of this study must be qualified and should be viewed as preliminary evidence. First, the use of a student sample requires that this study be replicated before any generalizations can be made. Student populations are often unstable in terms of both their relational schemata and their media consumption patterns. While it was felt that for an initial exploration of the role of attachment working models in imaginary relationships a student sample was adequate, it is important that the use of attachment models in developing PSR be tested in other populations as well. Indeed, it is quite reasonable to surmise that stronger and more consistent results may be identified in adult populations who have structured TV viewing habits as well as more stable working models of attachment. Nonetheless, the use of a student sample has the advantage of examining a group of subjects for whom interpersonal relations, both symbolic and social, are important and salient. Moreover, as compared with older adults, college students are more likely to look to symbolic relationships as models of adult relationships.

Second, although schema availability can explain why working models apply to PSR only for daters, we are still unsure what PSR represents for non-daters. Future research should attempt to identify theories of friendship or role-modeling that may shed light on this issue. Also, we know that PSR commonly develop with newscasters (Rubin, Perse, & Powell, 1985), talk-show hosts (Horton & Wohl, 1956), and salespeople on home-shopping networks (Auter & Moore, 1993). However, because of the predominance of fictional characters chosen by subjects in this study, the current data tell us little about the ways people experience PSR with other types of TV performers. Our analyses suggest that there are no systematic differences in who chooses fictional and non-fictional performers as favorites, but future research should examine more closely any possible differences in the ways PSR with different types of performers are experienced.

REFERENCES

Acitelli, L. K., & Young, A. M. (1996). Gender and thought in relationships. In G. J. Fletcher, & J. Fitness (Eds.), *Knowledge structures in close relationships: A social psychological approach* (pp. 147–168). Mahwah, NJ: Erlbaum.

Auter, P. J., & Moore, R. L. (1993). Buying from a friend: A content analysis of two teleshopping programs. *Journalism Quarterly, 70*(2), 425–436.

Bartholomew, K., & Horowitz, L. M. (1991). Attachment styles among young adults: A test of a four category model. *Journal of Personality and Social Psychology, 61*(2), 226–244.

Bowlby, J. (1969). *Attachment and loss: Vol. I. Attachment.* New York: Basic Books.

Bowlby, J. (1973). *Attachment and loss: Vol. II. Separation.* New York: Basic Books.

Bowlby, J. (1988). *A secure base: Parent-child attachment and healthy human development.* New York: Basic Books.

Burnett, R. (1987). Reflection in personal relationships. In R. Burnett, P. McGhee, & D. C. Clarke (Eds.), *Accounting for relationships: Explanation, representation and knowledge* (pp. 74–93). London: Methuen.

Caughey, J. L. (1984). *Imaginary social worlds: A cultural approach.* Lincoln: University of Nebraska Press.

Cialdini, R. B. (1993). *Influence: Science and practice* (3rd ed.). New York: Harper Collins.

Cohen, J., & Metzger, M. (1995). Social affiliation and the achievement of ontological security through interpersonal and mass communication. Paper presented at the annual conference of the International Communication Association. Albuquerque, New Mexico, 1995.

Collins, N. L. (1994). *Working models of attachment: Implications or explanation, emotion, and behavior.* Unpublished manuscript.

Collins, N. L., & Read, S. J. (1990). Adult attachment, working models, and relationship quality in dating couples. *Journal of Personality and Social Psychology, 58*(4), 644–663.

Collins, N. L., & Read, S. J. (1994). Cognitive representations of attachment: The structure and function of working models. In K. Bartholomew & D. Perlman (Eds.), *Advances in personal relationships: Vol. 5. Attachment processes in adulthood* (pp. 53–90). London: Kingsley.

Conway, J. C., & Rubin, A. M. (1991). Psychological predictors of viewing motivation. *Communication Research, 18*(4), 443–46.

Cortez, C. A. (1992). Mediated interpersonal communication: The role of attraction and perceived homophily in the development of parasocial relationships (Doctoral dissertation, University of Iowa, 1992). *Dissertation Abstracts International, 53*(1-A), 71848.

Devine, P. G. (1989). Stereotypes and prejudice: Their automatic and controlled components. *Journal of Personality and Social Psychology, 56*(1), 5–18.

Feeney, J. A., Noller, P., & Callan, V. J. (1994). Attachment style, communication and satisfaction in the early years of marriage. In K. Bartholomew & D. Perlman (Eds.) *Advances in personal relationships: Vol. 5. Attachment processes in adulthood* (pp. 269–308). London: Kingsley.

Fiske, S. T., & Taylor, S. E. (1984). *Social cognition.* Reading, MA: Addison-Wesley.

Fox, M., Gibbs, M., & Auerbach, D. (1983). Age and gender dimensions of friendship. *Psychology of Women Quarterly, 9*, 489–501.

Hazan, C., Collins, N., & Clark, C. L. (1996). Attachment styles and internal working models of self and relationship patterns. In G. J. O. Fletcher & J. Fitness (Eds.), *Knowledge structures in close relationship: A social psychological approach* (pp. 25–62). Mahwah, NJ: Erlbaum.

Hazan, C., & Shaver, P. R. (1987). Romantic love conceptualized as an attachment process. *Journal of Personality and Social Psychology, 52*, 511–524.

Hazan, C., & Shaver, P. R. (1990). Love and work: An attachment-theoretical perspective. *Journal of Personality and Social Psychology, 59*(2), 270–280.

Hazan, C., & Zeifner, D. (1994). Sex and the psychological tether. In K. Bartholomew & D. Perlman (Eds.), *Advances in personal relationships: Vol. 5 Attachment processes in adulthood* (pp. 151–180). London: Kingsley.

Helgeson, V. S. (1994). Long-distance romantic relationships: Sex differences in adjustment and breakup. *Personality and Social Psychology Bulletin, 20*(3), 254–265.

Higgins, E.T., & King, G. (1981). Accessibility of social constructs: Information processing consequences of individual and contextual variability. In N. Cantor & J. Kihlstrom (Eds.), *Personality, cognition, and social interaction* (pp. 69–121). Hillsdale, NJ: Erlbaum.

Hoijer, B. (1992). Socio-cognitive structures and television reception. *Media, Culture and Society, 14,* 583–603.

Horton, D., & Wohl, R. R. (1956). Mass communication and para-social interaction. *Psychiatry, 19,* 215–229.

Kirpatrick, L. A., (1994). The role of attachment in religious belief and behavior. In K. Bartholomew & D. Perlman (Eds.), *Advances in personal relationships: Vol. 5. Attachment processes in adulthood* (pp. 239–268). London: Kingsley.

Liebes, T., & Katz, E. (1990). *The export of meaning: Cross-cultural readings of Dallas.* New York: Oxford University Press.

Livingstone, S. M. (1991). *Making sense of television: The psychology of audience interpretation.* Oxford: Pergamon Press.

Livingstone, S. (1996). Relationships between media and audiences: Prospects for future research. Paper presented at the International Seminar in honor of Elihu Katz, Jerusalem, Israel.

Morley, D. (1986). *Family television: Cultural power and domestic leisure.* London: Comedia.

Perse, E. M., & Rubin, R. B. (1989). Attribution in social and parasocial relationships. *Communication Research, 16*(1), 59–77.

Reeves, B., & Nass, C. (1996). *The media equation: How people treat computers, television, and new media like real people and places.* New York: Cambridge University Press.

Rubin, A. M. (1985). Media gratifications through the life cycle. In K. E. Rosengren, L. A. Wenner, & P. Palmgreen (Eds.), *Media gratifications research: Current perspectives* (pp. 195–208). Beverly Hills, CA: Sage.

Rubin, R. B., & McHugh, M. P. (1987). Development of parasocial interaction relationships. *Journal of Broadcasting and Electronic Media, 31,* 279–292.

Rubin, A. M., & Perse, E. M. (1987). Audience activity and television news gratifications. *Communication Research, 14*(1), 58–84.

Rubin, A. M., Perse, E. M., & Powell, R. A. (1985). Loneliness, parasocial interaction, and local television news viewing. *Human Communication Research, 12,* 155–180.

Steever, G. S. (1994, August). Para-social attachments: Motivational antecedents. Paper presented at the meeting of the American Psychological Association. Los Angeles.

Wood, J. T. (1986). Different voices in relationship crises: An extension of Gillian's theory. *American Behavioral Scientist, 29*(3), 273–301.

Yanof, D. S. (1991). The para-social and interpersonal relationships of heavy, light, and nonviewers of daytime television serials (Doctoral dissertation, California School of Professional Psychology, Berkeley, 1991). *Dissertation Abstracts International, 52*(1-A), 71281.

CHAPTER 2 Functionalism, Uses, and Gratifications

The Nature and Functions of Mass Communication

Many studies in communication have been influenced by social science theories and methods from the fields of anthropology, psychology, and political science. Another discipline that has influenced media studies is sociology, which treats mass communication as a social phenomenon. In the following selection from *Mass Communication: A Sociological Perspective,* 3rd ed. (Random House, 1986), Charles R. Wright, a professor at the Annenberg School of Communications, investigates the way in which media functions in society. Functionalism is a theoretical approach that has been criticized for its apolitical stance and for the way it seems to confirm that what exists in the social/media relationship is positive. It assumes no ideological impact, and it supports a commonsense approach toward understanding the complex relationship. Functionalism offers both a language and concepts for relations between media and society that are generally not found in other theories.

In particular, the following selection explains the social consequences of mass communication and makes clear distinctions between functions and dysfunctions, as well as how manifest and latent content influence media users within the social context. In addition, the fourth function of mass communication, entertainment, has been added as a significant topic for analysis and study.

Key Concept: social aspects of mass media and functionalism

As a social process, communication is essential to society and to human survival. Every human society—so-called primitive or modern—depends on communication to enable its members to live together, to maintain and modify working arrangements about the social order and social regulation, and to cope with the environment. Participation in the communication process establishes a person as a social being and as a functioning member of society.

It is not surprising that a matter so basic to human life has been a topic for study and speculation throughout history. From antiquity to modern times, the subject of human communication has attracted the attention of a long line of authors representing a rich variety of intellectual orientations, and including artistic, humanistic, and political approaches. Only relatively recently, however, has it become a popular topic for investigation by social scientists. Communication has been studied by social scientists trained in anthropology, political science, psychology, social psychology, sociology, and other disciplines, in addition to those specializing in the study of communication itself....

FOUR MAJOR COMMUNICATION ACTIVITIES

Harold Lasswell, a political scientist who was a pioneer in mass communication research, once distinguished three major communication operations: (1) surveillance of the environment, (2) correlation of the parts of society in responding to the environment, and (3) transmission of the social heritage from one generation to the next.[1] Modifying Lasswell's categories somewhat and adding a fourth, entertainment, gives us the classification of the major communication activities with which we will be concerned....

Surveillance refers to the collection and distribution of information concerning events in the environment, both within a particular society and outside it. Coverage of events during a presidential election campaign is an example. To some extent, surveillance corresponds to what is commonly thought of as the handling of news. The news process, however, as we shall see later involves much more than "collecting" and distributing "facts" about self-evident events. There is a complex social process that produces what is accepted as news in a society.

Correlation includes interpretation of the information presented about the environment, prescriptions about what to do about it, and attempts to influence such interpretations, attitudes, and conduct. These operations are usually seen as editorial activity, propaganda, or attempts at persuasion. Although it is useful here to distinguish surveillance from correlation, in practice this may be difficult to do. Surveillance itself incorporates editorial judgments that determine what items qualify as news or information to be disbursed. Interpretation and value judgments are often implicit, sometimes explicit, in the "news" that is reported by mass media and by word of mouth. Linda Lannus, for example, reports that surveillance and correlation activities tended to be indistinguishable to the reporters, editors, and readers of two daily metropolitan newspapers that she studied in 1977.[2] True, the newspapers had special sections regarded as mainly editorial, such as the editorial page and signed columns of opinion or commentary. But the news people found it difficult and unrealistic to separate certain kinds of editorial judgments, such as the significance of an event and how much coverage to give it, from the surveillance process. Nevertheless, the distinction between surveillance and correlation is useful to our discussion—and easier to see in certain kinds of communication ventures, such as propaganda campaigns and mass persuasion. So we will keep it.

The third communication activity, transmission of the social heritage, focuses on the assimilation of people in society. It concerns the communicative processes by which society's store (or part of its store) of values, social norms, knowledge, and other cultural components is made known to and instilled in members and potential members. Our meaning goes beyond Lasswell's specification of transmission of the social heritage from one generation to the next and includes concern with communication relevant to the assimilation of children and adults into various social roles, immigrants into a new (new to them, that is) society, and related matters. This activity sometimes is called education or *socialization,* the term we will use.

Finally, *entertainment* refers here to communication activities primarily (even if arbitrarily) considered as amusement, irrespective of any other features they may seem to have. A television situation comedy, for example, may be regarded as an entertainment activity, even though it may contain some information.

It is good to remember that our four major communication activities are abstractions, useful for purposes of discussion and analysis. Clearly any specific case may be seen in terms of any or all four activities. A television news story, for example, may play a part in surveillance of events (A hurricane is coming this way!), evaluation of what to do (board up the windows), reflect social norms (people are responsible for protecting themselves and their property), and still be entertaining (It's a thrilling drama of humanity versus the elements!). Or a choice piece of gossip passed along to a friend may be informative, judgmental, reinforcing of some shared values, and titillating. (That's what makes gossip so much fun!) People may use the same materials in different ways—for entertainment or instruction. Life doesn't follow theory. Nonetheless our distinctions serve a useful purpose so long as we treat them as abstractions —convenient ways of looking at certain aspects of communication....

SOME FUNCTIONS OF MASS COMMUNICATION: AN OVERVIEW

The first lesson we can learn from functional theory is not to infer the social consequences of mass communication from its apparent or stated purposes. [Contemporary sociologist Robert K.] Merton stresses the need to distinguish between the significant consequences (functions) of a social activity and the apparent goals or aims given for it. The two matters need not be, and often are not, identical. This means that the functions of mass communication are not necessarily what is intended by the communicators.

Public health programs, for example, sometimes use mass communication in order to persuade people to get physical checkups, to get immunization shots against the flu, to stop smoking, and so on. This is the explicit purpose of regular local health campaigns. In pursuing these goals, the campaigns also may have important side effects. For example, as some research suggests, they could improve the social prestige and the morale of local public health workers, whose formerly unrecognized work now receives attention from the mass media and hence from the public. If this improvement in prestige and boost in morale leads to better community cooperation in public health efforts, that would be an important, but unexpected, consequence of the mass communication campaigns.

Merton labels significant intended consequences *manifest* and those that are unintended *latent.* Functional interpretation also distinguishes between those consequences that seem significantly useful to the maintenance and well-being of a system and those that seem harmful to it. Positive consequences are called *functions* and negative ones *dysfunctions.* (Those that seem irrelevant to the system under study are considered nonfunctions.) Any regular social activity, such as mass communication campaigns, can be analyzed in terms of what seem to be manifest or latent functions and dysfunctions for the society, its members, or its culture.

To return to our example of public health campaigns, we might look for such manifest functions as reductions in the risk of an epidemic, and for latent functions such as the boosts in prestige given to public health workers (thereby improving their occupational effectiveness in the community). We also might look for possible dysfunctions, such as frightening away potential health clients who fear they may learn that they have some incurable disease. Clearly the interpretation of social consequences as functional or dysfunctional involves judgment by the researcher. Are there some guidelines?

It seems important, to me, to avoid two problems if possible.[3] First, we should avoid trying to classify *every* possible effect of mass communication as functional or dysfunctional. It is more useful to limit functional analysis to those consequences that seem important to the maintenance and/or change of society, its members, or culture. For example, movie or television stories set in contemporary places might lead some viewers to learn a few new facts about the story's locale, such as some street names. But unless we can see how that minor effect is significant for the maintenance or change of society, its members, or culture, then simply calling it functional or dysfunctional does not increase our understanding of mass communication. Suppose, on the other hand, that movie and television settings influenced viewers' ideas about how attractive (or unattractive) a place is and thereby affected how many people sought to migrate to it. That could be a matter of considerable social significance and a potential topic for functional interpretation.

Second, it is important to avoid equating the terms functional and dysfunctional with our personal ideas of good and bad. We need not personally approve of some aspect of mass communication that we interpret as functional for a society. It does not have to fit our ideological preference. To call it functional means only that the practice seems to contribute to the strength and continuing operation of the society under study....

Consider what it means to a society for its members to have a constant stream of public information about events in the world. One positive consequence (function) of such surveillance is that it provides warnings about imminent threats of danger—a hurricane, earthquake, or military attack. Forewarned, the population can mobilize and protect itself from destruction. Furthermore, insofar as the information is available to all, rather than to a select few, warnings through mass communication may have the additional function of supporting feelings of egalitarianism within the society—everyone has had fair warning to escape from danger.[4] Such warnings also can be interpreted as functional for individual members of the society... insofar as personal (and family) safety is at stake.

A second social consequence of such communication is that it contributes to the everyday institutional operations of the society: it is instrumental in stock market activities, sales navigation, and recreation plans. The instrumental functions of news also apply to the individual. For instance, a group of social scientists took advantage of a local newspaper strike in New York City to study what people "missed" when they did not receive their regular newspaper. One clearly identifiable role of the newspaper for these urbanites was providing information about routine events: local radio programs and movie schedules, sales by local stores, weather forecasts, and so on. When people "missed" their daily newspapers, they were missing a multipurpose tool for daily living.[5]

Two important functions of mass-communicated news, suggested by sociologists Paul Lazarsfeld and Robert Merton are (1) status conferral and (2) ethicizing or the enforcement of social norms.[6] *Status conferral* means that news reports about persons, groups, or social issues increase their importance in the public's view by the very fact that they receive such attention. Presumably this is beneficial to society, in the case of certain social issues which thereby get put on the public agenda for consideration, discussion, and social action. Status conferral also benefits individuals and groups who receive the media's attention, since it certifies their importance and even may legitimize their real or aspired status as celebrities, leaders, and spokespersons for particular groups or about certain topics.

Mass-communicated news has an *ethicizing* effect when it strengthens social control by exposing deviant behavior to public view and possible censure. Newspaper crusades, for instance, publicize wrongdoings that might already have been known about privately by some people and silently borne, if not condoned, by them. Public disclosure of these wrongdoings makes them now a matter of public, not private, knowledge. Under these conditions, most people are obliged to condemn the misbehavior and to support public standards of morality. In this way, mass-communicated news strengthens social control, complementing other formal and informal methods for community detection and control of deviant behavior.

Mass-communicated surveillance can be dysfunctional for society and its members in a variety of ways. For example, the flow of world news could threaten the stability of a particular society or nation. Information about better living conditions elsewhere or about different ideologies might lead to invidious contrasts with conditions at home and to pressures for social change. Or, as another example, some people fear that mass-communicated news about impending danger, broadcast to the general public without local mediation and interpretation by someone, may lead to widespread panic (although contemporary sociological and social psychological research on disasters suggests that mass panic such as this rarely, if ever, happens.)[7]

Mass-communicated news may heighten an individual's anxieties, some say, especially concerning dangerous conditions in the world. What used to be called "war nerves" is an example. Perhaps "nuclear nerves" is the contemporary equivalent. Too much news—an information overload, as some call it—may lead to privatization. The individual overwhelmed by matters brought to his or her attention by mass communication, escapes to private concerns over which there seems to be more control—family or hobbies, cultivating one's own garden, so to speak. Mass-communicated news may lead to individual apathy about civic activity, it is said, because people spend so much time following the news that they have little time or energy left to try to solve social problems. They become so intent on keeping informed, mesmerized by the newscasts and newspapers, that they equate being an informed citizen with being an active citizen.

Lazarsfeld and Merton call this *narcotization*. Thus, for example, the person—feeling compelled to watch an hour or more of daily news (network or local) on television, read through the newspaper (maybe also the Sunday edition), several newsmagazines—ends up so numbed or self-satisfied by it all that he or she misses the local township meeting for public action to clean up toxic waste dumps in the neighborhood!

One also can analyze functions and dysfunctions of mass-communicated news for specific populations or subgroups, such as ethnic groups, minorities, workers, children, elderly people, or political elites. To illustrate . . . , news attention given to political leaders can confer status on them and legitimize their position. Mass-communicated news also may be instrumental for them by providing information that is useful for governance, by exposing subversive activities, and by gauging public opinion. On the other hand, one can think of some dysfunctions too. Uncensored mass-communicated news can threaten the political elite's power by presenting news that contradicts the leaders' claims about some situation (wartime victories, economic prosperity), or allows opponents (domestic or foreign) to present their message, or exposes wrongdoings (taking bribes).

Finally, one can consider possible consequences of mass communication surveillance for a society's cultural system—its body of social values, norms, folkways, beliefs, and other cultural features. Mass-communicated news and information about other societies and their cultures might enrich and add variety to one's own culture, and encourage cultural growth and adaptability. On the other hand, some people fear that the host culture will lose some or all of its distinctiveness and integrity as a result of such open cultural "invasion."

Many of the functions of the correlation activity in mass communication seem to prevent or limit some of the undesirable consequences of the mass communication of news. Correlation—including the selection, evaluation, and interpretation of events—imposes order on the surveillance activity and signifies the relative importance of what is reported. This helps to prevent an even greater flood of mass-communicated news than we already have, one that could overwhelm and confuse the public. Editorial activity also packages the news into categories (international news, sports, business) and signals a story's importance through the conventions of headlines, placement in the paper or newscast, and other devices.

We become more aware of such taken-for-granted management of the news when it is not provided. For example, in the study of what "missing" the newspaper means to readers, people said that they not only missed information about events, but also the evaluation and interpretation that the papers ordinarily provided. Some journalists believe it is their responsibility to evaluate and interpret events for the reader or listener—that is, to set events within their larger historical and social context, to evaluate the sources from which the "facts" came, and to suggest what the reader or listener may make of the facts reported. This could have the function, for example, of preventing undue public anxiety about news of impending danger.

One possible dysfunction of editorial-type activities through mass communication is that needed social changes may not get media support while social conformism does. Because of the public nature of mass communication, communicators risk sanctions if they publicly express social criticism or take an unpopular stand on issues. There may be political sanctions, economic ones, consumer boycotts, or other repercussions. Discretion may lead some mass communicators to avoid controversial topics and social criticism.[8] Certain practices associated with news reporting and interpretation may also work against social change, as for example when the mass media heavily rely on government, business, or other institutional sources for interpretations of events.

Another possible dysfunction would be the weakening of peoples' critical ability to find, sift, sort, interpret, and evaluate news for themselves. It can be argued that dependence on mass-communicated, prepackaged news, ideas, opinions, and views lessens people's effectiveness as citizens and makes them less capable of thinking for themselves. (It should be noted here, however, that people rarely, if ever, depend solely on mass communication, and frequently talk with one another in forming their opinions.)[9] ...

Socialization

In this section we simply note some possible functions and dysfunctions of handling socialization activities by mass communication. Such activities may help unify the society and increase social cohesion by providing a broad base of common social norms, values, and collective experiences to be shared by its members. That would be functional. Individuals too might be helped in their integration into the society through exposure to common social norms and other cultural matters. That could be especially functional for immigrants or other socially mobile persons. Mass communication also may contribute to the socialization of adults into new social values and changing social norms.

On the other hand, the presentation of a more or less standardized view of culture through mass communication could result in a loss of regional, ethnic, and other subcultural variety and could discourage cultural diversity and creativity. That would be dysfunctional. It can also be argued that mass communication makes the process of socialization seem less humane in some respects. David Riesman, for example, suggests that the moral lessons of tales told by mass media cannot be tailored to fit the capacity of the individual child hearing or seeing the story, as they might have been in traditional face-to-face storytelling. Hence some children might make unduly harsh demands on themselves if they try to internalize cultural lessons from movies, television, and other mass media.[10]

Entertainment

Mass entertainment offers some diversion and amusement for everybody, and relaxation and respite can be functional for people and beneficial to society. But too much escapism, too many TV circuses at one's fingertips, may distract people from important social issues and divert them from useful social participation and action. That would be dysfunctional. It would also be dysfunctional if people became so dependent on mass communication for entertainment that they no longer were able to entertain themselves and became permanent mass media spectators.

Some critics suggest that entertainment changes its nature and quality when mass-communicated. Mass entertainment, it is argued, lowers, or at least fails to raise, public taste to the level that might be achieved by less extensive forms of entertainment such as the theater, books, or opera.[11] There also may be significant changes in the social institutions of entertainment. Change in organized sports provides a case in point.

Mass communication, if nothing else, has vastly increased the number of people who witness a sports event (or, more accurately, the version of the event as presented by television, radio, or some other medium). Some 105 million television viewers saw the 1984 Super Bowl XVIII football game.[12] By comparison, personal attendance at professional football games usually averages in the thousands. Television, perhaps more than any other mass medium of communication, has affected this area of popular entertainment and its institutions.

Sociologists John Talamini and Charles Page remark that "the most spectacular rise of sport as mass entertainment, a post World War II development, has been largely the product of ... television."[13] Commenting on the functional and dysfunctional results of the increasing dependence of organized sports on the technology of television and on advertising funds, Talamini and Page see these consequences as including

> ... on the one hand, higher salaries and pensions for professional athletes geographical expansion, dividends for spectators such as instant replay and visibility of errors by officials, and improved quality of play; and, on the other hand, ruthless schedule manipulation, the conversion of athletes into ad men and salesman, and, in boxing and baseball, the undermining of local clubs and minor league teams—with tragic effects for apprentice players and journeyman fighters.[14]

These observations illustrate some of the potential consequences of mass-communicated sports for the sport itself as well as for individuals and society. How socially significant these effects seem depends on one's viewpoint. Certainly they are important to those directly involved (professional athletes, businessmen, amateurs).

The symbolic value of mass-communicated sports also should not be overlooked. For example, consider the political significance of the Olympics, which are televised throughout the world. The study of these and other social implications of mass-communicated sports presents a relatively unexplored but interesting area for research in the sociology of mass communication.

NOTES

1. Harold D. Lasswell, "The Structure and Function of Communication in Society," in Lyman Bryson, ed., *The Communication of Ideas* (New York: Harper & Brothers, 1948), pp. 37–51. Lasswell calls these operations "functions," a term we reserve for a different meaning later in this [selection.]

2. Linda Rush Lannus, "The News Organization and News Operations of the Urban Press: A Sociological Analysis based on Two Case Studies" (Ph. D. dissertation, University of Pennsylvania, 1977).

3. For a further brief discussion of these problems and other experiences in applying functional analysis to mass communication, see my "Commentary" on functional analysis in *The New Communications*, ed. Frederick Williams (Belmont, CA: Wadsworth, 1983), pp, 89–90.

4. I am indebted to Herbert H. Hyman for this suggestion.

5. Bernard Berelson, "What 'Missing the Newspaper' Means," in *Communications Research 1948–1949*, eds. Paul F. Lazarsfeld and Frank Stanton (New York: Harper & Brothers, 1949), pp. 111–129.

6. Several ideas about the functions of mass communication that we discuss here stem from this classic essay. Paul F. Lazarsfeld and Robert K. Merton, "Mass Communication, Popular Taste and Organized Social Action," in Bryson, *The Communication of Ideas*, pp. 95–118.

7. For a classic study, see Hadley Cantril, Hazel Gaudet, and Herta Herzog, *Invasion from Mars* (Princeton, NJ: Princeton University Press, 1940). For discussions of current research that questions earlier interpretations, see John F. Lofland, "Collective Behavior," in Morris Rosenberg and Ralph Turner, eds., *Social Psychology: Sociological Perspectives* (New York: Basic Books, 1981), and Joseph B. Perry, Jr., and Meredith

D. Pugh, *Collective Behavior: Response to Social Stress* (St. Paul, MN: West Publishing, 1978).

8. On the other hand, playing down socially divisive news and criticism may be interpreted as functional for keeping the society together. For an example, see Warren Breed, "Mass Communication and Socio-cultural Integration," *Social Forces* 37 (1958), pp. 109–116.

9. For a recently articulated theory of mass media dependency on the individual level, some of the conditions leading to it, and some functional and dysfunctional consequences, see Sandra J. Ball-Rokeach and Melvin De Fleur, "A Dependency Model of Mass Media Effects," *Communication Research,* 3 (1976), pp. 3–21. See also *Theories of Mass Communication,* 4th ed., by De Fleur and Ball-Rokeach (New York: Longman, 1982), pp. 236–251.

10. David Riesman et al., *The Lonely Crowd* (Garden City, NY: Doubleday, 1953), chap. 4.

11. For an examination of the mass culture critique and an alternative to it presenting a sociological analysis of the qualities of mass entertainment, see Herbert J. Gans, *Popular Culture and High Culture* (New York: Basic Books, 1974). For a sociological analysis of mass entertainment and its functions, see Harold Mendelsohn's *Mass Entertainment* (New Haven, CT: College and University Press, 1966), especially chapter II; and Harold Mendelsohn and H. T. Spetnagel, "Entertainment as a Sociological Enterprise," in *The Entertainment Functions of Television,* ed. Percy H. Tannenbaum (Hillsdale, NJ: Lawrence Erlbaum, 1980), pp. 13–29.

12. *Broadcasting,* January 14, 1985, p. 70.

13. John T. Talamini and Charles H. Page, *Sport and Society: An Anthology* (Boston: Little, Brown, 1973), p. 417.

14. Ibid., p. 418.

2.2 ELIHU KATZ, JAY G. BLUMLER, AND MICHAEL GUREVITCH

Utilization of Mass Communication by the Individual

Within the paradigm of functionalism is an approach loosely called "uses and gratifications" research. The following selection is from "Utilization of Mass Communication by the Individual," in Jay G. Blumler and Elihu Katz, eds., *The Uses of Mass Communications* (Sage Publications, 1974). In it, Elihu Katz, Jay G. Blumler, and Michael Gurevitch discuss how empirical research in uses and gratifications evolved. One of the important features about the uses and gratifications approach is that it examines the process of communication starting from the audience members' individual perceptions.

The uses and gratifications perspective investigates *why* individuals choose to use media. The areas of greatest difficulty for researchers following this approach is to understand and account for the audience's selective behavior: Why do they choose to watch a videotape rather than read a book? Is it the humor in a comedy they like, or is it an identification with the characters? Are people turning to media for reasons other than habit?

The coauthors of this selection are scholars in the field of mass communication research. Katz is currently a professor at the Hebrew University in Jerusalem and director of its Communications Institute. Blumler, a British researcher, is director of the Centre for Television Research and Reader in Mass Communications at the University of Leeds, England, where Gurevitch is a senior research fellow.

Key Concept: uses and gratifications

Suppose that we were studying not broadcasting-and-society in mid-twentieth-century America but opera-and-society in mid-nineteenth-century Italy. After all, opera in Italy, during that period, was a "mass" medium. What would we be studying? It seems likely, for one thing, that we would find interest in the attributes of the medium—what might today be called its "grammar"

—for example, the curious convention that makes it possible to sign contradictory emotions simultaneously. For another, we would be interested in the
functions of the medium for the individual and society: perceptions of the
values expressed and underlined; the phenomena of stardom, fanship, and
connoisseurship; the festive ambience which the medium created; and so on.
It seems quite unlikely that we would be studying the effects of the singing of
a particular opera on opinions and attitudes, even though some operas were
written with explicit political, social, and moral aims in mind. The study of
short-run effects, in other words, would not have had a high priority, although
it might have had a place. But the emphasis, by and large, would have been
on the medium as a cultural institution with its own social and psychological
functions and perhaps long-run effects.

We have all been over the reasons why much of mass communication research took a different turn, preferring to look at specific programs as specific
messages with, possibly, specific effects. We were social psychologists interested
in persuasion and attitude change. We were political scientists interested in
new forms of social control. We were commissioned to measure message effectiveness for marketing organizations, or public health agencies, or churches, or
political organizations, or for the broadcasting organizations themselves. And
we were asked whether the media were not causes of violent and criminal
behavior.

Yet even in the early days of empirical mass communication research this
preoccupation with short-term effects was supplemented by the growth of an
interest in the gratifications that the mass media provide their audiences. Such
studies were well represented in the Lazarsfeld-Stanton collections (1942, 1944,
1949); Herzog (1942) on quiz programs and the gratifications derived from listening to soap operas; Suchman (1942) on the motives for getting interested in
serious music on radio; Wolfe and Fiske (1949) on the development of children's
interest in comics; Berelson (1949) on the functions of newspaper reading; and
so on. Each of these investigations came up with a list of functions served either
by some specific contents or by the medium in question: to match one's wits
against others, to get information or advice for daily living, to provide a framework for one's day, to prepare oneself culturally for the demands of upward
mobility, or to be reassured about the dignity and usefulness of one's role.

What these early studies had in common was, first, a basically similar
methodological approach whereby statements about media functions were
elicited from the respondents in an essentially open-ended way. Second, they
shared a qualitative approach in their attempt to group gratification statements
into labelled categories, largely ignoring the distribution of their frequency in
the population. Third, they did not attempt to explore the links between the
gratifications thus detected and the psychological or sociological origins of the
needs that were so satisfied. Fourth, they failed to search for the interrelation-
ships among the various media functions, either quantitatively or conceptually,
in a manner that might have led to the detection of the latent structure of media
gratifications. Consequently, these studies did not result in a cumulatively more
detailed picture of media gratifications conducive to the eventual formulation
of theoretical statements.

The last few years have witnessed something of a revival of direct empirical investigations of audience uses and gratifications, not only in the United States but also in Britain, Sweden, Finland, Japan, and Israel. These... studies have a number of differing starting points, but each attempts to press toward a greater systematization of what is involved in conducting research in this field. Taken together, they make operational many of the logical steps that were only implicit in the earlier work. They are concerned with (1) the social and psychological origins of (2) needs, which generate (3) expectations of (4) the mass media or other sources, which lead to (5) differential patterns of media exposure (or engagement in other activities), resulting in (6) need gratifications and (7) other consequences, perhaps mostly unintended ones. Some of these investigations begin by specifying needs and then attempt to trace the extent to which they are gratified by the media or other sources. Others take observed gratifications as a starting point and attempt to reconstruct the needs that are being gratified. Yet others focus on the social origins of audience expectations and gratifications. But however varied their individual points of departure, they all strive toward an assessment of media consumption in audience-related terms, rather than in technological, aesthetic, ideological, or other more or less "elitist" terms. The convergence of their foci, as well as of their findings, indicates that there is a clear agenda here—part methodological and part theoretical—for a discussion of the future directions of this approach.

SOME BASIC ASSUMPTIONS OF THEORY, METHOD AND VALUE

Perhaps the place of "theory" and "method" in the study of audience uses and gratifications is not immediately apparent. The common tendency to attach the label "uses and gratifications approach" to work in this field appears to virtually disclaim any theoretical pretensions or methodological commitment. From this point of view the approach simply represents an attempt to explain something of the way in which individuals use communications, among other resources in their environment, to satisfy their needs and to achieve their goals, and to do so by simply asking them. Nevertheless, this effort does rest on a body of assumptions, explicit or implicit, that have some degree of internal coherence and that are arguable in the sense that not everyone contemplating them would find them self-evident. Lundberg and Hultén (1968) refer to them as jointly constituting a "uses and gratifications model." Five elements of this model in particular may be singled out for comment:

1. The audience is conceived of as active, that is, an important part of mass media use is assumed to be goal directed (McQuail, Blumler and Brown, 1972). This assumption may be contrasted with Bogart's (1965) thesis to the effect that "most mass media experiences represent pastime rather than purposeful activity, very often [reflecting] chance circumstances within the range of availabilities rather than the expression

of psychological motivation or need." Of course, it cannot be denied that media exposure often has a casual origin; the issue is whether, in addition, patterns of media use are shaped by more or less definite expectations of what certain kinds of content have to offer the audience member.

2. In the mass communication process much initiative in linking need gratification and media choice lies with the audience member. This places a strong limitation on theorizing about any form of straight-line effect of media content on attitudes and behavior. As Schramm, Lyle and Parker (1961) said:

> In a sense the term "effect" is misleading because it suggests that television "does something" to children.... Nothing can be further from the fact....

3. The media compete with other sources of need satisfaction. The needs served by mass communication constitute but a segment of the wider range of human needs, and the degree to which they can be adequately met through mass media consumption certainly varies. Consequently, a proper view of the role of the media in need satisfaction should take into account other functional alternatives—including different, more conventional, and "older" ways of fulfilling needs.

4. Methodologically speaking, many of the goals of mass media use can be derived from data supplied by individual audience members themselves—that is, people are sufficiently self-aware to be able to report their interests and motives in particular cases, or at least to recognize them when confronted with them in an intelligible and familiar verbal formulation.

5. Value judgments about the cultural significance of mass communication should be suspended while audience orientations are explored on their own terms. It is from the perspective of this assumption that certain affinities and contrasts between the uses and gratifications approach and much speculative writing about popular culture may be considered.

STATE OF THE ART: THEORETICAL ISSUES

From the few postulates outlined above, it is evident that further development of a theory of media gratification depends, first, on the clarification of its relationship to the theoretical traditions on which it so obviously draws and, second, on systematic efforts toward conceptual integration of empirical findings. Given the present state of the art, the following are priority issues in the development of an adequate theoretical basis.

Typologies of Audience Gratifications

Each major piece of uses and gratification research has yielded its own classification scheme of audience functions. When placed side by side, they reveal a mixture of shared gratification categories and notions peculiar to individual research teams. The differences are due in part to the fact that investigators have focused on different levels of study (e.g., medium or content) and different materials (e.g., different programs or program types on, say, television) in different cultures (e.g., Finland, Israel, Japan, Sweden, the United Kingdom, the United States, and Yugoslavia).

Unifunctional conceptions of audience interests have been expressed in various forms. Popular culture writers have often based their criticisms of the media on the ground that, in primarily serving the escapist desires of the audience, they deprived it of the more beneficial uses that might be made of communication (McDonald, 1957). Stephenson's analysis (1967) of mass communication exclusively in terms of "play" may be interpreted as an extension, albeit in a transformed and expanded expression, of this same notion. A more recent example has been provided by Nordenstreng (1970), who, while breaking away from conventional formulations, still opts for a unifunctional view when he claims that, "It has often been documented (e.g., during television and newspaper strikes in Finland in 1966–67) that perhaps the basic motivation for media use is just an unarticulated need for social contact."

The wide currency secured for a bifunctional view of audience concerns is reflected in Weiss' (1971) summary, which states that, "When... studies of uses and gratifications are carried out, the media or media content are usually viewed dichotomously as predominantly fantasist-escapist or informational-educational in significance." This dichotomy appears, for example, in Schramm's (1949) work (adopted subsequently by Schramm, Lyle and Parker, 1961: Pietila, 1969; and Furu, 1971), which distinguishes between sets of "immediate" and "deferred" gratifications, and in the distinction between informational and entertainment materials. In terms of audience gratifications specifically, it emerges in the distinction between surveillance and escape uses of the media.

The four-functional interpretation of the media was first proposed by Lasswell (1948) on a macro-sociological level and later developed by Wright (1960) on both the macro- and the micro-sociological levels. It postulated that the media served the functions of surveillance, correlation, entertainment, and cultural transmission (or socialization) for society as a whole, as well as for individuals and subgroups within society. An extension of the four-function approach can also be found in Wright's suggestive exploration of the potential dysfunctional equivalents of Lasswell's typology.

None of these statements, however, adequately reflects the full range of functions, which has been disclosed by the more recent investigations. McQuail, Blumler and Brown (1972) have put forward a typology consisting of the following categories: diversion (including escape from the constraints of routine and the burdens of problems, and emotional release); personal relationships (including substitute companionship as well as social utility); personal identity (including personal reference, reality exploration, and value reinforcement); and surveillance.

An effort to encompass the large variety of specific functions that have been proposed is made in the elaborate scheme of Katz, Gurevitch and Haas (1973). Their central notion is that mass communication is used by individuals to connect (or sometimes to disconnect) themselves—via instrumental, affective, or integrative relations—with different kinds of others (self, family, friends, nation, etc.). The scheme attempts to comprehend the whole range of individual gratifications of the many facets of the need "to be connected." And it finds empirical regularities in the preference for different media for different kinds of connections.

Gratification and Needs

The study of mass media use suffers at present from the absence of a relevant theory of social and psychological needs. It is not so much a catalogue of needs that is missing as a clustering of groups of needs, a sorting out of different levels of need, and a specification of hypotheses linking particular needs with particular media gratifications. It is true that the work of Schramm, Lyle and Parker (1961) draws on the distinction between the reality and pleasure principles in the socialization theories of Freud and others, but more recent studies suggest that those categories are too broad to be serviceable. Maslow's (1954) proposed hierarchy of human needs may hold more promise, but the relevance of his categories to expectations of communication has not yet been explored in detail. Lasswell's (1948) scheme to specify the needs that media satisfy has proven useful, and it may be helpful to examine Lasswell and Kaplan's (1950) broader classification of values as well.

Alternatively, students of uses and gratifications could try to work backwards, as it were, from gratifications to needs. In the informational field, for example, the surveillance function may be traced to a desire for security or the satisfaction of curiosity and the exploratory drive; seeking reinforcement of one's attitudes and values may derive from a need for reassurance that one is right; and attempts to correlate informational elements may stem from a more basic need to develop one's cognitive mastery of the environment. Similarly, the use of fictional (and other) media materials for "personal reference" may spring from a need for self-esteem; social utility functions may be traced to the need for affiliation; and escape functions may be related to the need to release tension and reduce anxiety. But whichever way one proceeds, it is inescapable that what is at issue here is the long-standing problem of social and psychological science: how to (and whether to bother to) systematize the long lists of human and societal needs. Thus far, gratifications research has stayed close to what we have been calling media-related needs (in the sense that the media have been observed to satisfy them, at least in part), but one wonders whether all this should not be put in the broader context of systematic studies of needs.

Sources of Media Gratifications

Studies have shown that audience gratifications can be derived from at least three distinct sources: media content, exposure to the media per se, and the social context that typifies the situation of exposure to different media. Although recognition of media content as a source of gratifications has provided the basis for research in this area from its inception, less attention has been paid to the other sources. Nevertheless, it is clear that the need to relax or to kill time can be satisfied by the act of watching television, that the need to feel that one is spending one's time in a worthwhile way may be associated with the act of reading (Waples, Berelson and Bradshaw, 1940; Berelson, 1949), and that the need to structure one's day may be satisfied merely by having the radio "on" (Mendelsohn, 1964). Similarly, a wish to spend time with one's family or friends can be served by watching television at home with the family or by going to the cinema with one's friends.

Each medium seems to offer a unique combination of (a) characteristic contents (at least stereotypically perceived in that way); (b) typical attributes (print vs. broadcasting modes of transmission, iconic vs. symbolic representation, reading vs. audio or audio-visual modes of reception); and (c) typical exposure situations (at home vs. out-of-home, alone vs. with others, control over the temporal aspects of exposure vs. absence of such control). The issue, then, is what combinations of attributes may render different media more or less adequate for the satisfaction of different needs (Katz, Gurevitch and Haas, 1973).

Gratification and Media Attributes

Much uses and gratifications research has still barely advanced beyond a sort of charting and profiling activity: findings are still typically presented to show that certain bodies of content serve certain functions or that one medium is deemed better at satisfying certain needs than another. The further step, which has hardly been ventured, is one of explanation. At issue here is the relationship between the unique "grammar" of different media—that is, their specific technological and aesthetic attributes—and the particular requirements of audience members that they are then capable, or incapable, of satisfying. Which, indeed, are the attributes that render some media more conducive than others to satisfying specific needs? And which elements of content help to attract the expectations for which they apparently cater?

It is possible to postulate the operation of some kind of division of labor among the media for the satisfaction of audience needs. This may be elaborated in two ways: taking media attributes as the starting point, the suggestion is that those media that differ (or are similar) in their attributes are more likely to serve different (or similar) needs; or, utilizing the latent structure of needs as a point of departure, the implication is that needs that are psychologically related or conceptually similar will be equally well served by the same media (or by media with similar attributes).

To illustrate the first approach, Robinson (1972) has demonstrated the interchangeability of television and print media for learning purposes. In the Israeli study, Katz, Gurevitch and Haas (1973) found five media ordered in a circumplex with respect to their functional similarities: books-newspapers-radio-television-cinema-books. In other words, books functioned most like newspapers, on the one hand, and like cinema, on the other. Radio was most similar in its usage to newspapers, on the one hand, and to television, on the other. The explanation would seem to lie not only with certain technological attributes that they have in common, but with similar aesthetic qualities as well. Thus, books share a technology and an informational function with newspapers, but are similar to films in their aesthetic function. Radio shares a technology, as well as informational and entertainment content, with television, but it is also very much like newspapers—providing a heavy dose of information and an orientation to reality.

An illustration of the second aspect of this division of labor may also be drawn from the same study. Here, the argument is that structurally related needs will tend to be serviced by certain media more often than by others. Thus, books and cinema have been found to cater to needs concerned with self-fulfilment and self-gratification: they help to "connect" individuals to themselves. Newspapers, radio, and television all seem to connect individuals to society. In fact, the function of newspapers for those interested in following what is going on in the world may have been grossly underestimated in the past (Edelstein, 1973; Lundberg and Hultén, 1968). Television, however, was found to be less frequently used as a medium of escape by Israeli respondents than were books and films. And a Swedish study of the "functional specialities of the respective media" reported that, "A retreat from the immediate environment and its demands—probably mainly by the act of reading itself—was characteristic of audience usage of weekly magazines" (Lundberg and Hultén, 1968).

REFERENCES

BERELSON, B. (1949) "What 'missing the newspaper' means," in P. F. Lazarsfeld and F. N. Stanton (eds.) Communications Research, 1948–9. New York: Duell, Sloan & Pearce.

BOGART, L. (1965) "The mass media and the blue-collar worker," in A. Bennett and W. Gomberg (eds.) Blue-Collar World: Studies of the American Worker. Engelwood Cliffs, N.J.: Prentice-Hall.

EDELSTEIN, A. (1973) "An alternative approach to the study of source effects in mass communication." Studies of Broadcasting 9.

FURU, T. (1971) The Function of Television for Children and Adolescents. Tokyo: Sophia University.

HERZOG, H. (1942) Professor quiz: a gratification study," in P. F. Lazarsfeld and F. N. Stanton (eds.) Radio Research, 1941. New York: Duell, Sloan & Pearce.

KATZ, E., M. GUREVITCH, and H. HAAS (1973) "On the use of mass media for important things." American Sociological Review 38.

LASSWELL, H. (1948) "The structure and function of communications in society," in L. Bryson (ed.) The Communication of Ideas. New York: Harper.

_____ and A. KAPLAN (1950) Power and Society. New Haven: Yale Univ. Press.

LAZARSFELD, P. F. and F. N. STANTON [eds.] (1949) Communications Research, 1948–9. New York: Harper.

_____ (1944) Radio Research, 1942–3. New York: Duell, Sloan & Pearce.

_____ (1942) Radio Research, 1941. New York: Duell, Sloan & Pearce.

LUNDBERG, D. and O. HULTEN (1968) Individen och Massmedia. Stockholm: EFI.

McDONALD, D. (1957) "A theory of mass culture," in D. M. White and B. Rosenberg (eds.) Mass Culture: the Popular Arts in America. Glencoe: Free Press.

McQUAIL, D., J. G. BLUMLER, and J. R. BROWN (1972) "The television audience: a revised perspective," in D. McQuail (ed.) Sociology of Mass Communications. Harmondsworth: Penguin.

MASLOW, A. H. (1954) Motivation and Personality. New York: Harper.

MENDELSOHN, H. (1964) "Listening to radio," in L. A. Dexter and D. M. White (eds.) People, Society and Mass Communications. Glencoe: Free Press.

NORDENSTRENG, K. (1970) "Comments on 'gratifications research' in broadcasting." Public Opinion Quarterly 34.

PIETILA, V. (1969) "Immediate versus delayed reward in newspaper reading." Acta Sociologica 12.

ROBINSON, J. P. (1972) "Toward defining the functions of television," in Television and Social Behavior, Vol. 4. Rockville, Md.: National Institute of Mental Health.

SCHRAMM, W. (1949) "The nature of news." Journalism Quarterly 26.

_____ J. LYLE, and E. B. PARKER (1961) Television in the Lives of Our Children. Stanford: Stanford Univ. Press.

STEPHENSON, W. (1967) The Play Theory of Mass Communication. Chicago: Univ. of Chicago Press.

SUCHMAN, E. (1942) "An invitation to music," In P. F. Lazarsfeld and F. N. Stanton (eds.) Radio Research, 1941. New York: Duell, Sloan & Pearce.

WAPLES, D., B. BERELSON, and F. R. BRADSHAW (1940) What Reading Does to People. Chicago: Univ. of Chicago Press.

WEISS, W. (1971) "Mass communication." Annual Review of Psychology 22.

WOLFE, K. M. and M. FISKE (1949) "Why children read comics," in P. F. Lazarsfeld and F. N. Stanton (eds.) Communications Research, 1948–9. New York: Harper.

WRIGHT, C. (1960) "Functional analysis and mass communication." Public Opinion Quarterly 24.

2.3 RICHARD C. VINCENT AND MICHAEL D. BASIL

College Students' News Gratifications, Media Use, and Current Events Knowledge

The following selection is from Richard C. Vincent and Michael D. Basil's "College Students' News Gratifications, Media Use, and Current Events Knowledge," *Journal of Broadcasting and Electronic Media* (vol. 41, 1997). In this study, the authors apply the uses and gratifications perspective to a current situation as they describe college students' use of news and current events as a socializing factor. Based on earlier studies, Vincent and Basil developed research hypotheses that reflected earlier literature on gratifications sought, news use, and current events knowledge.

It is interesting to see how the uses and gratifications perspective has developed to predict use of other forms of media as well as the form analyzed in this research study. This is becoming more and more an important factor as different distribution media enter the home. And, while many researchers claim that a proliferation of forms and channels of media (such as cable TV, VCRs, the Internet, and personal communication services) still reflect little diversity of content, the availability of a variety of media forms may play an increasingly important role in future uses and gratifications studies.

News has traditionally been a featured component in understanding the *surveillance* function of the media. This study questions how the surveillance function operates and extrapolates on other functions as reported by college students. The average use statistics in this report are also interesting.

Vincent teaches in the Department of Communication at the University of Hawaii. His research encompasses mass communication theory and international media. Basil teaches in the Department of Mass Communications and Journalism Studies at the University of Denver. His research deals with how individuals process messages.

Key Concept: uses and gratifications; surveillance and entertainment

The uses and gratifications perspective is often employed to examine audience uses of mass media according to social and psychological needs. It asks that we think of media exposure as an intervening variable in the study of traditional communication effects research (Katz, Blumler & Gurevitch, 1974). According to the uses and gratifications perspective, audiences differ in the gratifications they are seeking from the mass media, and these orientations may be related to certain social conditions and functions or personality dispositions and abilities. These orientations result in assorted media use patterns and a variety of media effects (Palmgreen, Wenner & Rosengren, 1985).

Various studies have examined the factors predicting adults' media use (Bantz, 1982; Becker, 1979; Conway & Rubin, 1991; Rubin, 1983; Rubin & Perse, 1987). The uses and gratifications approach has also been applied to television viewing needs and motives among children and adolescents (Greenberg, 1974; Rubin, 1977, 1979; Wade, 1973). Greenberg (1974) and Rubin (1977, 1979) found age to be a consistent predictor of viewing motivations among children and adolescents where motivations to escape or pass time were generally higher in younger viewers. Making use of these gratifications, Rubin (1981) found that motivations do determine television use. Generally, viewers who are seeking companionship or information tend to watch the most television. More recent research shows that the uses and gratifications approach is useful in predicting MTV (Rubin et al., 1986), magazine (Payne, Sever & Dozier, 1988), and telephone use (O'Keefe & Sulanowski, 1995). In some instances the nature of the gratifications are different from the traditional ones observed with regard to television news.

NEWS MEDIA USE AMONG COLLEGE STUDENTS

One genre that has been explored using the uses and gratifications approach is news media use. News has important implications in the creation of an informed electorate in areas including politics and international events. According to the uses and gratifications approach, predispositions such as an interest in current events drives news media use across the various media (Wenner, 1985).

College students make for an important sample of news use because they are in the midst of an important period of socialization to the news media during a dramatic yet predictable change in the life cycle (Henke, 1985; Rubin, 1985). This is a time when these young adults are unlearning childhood standards, experimenting with images of self, developing sex-roles, defining future roles, growing more independent, and moving toward establishing close relationships with peers (Bowerman & Kinch, 1959; Campbell, 1969; Cobb, 1986; Faber, Brown, & McLeod, 1979). They begin to vote. They also are anticipating their entry into the full-time work force.

O'Keefe and Spetnagel (1973) found that among college students, males viewed more television and read more newspapers than females, television viewing levels increased with age, and television was the preferred source for news of a national or international event with newspapers being second. Newspapers scored highest as a source for detailed information. Henke (1985) found that general media consumption and its perceived importance both increase with year in college. She also found an increase in the use of a new medium, CNN cable news, over this period. Presumably reflecting increased surveillance needs, the study found that CNN viewers read more newspapers, were more likely to watch a late night local news program, and read more weekly news magazines.

Richard C. Vincent and Michael D. Basil

This previous research by O'Keefe and Spetnagel (1973) and Henke (1985) has detailed specific college student patterns and perceptions of the news media, but did not use their data to test the uses and gratifications approach. So although these two studies show a pattern of increasing news media use through the college years, the reasons for this increased viewing were not explored. Use of college students helps us to partially avoid the potential pitfalls of limited media availability (Bogart, 1965) in a general audience. By comparing all media used, we may also have the advantage of looking at a potentially active audience whose media use may be responding more to active desires than to the force of habit (Goodhardt, Ehrenberg & Collins, 1975).

Hypotheses

The objective of the current study is to explore patterns of use of news media by college students and the relationship among traditional news gratifications functions. We propose that, according to uses and gratifications theory, gratifications sought will drive media use. Gratifications sought, combined with media use, will, in turn determine students' current events knowledge. For the present study, we have hypothesized that differences will emerge when attitudes on and use of various news media preferences and uses are examined in conjunction with current events knowledge.

Henke (1985) found that news media use shows an increase in college. We predict therefore:

H1: The use of news media will increase with year in college.

Uses and gratifications theory suggests that news use is rooted in viewing motivations. Therefore, based on the results reported by O'Keefe and Spetnagel (1973) and Henke (1985), an increase in news viewing should be caused by increasing surveillance needs. So we predict that:

H2: Demographic differences will affect gratifications sought. Generally, juniors and seniors, men, older students, and students with higher grade point averages will show higher surveillance needs.

Uses and gratifications theory also predicts that the medium used is also determined by viewers' motivations and satisfactions with previous use of that medium. This leads us to predict that:

H3: Gratifications sought will affect which medium viewers select for their consumption of news. Even more specifically, we predict that:

H3a: surveillance needs will show a positive relationship with print news use,

H3b: escapism and entertainment will show a positive relationship with broadcast news use.

Finally, previous studies of learning from the media (Chaffee & Choe, 1981; Chaffee & Schleuder, 1986) have shown that people learn more from print media than broadcast media. If the uses and gratifications theory is correct, this difference should be attributable to differing viewing motivations, which, in turn result in the use of different media. This leads us to predict that:

H4: The specific modality of news viewing will predict individual knowledge. Specifically, print media use will predict current events knowledge, broadcast news viewing will not.

Related to Hypothesis 4 we also wondered about the effects of CNN viewing. Because we predicted that it would be as similar to newspaper use as television viewing, we could not make a direction prediction. We did, however, pose a research question:

RQ: Is CNN viewing a significant predictor of current events knowledge?

METHODS

Subjects

A survey was used to gather data for this study. The sample for the study consisted of 1209 university students drawn from large state universities in the west, midwest and east during and after operations "Desert Shield" and "Desert Storm" during the Persian Gulf conflict—in late 1990 and early 1991. Of the entire sample, 54 percent (555) were female and 46 percent (468) were male. The age range was 18 to 72. The median age was 23.0.

Questionnaire

A 68-item questionnaire was distributed to Communication and Speech classes for all waves. Eleven questions collected demographic information including age, gender, and cultural orientation. Twenty-two items adapted questions about gratifications sought from previous instruments (largely based on studies of television use). Seventeen questions measured media use. For wave

3, 10 additional questions were added, 6 asking about their media use during the "Gulf War" and 4 asking about their own or their family connection to the military. In addition, for the second survey, administered in Summer 1990, students were also given a current events knowledge quiz. The quiz was adapted from *Time* magazine's education program's "Summer Current Events Quiz."

*Richard C.
Vincent and
Michael D.
Basil*

Measured Variables

The media use items... were subjected to preliminary analysis. Examination of responses suggested that less than 20% of students watched the Mac-Neil/Lehrer NewsHour or read opinion magazines. These variables, then, were eliminated from the subsequent factor analysis. These media use items resulted in two factors—print use and broadcast use. Based on this factor analysis, the reliabilities of these two scales were examined. The results suggested that the resulting print scale did not meet an acceptable level of reliability—the average correlation was .13, and the resulting alpha level was only .48. The broadcast scale, meanwhile, did result in a reliable scale—yielding an average correlation of .21 and an alpha coefficient of .65. Although the reliability of the broadcast scale was fairly low, it was deemed acceptable. The average correlation collapsing across broadcast and print media was .11.

The findings of the news scales suggest that the subjects tend to watch different sources of broadcast news similarly; that is, if they watched network news, they also tended to watch early and late local news. The students, however, were more likely to read one source of print news at the exclusion of others. The general "news viewing factor" also was too weak for standard criteria.

The gratification items... were also subjected to confirmatory factor analyses. Four factors emerged.... Based on this factor analysis, the reliabilities of these items were examined. All four scales yielded a minimum level of reliability. The resulting four gratification scales—surveillance, escape, boredom, and entertainment yielded alpha reliability coefficients of .89, .88, .85, and .85, respectively. These reliabilities were deemed acceptable.

The number correct on the current events quiz served as a measure of current events knowledge. The number correct ranged from 5 to 30, with the median number correct being 15.

RESULTS

Media Use

... On average, students read the newspaper 3.4 days a week, roughly comparable to O'Keefe and Spetnagel's (1973) 3.7 days. News magazine reading was less frequent, 1.3 versus 2.5, but there are more news sources today. In addition, students watched an average of a total of 7.4 television news programs, or 3.7 hours of broadcast news (assuming half hour news broadcasts), in an average week. Network news viewing was very similar (1.9 times/week now and 1.9 in 1973), as was local news (1.8 times/week now, 1.9 in 1973).

The gratifications questions... across the four factors (averaged across all questions) was: surveillance 4.73, escape 2.64, boredom 2.81, and entertainment 3.58.

Hypothesis Tests

The first hypothesis predicted that the use of news media would increase with year in college. Significant linear class effects were generally found....

[A] significant linear trend was found for newspaper reading..., news magazines..., broadcast..., CNN..., and MacNeil/Lehrer.... Hypothesis 1, therefore, was supported.

The second hypothesis predicted that demographic differences would affect gratifications sought. Generally, older students, men, students with higher grade point averages, and upperclassmen were expected to show higher surveillance needs than younger students, women, students with lower grade point averages, and lower classmen....

In this analysis, the respondent's age, gender, grade point average (GPA), and year in school were predictive of surveillance, escape, boredom, and entertainment needs. Age was negatively related to escape, boredom, and entertainment. Gender was a significant predictor of escape and entertainment needs. Females had lower levels of escapism and entertainment. Grade point average approached significance on escape, boredom, and entertainment. Most relevant to Hypothesis 2, although age, gender, and GPA showed no relationship with surveillance needs, year in school showed a positive relationship with surveillance needs. Because only year in school predicted surveillance needs, only the year in school findings do support Hypothesis 2.

The third hypothesis predicted that the gratifications sought would determine viewers' news media use. Specifically, hypothesis 3a predicted that surveillance needs would show a positive relationship with the use of print media. Hypothesis 3b predicted that escapism and entertainment would show a positive relationship with broadcast news viewing....

Here, demographics showed a significant relationship with news use, including a positive relationship with newspaper reading, television news and MacNeil/Lehrer viewing, but no significant relationship with CNN viewing. Gender showed a negative relationship with media use such that women showed lower news media use in all cases except news magazine reading. Students' grade point average was a significant predictor of some news media use; students with higher grade point averages were more likely to use newspapers, MacNeil/Lehrer, and CNN. GPA showed no relationship to news magazine or broadcast news media use, however. Year in school showed a positive relationship to newspaper reading and CNN viewing.

With regard to gratifications sought, surveillance was a significant predictor of news media use. Consistent with Hypothesis 3a, surveillance showed a positive relationship to use of all forms of news media. Boredom showed a negative relationship with news magazine use, and approached a significant relationship with newspaper reading. That is, people who reported boredom as a factor in choosing news media were less likely to read print. Consistent with Hypothesis 3b, entertainment showed a positive relationship with television news viewing and CNN viewing. Finally, escape was not a significant predictor of print media use.

... Hypothesis 3 in general, and Hypothesis 3a and 3b in particular, therefore, were supported.

The fourth hypothesis was that the specific modality of news viewing would predict individual knowledge, specifically that print media use, especially newspapers, would be a significant predictor of current events knowledge, while broadcast news viewing would not. In addition, a research question asked whether CNN viewing had a significant effect on current events knowledge. To test this hypothesis and research question, a third multiple regression examined determinants of current events knowledge. This analysis used a stepwise regression which first controlled for demographics. After demographics were entered, gratifications were entered. Finally, news media use was entered into the equation....

In this regression, all of the demographic variables were significant predictors of current events knowledge. The only gratifications factor that predicted knowledge was surveillance. Both forms of print media, meanwhile, were significant predictors of current events knowledge. Among these, however, newspaper reading showed a stronger relationship to current events knowledge than news magazine reading. This finding is consistent with other studies of learning from the news (e.g., Chaffee & Schleuder, 1986). It is also consistent with Hypothesis 4, formulated from uses and gratifications theory. The results of the research question support the importance of CNN as a source of knowledge about current events, at least during a time of crisis. In this way, the effects of CNN viewing can be more similar to newspaper reading than television news viewing.

CONCLUSIONS

This study conceptualized college students' news media use as a chain of events leading from news gratifications sought, to news media use, to current events knowledge. News media use levels were similar to those measured by O'Keefe and Spetnagel (1973) 18 years earlier with the exception of a drop in newspaper and news magazine reading. Consistent with media use levels found by Henke (1985), college appears to be a period of increasing levels of surveillance. College students appear to be socialized into using news media for specific purposes during these years. Age and gender differences reported by O'Keefe and Spetnagel (1973) did not materialize, however. This may suggest that the change in news use is more attributable to socialization than to chronological age and that women's roles and expectations in public policy have increased to levels comparable to men's.

This study also sought to discover the reasons for news media use. The most important demographic factor of gratifications sought was year in school on surveillance needs. Other demographic differences on gratifications sought were observed, including a decreasing importance of requiring the media to provide a source of escape, boredom release, and entertainment during the college years. This finding has implications not only for news media use, but also for entertainment media use.

After examining gratifications sought, this study examined predictors of media use. When demographic differences are controlled, it appears that news media use is accurately predicted by college students' surveillance needs. Those with high surveillance needs tend to use higher levels of all news media. Those students with higher entertainment needs, however, are more likely to use television than print as a source of their news.

Finally, this study examined predictors of current events knowledge. Consistent with earlier findings (Chaffee & Schleuder, 1986), current events knowledge was predicted by print media use and not by most electronic media. The exception to the pattern was that one electronic source, CNN, did have a positive relationship to current events knowledge, at least during the Gulf War. It is not clear whether this has to do with a difference in content, or may be due to the higher levels of surveillance reported by viewers during this period. But this finding suggests that it is not necessarily the medium of delivery that determines learning—people can learn from the broadcast media.

Two limitations of this study should be considered. First, the data were gathered from a sample of college students. Applications to a completely random sample of college students, or other populations may not be justified. Because these results are consistent with that reported from earlier studies of college students (Henke, 1985; O'Keefe & Spetnagel, 1973), however, the size of this sample may have provided a reasonable estimate. The data were also subjected to multivariate analysis, which controlled for other factors. This approach allows us to trust the correlational findings between gratifications sought, media use, and current events knowledge. The results, therefore, provide reliable support for the predictions of uses and gratifications theory. The second possible limitation is that these data were gathered during and after the Gulf War. It is possible that this period was atypical so that CNN viewing may have had a unique role during the war that it may not otherwise have, and that effect may have persisted through the data collection, perhaps even changing news expectations (Katz, 1992).

The results suggest four areas for further research. First, it would be useful to examine news viewing during other periods or transition. This should include the transition from college to work, or from the working years to retirement. Second, it would be useful to understand the effects of crises by comparing news uses during other wars and conflicts with that of times of peace. Third, what will be the effect of newer media such as the Internet on existing media use? Fourth, although this study used regression procedures to examine effects of gratifications sought on news media use and on current events knowledge, it would be useful to conduct a more detailed path analysis to verify whether these orderings appear justified. For example, whether people learn more from CNN than from other forms of broadcast news media may be due to differences in viewers' motivations, especially a higher need for surveillance, or differences in CNN news content. A path analysis may help us discover whether print's superiority is attributable to the medium itself, the differences in content, or in viewers' activity in processing the message.

REFERENCES

Bantz, C. (1982). Exploring uses and gratifications: A comparison of reported uses of television and reported uses of favorite program type. *Communication Research, 9,* 352–379.

Bogart, L. (1965). The mass media and the blue collar worker. In A. Bennett & W. Gomber (Eds.), *Blue-collar world: Studies of the American worker* (pp. 416–428). Englewood Cliffs, NJ: Prentice-Hall.

Bowerman, C. E., & Kinch, J. W. (1959). Changes in family and peer orientation of children between the fourth and tenth grades. *Social Forces, 37:* 206–211.

Campbell, E. Q. (1969). Adolescent socialization. In D. A. Goslin (Ed.), *Handbook of socialization theory and research.* Chicago: Rand McNally.

Chaffee, S. H., & Choe, S. Y. (1981). Newspaper reading in longitudinal perspective: Beyond structural constraints. *Journalism Quarterly, 58,* 201–211.

Chaffee, S. H., & Schleuder, J. (1986). Measurement and effects of attention to news media. *Human Communication Research, 13,* 76–107.

Cobb, C. J. (1986). Patterns of newspaper readership among teenagers. *Communication Research, 13,* 299–326.

Conway, J. C., & Rubin, A. M. (1991). Psychological predictors of television viewing motivation. *Communication Research, 18,* 443–463.

Faber, R. J., Brown, J. D., & McLeod, J. M. (1979). Coming of age in the global village: television and adolescence. In E. Wartella (Ed.), *Children communicating: Media and development of thought, speech, understanding* (pp. 215–249). Beverly Hills, CA: Sage.

Goodhardt, G., Ehrenberg, A., & Collins, M. (1975). *The television audience: Patterns of viewing.* Lexington, MA: D. C. Heath.

Greenberg, B. S. (1974). Gratifications of television viewing and their correlates for British children. In J. G. Blumler and E. Katz (Eds.), *The uses of mass communication: Current perspectives on gratifications research* (pp. 71–92). Beverly Hills: Sage.

Henke, L. L. (1985). Perceptions and use of news media by college students. *Journal of Broadcasting & Electronic Media, 29,* 431–436.

Katz, E. (1992). The end of journalism? Notes on watching the war. *Journal of Communication, 42,* 5–13.

Katz, E., Blumler, J. G., & Gurevitch, M. (1974). Utilization of mass communication by the individual. In J. G. Blumler & E. Katz (Eds.), *The uses of mass communications: Current perspectives on gratifications research* (pp. 19–32). Beverly Hills: Sage.

O'Keefe, G. J., & Spetnagel, H. T. (1973). Patterns of college students' use of selected news media. *Journalism Quarterly, 50,* 543–548.

O'Keefe, G. J., & Sulanowski, B. K. (1995). More than just talk: Uses, gratifications, and the telephone. *Journalism Quarterly, 72,* 922–933.

Palmgreen, P., Wenner, L. A., & Rosengren, K. E. (1985). Uses and gratifications research: The past ten years. In K. E. Rosengren, L. A. Wenner, & P. Palmgreen (Eds.), *Media gratifications research: Current perspectives* (pp. 11–37). Beverly Hills, CA: Sage.

Payne, G. A., Sever, J. J. H., & Dozier, D. M. (1988). Uses and gratifications motives as indicators of magazine readership. *Journalism Quarterly, 65,* 909–913, 959.

Rubin, A. M. (1977). Television usage, attitudes and viewing behaviors of children and adolescents. *Journal of Broadcasting, 21,* 355–369.

Rubin, A. M. (1979). Television use by children and adolescents. *Human Communication Research, 5,* 109–120.

Rubin, A. M. (1981). An examination of television viewing motivations. *Communication Research, 8,* 141–165.

Rubin, A. M. (1983). Television uses and gratifications: The interactions of viewing patterns and motivations. *Journal of Broadcasting, 27,* 37–51.

Rubin, A. M. (1985). Media gratifications through the life cycle. In K. E. Rosengren, L. A. Wenner, & P. Palmgreen (Eds.), *Media gratifications research: Current perspectives* (pp. 195–208). Beverly Hills, CA: Sage.

Rubin, A. M. (1994). Media uses and effects: A uses and gratifications perspective. In J. Bryant & D. Zillmann (Eds.), *Media effects: Advances in theory and research* (pp. 417–436). Hillsdale, NJ: Lawrence Erlbaum.

Rubin, A. M., & Perse, E. M. (1987). Audience activity and television news gratifications. *Communication Research, 14,* 58–84.

Rubin, R. B., Rubin, A. M., Perse, E. M., Armstrong, C., McHugh, M., & Faix, N. (1986). Media use and meaning of music video. *Journalism Quarterly, 63,* 353–359.

Wade, S. E. (1973). Interpersonal discussion: A critical predictor of leisure activity. *Journal of Communication, 23,* 426–445.

Wenner, L. A. (1985). The nature of news gratifications. In K. E. Rosengren, L. A. Wenner, & P. Palmgreen (Eds.), *Media gratifications research: Current perspectives* (pp. 171–194). Beverly Hills, CA: Sage.

CHAPTER 3 Long-Term Effects: Cultivation

3.1 GEORGE GERBNER ET AL.

The "Mainstreaming" of America: Violence Profile No. 11

George Gerbner is considered one of the most respected scholars in the field of mass media studies today. Now retired from a long tenure as dean of the Annenberg School of Communications at the University of Pennsylvania where he formed and directed the world-renowned Cultural Indicators project in the 1970s, he continues his mass media research and activism concerning the impact of mass media on everyday life. Gerbner has edited many books on such issues as media effects, government mass media policy, international communication, and media and education. The other members of the Cultural Indicators research team who worked with Gerbner on the study discussed in the following selection are Larry Gross, Michael Morgan, and Nancy Signorielli. Gross and Signorielli are both professors of communication, and all three carry on their own cultural indicators research.

Gerbner et al. argue that traditional media effects researchers err by focusing solely on the immediate "before and after" effects of exposure to media messages on people's behavior and attitudes. They suggest that in any culture it is the telling of stories that forms the *symbolic environment,* which gives order and meaning to human actions; growing up within a particular system of storytelling slowly but surely cultivates an individual's perceptions and judgments about society. Gerbner and his associates also argue that television provides a concentrated system of storytelling that rivals (and in modern societies supersedes) religion in its power to shape people's social perceptions.

Due to the unique nature of television, Gerbner et al. recommend what scientists term "longitudinal," or long-term, study of media effects. The Cultural Indicators project is itself a long-term study involving a three-pronged research effort: *institutional analysis,* which focuses on the structures of decision making that are involved in the production of media messages; *message system analysis,* which involves in-depth, quantitative content analysis aimed at discovering basic, social building blocks of TV content; and *cultivation analysis,* which focuses on TV viewers, correlating attitudes about the social world with, first, the amount of TV viewing and, second, the content of TV. Cultivation theory hypothesizes that perceptions of the social world on the part of heavy viewers will very closely resemble the structure of the "world of TV" content. In fact, Gerbner and his associates have gone on to posit a *mainstreaming effect* among heavy TV viewers.

The following selection is from "The 'Mainstreaming' of America: Violence Profile No. 11," *Journal of Communication* (vol. 30, no. 3, 1980). In it, Gerbner and his associates provide an annual report on their research and further expound the theory of cultivation.

Key Concept: theory of cultivation

*T*elevision makes specific and measurable contributions to viewers' conceptions of reality. These contributions relate both to the synthetic world television presents and to viewers' real life circumstances. These are the basic findings of our long-range research project called Cultural Indicators, and they have been supported, extended, and refined in a series of studies. Here we shall report new findings and introduce theoretical developments dealing with the dynamics of the cultivation of general concepts of social reality (which we shall call "mainstreaming") and of the amplification of issues particularly salient to certain groups of viewers (which we shall call "resonance").

The design of our research consists of two interrelated parts: message system analysis and cultivation analysis. Message system analysis is the annual monitoring of samples of prime-time and weekend daytime network dramatic programming (including series, other plays, comedies, movies, and cartoons). Cultivation analysis is the investigation of viewer conceptions of social reality associated with the most recurrent features of the world of television. Our studies since 1967–68 have traced some conceptual and behavioral correlates of growing up and living with a television world in which men outnumber women three to one, young people comprise one-third and old people one-fifth of their real numbers, professionals and law-enforcers dominate the occupations, and an average of five acts of violence per prime time hour (and four times that number per weekend daytime hour) involve more than half of all leading characters....

For purposes of this analysis, we define violence as the overt expression of physical force (with or without a weapon, against self or others) compelling action against one's will on pain of being hurt and/or killed or threatened to be so victimized as part of the plot. Idle threats, verbal abuse, or gestures without credible violent consequences are not coded as violence. However, "accidental" and "natural" violence (always purposeful dramatic actions that do victimize certain characters) are, of course, included.

A violent act that fits the definition is recorded, whatever the context. This definition includes violence that occurs in a fantasy or "humorous" context as well as violence presented in a realistic or "serious" context. There is substantial evidence that fantasy and comedy are effective forms in which to convey serious lessons (1, 3, 11). Thus eliminating fantasy or comic violence, as well as violence of an "accidental" nature, would be a major analytical error.

All items are coded by pairs of trained coders (see 4 and 5) and are subjected to an extensive reliability analysis (see 10). Only those items meeting acceptable standards of reliability (.6 or above) are included in the analysis.

The Violence Index combines three sets of observations in order to provide a single indicator sensitive to a range of program characteristics. These observations measure the extent to which violence occurs at all in the programs sampled, the frequency and rate of violent episodes, and the number of roles calling for characterization as violents, victims, or both. These three measures have achieved high inter-coder reliability over the years we have been collecting these data. Although here we report only the Index, the component measures are always reported in our full technical reports (e.g., 5)....

The frequency of violence and the patterns of victimization in the world of dramatic television are remarkably stable from year to year. Overall, the Fall 1979 Violence Index shows some decline over the 1978 Index, much of which can be accounted for by a reduction of violence on ABC. Violence also declined after 9 p.m. but rose in the 1979 "family viewing" time (8:00 to 9:00 p.m. EST) (see Figure 1). Although still way above the level in prime time, violence in weekend-daytime (children's) programs also declined. The largest increase in violence in the 1979 sample was in new prime-time programs, especially in the former "family hour" and particularly on NBC. The largest reductions in violence were in the late evening by ABC and NBC and on weekend-daytime programs by all networks, but especially NBC.

In prime time, 70 percent of all programs still contained violence. The rate of violent episodes was 5.7 per hour, up from 4.5 in 1978. Nearly 54 percent of all leading characters were involved in some violence, about the same as in 1978. In weekend-daytime (children's) programs, 92 percent of all programs contained some violence, down from 98 percent in 1978. The rate of violent episodes was 17 per hour, down from 25 the year before. Nearly 75 percent of all leading characters were involved in violence, down from 86 percent in 1978.

Overall, the percent of characters involved in violence has remained fairly steady since 1969. About two-thirds of the males and nearly half of the females are involved. When involved, female characters are more likely than male characters to be the victims rather than the perpetrators of violence. Only

FIGURE 1

Violence Index in Children's and Prime-Time Programming, 1967–1979

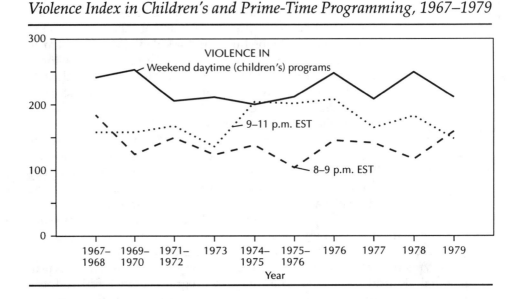

one group of male characters—young boys—are among the ten groups who are most likely to be victimized. Women cast in minority roles (old women, upper-class women, non-white women, young women, and lower-class women) are especially more likely to suffer rather than to inflict violence. Only two groups of characters—old men and "bad" women—are more likely to hurt others than to be hurt themselves (for details of these and other message analysis findings, see 5).

We now turn to the theory of cultivation and to findings relating to conceptions of a mean world and its dangers.

Television is the central and most pervasive mass medium in American culture and it plays a distinctive and historically unprecedented role. Other media are accessible to the individual (usually at the point of literacy and mobility) only after the socializing functions of home and family life have begun. In the case of television, however, the individual is introduced virtually at birth into its powerful flow of messages and images. The television set has become a key member of the family, the one who tells most of the stories most of the time. Its massive flow of stories showing what things are, how things work, and what to do about them has become the common socializer of our times. These stories form a coherent if mythical "world" in every home. Television dominates the symbolic environment of modern life.

Cultivation analysis is the investigation of the consequences of this ongoing and pervasive system of cultural messages. Given our premise that television's images cultivate the dominant tendencies of our culture's beliefs, ideologies, and world views, the observable independent contributions of television can only be relatively small. But just as an average temperature shift of a few degrees can lead to an ice age or the outcomes of elections can be determined by slight margins, so too can a relatively small but pervasive influence make a crucial difference. The "size" of an "effect" is far less critical than the direction of its steady contribution.

We have found that amount of exposure to television is an important indicator of the strength of its contributions to ways of thinking and acting. For heavy viewers, television virtually monopolizes and subsumes other sources of information, ideas, and consciousness. Thus, we have suggested that the more time one spends "living" in the world of television, the more likely one is to report perceptions of social reality which can be traced to (or are congruent with) television's most persistent representations of life and society. Accordingly, we have examined the difference that amount of viewing makes in people's images, expectations, assumptions, and behaviors.[1]

In previous reports, we have stressed across-the-board consequences of television viewing. Thus, we expected heavier viewers to be more likely to give the "television answers" to a series of informational and opinion questions than lighter viewers. This theoretical perspective still holds and provides some of the most compelling evidence for the existence of television's contributions to conceptions of social reality. But further examination of previously analyzed and new data reveals there are substantially different patterns of associations for different social groups between amount of viewing and certain conceptions of social reality.

Television's cultivation of conceptions and behaviors is a consistent process but is integrated in different ways and with different results into different patterns of life. Therefore, a fuller understanding of television's contribution may be achieved by paying particular attention to differences across different subgroups.

Many differences between groups of viewers can be explained in terms of one of two systematic processes which we call "mainstreaming" and "resonance."

The "mainstream" can be thought of as a relative commonality of outlooks that television tends to cultivate. By "mainstreaming" we mean the sharing of that commonality among heavy viewers in those demographic groups whose light viewers hold divergent views. In other words, differences deriving from other factors and social forces may be diminished or even absent among heavy viewers. Thus, in some cases we should only find evidence for cultivation within those groups who are "out" of the mainstream. In other cases, we may find that viewing "moderates" attitudes in groups whose light viewers tend to hold extreme views. But in all cases, more viewing appears to signal a convergence of outlooks rather than absolute, across-the-board increments in all groups.

For example, it is well documented that more educated, higher income groups have the most diversified patterns of cultural opportunities and activities; therefore, they tend to be lighter viewers. We found that, when they are light viewers, they also tend to be the least imbued with the television view of the world. But the heavy viewers in the higher education/high income groups respond differently. Their responses to our questions are more like those of other heavy viewers, most of whom have less education and income. It is the college-educated, higher income light viewers who diverge from the "mainstream" cultivated by television; heavy viewers of all groups tend to share a relatively homogeneous outlook.

But the relationship of real life experience to television's cultivation of conceptions of reality entails not only this generalized notion of "mainstreaming" but also special cases of particular salience to specific issues. This is what we call "resonance." When what people see on television is most congruent with everyday reality (or even *perceived* reality), the combination may result in a coherent and powerful "double dose" of the television message and significantly boost cultivation. Thus, the congruence of the television world and real-life circumstances may "resonate" and lead to markedly amplified cultivation patterns.

These processes are not the only possible mechanisms which might explain variations in susceptibility to cultivation. For example, related analyses of children and adolescents suggest that cultivation may be most pronounced when parents are not involved in their children's viewing (7) or when children are less integrated into cohesive peer groups (13). Furthermore, the constructs of "mainstreaming" and "resonance" are still being developed and investigated. Although the number of empirical instances of each is rapidly growing, too few have been accumulated to allow for predictions of when one or the other—or neither—will occur. Nonetheless, we believe that the results we will report here suggest that these concepts merit serious consideration.

Before we present findings further illuminating the two phenomena, it may help to illustrate them graphically. The data for this illustration come from our most recent sample of adults, collected in March 1979 by the Opinion Research Corporation (ORC).[2] In this sample we found instances of "mainstreaming" and "resonance" in the differential patterns of responses to a single question which may tap some conceptions cultivated by the violent and dangerous world of television. Figure 2 presents two examples of each in terms of the relationship between amount of viewing and responding that "fear of crime is a very serious personal problem."

As shown in Figure 2 this relationship holds only for respondents with medium or high incomes; low-income respondents are more likely to agree, regardless of viewing. The proportion of light viewers giving the "television answer" is much lower in the higher income groups; yet the middle- and high-income heavy viewers are in the "mainstream." When we look at the responses by race we see a consistent but different pattern. The relationship between viewing and fear is positive for whites but slightly negative for non-whites. Non-white light viewers are especially likely to express the notion that fear of crime is a "very serious personal problem." Heavy viewing among non-whites may moderate this outlook; thus, they are closer to the "mainstream."

... Figure 2 also shows that the association is strongest among females and among those who live in cities. To a large extent, this fear may be most salient to such respondents. Accordingly, real-life circumstances and environmental factors may "resonate" with television's messages and augment them.

FIGURE 2

Examples of Mainstreaming and Resonance in Terms of the Relationship Between Amount of Viewing and Percent of Respondents Saying That "Fear of Crime Is a Very Serious Personal Problem"

George Gerbner et al.

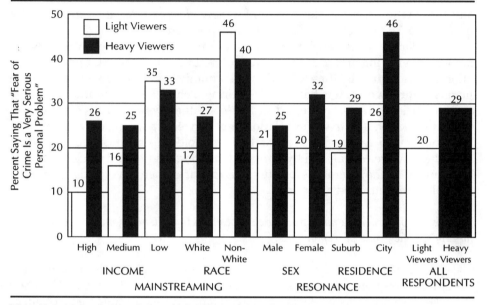

Note: *Data source:* Opinion Research Corporation, March 1979.

We shall now examine both mainstreaming and resonance in light of new data and in response to critiques of our earlier analyses.

Examples of "mainstreaming" can be found in analyses of questions relating to what we have called the "mean world syndrome." We combined three items from the 1975 and 1978 National Opinion Research Center (NORC) General Social Surveys to form an index of interpersonal mistrust (alpha = .68) similar to Rosenberg's "faith in people" scale (12). The three items—which form the Mean World Index—measure the degree to which respondents agree that most people are just looking out for themselves, that you can't be too careful in dealing with people, and that most people would take advantage of you if they got a chance.... [T]elevision viewing overall is significantly associated with the tendency to express mistrust (r = .12, p < .001). This relationship is not fully accounted for by any individual control. Simultaneous controls greatly reduce its strength, but the relationship remains statistically significant.

Even more revealing than this small overall correlation is the relationship between television viewing and mistrust for specific groups of the population. The relationship is strongest for respondents who have had some college education—those who are also least likely to express interpersonal mistrust. (The correlation between education and the Mean World Index is −.28, p < .001.) The most striking specifications emerge for whites and non-whites. As a group, non-whites score higher on the Mean World Index (r = .23, p < .001). Yet, there is a significant *negative* association among non-whites between television and this index (r = −.10, p < .05). The relationship for whites, however, remains positive. Thus, those groups who in general are *least* likely to hold a television-related attitude are *most* likely to be influenced toward the "mainstream" television view; and those who are most likely to hold a view *more* extreme than the TV view may be "coaxed back" to the "mainstream" position.

Similar patterns can be found by examining the relationship between amount of viewing and feelings of alienation. In the 1977 NORC survey, alienation was measured by three of Srole's (14) anomie items—the lot of the average man is getting worse, it is hardly fair to bring a child into the world, and most public officials are not interested in the lot of the average man. We had previously reported (4) that the relationship between amount of viewing and the tendency to agree with these statements holds up in most groups. When these items were reanalyzed by Stevens (15), Hughes (9), and Hirsch (8), they all found that the overall association disappears when several demographic variables are controlled all at once.

But the lack of an overall relationship does not mean that the relationship does not hold for any specific group of respondents.

We combined these items into an index (alpha = .61) and found that the best predictor of anomie appeared to be education (r = −.31, p < .001). When the relationship between television viewing and endorsing statements of alienation is examined within educational subgroups, the relationship persists for those respondents who, as a group, are far less likely to express alienation—again, those with some college education. This relationship withstands the implementation of a large number of controls, either singly or simultaneously (r = .14, p < .01). For respondents with less education, who are relatively alienated to begin with, television viewing has no apparent relationship with anomie. Again, we see that television may influence a convergence of outlooks toward its "mainstream" rather than cultivating absolute across-the-board changes.

New data from a national probability sample of adults (ORC) provide numerous examples of this "mainstreaming" phenomenon with regard to people's conceptions about crime and violence. Using a question that replicates some of our earlier work, we asked respondents whether chances of being involved in violence in any given week are one in ten or one in a hundred. Our basic expectation is that relatively more heavy than light viewers will answer that their chances of encountering violence are higher.

Heavy viewers are indeed significantly more likely to give this response, overall and within most subgroups. Yet, there are important specifications. A large majority (84 percent) of both light and heavy viewers *with low incomes* give the higher risk response, and thus show no evidence of a relationship between amount of viewing and responses to this question. When we examine the middle- and upper-income groups, however, we find that the proportion of light viewers giving the "television answer" drops; "only" 62 percent of light viewers with higher incomes overestimate their chances of being involved in violence. Yet, the *difference* between light and heavy viewers rises sharply. Light viewers with middle and upper incomes are considerably less likely to express a high expectation of encountering violence, while heavy viewers with middle or high incomes exhibit almost the same level of perceived risk as the low-income group.

Such differences could be explained in terms of a ceiling effect. However, we think that the results we have found are a strong indication that television does contribute to the cultivation of common perspectives. In particular, heavy viewing may serve to cultivate beliefs of otherwise disparate and divergent groups toward a more homogeneous "mainstream" view.

The other important refinement of our theory suggests that cultivation will be most pronounced when other aspects of one's social environment are most congruent and thereby "resonate" with television's message.

Among Canadians, Doob and Macdonald (2) found the strongest positive associations between amount of television viewing and fear of crime among those who live in high crime centers. Although they interpreted this finding as evidence of spuriousness of the relationship between television viewing and fear of crime, clearly the concept of neighborhood does not "explain" the observed relationship. Rather, it points to an important specification. For those urban dwellers who live in high crime centers, television's violent imagery may be most congruent with their real-life perceptions. These people receive a "double dose" of messages that the world is violent, and consequently show the strongest associations between viewing and fear.

We have found parallel results in an analysis of data from our most recent national survey of adults (ORC). We asked people about how safe they felt walking around alone, at night, in their own neighborhoods, and assumed that those who lived in urban areas would also be most likely to express fear. We found, as would be expected, that those who live in large cities are much more likely to be afraid in their own neighborhoods at night, regardless of amount of viewing. But city dwellers also "resonate" most—they show the strongest association between amount of viewing and expressing this fear.

To provide further evidence we tried to approximate Doob and Macdonald's high crime/low crime distinction for respondents who live in cities. We assumed that respondents who live in larger cities *and* have lower incomes are likely to live in areas with relatively high crime rates, while high-income urban residents arguably live in less dangerous areas. We used the five questions from the 1979 ORC survey* to form a Perceptions of Danger Index-I.[3] When amount of television viewing was correlated with the Perceptions of Danger Index-I scores, the relationship was much stronger for residents in low-income (presumably high crime) urban areas ($r = .26$, $p < .001$) than for those in high-income (presumably low crime) urban areas ($r = .05$).

---

* [The five questions from the 1979 ORC survey mesured (1) the percentage of respondents overestimating their chances of being involved in violence; (2) percentage agreeing that women are more likely to be victims of crime; (3) percentage saying that their neighborhoods are only somewhat safe or not safe at all; (4) percentage saying that fear of crime is a very serious problem; and (5) percentage agreeing that crime is rising.—Eds.]

This relationship remains positive and significant ($r = .13$ $p < .001$) for urban dwellers with low incomes and falls to zero for high-income urban residents when within-group controls for demographic factors are implemented simultaneously. While the correspondence between income and neighborhood crime is ambiguous in suburban and non-metropolitan areas, it is worth noting that the association between amount of viewing and these images of danger, crime, and violence remains significant despite controls. Thus, the role of television in the cultivation of attitudes and fears may be most pronounced when an issue has direct relevance to the respondent's life.

A further example of "resonance" from the same survey focuses upon the assumption that older people are more likely than younger people to be victims of crime (an assumption contrary to the facts). Young and middle-aged respondents show no overall relationship between amount of viewing and the tendency to think that the elderly are most likely to be victimized. But, among older respondents, there is a significant positive association between television viewing and expressing this belief (gamma $= .27$, $p < .001$). In particular, this holds for older respondents in those demographic groups in which light viewers are less likely to respond this way.

We must stress that these specifications do not exhaust cultivation results. Amount of viewing remains significantly related to scores on the Perceptions of Danger Index-I, over and above the effects of education, income, sex, race, age, urban proximity, and newspaper reading (seventh order partial $r = .11$, $p < .001$). Although the amount of the variance in these scores explained by television viewing is small, with other things being held constant its predictive power is equal to or greater than that of age, race, urban proximity, income, or newspaper reading. But even where a relationship disappears for an entire sample, as Hirsch (8), Hughes (9), and Stevens (15) have found, it may quite clearly hold up in certain groups.

Thus, we have seen two distinct processes which help explain differential susceptibility to cultivation. "Resonance" may occur when a feature of the television world has special salience for a group, e.g., greater fear among city dwellers, or perceived over-victimization by the elderly. In these cases, the correlates of heavy viewing are most apparent among those for whom the topic holds considerable personal relevance. "Mainstreaming," on the other hand, may be related more to general and widespread images and norms of social reality.

Data from our three-year longitudinal study of adolescents also provide strong evidence for both an overall effect of viewing and important specification/interaction effects.

In the second and third years of this study we included two dependent measures—the Mean World Index (see above) and an index of Perceptions of Danger-II. The Perceptions of Danger Index-II was composed of four questions relating to estimates of the chances of encountering violence, aspects of murders and killings, and the importance of knowing self-defense. Agreement with these beliefs was interpreted as reflecting a strong image of the world as a dangerous place.

... Among boys, there is an interaction between second year viewing and second year scores on the Perceptions of Danger Index-II upon the third Perceptions of Danger Index-II scores. With IQ, SES, grade, early viewing, and early scores on the Perceptions of Danger Index-II already in a regression equation, there is still a negative and significant interaction (partial $r = -.30$, $F = 6.26$, d.f. $= 1, 64$, $p < .05$). This means that for those boys who had low Perceptions of Danger Index-II scores and watched more television in the second year, third year scores increased. But among those who were initially *more* afraid, heavy viewing led to less fear.

This is a dramatic and significant demonstration of the power of television to cultivate mainstream outlooks. There are, to be sure, significant "main effects," in a generally positive direction. But perhaps the more fundamental underlying process is that of convergence into a "mainstream" television view of the world, regardless of starting points. The ultimate homogenization of initially different perspectives may be the critical consequence of living with television.

The results reported here confirm, amplify, extend, and specify previous findings. The basic stability of the Violence Index and the apparent convergence of different programming parts (with the disappearance of the former "family hour" as a relatively low-violence zone) are the most noteworthy findings of message analysis. The cultivation analysis provides further strong support for the theory of pervasive cultivation of mistrust, apprehension, danger, and exaggerated "mean world" perceptions. Important specifications suggest that television viewing is associated with a cultural "mainstream" that tends to absorb or assimilate groups that otherwise diverge from it, and that the salience of certain real-life circumstances is likely to boost television's cultivating potential.

NOTES

1. We refer to this difference as the "cultivation differential" (CD) which is the spread between the percentages of light and heavy viewers who give a "television answer" to questions about social reality. The classification of respondents as relatively light, medium, and heavy viewers is determined by the distribution of amount of viewing in a given sample. Consequently, the actual proportions of lighter and heavier viewers will vary from one sample to another.

2. These data were collected as part of an Administration on Aging research grant (No. 90-A-1299) on "Aging with Television." George Gerbner, Larry Gross, and Nancy Signorielli were co-principal investigators (see 6).

3. These items essentially tap discrete dimensions; their conceptual link, however, is that they examine various aspects of television's portrayal of violence. Thus, it is not surprising that while these questions are all positively and significantly related to each other, their additive index has relatively low internal homogeneity (alpha = .34). At the same time, there is only one factor underlying the five items, indicating a high degree of unidimensionality. This index is called the Images of Violence Index in Violence Profile No. 11 (5).

Chapter 3
Long-Term
Effects:
Cultivation

1. Bandura, Albert, Dorothea Ross, and Sheila Ross. "Transmission of Aggression through Imitation of Aggressive Models." *Journal of Abnormal and Social Psychology* 63, 1967, pp. 575–582.

2. Doob, Anthony N. and Glenn E. Macdonald. "Television Viewing and Fear of Victimization: Is the Relationship Causal?" *Journal of Personality and Social Psychology* 37(2), 1979, pp. 170–179.

3. Ellis, Glenn T. and Francis Sekura III. "The Effect of Aggressive Cartoons on the Behavior of First Grade Children." *Journal of Psychology* 81, 1972, pp. 7–43.

4. Gerbner, George, Larry Gross, Marilyn Jackson-Beeck, Suzanne Jeffries-Fox, and Nancy Signorielli. "Cultural Indicators: Violence Profile No. 9." *Journal of Communication* 28(3), Summer 1978, pp. 176–207.

5. Gerbner, George, Larry Gross, Michael Morgan, and Nancy Signorielli. "Violence Profile No. 11: Trends in Network Television Drama and Viewer Conceptions of Social Reality, 1967–1979." Technical Report, The Annenberg School of Communications, University of Pennsylvania, May 1980.

6. Gerbner, George, Larry Gross, Nancy Signorielli, and Michael Morgan. "Aging with Television: Images on Television Drama and Conceptions of Social Reality." *Journal of Communication* 30(1), Winter 1980, pp. 37–47.

7. Gross, Larry and Michael Morgan. "Television and Enculturation." In J. R. Dominick and J. Fletcher (Eds.) *Broadcasting Research Methods: A Reader.* Boston: Allyn and Bacon, in press.

8. Hirsch, Paul. "The 'Scary World' of the Nonviewer and Other Anomalies: A Reanalysis of Findings on the Cultivation Hypothesis, Part I." Paper presented at the 35th Annual Conference of the American Association for Public Opinion Research, Cincinnati, May 1980. Also, *Communication Research*, in press.

9. Hughes, Michael. "The Fruits of Cultivation Analysis: A Re-examination of the Effects of Television Watching on Fear of Victimization, Alienation, and the Approval of Violence." *Public Opinion Quarterly*, in press.

10. Krippendorff, Klaus. "Bivariate Agreement Coefficients for the Reliability of Data." In E. F. Borgatta and G. W. Bohrnstedt (Eds.) *Sociological Methodology 1970.* San Francisco: Jossey-Bass, 1970.

11. Lovas, O. I. "Effects of Exposure to Symbolic Aggression on Aggressive Behavior." *Child Development* 32, 1961, pp. 37–44.

12. Rosenberg, Morris. *Occupations and Values.* Glencoe, Ill.: Free Press, 1957.

13. Rothschild, Nancy F. "Group as a Mediating Factor in the Cultivation Process Among Young Children." Unpublished master's thesis, The Annenberg School of Communications, University of Pennsylvania, 1979.

14. Srole, Leo. "Social Integration and Certain Correlaries: An Exploratory Study." *American Sociological Review* 21, 1956, pp. 709–712.

15. Stevens, Geoffrey. "TV and Attitudes of Fear and Alienation." Unpublished master's thesis, The Annenberg School of Communications, University of Pennsylvania, 1980.

3.2 MICHAEL MORGAN

Television and Democracy

Michael Morgan has expanded the focus of cultivation research to include such issues as computers in the home, television and academic achievement, media and the family, and TV in the classroom. He is an associate professor of communication at the University of Massachusetts, Amherst, and he has published many scholarly articles.

In the following excerpt from his essay "Television and Democracy," in Ian Angus and Sut Jhally, eds., *Cultural Politics in Contemporary America* (Routledge, 1989), Morgan focuses on the relationship between television and the democratic process. His cultivation analysis shows that heavy TV viewers, no matter what their actual political party affiliation, tend to identify themselves as "middle of the road" or "moderate." Likewise, and perhaps more troubling, heavy TV viewers from all classes tend to describe themselves as middle class. These viewer perceptions closely resemble the world of TV content, which systematically avoids representing "extreme" or "deviant" viewpoints. Morgan argues that this convergence of viewpoints toward a mythical "middle" represents a narrowing-down and homogenization of the political culture of the United States and that it is dangerous for democracy.

Key Concept: mainstreaming

*T*his essay explores the implications of television for a democratic system based on some theories and empirical findings from a long-term, ongoing research project called Cultural Indicators. Cultural Indicators is a three-pronged research strategy designed to investigate (1) the institutional processes underlying the production of television content, (2) the most common and stable "facts of life" in the world of television content (called *message system analysis*), and (3) relationships between exposure to television's messages and audience beliefs and behavior (called *cultivation analysis*). In particular, this essay will draw upon findings from the cultivation analysis aspects of the project.

The basic hypothesis guiding cultivation analysis is that the more time one spends watching television (that is, the more television dominates one's sources of information and consciousness), the more likely one is to hold conceptions of reality that can be traced to television's most stable and recurrent portrayals of life and society. For more than 15 years, cultivation analyses have produced consistent evidence that television viewing makes an independent contribution to people's images and assumptions about violence, sex roles, aging, occupations, education, science, health, religion, and other issues.

This essay highlights some findings from this research that relate to television's impact on political orientations, beliefs, and behavior. To most people in the United States, "politics" is a very narrow term relating to elections, campaigns, and running for office; but "politics" here is also used in the broader sense to encompass the allocation and distribution of social resources and the structures of social power. The data from these studies suggest that television does cultivate underlying values and ideologies about social power in the United States. These outcomes sometimes support but often pose a challenge to democratic principles and practices.

There are several reasons why television in America does not fit well the traditional concept of the role mass communication should play in a democratic society. The press in a democracy is supposed to be a selectively used medium, with readers searching out material which confirms and expands their point of view. Television, however, provides a relatively restricted set of choices for an almost unlimited variety of interests. Unlike print media, television is viewed relatively *non*-selectively; most people watch by the clock, not the program. Television does not require either literacy or mobility, and it provides a steady stream of politically relevant messages to nearly everyone, whether they actively seek them or not.

As with all cultural artifacts and products, television programs reflect and are shaped by cultural assumptions which are often invisible simply because they are so taken for granted. Patterns of casting and demography, conventions of portraying "human nature," and incidental, backdrop images of "reality" carry political and cultural significance.

The stories of a culture reflect and cultivate its most basic and fundamental assumptions, ideologies, and values. From myths and legends to fairy tales and nursery rhymes, from religious parables to fast-food commercials, the function of stories is to enculturate children and provide continual socialization for adults, to remind them what exists and what doesn't, what is important, good and bad, right and wrong.

Television is most of all a centralized system of storytelling. It brings a stable and coherent world of common images and messages into virtually every home in the United States. Television has become the primary, *common* source of everyday culture, politics, and values of an otherwise heterogeneous population. Tens of millions of people who had been scattered, isolated, provincial, and culturally and politically distant, are now brought into the mainstream by television.

In the average U.S. home, the television is on for more than seven hours a day. As we often hear, by the time children finish high school, they will have spent more time watching television than in school; they will have seen about 18,000 violent deaths and will have spent thousands of *hours* of their lives watching commercials. Adults spend more time watching television than doing anything else except sleeping and working. Storytelling traditionally relies upon repetition; the extent to which we are exposed to repetitive lessons through television is historically unprecedented.

The television system in the United States attracts its massive audiences by offering to all, no matter how young or old, rich or poor, the most broadly acceptable world of stories and action. Each night, 90 million people sit down and spend several hours watching mostly the same programs. Television provides, perhaps for the first time since pre-industrial religion, a strong cultural and political link between the elites and all other publics, in a shared daily ritual. As George Gerbner has put it, television is like religion, except most people watch TV more religiously....

I have looked at the relationship between amount of television viewing and voting behavior over the last four U.S. presidential elections, by reanalyzing data from large national surveys. Each year, the National Opinion Research Center asks a sample of about 1500 people whether they voted in recent presidential elections, who they voted for, and, for non-voters, who they *would* have voted for if they had voted. The responses can then be compared across light, medium, and heavy television viewers.

The patterns are strong, consistent, and clear: those who watch more television are less likely to say they voted, by an average margin of about 10 percent. The relationship holds up despite statistical controls for age, income, education, sex, race, political orientation, party identification, and other powerful factors.

Over the last 12 years, heavy viewers were also more likely than light viewers to say that they either *did* or *would have* voted for the *loser.* The longer the time from the election, the wider the gap; that is, for each year that passes following an election, the more heavy viewers turn against the incumbent—including Ronald Reagan. Despite the fact that the vast bulk of political campaign money is spent on television, those who watch more television are less likely to vote, and less likely to say they voted for the winner.

This is not to imply that television alone is responsible for the steady declines in voter turnout since the 1940s. But television has turned political campaigns into a kind of spectator sport, where the only thing the viewer has to do is to tune in to see who won—even if the media have already announced it *before* the election....

But the implications of television in a democratic political system go deeper than voting, candidates, and elections. Over the last 35 years television has transformed political reality in the United States, but the actual nature of that transformation has gone almost unnoticed. In part, this is because we've been asking the wrong questions.

Much research and debate on the impact of mass communication has tended to focus on individual messages, programs, series, or genres, usually in terms of their ability to produce immediate changes in audience attitudes and behavior. Also, it has been assumed that news and information programs are the major sources of people's political orientations, attitudes, and opinions.

In contrast, cultivation analysis is concerned with more general and pervasive consequences of overall immersion in a cumulative exposure to television. It sees television's impact not so much in change among individuals as in *resistance* to change, or in slow but steady shifts across generations. What cuts across most programs, what is largely inescapable regardless of whatever content "types" are "selected," is what counts. Focusing on plots and surface features may distract from what we really absorb.

The underlying political messages of regular entertainment may be among the least visible aspects of television, but they may also be among the most significant. The amount of attention given to such controversial fare as "Rambo," "White Knights," and "Amerika" may deflect attention away from the day-to-day political messages which permeate prime-time drama. From the cultivation perspective, regular, everyday entertainment may be a tremendously powerful means for expressing and sustaining cultural beliefs and values. Most people, most of the time, watch dramatic, fictional entertainment, which teaches them many basic lessons, facts, and values about social and political reality.

Television tells us, over and over, what different social types can and should do, and what fate has in store for them. Its dramatic portrayals of crime, adventure, sex roles, minorities, courtrooms and the conflicts of urban life provide vivid and consistent lessons for viewers. Those basic lessons contribute to broadly shared, common assumptions about risks and opportunities, vulnerabilities and power—the building blocks of political orientations....

Institutional and economic pressures mean that these basic underlying features of the television world are remarkably stable and consistent over time, despite surface-level novelties and fads that come and go. In the United States, about $55 million of revenue rides on every rating point. So, program producers *have* to create programs with the broadest possible appeal. That means avoiding political (and most other) "extremes," or making them as bland and non-threatening as possible, glorifying conventional consumer values, and striving for a safe, respectable, "middle-of-the-road" balance in most things.

Avoiding perceived extremes has always been television's strategy, as networks and advertisers expect attacks from special interest groups on the right *and* the left. What the television industry fears most is that people might get upset with what they watch and turn off the TV; so industry takes the obvious way out—navigating between (relative) extremes, safely in the comfortable mainstream that alienates no one and attracts the largest possible audience. "Deviant" or "extreme" groups are rarely shown, or are harshly criticized. All presentations *must* appear "objective," "moderate," "non-ideological," and otherwise suitable for mass marketing.

Some people are to the left of the television mainstream, and others are to the right; in order to maximize its audience, television attempts to steer a middle course—and in the process absorbs and homogenizes people with otherwise divergent orientations. This process of convergence is called "mainstreaming." One result is that those who watch more television are more likely to call themselves moderate (and less likely to say they are liberal or conservative) than light viewers. That is, the more time people spend watching television, the less they claim to be either liberal *or* conservative, and the more they say they are "moderate, middle-of-the-road."

The images of political reality television presents to people in the United States are highly constricted. We are given a basic continuum running from a "liberal left" to a "conservative right." It's a simple continuum, not multidimensional, and has a fairly narrow range. Positions and perspectives *outside* that narrow range of political discourse essentially do not exist.

Every issue is presented as having a "liberal" and a "conservative" side —e.g., abortion, homosexuality, school prayer, gun control, racial equality, women's rights, etc.—and the most consistent message is that the "truth" always lies somewhere in between—in the middle, in the mainstream. And the more that people watch television, the more they place themselves in that moderate, middle position.

The mainstreaming effects of television are extremely interesting within groups defined by party affiliation....

The more that members of all three parties watch television, the more they choose the moderate label.... Heavy viewing Democrats and Independents are less likely to choose either the liberal *or* conservative label. Among Republicans, heavy viewers are less likely to call themselves conservatives, and more likely to say they are either moderate or liberal. Television blurs and distorts the impact of party on where people place themselves on the political spectrum—all groups say they are "moderate" if they watch more TV.

This finding that heavy viewers see themselves as "moderate" holds up in survey after survey, in subgroup after subgroup. And, it's specific to television, not a correlate of general media use; the same results do *not* apply to radio listening or newspaper reading. It is television, and television alone, which cultivates "moderate" self-perceptions in its audiences, in line with the mainstream political lessons of television.

This may be part of a more general phenomenon: the cultivation of homogeneous, "average" self-perceptions. In addition to political moderation, the television world is dominated by characters who fit squarely in the "middle-middle" of a five-point social class category scale; middle-class characters vastly outnumber all others.

Cultivation research has found that when people whose objective social class is low watch more television, they are more likely to call themselves "middle class" as opposed to "working class." Middle-class viewers show the least sense of class distinction at different viewing levels; they are already "in" the mainstream. The upper classes, however, like the lower, show a pattern that is strongly associated with amount of television viewing; the more they watch, the *lower* their self-designated class. Heavy viewers are also more likely to say they have "average" incomes, particularly as real income increases.

Thus, the television experience seems to swamp other circumstances in thinking of one's class. Television viewing tends to blur class distinctions as it does political labels, and to make more affluent heavy viewers think of themselves as just working people of average income. Long-term, cumulative exposure to the consumer-oriented demography and middle-class supremacy of television tends to confound real class distinctions and to cultivate "average" or "middle class" self-perceptions as the norm of the television mainstream.

On the surface, mainstreaming looks like a "centering" or "middling" of political tendencies. But if we look at the actual positions heavy viewers take on specific political issues, we see that the mainstream does not run down the "middle-of-the-road."

Television viewing makes an independent contribution to what people in the United States think about the hard political issues of our times such as women and minorities, fairness and individual rights, defense spending and welfare, taxes and other issues. Its contribution reflects the most common, stable, and repetitive messages of the fictional world of dramatic television. . . .

But the patterns are for different groups; cultivation depends upon where one is in relation to the mainstream. . . . On . . . issues [such as busing, open housing, laws against intermarriage, homosexuality, abortion, and the legalization of marijuana], the traditional polarization of liberals and conservatives turns into a homogenization of views, in the direction of the television mainstream. These otherwise disparate groups find common ground in, converge, and blend into, the television mainstream.

For example, in terms of attitudes towards racial segregation, [there is a] relationship between amount of viewing and respondents' opposition to busing. Heavy viewing conservatives are more "liberal" and heavy viewing liberals more "conservative" than their respective light viewing counterparts. . . . [H]eavy viewers of all three groups are more likely to oppose laws about open housing, but . . . the relationship is strongest among those who call themselves liberal. . . . [Regarding] laws against marriages between blacks and whites, television viewing cultivates a more restrictive attitude among all three political subgroups, but this is significantly more pronounced for liberals, whose heavy viewers join in the anti-integration mainstream. Again and again, light viewers are more diverse and heavy viewers more concentrated, and the three groups converge upon the conservative position.

. . . The sample patterns show up in terms of many other issues—sexual tolerance, freedom of speech, approval of legalizing marijuana, and many, many others.

Among heavy viewers, the difference between liberals, moderates, and conservatives are greatly reduced. But the most notable trend is the erosion of the traditionally "liberal" view among heavy viewers. In general, those who call themselves conservatives are "already" in the television mainstream. But liberals express traditionally "liberal" views *only* if they are light viewers. Mainstreaming means not only a narrowing of political differences but also a significant tilt in a conservative direction. Most consistently it reveals a significant loss of support for personal and political freedoms among liberals.

Something entirely different occurs when we look at responses to questions about *economic* issues of government spending and taxes. Instead of heavy viewing liberals taking positions closer to conservatives, the opposite happens: heavy viewing conservatives, as well as moderates, converge toward the traditionally *liberal* position of wanting the government to spend *more* on social programs, such as health, the environment, welfare, the cities, etc. The more people watch, the less they say we spend "too much"; heavy viewers endorse greater government spending, rather than cuts. (Needless to say, heavy viewers are also more likely to think we should be spending more on arms and defense, although here we see the familiar pattern of liberals converging with conservatives.)

At the same time, heavy viewers are more likely to feel their taxes are too high. Those who watch more television are more likely to hold these contradictory positions simultaneously—within every demographic subgroup, heavy viewers are more likely to want more social spending *and* lower taxes.

All this relates to and clarifies television's contribution to many other conceptions of social reality. The more people watch television, the more they are fearful and afraid. They are more willing to accept repressive measures in the name of security, and to approve of more extreme ways to punish those who break the rules of the system. They are alienated, depoliticized, and afraid both of crime in the streets and of world war. They want more protection, more money for fighting crime and drug abuse, more money for defense, but—of course—no more taxes. Heavy viewers of all political persuasions hold these conflicting beliefs more than do light viewers in the same groups.

Television thus contributes to the current political scene in the United States in three ways. First, it blurs the impact of traditional party, class, regional, and other social differences. Among light viewers, factors such as whether you call yourself a liberal, moderate, or conservative, or your social class, or what region of the country you live in, are all powerful determinants of political beliefs. But if you're a heavy viewer, these factors play a much smaller role. Living in the cultural and political mainstream of television thus appears to be diminishing the influence of social forces that traditionally governed political behavior.

Second, television blends otherwise divergent perspectives and ways of labeling one's self into its own mainstream. That is, heavy viewers of all groups are more likely to call themselves moderate, average, middle class.

And third, television bends that mainstream to the purposes of the medium's own marketing and other commercial interests. The result is that heavy viewers are conservative on social issues but liberal on economic issues.

Television cultivates a set of paradoxical currents. In a nutshell, heavy viewers think like conservatives, want like liberals, and yet call themselves moderates. They are less likely to vote but quicker to turn against an incumbent. They think elected officials don't care about what happens to them but are more interested in their personal lives than in their policies. They want to cut taxes but improve education, medical care, social security. They distrust big government but want it to fix things for them, to protect them at home and from foreign threats. They praise freedom but want to restrict anyone who uses it in an unconventional way. They are losing confidence in people who run virtually all institutions, including religion, but they express trust in God, America—and television.

Taken together, these findings suggest that democracy itself may be compromised by these unintended and incidental effects of television. Some may believe that democracy works best when the people don't care much about politics but are deeply concerned about hair spray and deodorants. But the important question, and the critical challenge to democracy, is whether or not citizens are helpless in the tidal wave of the television mainstream.

The answer will depend on the ability of people whose interests are not well served by the television mainstream to mobilize and activate voters to influence both television and public policy. It will depend on our ability to equalize the flow of influence between television and the citizenry, to make television more responsive to rewards besides commercial profit. And it will depend on the extent to which this centralized system of storytelling continues to dominate the symbolic environment and our political consciousness—because these patterns are not *necessary* effects of television *per se,* but the consequences of particular institutional and commercial arrangements which have made television the mainstream of American culture.

The concept of democracy implies that citizens can participate in their political governance on a basis of equality. Numerous studies suggest that even the youngest North Americans value highly the principles of popular government, voting, equality, pluralism. But television—again, not by design, not by conspiracy, but by commercial imperative—tends to work against these principles in practice, while probably strengthening support of the principles.

Any democratic system requires communication for stability, growth, and survival. Democracy in a large and complex society depends upon mass communication to tell us things we "need" to know in a relatively "objective" and comprehensive fashion, since in a large and complex society it is virtually impossible to find out such things for ourselves *without* mass media.

Television is by no means the most powerful influence on people, but it is the most *common;* what it teaches most people, most of the time, is of the highest political, cultural, and moral importance. As mass media become more centralized and homogeneous, the cultural currents become narrower, more standardized, and more sharply defined, and mass communication becomes a more effective mechanism of social control.

In a commercial mass communication system, corporate interests rarely give way to the *public* interest. Concentration of ownership in fewer and fewer hands, and the need to attract larger and larger heterogeneous audiences, together create blander and less diverse content; when nothing but ratings and commercial profit drive the media, the result can be apathetic and alienated citizens, who nonetheless remain obedient to the authority of the marketplace.

Mass communication is the mass production of the symbolic environment, of the cultural contexts within which we live and define ourselves and others. Earlier media did give us a broader range of sometimes antagonistic perspectives and ideologies. But television has meant that more and more people are exposed to messages created and controlled by fewer and fewer, and in far greater doses, than ever before.

The television mainstream is turning out to be the true twentieth-century melting pot of the United States. Increasingly, it may be having similar consequences around the globe, as dozens and dozens of countries have found that importing U.S. programs is easier and cheaper than producing their own. International and cross-cultural extensions of the research summarized here is now being conducted or planned in numerous other countries, including Argentina, China, India, and others. The results in the United States and elsewhere will be of central significance for the theory as well as for the practice of popular democratic self-government in the television age.

*Michael
Morgan*

The theories and research findings discussed in this paper are derived from the work of the Cultural Indicators Project, directed by George Gerbner and Larry Gross (The Annenberg School of Communications, University of Pennsylvania), Michael Morgan (Department of Communication, University of Massachusetts), and Nancy Signorielli (Department of Communication, University of Delaware). See George Gerbner, Larry Gross, Michael Morgan, and Nancy Signorielli, "The Dynamics of the Cultivation Process," in J. Bryant and D. Zillman, eds., *Perspective on Media Effects* (Hillsdale, NJ: Erlbaum, 1986), pp. 17–40; "Political Correlates of Television Viewing," *Public Opinion Quarterly*, 48 (Spring 1984), 283–300; "Charting the Mainstream: Television's Contributions to Political Orientations," *Journal of Communication*, 32:2 (Spring 1982), 100–127; "The 'Mainstreaming' of America: Violence Profile No. 11," *Journal of Communication*, 30:3 (Summer 1980), 10–29; "Television Violence, Victimization, and Power," *American Behavioral Scientists*, 23:5 (1980), 705–716; Larry Gross, "The Cultivation of Intolerance: Television, Blacks, and Gays," in G. Melischek, K. E. Rosengren, and J. Stappers, eds., *Cultural Indicators: An International Symposium* (Vienna: Austrian Academy of Sciences, 1984), pp. 345–364; Larry Gross and Michael Morgan, "Television and Enculturation," in J. Dominick and J. Fletcher, eds., *Broadcasting Research Methods* (Boston: Allyn and Bacon, 1985), pp. 221–234; Michael Morgan, "Television and the Erosion of Regional Diversity," *Journal of Broadcasting and Electronic Media*, 30:2 (Spring 1986), 123–139; and Michael Morgan, "Symbolic Victimization and Real-World Fear," *Human Communication Research*, 9:2 (1983), 146–157.

CHAPTER **4**

Communication and the Political Process

4.1   MAXWELL E. McCOMBS AND
DONALD L. SHAW

The Agenda-Setting Function of Mass Media

How people interpret and are affected by political messages has long been a part of public opinion research. When Maxwell E. McCombs and Donald L. Shaw conducted the study that is described in the following selection, they assumed that the producers of news (reporters, editors, and broadcasters) would contribute to the ways in which "reality" was shaped. The "agenda-setting function" the authors discuss has been considered invaluable for understanding that producers and consumers of messages each contribute to the media's impact.

In the following selection from "The Agenda-Setting Function of Mass Media," *Public Opinion Quarterly* (Spring 1972), McCombs and Shaw demonstrate how they drew from earlier research to better understand the mutual tensions in presenting and making sense of information that is distributed during an election campaign. Their combination of content analysis and audience surveys involves a rigorous methodology that encouraged future researchers to ask questions related to their agenda, such as "What constitutes news?" and "How can something get on the agenda?"

McCombs is currently a professor in the Department of Journalism at the University of Texas at Austin, and Shaw is a professor in the School of Journalism at the University of North Carolina, Chapel Hill.

Key Concept: agenda setting

*Maxwell E.
McCombs and
Donald L. Shaw*

In choosing and displaying news, editors, newsroom staff, and broadcasters play an important part in shaping political reality. Readers learn not only about a given issue, but also how much importance to attach to that issue from the amount of information in a news story and its position. In reflecting what candidates are saying during a campaign, the mass media may well determine the important issues—that is, the media may set the "agenda" of the campaign....

In our day, more than ever before, candidates go before the people through the mass media rather than in person.[1] The information in the mass media becomes the only contact many have with politics. The pledges, promises, and rhetoric encapsulated in news stories, columns, and editorials constitute much of the information upon which a voting decision has to be made. Most of what people know comes to them "second" or "third" hand from the mass media or from other people.[2]

Although the evidence that mass media deeply change attitudes in a campaign is far from conclusive,[3] the evidence is much stronger that voters learn from the immense quantity of information available during each campaign.[4] People, of course, vary greatly in their attention to mass media political information. Some, normally the better educated and most politically interested (and those least likely to change political beliefs), actively seek information; but most seem to acquire it, if at all, without much effort. It just comes in. As Berelson succinctly puts it: "On any single subject many 'hear' but few 'listen'." But Berelson also found that those with the greatest mass media exposure are most likely to know where the candidates stand on different issues.[5] Trenaman and McQuail found the same thing in a study of the 1959 General Election in England.[6] Voters do learn.

They apparently learn, furthermore, in direct proportion to the emphasis placed on the campaign issues by the mass media. Specifically focusing on the agenda-setting function of the media, Lang and Lang observe:

> The mass media force attention to certain issues. They build up public images of political figures. They are constantly presenting objects suggesting what individuals in the mass should think about, know about, have feelings about.[7]

Perhaps this hypothesized agenda-setting function of the mass media is most succinctly stated by Cohen, who noted that the press "may not be successful much of the time in telling people what to think, but it is stunningly successful in telling its readers what to think *about.* "[8] While the mass media may have little influence on the direction or intensity of attitudes, it is hypothesized that *the mass media set the agenda for each political campaign, influencing the salience of attitudes toward the political issues.*

METHOD

To investigate the agenda-setting capacity of the mass media in the 1968 presidential campaign, this study attempted to match what Chapel Hill voters *said* were key issues of the campaign with the *actual content* of the mass media used by them during the campaign. Respondents were selected randomly from lists of registered voters in five Chapel Hill precincts economically, socially, and racially representative of the community. By restricting this study to one community, numerous other sources of variation—for example, regional differences or variations in media performance—were controlled.

Between September 18 and October 6, 100 interviews were completed. To select these 100 respondents a filter question was used to identify those who had not yet definitely decided how to vote—presumably those most open or susceptible to campaign information. Only those not yet fully committed to a particular candidate were interviewed. Borrowing from the Trenaman and McQuail strategy, this study asked each respondent to outline the key issues as he saw them regardless of what the candidates might be saying at the moment.[9] Interviewers recorded the answers as exactly as possible.

Concurrently with the voter interviews, the mass media serving these voters were collected and content analyzed. A pretest in spring 1968 found that for the Chapel Hill community almost all the mass media political information was provided by the following sources: Durham *Morning Herald*, Durham *Sun*, Raleigh *News and Observer*, Raleigh *Times*, New York *Times*, *Time*, *Newsweek*, and NBC and CBS evening news broadcasts.

The answers of respondents regarding major problems as they saw them and the news and editorial comment appearing between September 12 and October 6 in the sampled newspapers, magazines, and news broadcasts were coded into 15 categories representing the key issues and other kinds of campaign news. Media news content also was divided into "major" and "minor" levels to see whether there was any substantial difference in mass media emphasis across topics.[10] For the print media, this major/minor division was in terms of space and position; for television, it was made in terms of position and time allowed. More specifically, *major* items were defined as follows:

1. Television: Any story 45 seconds or more in length and/or one of the three lead stories.
2. Newspapers: Any story which appeared as the lead on the front page or on any page under a three-column headline in which at least one-third of the story (a minimum of five paragraphs) was devoted to political news coverage.

3. News Magazines: Any story more than one column or any item which appeared in the lead at the beginning of the news section of the magazine.
4. Editorial Page Coverage of Newspapers and Magazines: Any item in the lead editorial position (the top left corner of the editorial page) plus all items in which one-third (at least five paragraphs) of an editorial or columnist comment was devoted to political campaign coverage.

Minor items are those stories which are political in nature and included in the study but which are smaller in terms of space, time, or display than major items.

FINDINGS

The over-all *major* item emphasis of the selected mass media on different topics and candidates during the campaign... indicates that a considerable amount of campaign news was *not* devoted to discussion of the major political issues but rather to *analysis of the campaign itself.* This may give pause to those who think of campaign news as being primarily about the *issues.* ...

The media appear to have exerted a considerable impact on voters' judgments of what they considered the major issues of the campaign (even though the questionnaire specifically asked them to make judgments without regard to what politicians might be saying at the moment)....

But while the three presidential candidates placed widely different emphasis upon different issues, the judgments of the voters seem to reflect the *composite* of the mass media coverage.... [V]oters pay some attention to all the political news *regardless* of whether it is from, or about, any particular favored candidate.... [I]t is possible that individual differences, reflected in party preferences and in a predisposition to look mainly at material favorable to one's own party, are lost by lumping all the voters together in the analysis. Therefore, answers of respondents who indicated a preference (but not commitment) for one of the candidates during the September-October period studied (45 of the respondents; the others were undecided) were analyzed separately....

If one expected voters to pay more attention to the major and minor issues oriented to their own party—that is, to read or view *selectively*—the correlations between the voters and news/opinion about their own party should be strongest. This would be evidence of selective perception.[11] If, on the other hand, the voters attend reasonably well to *all* the news, *regardless* of which candidate or party issue is stressed, the correlations between the voter and total media content would be strongest. This would be evidence of the agenda-setting function. The crucial question is which set of correlations is stronger.

In general.... voters who were not firmly committed early in the campaign attended well to *all* the news. For major news items, correlations were more often higher between voter judgments of important issues and the issues reflected in all the news (including of course news about their favored candidate/party) than were voter judgments of issues reflected in news *only* about their candidate/party. For minor news items, again voters more often correlated highest with the emphasis reflected in all the news than with the emphasis reflected in news about a favored candidate. Considering both major and minor item coverage, 18 of 24 possible comparisons show voters more in agreement with all the news rather than with news only about their own party/candidate preference. This finding is better explained by the agenda-setting function of the mass media than by selective perception. . . .

Two sets of factors, at least, reduce consensus among the news media. First, the basic characteristics of newspapers, television, and newsmagazines differ. Newspapers appear daily and have lots of space. Television is daily but has a severe time constraint. Newsmagazines appear weekly; news therefore cannot be as "timely." . . .

Second, news media do have a point of view, sometimes extreme biases. However, the high correlations . . . (especially among like media) suggest consensus on news values, especially on major news items. Although there is no explicit, commonly agreed-upon definition of news, there is a professional norm regarding major news stories from day to day. These major-story norms doubtless are greatly influenced today by widespread use of the major wire services—especially by newspapers and television—for much political information.[12] But as we move from major events of the campaign, upon which nearly everyone agrees, there is more room for individual interpretation, reflected in the lower correlations for minor item agreement among media. . . . Since a newspaper, for example, uses only about 15 percent of the material available on any given day, there is considerable latitude for selection among minor items.

In short, the political world is reproduced imperfectly by individual news media. Yet the evidence in this study that voters tend to share the media's *composite* definition of what is important strongly suggests an agenda-setting function of the mass media.

DISCUSSION

The existence of an agenda-setting function of the mass media is not *proved* by the correlations reported here, of course, but the evidence is in line with the conditions that must exist if agenda-setting by the mass media does occur. This study has compared aggregate units—Chapel Hill voters as a group compared to the aggregate performance of several mass media. This is satisfactory as a first test of the agenda-setting hypothesis, but subsequent research must move from a broad societal level to the social psychological level, matching individual attitudes with individual use of the mass media. Yet even the present study refines the evidence in several respects. Efforts were made to match respondent attitudes only with media actually used by Chapel Hill voters. Further, the analysis includes a juxtaposition of the agenda-setting and selective perception hypotheses. Comparison of these correlations too supports the agenda-setting hypothesis.

Interpreting the evidence from this study as indicating mass media influence seems more plausible than alternative explanations. Any argument that

*Maxwell E.
McCombs and
Donald L. Shaw*

the correlations between media and voter emphasis are spurious—that they are simply responding to the same events and not influencing each other one way or the other—assumes that voters have alternative means of observing the day-to-day changes in the political arena. This assumption is not plausible; since few directly participate in presidential election campaigns, and fewer still see presidential candidates in person, the information flowing in interpersonal communication channels is primarily relayed from, and based upon, mass media news coverage. The media are the major primary sources of national political information; for most, mass media provide the best—and only—easily available approximation of ever-changing political realities.

It might also be argued that the high correlations indicate that the media simply were successful in matching their messages to audience interests. Yet since numerous studies indicate a sharp divergence between the news values of professional journalists and their audiences, it would be remarkable to find a near perfect fit in this one case.[13] It seems more likely that the media have prevailed in this area of major coverage.

While this study is primarily a sociology of politics and mass communication, some psychological data were collected on each voter's personal cognitive representation of the issues. Shrauger has suggested that the salience of the evaluative dimension—not the sheer number of attributes—is the essential feature of cognitive differentiation.[14] So a content analysis classified respondents according to the *salience of affect* in their responses to open-ended questions about the candidates and issues.[15] Some voters described the issues and candidates in highly affective terms. Others were much more matter-of-fact. Each respondent's answers were classified by the coders as "all affect," "affect dominant," "some affect but not dominant," or "no affect at all."[16] Regarding each voter's salience of affect as his cognitive style of storing political information, the study hypothesized that cognitive style also influences patterns of information-seeking.

Eschewing causal language to discuss this relationship, the hypothesis states that salience of affect will index or locate differences in the communication behavior of voters. But a number of highly efficient locator variables for voter communication behavior already are well documented in the research literature. Among these are level of formal education and interest in politics generally. However, in terms of *The American Voter*'s model of a "funnel" stretching across time, education and political interest are located some distance back from the particular campaign being considered.[17] Cognitive style is located closer to the end of the funnel, closer to the time of actual participation in a campaign. It also would seem to have the advantage of a more functional relationship to voter behavior.

Examination of the relationship between salience of affect and this pair of traditional locators, education and political interest, showed no significant correlations. The independent effects of political interest and salience of affect on media use are demonstrated in Table 1. Also demonstrated is the efficacy of salience of affect as a locator or predictor of media use, especially among persons with high political interest.[18]

Both salience of affect and media use in Table 1 are based on the issue that respondents designated as the most important to them personally. Salience of

TABLE 1

Proportion of Media Users by Political Interest and Salience of Affect

Media	Low Political Interest		High Political Interest	
	High Affect (N = 40)	*Low Affect* (N = 17)	*High Affect* (N = 25)	*Low Affect* (N = 12)
TV	15.0%	17.7%	20.0%	41.7%
Newspapers	25.7	35.4	36.0	58.3
News Magazines	7.5	11.8	24.0	33.3
Radio	12.5	11.8	8.0	33.3
Talk	20.0	17.7	64.0	75.0

affect was coded from their discussion of why the issue was important. Use of each communication medium is based on whether or not the respondent had seen or heard anything via that medium about that particular issue in the past twenty-four hours.

High salience of affect tends to block use of communication media to acquire further information about issues with high personal importance. At least, survey respondents with high salience of affect do not recall acquiring recent information. This is true both for persons with low and high political interest, but especially among those with high political interest. For example, among respondents with high political interest *and* high salience of affect only 36 percent reported reading anything in the newspaper recently about the issue they believed to be most important. But among high political interest respondents with low salience of affect nearly six of ten (58.3 percent) said they acquired information from the newspaper. Similar patterns hold for all the communication media.

Future studies of communication behavior and political agenda-setting must consider both psychological and sociological variables; knowledge of both is crucial to establishment of sound theoretical constructs. Considered at both levels as a communication concept, agenda-setting seems useful for study of the process of political consensus.

NOTES

1. See Bernard R. Berelson, Paul F. Lazarsfeld, and William N. McPhee, *Voting,* Chicago, University of Chicago Press, 1954, p. 234. Of course to some degree candidates have always depended upon the mass media, but radio and television brought a new intimacy into politics.
2. Kurt Lang and Gladys Engel Lang, "The Mass Media and Voting," in Bernard Berelson and Morris Janowitz, eds., *Reader in Public Opinion and Communication,* 2d ed., New York, Free Press, 1966, p. 466.

3. See Berelson *et al., op. cit.,* p. 223; Paul F. Lazarsfeld, Bernard Berelson, and Hazel Gaudet, *The People's Choice,* New York, Columbia University Press, 1948. p. xx; and Joseph Trenaman and Denis McQuail, *Television and the Political Image,* London, Methuen and Co., 1961, pp. 147, 191.

4. See Bernard C. Cohen, *The Press and Foreign Policy,* Princeton, Princeton University Press, 1963, p. 120.

5. Berelson *et al., op. cit.,* pp. 244, 228.

6. Trenaman and McQuail, *op. cit.,* p. 165.

7. Lang and Lang, *op. cit.,* p. 468. Trenaman and McQuail warn that there was little evidence in their study that television (or any other mass medium) did anything other than provide information; there was little or no attitude change on significant issues. "People are aware of what is being said, and who is saying it, but they do not necessarily take it at face value." See *op. cit.,* p. 168. In a more recent study, however, Blumler and McQuail found that high exposure to Liberal party television broadcasts in the British General Election of 1964 was positively related to a more favorable attitude toward the Liberal party for those with medium or weak motivation to follow the campaign. The more strongly motivated were much more stable in political attitude. See Jay G. Blumler and Denis McQuail, *Television in Politics: Its Uses and Influence,* Chicago, University of Chicago Press, 1969, p. 200.

8. Cohen, *op. cit.,* p. 13.

9. See Trenaman and McQuail, *op. cit.,* p. 172. The survey question was: "What are you *most* concerned about these days? That is, regardless of what politicians say, what are the two or three *main* things which you think the government *should* concentrate on doing something about?"

10. Intercoder reliability was above .90 for content analysis of both "major" and "minor" items. Details of categorization are described in the full report of this project. A small number of copies of the full report is available for distribution and may be obtained by writing the authors.

11. While recent reviews of the literature and new experiments have questioned the validity of the selective perception hypothesis, this has nevertheless been the focus of much communication research. For example, see Richard F. Carter, Ronald H. Pyszka, and Jose L. Guerrero, "Dissonance and Exposure to Arousive Information," *Journalism Quarterly,* Vol. 46, 1969, pp. 37–42; and David O. Sears and Jonathan L. Freedman, "Selective Exposure to Information: A Critical Review," *Public Opinion Quarterly,* Vol. 31, 1967, pp. 194–213.

12. A number of studies have focused on the influence of the wire services. For example, see David Gold and Jerry L. Simmons, "News Selection Patterns among Iowa Dailies," *Public Opinion Quarterly,* Vol. 29, 1965, pp. 425–430; Guido H. Stempel III, "How Newspapers Use the Associated Press Afternoon A-Wire." *Journalism Quarterly,* Vol. 41, 1964, pp. 380–384; Ralph D. Casey and Thomas H. Copeland Jr., "Use of Foreign News by 19 Minnesota Dailies," *Journalism Quarterly,* Vol. 35, 1958, pp. 87–89; Howard L. Lewis, "The Cuban Revolt Story: AP, UPI, and Three Papers," *Journalism Quarterly,* Vol. 37, 1960, pp. 573–578; George A. Van Horn, "Analysis of AP News on Trunk and Wisconsin State Wires," *Journalism Quarterly,* Vol. 29, 1952, pp. 426–432; and Scott M. Cutlip, "Content and Flow of AP News—From Trunk to TTS to Reader," *Journalism Quarterly,* Vol. 31, 1954, pp. 434–446.

13. Furthermore, five of the nine media studied here are national media and none of the remaining four originate in Chapel Hill. It is easier to argue that Chapel Hill voters fit their judgments of issue salience to the mass media than the reverse. An interesting study which discusses the problems of trying to fit day-to-day news judgments to

reader interest is Guido H. Stempel III, "A Factor Analytic Study of Reader Interest in News," *Journalism Quarterly*, Vol. 44, 1967, pp. 326–330. An older study is Philip F. Griffin, "Reader Comprehension of News Stories: A Preliminary Study," *Journalism Quarterly*, Vol. 26, 1949, pp. 389–396.

14. Sid Shrauger, "Cognitive Differentiation and the Impression-Formation Process," *Journal of Personality*, Vol. 35, 1967, pp. 402–414.

15. Affect denotes a "pro/con" orientation, a feeling of liking or disliking something. Cognition, by contrast, denotes the individual's perception of the attitude object, his "image" or organized set of information and beliefs about a political object.

16. Coder reliability exceeded .90.

17. Angus Campbell, Philip Converse, Warren Miller, and Donald Stokes, *The American Voter*, New York, Wiley, 1960, chap. 2.

18. No statistical analysis is reported for the five separate three-way analyses in the Table because of small *N*'s in some cells, but despite these small *N*'s the pattern of results is consistent across all media.

4.2 KATHLEEN HALL JAMIESON

Packaging the Presidency

In the most recent phase of political communication research, many authors have moved beyond theories and methodologies that are closely aligned with psychology and sociology. In the current phase of political research, attention has become focused on how media influence the political process by using techniques that have become familiar to audiences over time. In particular, television has assumed a place in culture that allows researchers to investigate how real-world issues, like politics, become "packaged" like products.

Kathleen Hall Jamieson, professor and dean of the Annenberg School of Communications at the University of Pennsylvania, Philadelphia, has produced a number of works on rhetorical style in the television age, including *Packaging the Presidency: A History and Criticism of Presidential Campaign Advertising,* 3rd ed. (Oxford University Press, 1996), from which the following selection is taken, and *Dirty Politics: Deception, Distraction, and Democracy* (Oxford University Press, 1992). Her work examines the images and the words used by candidates and their managers to influence the public's perception of issues in the political world.

The following selection shows how television has become regarded as a central mediating technology in the political process. Jamieson's links between the content of advertising, political speeches, and the political process demonstrate an evolution in the media.

Key Concept: political advertising

*P*olitical advertising is now the major means by which candidates for the presidency communicate their messages to voters. As a conduit of this advertising, television attracts both more candidate dollars and more audience attention than radio or print. Unsurprisingly, the spot ad is the most used and the most viewed of all available forms of advertising. By 1980 the half-hour broadcast speech—the norm in 1952—had been replaced by the 60-second spot.

Ads enable candidates to build name recognition, frame the questions they view as central to the election, expose their temperaments, talents, and agendas for the future in a favorable light, and attack what they perceive as their opponent's fatal flaws. In part because more voters attend to spot ads than to network news and in part because reporters are fixated with who's winning and losing instead of what the candidates are proposing, some scholars believe that ads provide the electorate with more information than network news. Still, ads more often successfully reinforce existing dispositions than create new ones.

By personalizing issues, ads also assert their relevance to our lives. In the 1950s the public at large did not find political matters salient to it. From the late 1950s to the early 1970s our perception of the relevances of political matters to one's day-to-day life increased at all educational levels. Citizens saw a greater connection between what occurred in the political world and what occurred at home and work. Television ads' ability to personalize and the tendency of TV news to reduce issues to personal impact have, in my judgment, facilitated that change. Democratic ads argued in 1964, for example, that a vote against nonproliferation could increase the Strontium 90 in children's ice cream.

As the salience of political issues increased so too did the consistency of the beliefs of individual voters. Dissonant views are less likely to be simultaneously held now than before. This tendency is also reinforced by political advertising, for politicians have increasingly argued the interconnection of issues of importance to them. In 1980 Reagan predicated a strong defense on a strong economy. In 1968 Nixon tied crime, lawlessness, and the war in Vietnam into a single bundle and laid it on Humphrey's doorstep.

Ads also define the nature of the presidency by stipulating the attributes a president should have. In the process they legitimize certain occupations. Ike polished the assumption that being a general was a suitable qualification. Carter argued that being an outsider as well as an engineer, a farmer, a businessman but not a lawyer qualified him. Reagan contended that being the governor of a large state and a union leader were stronger qualifications than being an incumbent president. Clinton made the same case for being the governor of a small state. In their bids for second terms Eisenhower, Nixon, Johnson, Ford, and Carter argued that being the incumbent qualified one for the presidency.

... Where Nixon maintained tight control over advertising decisions in 1960, Kennedy delegated all responsibility for advertising to others. At the same time, ad campaigns that lurched uncertainly from one message to another and from one set of strategists to another (as did Ford's, Mondale's, Dukakis's, and Bush's in 1992) suggested perhaps that the candidate and his advisors were unable to provide a clear sense of the direction in which they wanted to take the country, an observation consistent with the failure of these campaigns to forecast their candidates' visions of the future.

Occasionally, a candidate's response to the requirements of advertising raises troublesome questions about his suitability for the office or, perhaps, about the intensity of his desire to hold it. Adlai Stevenson's perpetual quest for the perfect word or precisely phrased argument and his apparent need to perfect texts even as he was walking to the stage invite doubts about his ability to act decisively.

When the acceptance speech and the election eve telecasts are taken as the brackets bounding advertising, a focus on paid messages can reveal a campaign's fundamental coherence or incoherence. In a coherent campaign, the acceptance speech at the convention synopsizes and polishes the message the candidate has communicated in the primaries as a means of forecasting both the themes of the general election campaign and this person's presidency. The

Kathleen Hall
Jamieson

message is then systematically developed in the advertising of the general election and placed in its final form on election eve where the candidate tries on the presidency by indicating for the country his vision of the next four years under his leadership. From the first campaign advertising of January through the last on election eve in November, when candidates offer consistent, coherent messages about themselves and the future as they envision it, they both minimize the likelihood that their record or plans will be distorted effectively by opponents and create a clear set of expectations to govern their conduct in office. However, these same expectations may haunt them when they seek reelection. So, for example, Bush's 1988 "Read my lips. No new taxes" pledge was recycled as an indictment by Pat Buchanan in the 1992 New Hampshire primary.

Viewing campaign advertising as an extended message instead of a series of individual ones also enables us to see how a candidate's response to attacks in the primaries can either strengthen or strangle the candidate's chances in the general election. When attacks are raised in the primaries and effectively neutralized, as were questions about Kennedy's age and religion in 1960, the issue can be effectively dispatched in the general election. Kennedy's widely aired speech to the Houston ministers builds on a structure of beliefs first cemented in Kennedy's speeches and ads in the West Virginia primary. And the thorough discussion of Clinton's draft record in the 1992 primaries made the charges less damaging when broadcast in Bush ads in the general election.

Preventing candidates from using advertising to create a sense of themselves discrepant from who they are and what they have done is the vigilant presence of opponents and the potentially vigilant presence of the press. Throughout we have seen instances in which candidates' words and actions in settings they did not control undermined the crafted images of their ads. So, for example, the image of the sweating, gaunt, pale Nixon of the first debate in 1960 clashed with the polished presence in his ads.

When ads lie, the vigilance of press and opponents can, but does not necessarily, protect the public. When NBC and CNN joined the *Atlanta Constitution* in exposing false inferences invited by an anti-Bush ad aired by Buchanan in the 1992 Georgia primary, a CNN survey showed a public backlash against the criticized ad. And a study that Joseph N. Cappella and I conducted of another CNN adwatch confirmed that the analysis did minimize the power of the offending ad.

In many ways televised political advertising is the direct descendant of the advertised messages carried in song and on banners, torches, bandannas, and broadsides. Ads continue to ally the candidate with the people, only now that takes the form of showing the candidate pressing the flesh or answering questions from groups of citizens. Candidates continue to digest their messages into slogans, yet these now appear at the end of broadcast ads rather than on banners and torches. Candidates continue to overstate their accomplishments and understate their failures. So, for example, as governor, despite his claims to the contrary, Ronald Reagan did not increase welfare benefits 43%, although he did increase them just as, contrary to his advertising, Andy Jackson had served in one, not two wars.

What differentiates the claims of Jackson's time from those aired today is the role the press has now assumed as monitor of presidential advertising.

While the partisan papers controlled by his opponent revealed Jackson's actual war record and noted that his was not the hand that guided the plow, those papers were not a credible source of information for Jackson's likely supporters. By contrast, in the 1992 presidential race, articles and news stories—bearing the imprint of neither party—publicly scrutinized the adequacy of candidates' claims. The difficulty in relying on news to correct distortions in advertising is, of course, that comparatively few people consume news while many are exposed to ads. The impact of adwatches is not lost on consultants, however, who justifiably fear that their content will appear in opponent's ads.

One of the argumentative ploys born in the political and product advertising of the nineteenth century was refined by politicians in the age of television and then shunted aside by Watergate. By visually associating the favored candidate with pictures of well-fed cattle, happy families, large bundles of grain, and bulging factories, banners and broadsides argued to literate and illiterate alike that this candidate stood for prosperity. The opponent, on the other hand, was visually tied to drawings of starving cattle, poverty-ravished families, empty grain bins, and deserted factories. Some of these associations obviously had no direct bearing on what sort of president the candidate would make.

Political argument by visual association flowered for the same reason it appeared in product advertising. Initially, advertising for products simply identified the existence, cost, function, and way to obtain the product. As success bred success, products performing the same function proliferated. Distinguishing attributes—some real, some fictional—were sought to persuade customers that one product rather than its twin should be purchased. Van Buren and Harrison were parity products, differentiated by the associations sculpted by their respective campaigns. Since the advertising of the early nineteenth century relied on drawings rather than photographs, the range of possible associations was limited only by the artist's imagination.

The wizardry of videotape and film editing did not change the nature of argument from visual association—it simply increased its subtlety. In the process, the evidentiary burden that candidates should assume dropped. So, for example, Goldwater's ads juxtaposed a picture of Billie Sol Estes with scenes of street riots and intercut a picture of Bobby Baker. Goldwater then appeared on screen to indict the Democrats for their disregard of law, order, and morality. Estes' relation to Baker, the relation of either to the street riots, or the relation among the three and Lyndon Johnson are not explicitly argued.

In 1968 this type of argument reached a new level of complexity in the Republican ad that intercut scenes from the Vietnam War and from the riots outside the Democratic convention with pictures of Hubert Humphrey, including one in which he appears to be smiling. The juxtaposition of highly evocative images invites the audience to impute causality.

The form of argument embodied in this ad is as powerful as it is irrational. It solicits a visceral, not an intellectual response. As a vehicle of attack this type of ad was vanquished by Watergate, which forced politicians and the public to consider what is and is not fair attack in a political campaign. Lurking in the McGovern campaign of 1972 and Bush campaign of 1988 are the forms of attack that replace it: the personal witness, neutral reporter, and pseudo-documentary ads. These mimic some features of actual news. The personal testimony ads consist of real individuals reporting their opinions of the opposing candidate's performance. They resemble person-in-the-street interviews and pose as a report of a survey; the opinions expressed are not scripted —indeed, their ungrammatical nature underscores their spontaneity. They do not appear to be unfair because, first, we are taught that everyone is entitled to express his or her opinion and, second, these people are voicing opinions that the electorate presumably is disposed to share. In 1976 Ford pioneered this form against Carter. Carter used it less successfully against Reagan. Bush used it against Dukakis in 1988 and Clinton in 1992.

In the neutral reporter spot, an announcer whose delivery is deliberately low key details facts about the opponent. The ad itself rarely draws any conclusion from the data. That task is left to the audience. Ford did this in a 1976 ad comparing Carter's statements in the campaign with his actual record as governor of Georgia. An ad by Carter did the same to Reagan in 1980. And the neutral reporter form—recapping optimistic statements made by Bush about the economy—was the stock-in-trade of Democratic ads in the 1992 general election.

Pseudo-documentary ads dramatize supposedly real conditions. Here the "revolving door" ad of 1988 is a prime illustration.

By replacing attack ads that use visual, not verbal, means to prompt sweeping inferences with attack ads that verbally and visually invite judgments based on verifiable facts, Watergate temporarily transformed a form of presidential attack advertising from an exercise in the prompting of false inferences to an exercise in traditional argument. In 1988, invitations to false inference were back with a vengeance.

The widespread perception that being able to present broadcast messages persuasively to a mass public would emerge as a criterion governing selection of presidential candidates is not convincingly confirmed from 1952 to 1992. Of the candidates to receive their party's nomination since 1952, Kennedy, Bush, and Dukakis were adequate speakers, Goldwater and Nixon often excellent, and only Reagan a master. While Clinton's extemporaneous delivery rivals Reagan's for its sense of personal conviction, his scripted delivery is considerably less compelling. In short, the ability to deliver televised messages artfully, while certainly an asset for those who possess it, has not become so central a qualification for the presidency that it has exiled candidates who lack it.

Another misconception about political advertising holds that spots and paid programming are somehow alien to the political speech, a thing apart, a bad dream, an aberration. An analysis of both the stock campaign speeches and the acceptance addresses of the presidential candidates suggests instead that the advertising is rarely anything but a digest of the speeches being delivered throughout the country. Occasionally, but not often, the candidate will say something important in a stump speech that does not appear in the paid broadcasting. But these things are usually strategic blunders such as Carter's assertion in 1980 that Reagan would rend the country North from South.

[T]he convention acceptance speeches are a reliable predictor of the content of the candidate's ads in the general election. Indeed in both 1988 and 1992 sections of Bush's acceptance speeches reappeared in his ads. For those who read the campaign's position papers, examine its brochures, and listen to its stump speeches, the ads function as reinforcement. Those who ignore the other campaign-produced materials receive a digest of them in the ads. This is true both of the advertising against the opponent and that supporting the candidate.

The cost of reaching voters through broadcast advertising poses other problems. Since spot advertising is both costly and often the most cost-efficient means of reaching a mass of voters, the contemporary reliance on spots means that those who cannot afford to purchase them, with rare exceptions, are denied the ability to have their ideas either heard or taken seriously in presidential primaries.

For these and related reasons public concern over the nature and influence of political advertising has been rising. Responding to this escalating public concern, legislators drafted or considered drafting bills that can be grouped into three broad categories. The first would have either the public or the radio and TV stations assume the burden of financing some or all of candidate advertising; the second would give candidates attacked by PACs free response time or —regardless of the origin of attack—would give the attacked candidate free response time; the third would promote changes in the form by offering free time to those agreeing to certain formats (e.g., talking head ads) or lengths (e.g., a minimum length or free time in no less than five-minute and half-hour blocks).

Underlying the debate over these and similar proposals is widening consensus that the electoral process would benefit if the candidates' cost of reaching a mass audience could be reduced; if all bona-fide candidates could be provided with sufficient access to communicate their basic ideas; if politicians made greater use of longer forms of communication and the electorate as a whole attended more readily to such forms; if candidates assumed or could be enticed to assume the obligation of being viewed by the public in forms that they do not control such as debates; if the advantage PACs can bring to a presidential candidate could be countered or muted.

Still, if political advertising did not exist, we would have to invent it. Political advertising legitimizes our political institutions by affirming that change is possible within the political system, that the president can effect change, that votes can make a difference. As a result, like campaigns in general, advertising channels discontent into the avenues provided by the government and acts as a safety valve for pressures that otherwise turn against the system to demand its substantial modification or overthrow.

Political advertising does this, in part, by underscoring the power of the ballot. Your vote makes a difference, it says, at the same time as its carefully targeted messages imply that the votes that would go to the opponent are best left uncast.

Political ads affirm that the country is great, has a future, is respected. The contest they reflect is over who should be elected, not over whether there should be an election. The very existence of the contest suggests that there is a choice, that the voters' selection of one candidate over the other will make a difference.

PART TWO

The Media of Communication

On the Internet . . .

Sites appropriate to Part Two

This University of Iowa Communication Studies site contains several links to useful references regarding media and technology.

```
http://www.uiowa.edu/~commstud/resources/
    digitalmedia/
```

The Technology Page links to pages that profile new communication technologies as well as technology in science. The latest information on such topics as digital audio, HDTV, and cellular technologies can be found here.

```
http://www.dvtech.com/pages/pages/
    TecNew.htm
```

The Media Futures Archive provides forecasts on television, film, radio, computers, the Internet, and the world of tomorrow, using statements from business, industry, government officials, and popular authors. An excellent resource for appropriate quotes from officials, this site also allows users to post quotes.

```
http://www.hfac.uh.edu/MediaFutures/
    home.html
```

From this Netcraft site you can research some recent history on the Internet and find related links that show the breadth of coverage and the extent to which the Internet is utilized.

```
http://www.netcraft.co.uk/
```

CHAPTER 5

Media Bias and Sense Extension

5.1 MARSHALL McLUHAN

Understanding Media

The media theories of Canadian literary critic Marshall McLuhan (1911–1980) have been hailed by some as the work of a "visionary" and by others as the work of a "crackpot." His work was influenced by the turbulent 1960s, when many new electronic forms of communication—including VCRs, satellites, portable audio technologies, and microcomputers—were becoming more widespread. McLuhan broke away from issues of media content and focused on technological form. His famous statement "The medium is the message" is an indication of the way McLuhan looked for the unique characteristics of a medium to understand how it communicates messages and influences users' perspectives. With his novel viewpoint, McLuhan influenced a host of scholars who were attracted to the idea that the medium itself has the ability to influence users' senses of space and time.

In the following selection from the introduction and a chapter of his well-known book *Understanding Media: The Extensions of Man* (McGraw-Hill, 1964), McLuhan discusses some of his most controversial ideas. Taking the perspective that media creates and influences new environments, he asserts that the individual is "hypnotized" by the media experience and is unaware of the ways technology influences the environment and the content of media.

Key Concept: media form and sensory extension

*A*ny technology gradually creates a totally new human environment. Environments are not passive wrappings but active processes. In his splendid work *Preface to Plato* (Harvard University Press, 1963), Eric Havelock contrasts the oral and written cultures of the Greeks. By Plato's time the written word had created a new environment that had begun to detribalize man. Previously the Greeks had grown up by benefit of the process of the *tribal encyclopedia.* They had memorized the poets. The poets provided specific operational wisdom for all the contingencies of life—Ann Landers in verse. With the advent of individual detribalized man, a new education was needed. Plato devised such a new program for literate men. It was based on the Ideas. With the phonetic alphabet, classified wisdom took over from the operational wisdom of Homer and Hesiod and the tribal encyclopedia. Education by classified data has been the Western program ever since.

Now, however, in the electronic age, data classification yields to pattern recognition, the key phrase at IBM. When data move instantly, classification is too fragmentary. In order to cope with data at electric speed in typical situations of "information overload," men resort to the study of configurations, like the sailor in Edgar Allan Poe's *Maelstrom.* The drop-out situation in our schools at present has only begun to develop. The young student today grows up in an electrically configured world. It is a world not of wheels but of circuits, not of fragments but of integral patterns. The student today *lives* mythically and in depth. At school, however, he encounters a situation organized by means of classified information. The subjects are unrelated. They are visually conceived in terms of a blueprint. The student can find no possible means of involvement for himself, nor can he discover how the educational scene relates to the "mythic" world of electronically processed data and experience that he takes for granted. As one IBM executive puts it, "My children had lived several lifetimes compared to their grandparents when they began grade one."

"The medium is the message" means, in terms of the electronic age, that a totally new environment has been created. The "content" of this new environment is the old mechanized environment of the industrial age. The new environment reprocesses the old one as radically as TV is reprocessing the film. For the "content" of TV is the movie. TV is environmental and imperceptible, like all environments. We are aware only of the "content" or the old environment. When machine production was new, it gradually created an environment whose content was the old environment of agrarian life and the arts and crafts. This older environment was elevated to an art form by the new mechanical environment. The machine turned Nature into an art form. For the first time men began to regard Nature as a source of aesthetic and spiritual values. They began to marvel that earlier ages had been so unaware of the world of Nature as Art. Each new technology creates an environment that is itself regarded as corrupt and degrading. Yet the new one turns its predecessor into an art form. When writing was new, Plato transformed the old oral dialogue into an art form. When printing was new the Middle Ages became an art form. "The Elizabethan world view" was a view of the Middle Ages. And the industrial age turned the Renaissance into an art form as seen in the work of Jacob Burckhardt. Siegfried Giedion, in turn, has in the electric age taught us how to see the entire process of mechanization as an art process. (*Mechanization Takes Command*)....

INTRODUCTION

James Reston wrote in *The New York Times* (July 7, 1957):

> A health director... reported this week that a small mouse, which presumably had been watching television, attacked a little girl and her full-grown cat.... Both mouse and cat survived, and the incident is recorded here as a reminder that things seem to be changing.

After three thousand years of explosion, by means of fragmentary and mechanical technologies, the Western world is imploding. During the mechanical ages we had extended our bodies in space. Today, after more than a century of electric technology, we have extended our central nervous system itself in a global embrace, abolishing both space and time as far as our planet is concerned. Rapidly, we approach the final phase of the extensions of man—the technological simulation of consciousness, when the creative process of knowing will be collectively and corporately extended to the whole of human society, much as we have already extended our senses and our nerves by the various media. Whether the extension of consciousness, so long sought by advertisers for specific products, will be "a good thing" is a question that admits of a wide solution. There is little possibility of answering such questions about the extensions of man without considering all of them together. Any extension, whether of skin, hand, or foot, affects the whole psychic and social complex.

Some of the principal extensions, together with some of their psychic and social consequences, are studied [here]. Just how little consideration has been given to such matters in the past can be gathered from the consternation of one of the editors of this [selection]. He noted in dismay that "seventy-five per cent of your material is new. A successful book cannot venture to be more than ten per cent new." Such a risk seems quite worth taking at the present time when the stakes are very high, and the need to understand the effects of the extensions of man becomes more urgent by the hour.

In the mechanical age now receding, many actions could be taken without too much concern. Slow movement insured that the reactions were delayed for considerable periods of time. Today the action and the reaction occur almost at the same time. We actually live mythically and integrally, as it were, but we continue to think in the old, fragmented space and time patterns of the pre-electric age.

Western man acquired from the technology of literacy the power to act without reacting. The advantages of fragmenting himself in this way are seen in the case of the surgeon who would be quite helpless if he were to become humanly involved in his operation. We acquired the art of carrying out the most dangerous social operations with complete detachment. But our detachment was a posture of noninvolvement. In the electric age, when our central nervous system is technologically extended to involve us in the whole of mankind and to incorporate the whole of mankind in us, we necessarily participate, in depth, in the consequences of our every action. It is no longer possible to adopt the aloof and dissociated role of the literate Westerner....

THE MEDIUM IS THE MESSAGE

In a culture like ours, long accustomed to splitting and dividing all things as a means of control, it is sometimes a bit of a shock to be reminded that, in operational and practical fact, the medium is the message. This is merely to say that the personal and social consequences of any medium—that is, of any extension of ourselves—result from the new scale that is introduced into our affairs by each extension of ourselves, or by any new technology. Thus, with automation, for example the new patterns of human association tend to eliminate jobs, it is true. That is the negative result. Positively, automation creates roles for people, which is to say depth of involvement in their work and human association that our preceding mechanical technology had destroyed. Many people would be disposed to say that it was not the machine, but what one did with the machine, that was its meaning or message. In terms of the ways in which the machine altered our relations to one another and to ourselves, it mattered not in the least whether it turned out cornflakes or Cadillacs. The restructuring of human work and association was shaped by the technique of fragmentation that is the essence of machine technology. The essence of automation technology is the opposite. It is integral and decentralist in depth, just as the machine was fragmentary, centralist, and superficial in its patterning of human relationships.

The instance of the electric light may prove illuminating in this connection. The electric light is pure information. It is a medium without a message, as it were, unless it is used to spell out some verbal ad or name. This fact, characteristic of all media, means that the "content" of any medium is always another medium. The content of writing is speech, just as the written word is the content of print, and print is the content of the telegraph. If it is asked, "What is the content of speech?," it is necessary to say, "It is an actual process of thought, which is in itself nonverbal." An abstract painting represents direct manifestation of creative thought processes as they might appear in computer designs. What we are considering here, however, are the psychic and social consequences of the designs or patterns as they amplify or accelerate existing processes. For the "message" of any medium or technology is the change of sale or pace or pattern that it introduces into human affairs. The railway did not introduce movement or transportation or wheel or road into human society, but it accelerated and enlarged the scale of previous human functions, creating totally new kinds of cities and new kinds of work and leisure. This happened whether the railway functioned in a tropical or a northern environment, and is quite independent of the freight or content of the railway medium. The airplane, on the other hand, by accelerating the rate of transportation, tends to dissolve the railway form of city, politics, and association, quite independently of what the airplane is used for.

Let us return to the electric light. Whether the light is being used for brain surgery or night baseball is a matter of indifference. It could be argued that these activities are in some way the "content" of the electric light, since they could not exist without the electric light. This fact merely underlines the point that "the medium is the message" because it is the medium that shapes and controls the scale and form of human association and action. The content or uses of such media are as diverse as they are ineffectual in shaping the form of human association. Indeed, it is only too typical that the "content" of any medium blinds us to the character of the medium. It is only today that industries have become aware of the various kinds of business in which they are engaged. When IBM discovered that it was not in the business of making office equipment or business machines, but that it was in the business of processing information, then it began to navigate with clear vision. The General Electric Company makes a considerable portion of its profits from electric light bulbs and lighting systems. It has not yet discovered that, quite as much as A.T.&T., it is in the business of moving information. . . .

In accepting an honorary degree from the University of Notre Dame . . . , General David Sarnoff made this statement: "We are too prone to make technological instruments the scapegoats for the sins of those who wield them. The products of modern science are not in themselves good or bad; it is the way they are used that determines their value." That is the voice of the current somnambulism. Suppose we were to say, "Apple pie is in itself neither good nor bad; it is the way it is used that determines its value." Or, "The smallpox virus is in itself neither good nor bad; it is the way it is used the determines its value." Again, "Firearms are in themselves neither good nor bad; it is the way they are used that determines their value." That is, if the slugs reach the right people firearms are good. If the TV tube fires the right ammunition at the right people it is good. I am not being perverse. There is simply nothing in the Sarnoff statement that will bear scrutiny, for it ignores the nature of the medium, of any and all media, in the true Narcissus style of one hypnotized by the amputation and extension of its own being in a new technical form. General Sarnoff went on to explain his attitude to the technology of print, saying that it was true that print caused much trash to circulate, but it had also disseminated the Bible and the thoughts of seers and philosophers. It has never occurred to General Sarnoff that any technology could do anything but *add* itself on to what we already are. . . .

Just before an airplane breaks the sound barrier, sound waves become visible on the wings of the plane. The sudden visibility of sound just as sound ends is an apt instance of that great pattern of being that reveals new and opposite forms just as the earlier forms reach their peak performance. Mechanization was never so vividly fragmented or sequential as in the birth of the movies, the moment that translated us beyond mechanism into the world of growth and organic interrelation. The movie, by sheer speeding up the mechanical, carried us from the world of sequence and connections into the world of creative configuration and structure. The message of the movie medium is that of transition from lineal connections to configurations. It is the transition that produced the now quite correct observation: "If it works, it's obsolete." When electric speed further takes over from mechanical movie sequences, then the lines of force in structures and in media become loud and clear. We return to the inclusive from of the icon.

To a highly literate and mechanized culture the movie appeared as a world of triumphant illusions and dreams that money could buy. It was at this moment of the movie that cubism occurred, and it has been described by E. H. Gombrich (*Art and Illusion*) as "the most radical attempt to stamp out ambiguity and to enforce one reading of the picture—that of a man-made construction, a colored canvas." For cubism substitutes all facets of an object simultaneously for the "point of view" or facet of perspective illusion. Instead of the specialized illusion of the third dimension on canvas, cubism sets up an interplay of planes and contradiction or dramatic conflict of patterns, lights, textures that "drives home the message" by involvement. This is held by many to be an exercise in painting, not in illusion.

In other words, cubism, by giving the inside and outside, the top, bottom, back, and front and the rest, in two dimensions, drops the illusion of perspective in favor of instant sensory awareness of the whole. Cubism, by seizing on instant total awareness, suddenly announced that *the medium is the message.* Is it not evident that the moment that sequence yields to the simultaneous, one is in the world of the structure and of configuration? Is that not what has happened in physics as in painting, poetry, and in communication? Specialized segments of attention have shifted to total field, and we can now say, "The medium is the message" quite naturally. Before the electric speed and total field, it was not obvious that the medium is the message. The message, it seemed, was the "content," as people used to ask what a painting was *about.* Yet they never thought to ask what a melody was about, nor what a house or a dress was about. In such matters, people retained some sense of the whole pattern, of form and function as a unity. But in the electric age this integral idea of structure and configuration has become so prevalent that educational theory has taken up the matter. Instead of working with specialized "problems" in arithmetic, the structural approach now follows the lines of force in the field of number and has small children meditating about number theory and "sets."

Cardinal Newman said of Napoleon, "He understood the grammar of gunpowder." Napoleon had paid some attention to other media as well, especially the semaphore telegraph that gave him a great advantage over his enemies. He is on record for saying that "Three hostile newspapers are more to be feared than a thousand bayonets."

... [Alexis] de Tocqueville, in earlier work on the French Revolution, had explained how it was the printed word that, achieving cultural saturation in the eighteenth century, had homogenized the French nation. Frenchmen were the same kind of people from north to south. The typographic principles of uniformity, continuity, and lineality had overlaid the complexities of ancient feudal and oral society. The Revolution was carried out by the new literati and lawyers.

In England, however, such was the power of the ancient oral traditions of common law, backed by the medieval institution of Parliament, that no uniformity or continuity of the new visual print culture could take complete hold. The result was that the most important event in English history has never taken place; namely, the English Revolution on the lines of the French Revolution. The American Revolution had no medieval legal institutions to discard or to root out, apart from monarchy. And many have held that the American Presidency has become very much more personal and monarchical than any European monarch ever could be.

De Tocqueville's contrast between England and America is clearly based on the fact of typography and of print culture creating uniformity and continuity. England, he says, has rejected this principle and clung to the dynamic or oral common-law tradition. Hence the discontinuity and unpredictable quality of English culture. The grammar of print cannot help to construe the message of oral and nonwritten culture and institutions. The English aristocracy was properly classified as barbarian by Matthew Arnold because its power and status had nothing to do with literacy or with the cultural forms of typography. Said the Duke of Gloucester to Edward Gibbon upon the publication of his *Decline and Fall:* "Another damned fat book, eh, Mr. Gibbon? Scribble, scribble, scribble, eh, Mr. Gibbon?" De Tocqueville was a highly literate aristocrat who was quite able to be detached from the values and assumptions of typography. That is why he alone understood the grammar of typography. And it is only on those terms, standing aside from any structure or medium, that its principles and lines of force can be discerned. For any medium has the power of imposing its own assumption on the unwary. Prediction and control consist in avoiding this subliminal state of Narcissus trance. But the greatest aid to this end is simply in knowing that the spell can occur immediately upon contact, as in the first bars of a melody.

... Our conventional response to all media, namely that it is how they are used that counts, is the numb stance of the technological idiot. For the "content" of a medium is like the juicy piece of meat carried by the burglar to distract the watchdog of the mind. The effect of the medium is made strong and intense just because it is given another medium as "content." The content of a movie is a novel or a play or an opera. The effect of the movie form is not related to its program content. The "content" of writing or print is speech, but the reader is almost entirely unaware either of print or of speech.

The Age of Show Business

New York University professor Neil Postman has written extensively on the way media environments influence and change social practices. Some of his books include *The Disappearance of Childhood* (Vintage Books, 1982), *Conscientious Objections* (Vintage Books, 1988), and *Technopoly* (Alfred A. Knopf, 1992).

The following selection is taken from one of his most influential books, *Amusing Ourselves to Death: Public Discourse in the Age of Show Business* (Penguin, 1985). In it, Postman shows how practices of public discourse are repackaged in media environments to be presented as forms of entertainment. He claims that when media present serious issues, television audiences in particular are left with an impression formed by television's bias for entertainment programming.

Postman focuses on the unique characteristics of media form and its ability to influence both the message and the audience's perception of the message. He points out that various cultures use television for different purposes; thus, the medium helps shape, and is also shaped by, the North American cultural experience. Finally, Postman calls for more criticism of the way media packages and presents content.

Key Concept: entertainment and media bias

A dedicated graduate student I know returned to his small apartment the night before a major examination only to discover that his solitary lamp was broken beyond repair. After a whiff of panic, he was able to restore both his equanimity and his chances for a satisfactory grade by turning on the television set, turning off the sound, and with his back to the set, using its light to read important passages on which he was to be tested. This is one use of television —as a source of illuminating the printed page.

But the television screen is more than a light source. It is also a smooth, nearly flat surface on which the printed word may be displayed. We have all stayed at hotels in which the TV set has had a special channel for describing the day's events in letters rolled endlessly across the screen. This is another use of television—as an electronic bulletin board.

Many television sets are also large and sturdy enough to bear the weight of a small library. The top of an old-fashioned RCA console can handle as many as thirty books, and I know one woman who has securely placed her entire collection of Dickens, Flaubert, and Turgenev on the top of a 21-inch Westinghouse. Here is still another use of television—as bookcase.

I bring forward these quixotic uses of television to ridicule the hope harbored by some that television can be used to support the literate tradition. Such a hope represents exactly what Marshall McLuhan used to call "rear-view mirror" thinking: the assumption that a new medium is merely an extension or amplification of an older one; that an automobile, for example, is only a fast horse, or an electric light a powerful candle. To make such a mistake in the matter at hand is to misconstrue entirely how television redefines the meaning of public discourse. Television does not extend or amplify literate culture. It attacks it. If television is a continuation of anything, it is of a tradition begun by the telegraph and photograph in the mid-nineteenth century, not by the printing press in the fifteenth.

What is television? What kinds of conversations does it permit? What are the intellectual tendencies it encourages? What sort of culture does it produce?

... We might say that a technology is to a medium as the brain is to the mind. Like the brain, a technology is a physical apparatus. Like the mind, a medium is a use to which a physical apparatus is put. A technology becomes a medium as it employs a particular symbolic code, as it finds its place in a particular social setting, as it insinuates itself into economic and political contexts. A technology, in other words, is merely a machine. A medium is the social and intellectual environment a machine creates.

Of course, like the brain itself, every technology has an inherent bias. It has within its physical form a predisposition toward being used in certain ways and not others. Only those who know nothing of the history of technology believe that a technology is entirely neutral. There is an old joke that mocks that naive belief. Thomas Edison, it goes, would have revealed his discovery of the electric light much sooner than he did except for the fact that every time he turned it on, he held it to his mouth and said, "Hello? Hello?"

Not very likely. Each technology has an agenda of its own. It is, as I have suggested, a metaphor waiting to unfold. The printing press, for example, had a clear bias toward being used as a linguistic medium. It is *conceivable* to use it exclusively for the reproduction of pictures. And, one imagines, the Roman Catholic Church would not have objected to its being so used in the sixteenth century. Had that been the case, the Protestant Reformation might not have occurred, for as Luther contended, with the word of God on every family's kitchen table, Christians do not require the Papacy to interpret it for them. But in fact there never was much chance that the press would be used solely, or even very much, for the duplication of icons. From its beginning in the fifteenth century, the press was perceived as an extraordinary opportunity for the display and mass distribution of written language. Everything about its technical possibilities led in that direction. One might even say it was invented for that purpose.

The technology of television has a bias, as well. It is conceivable to use television as a lamp, a surface for texts, a bookcase, even as radio. But it has not been so used and will not be so used, at least in America. Thus, in answering the question, What is television?, we must understand as a first point that we are not talking about television as a technology but television as a medium. There are many places in the world where television, though the same technology as it is in America, is an entirely different medium from that which we know. I refer to places where the majority of people do not have television sets, and those who do have only one; where only one station is available; where television does not operate around the clock; where most programs have as their purpose the direct furtherance of government ideology and policy; where commercials are unknown, and "talking heads" are the principal image; where television is mostly used as if it were radio. For these reasons and more television will not have the same meaning or power as it does in America, which is to say, it is possible for a technology to be so used that its potentialities are prevented from developing and its social consequences kept to a minimum.

But in America, this has not been the case. Television has found in liberal democracy and a relatively free market economy a nurturing climate in which its full potentialities as a technology of images could be exploited. One result of this has been that American television programs are in demand all over the world. The total estimate of U.S. television program exports is approximately 100,000 to 200,000 hours, equally divided among Latin America, Asia and Europe. Over the years, programs like "Gunsmoke," "Bonanza," "Mission: Impossible," "Star Trek," "Kojak," and more recently, "Dallas" and "Dynasty" have been as popular in England, Japan, Israel and Norway as in Omaha, Nebraska. I have heard (but not verified) that some years ago the Lapps postponed for several days their annual and, one supposes, essential migratory journey so that they could find out who shot J.R.* All of this has occurred simultaneously with the decline of America's moral and political prestige, worldwide. American television programs are in demand not because America is loved but because American television is loved.

We need not be detained too long in figuring out why. In watching American television, one is reminded of George Bernard Shaw's remark on his first seeing the glittering neon signs of Broadway and 42nd Street at night. It must be beautiful, he said, if you cannot read. American television is, indeed, a beautiful spectacle, a visual delight, pouring forth thousands of images on any given day. The average length of a shot on network television is only 3.5 seconds, so that the eye never rests, always has something new to see. Moreover, television offers viewers a variety of subject matter, requires minimal skills to comprehend it, and is largely aimed at emotional gratification. Even commercials, which some regard as an annoyance, are exquisitely crafted, always pleasing to the eye and accompanied by exciting music. There is no question but that the best photography in the world is presently seen on television commercials. American television, in other words, is devoted entirely to supplying its audience with entertainment.

Of course, to say that television is entertaining is merely banal. Such a fact is hardly threatening to a culture, not even worth writing a book about. It may even be a reason for rejoicing. Life, as we like to say, is not a highway strewn

* [J.R. Ewing, a character on the prime-time soap opera "Dallas," was shot during the final episode of the 1979–1980 season. The November 21, 1980, episode, in which the identity of the shooter was revealed, became the highest-rated entertainment program in television history.—Eds.]

with flowers. The sight of a few blossoms here and there may make our journey a trifle more endurable. The Lapps undoubtedly thought so. We may surmise that the ninety million Americans who watch television every night also think so. But what I am claiming here is not that television is entertaining but that it has made entertainment itself the natural format for the representation of all experience. Our television set keeps us in constant communion with the world, but it does so with a face whose smiling countenance is unalterable. The problem is not that television presents us with entertaining subject matter but that all subject matter is presented as entertaining, which is another issue altogether.

To say it still another way: Entertainment is the supraideology of all discourse on television. No matter what is depicted or from what point of view, the overarching presumption is that it is there for our amusement and pleasure. That is why even on news shows which provide us daily with fragments of tragedy and barbarism, we are urged by the newscasters to "join them tomorrow." What for? One would think that several minutes of murder and mayhem would suffice as material for a month of sleepless nights. We accept the newscasters' invitation because we know that the "news" is not to be taken seriously, that it is all in fun, so to say. Everything about a news show tells us this—the good looks and amiability of the cast, their pleasant banter, the exciting music that opens and closes the show, the vivid film footage, the attractive commercials—all these and more suggest that what we have just seen is no cause for weeping. A news show, to put it plainly, is a format for entertainment, not for education, reflection or catharsis. And we must not judge too harshly those who have framed it in this way. They are not assembling the news to be read, or broadcasting it to be heard. They are televising the news to be seen. They must follow where their medium leads. There is no conspiracy here, no lack of intelligence, only a straightforward recognition that "good television" has little to do with what is "good" about exposition or other forms of verbal communication but everything to do with what the pictorial images look like.

I should like to illustrate this point by offering the case of the eighty-minute discussion provided by the ABC network on November 20, 1983, following its controversial movie *The Day After*. Though the memory of this telecast has receded for most, I choose this case because, clearly, here was television taking its most "serious" and "responsible" stance. Everything that made up this broadcast recommended it as a critical test of television's capacity to depart from an entertainment mode and rise to the level of public instruction. In the first place, the subject was the possibility of a nuclear holocaust. Second, the film itself had been attacked by several influential bodies politic, including the Reverend Jerry Falwell's Moral Majority. Thus, it was important that the network display television's value and serious intentions as a medium of information and coherent discourse. Third, on the program itself no musical theme was used as background—a significant point since almost all television programs are embedded in music, which helps to tell the audience what emotions are to be called forth. This is a standard theatrical device, and its absence on television is always ominous. Fourth, there were no commercials during the discussion, thus elevating the tone of the event to the state of reverence usually reserved for the funerals of assassinated Presidents. And finally, the participants included Henry Kissinger, Robert McNamara, and Elie Wiesel, each of whom is a symbol of sorts of serious discourse. Although Kissinger, somewhat later, made an appearance on the hit show "Dynasty," he was then and still is a paradigm of intellectual sobriety; and Wiesel, practically a walking metaphor of social conscience. Indeed, the other members of the cast—Carl Sagan, William Buckley and General Brent Scowcroft—are, each in his way, men of intellectual bearing who are not expected to participate in trivial public matters.

The program began with Ted Koppel, master of ceremonies, so to speak, indicating that what followed was not intended to be a debate but a *discussion*. And so those who are interested in philosophies of discourse had an excellent opportunity to observe what serious television means by the word "discussion." Here is what it means: Each of six men was given approximately five minutes to say something about the subject. There was, however, no agreement on exactly what the subject was, and no one felt obliged to respond to anything anyone else said. In fact, it would have been difficult to do so, since the participants were called upon seriatim, as if they were finalists in a beauty contest, each being given his share of minutes in front of the camera. Thus, if Mr. Wiesel, who was called upon last, had a response to Mr. Buckley, who was called upon first, there would have been four commentaries in between, occupying about twenty minutes, so that the audience (if not Mr. Wiesel himself) would have had difficulty remembering the argument which prompted his response. In fact, the participants—most of whom were no strangers to television—largely avoided addressing each other's points. They used their initial minutes and then their subsequent ones to intimate their position or give an impression. Dr. Kissinger, for example, seemed intent on making viewers feel sorry that he was no longer their Secretary of State by reminding everyone of books he had once written, proposals he had once made, and negotiations he had once conducted. Mr. McNamara informed the audience that he had eaten lunch in Germany that very afternoon, and went on to say that he had at least fifteen proposals to reduce nuclear arms. One would have thought that the discussion would turn on this issue, but the others seemed about as interested in it as they were in what he had for lunch in Germany. (Later, he took the initiative to mention three of his proposals but they were not discussed.) Elie Wiesel, in a series of quasi-parables and paradoxes, stressed the tragic nature of the human condition, but because he did not have the time to provide a context for his remarks, he seemed quixotic and confused, conveying an impression of an itinerant rabbi who has wandered into a coven of Gentiles.

In other words, this was no discussion as we normally use the word. Even when the "discussion" period began, there were no arguments or counterarguments, no scrutiny of assumptions, no explanations, no elaborations, no definitions. Carl Sagan made, in my opinion, the most coherent statement —a four-minute rationale for a nuclear freeze—but it contained at least two questionable assumptions and was not carefully examined. Apparently, no one wanted to take time from his own few minutes to call attention to someone else's. Mr. Koppel, for his part, felt obliged to keep the "show" moving, and though he occasionally pursued what he discerned as a line of thought, he was more concerned to give each man his fair allotment of time.

But it is not time constraints alone that produce such fragmented and discontinuous language. When a television show is in process, it is very nearly impermissible to say, "Let me think about that" or "I don't know" or "What do you mean when you say ... ?" or "From what sources does your information come?" This type of discourse not only slows down the tempo of the show but creates the impression of uncertainty or lack of finish. It tends to reveal people in the *act of thinking,* which is as disconcerting and boring on television as it is on a Las Vegas stage. Thinking does not play well on television, a fact that television directors discovered long ago. There is not much to *see* in it. It is, in a phrase, not a performing art. But television demands a performing art, and so what the ABC network gave us was a picture of men of sophisticated verbal skills and political understanding being brought to heel by a medium that requires them to fashion performances rather than ideas. Which accounts for why the eighty minutes were very entertaining, in the way of a Samuel Beckett play: The intimations of gravity hung heavy, the meaning passeth all understanding. The performances, of course, were highly professional. Sagan abjured the turtle-neck sweater in which he starred when he did "Cosmos." He even had his hair cut for the event. His part was that of the logical scientist speaking in behalf of the planet. It is to be doubted that Paul Newman could have done better in the role, although Leonard Nimoy might have. Scowcroft was suitably military in his bearing—terse and distant, the unbreakable defender of national security. Kissinger, as always, was superb in the part of the knowing world statesman, weary of the sheer responsibility of keeping disaster at bay. Koppel played to perfection the part of a moderator, pretending, as it were, that he was sorting out ideas while, in fact, he was merely directing the performances. At the end, one could only applaud those performances, which is what a good television program always aims to achieve; that is to say, applause, not reflection.

I do not say categorically that it is impossible to use television as a carrier of coherent language or thought in process. William Buckley's own program, "Firing Line," occasionally shows people in the act of thinking but who also happen to have television cameras pointed at them. There are other programs, such as "Meet the Press" or "The Open Mind," which clearly strive to maintain a sense of intellectual decorum and typographic tradition, but they are scheduled so that they do not compete with programs of great visual interest, since otherwise, they will not be watched. After all, it is not unheard of that a format will occasionally go against the bias of its medium. For example, the most popular radio program of the early 1940's featured a ventriloquist, and in those days, I heard more than once the feet of a tap dancer on the "Major Bowes' Amateur Hour." (Indeed, if I am not mistaken, he even once featured a pantomimist.) But ventriloquism, dancing and mime do not play well on radio, just as sustained, complex talk does not play well on television. It can be made to play tolerably well if only one camera is used and the visual image is kept constant—as when the President gives a speech. But this is not television at its best, and it is not television that most people will choose to watch. The single most important fact about television is that people *watch* it, which is why it is called *"television."* And what they watch, and like to watch, are moving pictures—millions of them, of short duration and dynamic variety. It is in the nature of the medium that it must suppress the content of ideas in order to accommodate the requirements of visual interest; that is to say, to accommodate the values of show business.

Film, records and radio (now that it is an adjunct of the music industry) are, of course, equally devoted to entertaining the culture, and their effects in altering the style of American discourse are not insignificant. But television is different because it encompasses all forms of discourse. No one goes to a movie to find out about government policy or the latest scientific advances. No one buys a record to find out the baseball scores or the weather or the latest murder. No one turns on radio anymore for soap operas or a presidential address (if a television set is at hand). But everyone goes to television for all these things and more, which is why television resonates so powerfully throughout the culture. Television is our culture's principal mode of knowing about itself. Therefore —and this is the critical point—how television stages the world becomes the model for how the world is properly to be staged. It is not merely that on the television screen entertainment is the metaphor for all discourse. It is that off the screen the same metaphor prevails. As typography once dictated the style of conducting politics, religion, business, education, law and other important social matters, television now takes command. In courtrooms, classrooms, operating rooms, board rooms, churches and even airplanes, Americans no longer talk to each other, they entertain each other. They do not exchange ideas; they exchange images. They do not argue with propositions; they argue with good looks, celebrities and commercials. For the message of television as metaphor is not only that all the world is a stage but that the stage is located in Las Vegas, Nevada.

In Chicago, for example, the Reverend Greg Sakowicz, a Roman Catholic priest, mixes his religious teaching with rock 'n' roll music. According to the Associated Press, the Reverend Sakowicz is both an associate pastor at the Church of the Holy Spirit in Schaumberg (a suburb of Chicago) and a disc jockey at WKQX. On his show, "The Journey Inward," Father Sakowicz chats in soft tones about such topics as family relationships or commitment, and interposes his sermons with "the sound of *Billboard*'s Top 10." He says that his preaching is not done "in a churchy way," and adds, "You don't have to be boring in order to be holy."

Meanwhile in New York City at St. Patrick's Cathedral, Father John J. O'Connor put on a New York Yankee baseball cap as he mugged his way through his installation as Archbishop of the New York Archdiocese. He got off some excellent gags, at least one of which was specifically directed at Mayor Edward Koch, who was a member of his audience; that is to say, he was a congregant. At his next public performance, the new archbishop donned a New York Mets baseball cap. These events were, of course, televised, and were vastly entertaining, largely because Archbishop (now Cardinal) O'Connor has gone Father Sakowicz one better: Whereas the latter believes that you don't have to be boring to be holy, the former apparently believes you don't have to be holy at all.

In Phoenix, Arizona, Dr. Edward Dietrich performed triple bypass surgery on Bernard Schuler. The operation was successful, which was nice for Mr. Schuler. It was also on television, which was nice for America. The operation was carried by at least fifty television stations in the United States, and also by the British Broadcasting Corporation. A two-man panel of narrators (a play-by-play and color man, so to speak) kept viewers informed about what they were seeing. It was not clear as to why this event was televised, but it resulted in transforming both Dr. Dietrich and Mr. Schuler's chest into celebrities. Perhaps because he has seen too many doctor shows on television, Mr. Schuler was uncommonly confident about the outcome of his surgery. "There is no way in hell they are going to lose me on live TV," he said.

As reported with great enthusiasm by both WCBS-TV and WNBC-TV in 1984, the Philadelphia public schools have embarked on an experiment in which children will have their curriculum sung to them. Wearing Walkman equipment, students were shown listening to rock music whose lyrics were about the eight parts of speech. Mr. Jocko Henderson, who thought of this idea, is planning to delight students further by subjecting mathematics and history, as well as English, to the rigors of a rock music format. In fact, this is not Mr. Henderson's idea at all. It was pioneered by the Children's Television Workshop, whose television show "Sesame Street" is an expensive illustration of the idea that education is indistinguishable from entertainment. Nonetheless, Mr. Henderson has a point in his favor. Whereas "Sesame Street" merely attempts to make learning to read a form of light entertainment, the Philadelphia experiment aims to make the classroom itself into a rock concert.

In New Bedford, Massachusetts, a rape trial was televised, to the delight of audiences who could barely tell the difference between the trial and their favorite mid-day soap opera. In Florida, trials of varying degrees of seriousness, including murder, are regularly televised and are considered to be more entertaining than most fictional courtroom dramas. All of this is done in the interests of "public education." For the same high purpose, plans are afoot, it is rumored, to televise confessionals. To be called "Secrets of the Confessional Box," the program will, of course, carry the warning that some of its material may be offensive to children and therefore parental guidance is suggested.

On a United Airlines flight from Chicago to Vancouver, a stewardess announces that its passengers will play a game. The passenger with the most credit cards will win a bottle of champagne. A man from Boston with twelve credit cards wins. A second game requires the passengers to guess the collective age of the cabin crew. A man from Chicago guesses 128, and wins another bottle of wine. During the second game, the air turns choppy and the Fasten Seat Belt sign goes on. Very few people notice, least of all the cabin crew, who keep up a steady flow of gags on the intercom. When the plane reaches its destination, everyone seems to agree that it's fun to fly from Chicago to Vancouver.

On February 7, 1985, *The New York Times* reported that Professor Charles Pine of Rutgers University (Newark campus) was named Professor of the Year by the Council for the Support and Advancement of Education. In explaining why he has such a great impact on his students, Professor Pine said: "I have some gimmicks I use all the time. If you reach the end of the blackboard, I keep writing on the wall. It always gets a laugh. The way I show what a glass molecule does is to run over to one wall and bounce off it, and run over to the other wall." His students are, perhaps, too young to recall that James Cagney used this "molecule move" to great effect in *Yankee Doodle Dandy*. If I am not mistaken, Donald O'Connor duplicated it in *Singin' in the Rain*. So far as I know, it has been used only once before in a classroom: Hegel tried it several times in demonstrating how the dialectical method works.

The Pennsylvania Amish try to live in isolation from mainstream American culture. Among other things, their religion opposes the veneration of graven images, which means that the Amish are forbidden to see movies or to be photographed. But apparently their religion has not got around to disallowing seeing movies *when* they are being photographed. In the summer of 1984, for example, a Paramount Pictures crew descended upon Lancaster County to film the movie *Witness,* which is about a detective, played by Harrison Ford, who falls in love with an Amish woman. Although the Amish were warned by their church not to interfere with the film makers, it turned out that some Amish welders ran to see the action as soon as their work was done. Other devouts lay in the grass some distance away, and looked down on the set with binoculars. "We read about the movie in the paper," said an Amish woman. "The kids even cut out Harrison Ford's picture." She added: "But it doesn't really matter that much to them. Somebody told us he was in *Star Wars* but that doesn't mean anything to us." The last time a similar conclusion was drawn was when the executive director of the American Association of Blacksmiths remarked that he had read about the automobile but that he was convinced it would have no consequences for the future of his organization....

Prior to the 1984 presidential elections, the two candidates confronted each other on television in what were called "debates." These events were not in the least like the Lincoln-Douglas debates or anything else that goes by the name. Each candidate was given five minutes to address such questions as, What is (or would be) your policy in Central America? His opposite number was then given one minute for a rebuttal. In such circumstances, complexity, documentation and logic can play no role, and, indeed, on several occasions syntax itself was abandoned entirely. It is no matter. The men were less concerned with giving arguments than with "giving off" impressions, which is what television does best. Post-debate commentary largely avoided any evaluation of the candidates' ideas, since there were none to evaluate. Instead, the debates were conceived as boxing matches, the relevant question being, Who KO'd whom? The answer was determined by the "style" of the men—how they looked, fixed their gaze, smiled, and delivered one-liners. In the second debate, President Reagan got off a swell one-liner when asked a question about his age. The following day, several newspapers indicated that Ron had KO'd Fritz with his joke. Thus, the leader of the free world is chosen by the people in the Age of Television.

What all of this means is that our culture has moved toward a new way of conducting its business, especially its important business. The nature of its discourse is changing as the demarcation line between what is show business and what is not becomes harder to see with each passing day. Our priests and presidents, our surgeons and lawyers, our educators and newscasters need worry less about satisfying the demands of their discipline than the demands of good showmanship. Had Irving Berlin changed one word in the title of his celebrated song, he would have been as prophetic, albeit more terse, as Aldous Huxley. He need only have written, There's No Business But Show Business.

New Group Identities

Joshua Meyrowitz, who received his Ph.D. from New York University, is a professor at the University of New Hampshire. In the following selection from Meyrowitz's award-winning book *No Sense of Place: The Impact of Electronic Media on Social Behavior* (Oxford University Press, 1985), the author stresses how the characteristics of electronic media ultimately influence the ways individuals perceive themselves in relation to others through group identity, tolerance for diversity, and a sense of shared culture.

Meyrowitz's thesis is that electronic media influence the way people relate to physical location and access to information, and he explains how familiarity with media form influences interpersonal social dynamics. In some ways, his work reflects the concept of media having the ability to influence spatial and temporal reality. Meyrowitz addresses the long-term effects of living with electronic media by looking at the ways individuals have internalized mediated messages, but he also points to the positive and negative results of media's time- and space-binding qualities. His work further elaborates on the concepts of media form and sense extension.

Meyrowitz's work, as well as the work of recent political communication researchers, looks at the long-term effects of living with media—how people have internalized certain behaviors and standards that media have conditioned us to accept.

Key Concept: group affiliation and media bias

Group identity is based on "shared but special" information-systems. The greater the number of distinct social information-systems, the greater the number of distinct "groups"; the smaller the number of distinct information-systems, the smaller the number of distinct group identities. The merging of many formerly distinct situations through electronic media, therefore, should have an homogenizing effect on group identities.

As a result of the widespread use of television, for example, the social information available to the ghetto family now more closely resembles the information available to the middle class family. Information available to women now more closely resembles information available to men. Formerly distinct groups not only share very similar information about society in general, they also share more information about each other—information that once distinguished "insiders" from "outsiders." As a consequence, traditional distinctions among groups become partially blurred.

The change in the information characteristic of traditional groups leads to two complementary phenomena: the decreasing importance of traditional group ties and the increasing importance of other types of association.

The homogenized information networks fostered by electronic media offer individuals a comparatively holistic view of society and a wider field within which to measure their relative lot. To use George Herbert Mead's term, electronic media alter one's "generalized other"—the general sense of how other people think and evaluate one's actions. The "mediated generalized other" includes standards, values, and beliefs from outside traditional group spheres, and it thereby presents people with a new perspective from which to view their actions and identities. The new mediated generalized other bypasses face-to-face encounters in family and community and is shared by millions of others.

One result of this shared perspective and more common set of situations is that members of formerly isolated and distinct groups begin to demand "equal" rights and treatment. This analysis, therefore, offers one possible explanation for the recent, sudden rise of "minorities" as potent social and political forces. Blacks, women, hispanics, Native Americans, gays, children, prisoners, and the disabled are all groups composed of people who now feel or are seen as isolated in a corner of the larger environment, restricted and disenfranchised.

The rise of minority consciousness, according to this analysis, actually indicates the demise of one aspect of minority status in the traditional sense. Minority affiliations were once based on *isolated* information-systems and very *distinct* group experiences. The demand for full equality in roles and rights dramatizes the development, in a way, of a mass "majority," a single large "group" whose members will not tolerate any great distinctions in roles and privileges.

Today's minority consciousness is something of a paradox. Many people take renewed pride in their special identity, yet the heightened consciousness of the special group is the result of being able to view one's group from the outside; that is, it is the result of no longer being fully *in* the group. Members of today's minority groups are united in their feelings of *restriction* from certain rights and experiences. People sense they are in a minority group because they feel excluded from the larger reference group. The diminutive connotation of the term "minority" does not refer to the small number of people in the group, but rather to the limited degree of access the members feel they have to the larger society. The term "minority" as it is sometimes applied to women[1]—the majority of the population—is meaningless in any other sense....

Many minorities consciously proclaim their special identity in the unconscious hope of losing at least part of it. When gays, for example, publicly protest for equal treatment under the law, including the right to teach and the recognition of homosexual marriages, they are not only saying, "I'm different and I'm proud of it," they are also saying, "I should be treated as if I'm the same as everyone else." So there is a paradoxical call for both consciousness of differences and blindness to them.

Ironically, the sense of restriction felt by many minority group members may be the result of the sudden *increase* in access to a larger, more inclusive information environment. For to know about and be constantly exposed to places you cannot go and things you are not allowed to do makes you feel more isolated than you were before. My uncle has told me many times that when he was young, he did not realize how poor his family was because everyone he knew was poor. Through television, today's ghetto children have more points of reference and higher standards for comparison. They see what they are being deprived of in every program and commercial. . . .

THE UNDERMINING OF GROUP LOCATIONS

Electronic media have had a tremendous impact on group identity by undermining the relationship between physical location and information access. Many categories of people—women, ghetto dwellers, prisoners, children—were once "naturally" restricted from much social information by being isolated in particular places. The identity and cohesion of many groupings and associations were fostered by the fact that members were "isolated together" in the same or similar locations: homes or offices, ghettos or suburbs, prisons or stores, playgrounds or bars. Such physical segregation worked to create social segregation for as long as place and situation were still closely linked. Now, however, electronic messages on television, telephone, and radio democratize and homogenize places by allowing people to experience and interact with others in spite of physical isolation. As a result, physical location now creates only one type of information-system, only one type of shared but special group experience. Electronic media begin to override group identities based on "co-presence," and they create many new forms of access and "association" that have little to do with physical location.

Electronic media have an impact on group identity by distancing people from traditional group perspectives. The use of the word "perspective" to mean both what one sees from a given location as well as one's social attitudes suggests the strong traditional relationship between physical place and social belief. Shared physical location fosters a shared perspective which, in turn, reinforces group solidarity. A shift in physical position generally leads to a shift in attitude. A common example is the change in our perception of a street or intersection as we switch from pedestrian to driver. The same principle, however, provides the basis for one of the subtlest techniques of cinematic persuasion and propaganda: the shifting of perspective and position rather than the altering of content. In the celebrated film *The Godfather*, for example, we are not asked to believe that the mafia family members are good people; we are simply "put" in their home and given their view of the world. As a result, we find ourselves in the unusual position of rooting for the criminals and cheering when government agents are killed. Similar techniques are used in war movies and westerns where, regardless of "plot," viewers tend to take the side of those whose perspective they are shown.[2]

Through visual portrayal of real and fictional events, television presents most members of our society with a crazy-quilt pattern of perspectives. Regardless of physical location and traditional group ties, people experience how the world looks and feels from other places and other role perspectives. Television's views are, to be sure, distorted and incomplete, and often they are purposefully biased for political or economic reasons. Nevertheless, television "removes" viewers from their physical locales and offers them alternative views of other people and the physical environment. The "view from no place" that television permits may have been a stimulus for the growth of such groups as Amnesty International, for the increasing awareness of ecological issues, and for the growing demand for nuclear disarmament. Such issues require an "overview," an overriding of traditional group concerns and a bypassing of needs as seen from one's particular place. (Ironically, the "liberalizing" effect of the multiple perspective view may still give a political advantage to conservatives, reactionaries, and special interest groups. After all, multiple perspectives often lead many people to an overabundance of empathy and, therefore, to political ambivalence and inaction.

The impact of electronic media on group identity may be most apparent in large cities where traditional community ties are often already weak, where people do not know all their neighbors, nor speak to everyone they see. But small towns too are experiencing a change in perspective. Media ties compete with family, church, school, and community. Media create new "communities," and a large portion of their content is shared by most people in the country. Many jokes, phrases, expression, and events heard and seen on television provide a common set of "experience" for people across the land. It is not surprising, therefore, that what sociologists refer to as the "urbanization" of America includes not only population shifts to large cities but also a general urbanization of attitudes and behaviors throughout the country.[3] Electronic media move people informationally to the same "place."

The homogenization of regional spheres is, of course, only a matter of degree. Different places are still different, but they are not as different as they once were. The psychological distinctions between states and regions were once very great. As late as the 1940s, one coast of America was something of a mystery to the other. A cross-country trip was a true adventure into the unknown.[4] But television has removed much of this sense of mystery.

The telegraph began the breakdown of communication barriers between different places. But is presented terse coded messages that had to follow the telegraph lines. Radio enhanced the process, first by sending Morse Code through the air rather than through wires and later by adding the human voice. But radio merely *reported* verbally on events in other parts of the world or country. The information was still descriptive and "second-hand," a linguistic abstraction. Radio provided "word-pictures," but the pictures had to be redrawn in each listeners's imagination. It is difficult to imagine something new and mysterious without picturing it as some variation of what one has already seen. Further, with radio each listener creates his or her own unique and subjective picture. Television, in contrast, seemingly allows the viewer to experience distant events and places directly and "objectively." It is significant that when Edward R. Murrow's radio program "Hear It Now" became television's "See It Now," the premiere show featured a live hookup between California and New York; viewers saw the Golden Gate Bridge and the Brooklyn Bridge simultaneously on a split screen.[5] With television, the final demystification of other parts of the country began.

Electronic media, of course, are not the only causes of merging situations. High speed travel and mass production of identical clothes, appliances, and other products also have had their impact. As Daniel Boorstin's history of America suggests, the development and use of electronic media may be part of a larger trend of the homogenizing of here and there.[6] But electronic media have an effect that goes beyond other variables. Travel allows people to get from *place to place*. Identical products give *different places* the same surface look. These changes are physical not informational. Electronic media, in contrast, eat away at the very meaning of distinct places: shared by special *experience*. To be "with" other people is very different from using the same products or eating similar foods. . . .

Television's "national embrace" has an effect on local media content and local behavior. National weather reports, for example, are now included even in local news programs. And a disaster in another state—such as California mud slides or sink-holes in Florida—often receives more attention in local news and conversation than a house fire in one's home town. One result of this national and sometimes international view is that the total strangeness of "strangers" as well as the special meaning of "neighbor"—both important elements in the "them vs. us" feelings of group identity—have been muted.

It is difficult to isolate oneself from the metaphysical arena created by television. In the early days of television, the low quality of programming made it embarrassing for professors and other "highbrows" to admit that they even owned a television set, let alone that they spent any valuable time watching it. Today, however, the massive saturation of television into virtually every American home imbues the activity of watching television with multiple levels of social significance (and therefore offers convenient justifications as well). To watch television is now to hook into part of the "American experience." One can watch popular programs, not merely to see the program, but to see what others are watching. One can watch, not necessarily to stare into the eyes of America, but at least to look over the shoulders of Americans and see what they see. Television watching may not allow you to keep your finger directly on the pulse of the nation, but it does allow you to keep your finger on the pulse the nation is keeping its finger on.

Television today has a social function similar to the weather. No one takes responsibility for it, often it is bad, but nearly everyone pays attention to it and sees it as a basis of common experience and a source of topics of conversation.

The ease and speed with which one can tune into the national television forum or be in touch with other people through the telephone make it more difficult for people to isolate themselves in specific places. With electronic media, one is always "in range," others are always "within reach." To be "out of touch" today is to be abnormal. Many people now carry portable radios, or even television sets while on vacations or "retreats," and many isolated camping sites advertise that they have a TV room and a telephone. Similarly, for a person to live or vacation in a place that has no telephone is often thought to be an implicit insult to friends, relatives, and co-workers. Taking one's phone off the hook may be seen as a mark of a misanthrope. In some occupations, people are expected to wear "beepers" that make them accessible at any time wherever they are and whatever they are doing. Thus, many of the traditional behavioral characteristics of "place"—those dependent on isolation—are overridden. Indeed, electronic media have given insularity of thought and place a bad name.

It now seems unnatural to be completely unaware or inaccessible. This may partially explain why the television set and the telephone recently have become fixtures even in the recreation rooms of convents and in the formerly silent halls of the Trappist monks.[7]

Electronic media create ties and associations that compete with those formed through live interaction in specific locations. Live encounters are certainly more "special" and provide stronger and deeper relationships, but their relative number is decreasing. Many business, social, and even intimate family encounters now take place through electronic media ("Long distance is the next best thing to being there.") Although close physical ties in the home are important enough to compete successfully with a small number of electronic links, the many contacts through radio, television, and telephone begin to outweigh personal interactions through sheer number. Indeed, many "family encounters" now take place in from of the television set. Whether media have actually affected the *amount* of family interaction may be less of an issue than the fact that they have changed the *uniqueness* of what goes on in the home. Because many electronic messages within a given home are also experienced simultaneously by many other families, the shared but secret behavior of the family unit is further diluted. A person's psychological affiliation with his or her nuclear family is weakened when the families of friends, co-workers, and relatives share much of the same information at the same time. The common backdrop of social experience provided by electronic media creates broader (and therefore shallower) ties and associations.

Electronic media's impact on the uniqueness of family interactions suggests a common element underlying both the 1960s fad of communal living and the stronger current trend toward single-member households.[8] Both communal living and living alone represent a breakdown of traditional family ties; both represent treating large numbers of others with equal intimacy. The commune movement involved treating strangers like family; living alone involves treating even family members like partial strangers. In an electronic society, it makes sense that the single-member household arrangement has become the stronger of the two trends. Living alone more closely reflects, in physical terms, the patterns of association fostered by electronically created information-systems. Communes, like extended families before them, involve deep, long-term, place-bound commitments with a stable group of others. In both electronic communication and single-living, however, the options of association are large and shared, but the choice is individual and idiosyncratic. Just as electronic interactions do not saturate a time/space frame, so now do many live relationships take on an ephemeral and sporadic quality.

The integration of social spheres does not simply give people new places to play their old roles; it changes the roles that are played. As place and information access become disconnected, place-specific behaviors and activities begin to fade. The psychological and social distance among physical places is muted. As a result, dress codes in schools and restaurants have come to seem antiquated or phony. And when people do "dress up" today, it is more likely than in the past to be viewed as a "costume" rather than as a clear sign of personal identity. Further, people are less likely to wear the once "appropriate" dress for their role in a given place because places and roles no longer seem that distinct. Presidents wear jeans in public and nuns shed their habits.

As different places become informationally similar, the social definitions of different locations begin to merge. Factories and lavishly decorated residential lofts can coexist in the same buildings because location now has much less to do with group identity and interaction. The workplace begins to move back into the home because business interactions and information flow are now less dependent on the physical presence of co-workers and clients. As previously distinct situations are combined, formerly distinct behavior patterns merge. One of the contingencies of establishing an office at home, for example, is the need to develop a new social role that is neither "executive-in-office" nor "spouse/parent-at-home."

Traditional groups were formed on the basis of long-term shared locations and live experience. Workers in a factory, women at home, children in school, and shoppers in a store often defined themselves in terms of the physical defined "group": the factory, the family, the school, the neighborhood. Problems with a supervisor, a husband, a teacher, or a shopkeeper were once likely to be considered personal problems between individuals. Today, however, the mediated "view from above" redefines many problems into "social issues" and into battles between "social categories." When a promotion is denied, it is now likely to be liked to sex discrimination or racism; a problem with a spouse is likely to be defined in terms of spouse abuse or sexism. A child's problem in school may end up as a court battle over educational malpractice, and an interaction with a shopkeeper may be seen as a "consumer" issue. I am not suggesting that these perceptions are necessarily "false," only that they certainly are *different*. While interactions continue to occur in specific places, they are now conceived of as taking place in a much larger social arena.

Many of today's groupings are based on single, superficial attributes shared in common rather than on an intimate web of complicated interactions and long-term shared experience. The current battles over the rights of "smokers" versus "nonsmokers," for example, suggest how removed many current groupings are from traditional place-bound group ties.

Audiences for particular group behaviors are no longer determined by physical presence, and the performance of roles on all social levels shifts as a result. Police who negotiate with the city "through the media," for example, can no longer clearly distinguish their front region image of dedicated and selfless protectors of the people from their back region haggling for more sick days, vacation time, and higher salaries. Similarly, when the U.S. Senate's debate on the Panama Canal Treaty was broadcast live in Panama, there was a merging of the back region of American-American dealings into the front region of American-Panamanian interaction. The United States could no longer conduct its internal arguments with all due intensity and bitterness without insulting Panamanians, nor could it present a unified and diplomatic front to Panama without diminishing internal debate and discussion. Thus, the undermining of group locations leads to the dilution of traditional group behaviors and the development of "middle region" compromise behavior patterns.

1. For an early article on "Women as a Minority Group," see Hacker, 1951.

2. Meyrowitz, 1979, pp. 71–72. A more recent example of a "disturbing identification" for many Americans is the movie "Das Boot" in which the adventures of a World War II German U-Boat crew are chronicled. In direct contrast to virtually all *our* World War II movies, the Germans become "us" and the British and Americans become "them."

3. See, for example, Popenoe, 1980, pp. 513–514.

4. One indication of this was the role that cross-country travel could still play in radio dramas. The classic 1942 radio thriller with Orson Wells, "The Hitchhiker," for example, begins with the main character assuring his mother that her fears about his planned drive from New York to California are unfounded; the drama ends with his trip transformed into a journey from sanity to near-insanity, from normal life to a sort of purgatory. And, interestingly, his one hope for remaining sane is the telephone that will link him to the known world—his mother's house.

5. Barnouw, 1970, p. 45.

6. Boorstin, 1973, pp. 307–410.

7. Since the "renewal movement" spurred by Vatican Council II in the 1960s, there has been a dramatic increase in access to electronic media among nuns and monastery brothers. Although media use varies from place to place, most nuns now have relatively free access to radio, telephone, and television (Father Francis L. Demers, Vicar for Religious, Diocese of Manchester, personal communication, May 1984). Communication among the Trappist monks was once highly restricted; brothers could not even speak to each other except in emergencies or with special permission from the Abbot. This changed in the late 1960s, however, and along with the increase in face-to-face communication has come an increase in access to electronic media. At the Abbey of the Genesee in Piffard, New York, for example, brothers now have access to a telephone (once the prerogative of the Abbot alone). The monks also use a computer for word processing and for running their bakery business, a video taping system is used to give "tours" of the facilities, and one brother is in charge of taping appropriate television programs off the air for later viewing by the monks. The Abbey also subscribes to weekly newspapers and new magazines. To maintain their goal of "solitude," however, the monks avoid watching regular broadcast television or reading daily newspapers (Brother Anthony, Guestmaster, Abbey of the Genesee, personal communication, May 1984).

8. Between 1960 and 1981 the number of people living alone in the United States nearly tripled. In 1982, the U.S. Bureau of the Census reported that nearly one out of every four households in the United States consisted of a person living alone. U.S. Bureau of the Census, 1982, p. 44. In a recent study on single-member households, Hughes and Gove, 1981, are surprised to discover that, contrary to earlier findings, people who live alone are no longer associated with many pathological behaviors, including higher rates of suicide. They suggest that their findings undermine previous thinking concerning the importance of "social integration" and the detrimental effects of "social isolation." What they overlook, however, is the opportunity that electronic media have provided for "selective integration." In an electronic age, people who live alone *physically* are no longer necessarily isolated *informationally.*

REFERENCES

Barnouw, Erik. *The Image Empire: A History of Broadcasting in the United States, Vol. 3— From 1953.* New York: Oxford Univ. Press, 1970.

Boorstin, Daniel J. *The Americans: The Democratic Experience.* New York: Random House, 1973.

Hacker, Helen M. "Women as a Minority Group." *Social Forces,* 30 (1951), 60–69.

Meyrowitz, Joshua. "Television and Interpersonal Behavior: Codes of Perception and Response." In *Inter/Media: Interpersonal Communication in a Media World.* Ed. Gary Gumpert and Robert Cathcart. New York: Oxford Univ. Press, 1979, pp. 56–76.

A.C. Nielsen, *Nielsen Report on Television.* Northbrook, IL: A.C. Nielsen Co. (An edition of this booklet is published every year.)

Popenoe, David. *Sociology.* 4rth ed. Englewood Cliffs, NJ: Prentice-Hall, 1980.

U.S. Bureau of the Census. *Statistical Abstract of the United States: 1982–83.* 103rd Ed. Washington, D.C.: U.S. Government Printing Office, 1982.

CHAPTER 6 Regulation and Control

6.1 DAVID EASTER AND JARICE HANSON

Deregulation and the Information Society

When radio became a mass medium, many governments established rules and regulations for the effective use of the airwaves. In the United States, the Radio Act of 1927 and the Communications Act of 1934 asserted that the "airwaves belong to the people." This philosophy, which held that the airwaves were a public trust, supported many of the regulations that sought to ensure fair access to the airwaves by broadcasters *and* a diversity of content for listeners.

Later, other forms of media were developed that used airwaves (television, satellites, and wireless telephony, for example), but these communication media were developed at a time in which a different philosophy began to dominate. "The marketplace" became a metaphor for an economic system in which free trade practices dominated. The new philosophy espoused a system in which competition was viewed as the best way to reduce costs and to ensure a diversity of products—or, in media, a diversity of content. At the same time, limited or no regulation by the government was viewed as the best way to allow trade practices to grow quickly and fairly.

The "marketplace" philosophy dominated many aspects of economic life in the United States starting in the 1970s. The deregulation of media industries throughout the 1980s had a significant impact on the way the media industries operated in the United States. The airwaves no longer belonged to "the people" but, instead, to those who held licenses to broadcast, or to operate media. The primary architect of the deregulation of the media industries was Federal Communications Commission chair Mark Fowler, who outlined his deregulatory plan and rationale in a 1988 article coauthored with Daniel Brenner, his former legal assistant, entitled "A Marketplace Approach to Broadcast Regulation."

Deregulation in many industries is a controversial topic. While some people subscribe to the marketplace "rules" and reject government intervention through regulation, many others feel that deregulation unavoidably leads to less diversity of content, greater concentration of ownership, and fewer actions in the public interest.

The following selection is from "Deregulation and the Information Society: Assessing the Marketplace Philosophy," in Jarice Hanson, ed., *Advances in Telematics* (Ablex, 1994). Authored by David Easter, an associate professor at the University of Ohio, Lima, and Jarice Hanson, a professor of communication at the University of Massachusetts–Amherst, it outlines the pros and cons of deregulation and the marketplace philosophy that has dominated media in the United States.

Key Concept: marketplace rules and deregulation of the media industries

Since the 1970s, the United States has embraced the theme of deregulation as a means of opening markets for competition while restricting government intervention in business affairs. While the free market philosophy may be better suited to some businesses than others, the attempt to create a deregulated marketplace in telecommunications has caused controversy in Congress, federal agencies, communications industries, and among groups of concerned citizens.

The trend in telecommunications deregulation has ranged in depth and breadth from the relaxation of structural regulations regarding the ownership and sale of communication licenses, to an attack on the legitimacy of content regulations such as the Fairness Doctrine. Changing licensing arrangements so drastically that some licenses (i.e., LPTV [Low Power Television]) are now disbursed in a lottery system, the FCC [Federal Communications Commission] sought to fundamentally reorder the way in which the communications marketplace operates and is regulated in this country. Invoking Adam Smith, the core of this program was based on the call for a "return" to free market principles in communications, in which the market is steered by the laws of supply and demand rather than by the laws of Washington.

Against what it saw as the social and economic forms of engineering as embodied in the "public trustee" doctrine, the FCC asserted that its free market approach would better meet the social and economic policy goals of the Communications Act of 1934: universal and affordable access to a diversity of information sources and services.

Specifically, proponents of a transition to a marketplace approach to communication asserted that deregulation would achieve three main goals addressing issues of structure, access, and content. Structurally, deregulation would lead to greater competition by opening markets to new players and in doing so, encourage development of alternative systems and services that could better meet the needs and desires of consumers. In terms of access, it would, through increased competition, lead to lower prices and thus more affordable access to communication services. In terms of content, it would lead to a greater diversity of information, thus enhancing First Amendment goals.

With almost 20 years of deregulation upon which to reflect, it is now important to consider how effective deregulation has been at meeting its specified goals. In this [selection] we examine the turn to a deregulatory perspective, both in terms of its ideological impact and its effect on the telecommunications marketplace since deregulation targeted these industries in the 1980s. To focus on the ongoing controversy, we will examine Congress's moves to "reregulate" certain areas, as exemplified by the cable television industry. We will attempt to situate the drive to deregulation and reregulation against the backdrop of a broader social dialogue concerning the emergence of the so-called *information society*.

Examining the move toward deregulation in the context of this broader dialogue is important, in that, all too often, analyses of policy debates remain at the level of policy rhetoric, while failing to assess the manner in which these policies reverberate with fundamental shifts in society. Thus, most popular debate continues to focus on questions such as: Is deregulation for or against the "public interest"; does it offer a more "efficient" way of organizing communication markets and the "marketplace of ideas"; and does it maximize or diminish "diversity of information" in society? It is important to contextualize deregulation as a force that both drives and echoes developments and imperatives within the social formation as a whole, in the service of the general transition to an information society.

THE IDEOLOGY OF DEREGULATION

Though the trend toward deregulation of business emerged during the Carter administration, the efforts were duly supported by Ronald Reagan. The chief architect of deregulation in the field of communications was Mark S. Fowler, Chair of the Federal Communications Commission from 1981–1987. Fowler's deregulatory scheme was articulated in its full state in "A Marketplace Approach to Broadcast Regulation" (Fowler & Brenner, 1988, pp. 209–257).

Fowler's analysis, and comments made during his tenure as chair of the FCC, project a political vision of some of the most basic questions concerning the fundamentals of communications policy. His articulation of "marketplace" ideology is developed in three major themes: (a) a literal, rather than metaphorical, linkage of the terms in the phrase *the marketplace of ideas*; (b) a definition of communication technology and the information transmitted as commodities (related to this is the articulation that *product* diversity equals *idea* diversity) (Entman & Wildman, 1992); and (c) the consumer interest equated with the "public interest."

The phrase *a marketplace of ideas* has long served as the benchmark of First Amendment law in communication policy, though it has been defined in a variety of ways, depending upon issue and time in history, and by judicial review. The fundamental principle of the political theory of liberalism, grounded in Enlightenment thought, was that a vibrant, open marketplace of ideas was essential to the construction of a diverse and democratic public sphere. Ideally, the emergence of such an idea marketplace involved "all voices having equal access to a neutral public sphere, where their unfettered rational discourse would culminate in the articulation of popular will" (Dahlgren, 1987, p. 25).

While theorists such as Habermas (1974) have noted that the expansion of industrial capitalism and commercial enterprise into virtually every domain of society has threatened the ideal goal of an autonomous public sphere, the principle of autonomy has continued to inform public policy in communication, as embodied in policies grounded in the public trustee doctrine. To this extent, the phrase *marketplace of ideas* has traditionally functioned metaphorically, with the marketplace seen not merely as involving business transactions among private owners but as involving the open exchange of ideas. In fact, since the Radio Act of 1912, communication law focused on the dangers of tipping the scales too greatly in the favor of private powers—hence, the popularity of the term *the public owns the airwaves.* Nonetheless, as evidenced by the ongoing debates concerning public and private rights in the communication marketplace, there has been a constant tension arising from the dual interests of a communication infrastructure that both promotes commercial enterprise and also ideals concerning an autonomous public sphere.

The deregulatory position, as articulated by Fowler, seeks to resolve this tension by forwarding a new, literal definition of *the marketplace of ideas.* The idea marketplace is just that, a marketplace, and it should operate like any other marketplace, according to the principle of private property and the dictates of maximizing economic efficiency. Similarly, communication players should be defined, not primarily as public fiduciaries, but rather as businesspeople who are also protected by the First Amendment. This interpretation sees vendors in a marketplace as equals but ignores the fact that some vendors are in a better position than others to operate. Thus, the idea that markets could operate in equal terms is fallacious; power relations always privilege some players, even in a market.

Similarly, while political theory based on the public trustee doctrine sought to maintain a distinction between the economic and informational aspects of the communications sphere, often asserting that economic imperatives may undermine rather than enhance informational goals, Fowler collapsed the distinction between the two realms. The achievement of market efficiency, in this view, will (naturally and unproblematically) achieve the promotion of social/informational goals, specifically the creation of a diverse marketplace of ideas from which a well-informed citizenry emerges and is nurtured. With this view, prior policies based on the public trustee doctrine introduced "distortions" in the idea marketplace. Policies like the Fairness Doctrine wrongly intervened in the marketplace, mistakenly attempting to replace market workings with information subsidies, if you will, both violating the laws of the market and raising First Amendment concerns.

INFORMATION AS A COMMODITY

The notion that market efficiency is synonymous with idea diversity is grounded in the treatment of technology and information as commodities. To the extent that information is treated as an economic category from this perspective, its diversity and abundance can be gauged through marketplace means, leading to the articulation that product diversity equals idea diversity. This view is made explicit in Fowler's controversial claim that television "is just another product. It's a toaster with pictures" ("Evangelist," 1983, p. 58). The distinction between television as a physical product (the set) and a means of communication (the words and images) is virtually eliminated. Implicit in Fowler's analogy is a recognition, however blithe, of the commodity nature of television —both the set itself and the information it carries as nothing more (or less) than commodities to be bought and sold in the marketplace.

In proposing the idea of auctioning licenses for future technologies relying on the electromagnetic spectrum, Fowler and Brenner wrote:

> A marketplace approach to exclusive use of radio frequencies would open all positions in the electromagnetic spectrum to bidding by those who want them. As with the allocation of other goods in society, the highest bidder would acquire exclusive rights to a particular frequency. In a fully deregulated marketplace, the highest bidder would make the best and highest use of the resource. (1982, p. 211)

The assumption here is that if frequencies were awarded to those with the economic means to optimally "manage" them, this would translate into maximal informational benefits accruing over that spectrum as well. While controversial at first, this proposal, for a variety of reasons, has received a warmer hearing among congressional Democrats in recent years. In fact, in a recent proposal to transfer 200 MHZ of spectrum from the government to the private sector (Emerging Technologies Act, H. R. 1407), there is growing support to award these frequencies via auctions. Reflecting the new bipartisan consensus, Representative Edward Markey (D-Mass.), House Telecommunications Subcommittee chair, said, "I think we can work this out. The philosophical basis for understanding is there" ("Spectrum Auction," 1991, p. 34).

Furthermore, a central argument of the Fowler FCC was that to the extent that a plethora of new communication technologies and outlets were developed and introduced, there would be a subsequent flourishing of the marketplace of ideas as well. Deregulation advocates then claim that the amount of product diversity provides an adequate index of the amount of idea diversity in society (Entman & Wildman, 1992, p. 8). Product diversity means that the best competitive conditions for promoting economic efficiency are being created, which will in turn lead to greater consumer choice and thus a strengthening of political will.

When the public is defined as synonymous with the consumer, actions once regarded as distinct from the commercial sphere, such as political decisions, become viewed purely in terms of consumption.

One might respond to this assertion by stating that while there may be an increase in the quantity of products and therefore information, the key question is, what kind of information? In other words, one could pose the issue of quantity versus quality. However, such an approach maintains a distinction between information as a social utility and information as a commodity, a distinction that the deregulationist camp does not accept. Perhaps, then, this question must be reformulated in terms of the relationship between communication deregulation and broader societal trends.

THE IDEOLOGICAL DOUBLE-BLIND

What are the ideological underpinnings of the move toward deregulation of the communication marketplace, what have been the consequences of this move in the market, and how does this comport with predictions concerning the rise of a new information economy? We can begin with the assumption that deregulation was designed to fuel the transition to an information economy, and in fact to transform American political economy generally.

Furthermore, it is clear that the move to "marketplace principles" in communication comports with notions concerning the accelerating privatization of the information economy. However, deregulatory philosophy does not agree with its critics that the result will be the creation of a society of information "haves" and "have-nots." To the contrary, it is argued that deregulation will usher in the democratization of benefits, in terms of economic growth and informational abundance, that the prior public trustee doctrine claimed to champion. However, as analyzed later, the impact of deregulation has called into question this claim. If we examine the ideological perspective and key philosophical assumptions underlying deregulation, we find that the attainment of these goals becomes deeply problematic.

Fejes and Schwoch (1987) and others have written that the ideological underpinning of much of the literature on the information society involves an assumption that technology equals progress. As Slack (1989) points out, there is no necessary connection between these two terms; a society could just as easily orient itself around the notion that technology undermines progress. Yet, such "articulations" reach the status of ideology when they become "naturalized" as unproblematic, over and against other possible alternative articulations that are rendered subordinate. As Slack (p. 333) states, "ideology is the mechanism that organizes the multiplicity of connections into a temporarily essentialized system of representation within which we live out those connections as real." We can analyze the ideology of deregulation in terms of how its discourse on the information society has become dominant and thus naturalized, and thus how it has subordinated other perspectives. Specifically, this ideology functions to naturalize the move toward the commodification of the information sphere: The idea marketplace is viewed as operating under the same principles as the business marketplace, ideas are viewed as commodities, and the public exerts its political will through consumption decisions.

Generally, this ideological perspective deviates significantly from Enlightenment principles and underscores Habermas's fears about the erosion of this sphere. The public sphere, and marketplace within it, was supposed to be autonomous from commerce and political coercion. Also, *public* was defined as distinct from consumption. Furthermore, information was defined not as a good but a social utility, not a commodity but a social relation. At least in theory, if not always in practice, these "articulations" have formed the basis for U.S. communications policy.

Deregulation advocates might respond to this by stating that such assertions take place at the level of rhetoric, while one must look to the actual marketplace to see that a marketplace approach actually achieves these goals. However, there is little evidence to indicate that deregulation, as it has been implemented, achieves anything but a further privatization and commodification of the information sphere.

THE IDEOLOGY OF THE INFORMATION AGE

If, as noted earlier, U.S. communications policy has always been anchored precariously on the divide between private interests and the public good, and if, as also noted, there has been a general ideological commitment to the belief that technological progress ultimately will serve as the mediator of conflicts along this divide, then Fejes and Schwoch's scenario of the coming information society is a sobering one. In fact, it is the realization that the new information technology will not solve all the problems of its introduction (e.g., the problem of massive structural unemployment) that may fuel the transition to what they call a "two-sector" information society. Specifically, what the authors predict is not an entire transformation but rather a shift in the political, economic, and social principles governing the material and informational sectors of the social formation. Most fundamentally, they see an overturning of the two sectors: The material sector will no longer function under free market principles as it has traditionally.

Instead, in response to endemic problems such as structural unemployment and the decline of the material manufacturing base, the state will be compelled to intervene in the material sector through industrial planning and social welfare policies. In the face of growing scarcity of material resources, material production will be reorganized and spread to material consumption. The result will be less diversity and controlled consumption of consumer products. In this sense, while scarcity will be the operating principle, the material sector will become more egalitarian, compared to the prior organization in which ability-to-pay served as the criteria of access to material wealth and status.

Fejes and Schwoch predict that the information sector, on the other hand, will be characterized by increasing privatization and commodification: "Information itself will become a commodity to be produced according to market demand" (p. 165). The information sector, once envisioned as a social good, will now be under the principles of the private sector.

The state will intervene strongly to protect property rights and also to protect American companies from foreign competition; however, the information economy will otherwise be left to governance via private ownership and market competition. Thus, historic policies/ideologies concerning the material and information sectors will be inverted:

> With information fully defined as private property, the production of information products will be owned and controlled by private interests. The distribution and consumption of information products will be organized primarily on the basis of effective market demand and not socially defined need. Thus the information economy will be highly inegalitarian with highly stratified consumption patterns. Where the material economy will be an entitlement economy, the information economy will be a commodity economy. (p. 166)

As such, social/class status will no longer be defined by access to the material economy but rather to the information economy: "It will be the workings of the information economy that will define the overall class structure of the entire society" (p. 167). In this sense, the authors believe, contrary to certain notions of the information society as freeing us from material constraints and inequities and class divisions, these will be reproduced but in an inverted form. The material sector, traditionally operated under the principles of private property, will become "socialized"; the information sector, traditionally operated under Enlightenment notions of information as a common good, will become privatized.

While Fejes and Schwoch do not claim that their scenario describes exactly the form that the information society will take, it questions key optimistic assumptions, and it serves to highlight a major risk in the transition: that our Enlightenment-based concepts of *information* and *knowledge* will be redefined, threatening a total loss of the autonomy of this sphere to privatization and commodification.

EVALUATING DEREGULATION

As we have discussed, deregulation was intended to achieve three main goals: (a) structurally, to create a more level playing field by opening markets to competition and a host of new players; (b) in terms of access, to drive down prices, making communications services more affordable; and (c) in terms of content, to lead to a greater diversity of information.

While political and ideological posturing influences the perceived success of deregulation in achieving these goals, it is interesting to hear the views of Mark Fowler, who now looks back at his tenure as FCC chair with a different eye. When asked in early 1992 whether he thought that deregulation in the communications industries had worked as well as he had hoped, he responded with an emphatic "No." He elaborated by stating that it could have worked if the lobbyists and politicians had maintained the original vision of what deregulation had intended (Fowler, personal communication, February 3, 1992). Fowler sharply criticized Washington for losing perspective and allowing special interest groups and politics to muddle the implementation of policy.

Whatever the merits of this critique, it reveals Fowler's characteristic tendency to apply the theoretical principles of free market theory to solve the problem of "inefficiency" generally, including in the government sphere. In other words, we can see here a vision of a policy "marketplace" that runs with the same systemic pristineness as the "open" economic marketplace, somehow released from the distorting effects of power brokerage and vested interests. As an economic model, the image is one of rational action, but as a social phenomenon, it is too restricted to address the vicissitudes of real action.

The battle over deregulation of the cable industry in the 1980s certainly exemplified the less pristine manner in which the policy-making process generally unfolds, with Congress attempting to enact a major deregulatory initiative while coterminously seeking to appease the various special interests involved.

CABLE DEREGULATION AND REREGULATION

An analysis of cable policy not only brings into question the assumption that deregulation will increase the number of players in the marketplace and therefore enhance competition and product innovation, it also casts doubt on whether economic efficiency will promote social/informational goals.

The cable television industry was originally regulated in a patchwork, case-by-case basis, stemming from the explosion of cable stations in the 1970s. The FCC, claiming that cable delivery was not a threat to the dominance of broadcast television, was initially reluctant to assume the task of overseeing cable's development. Because cable did not use the electromagnetic spectrum for distribution, it was touted as an example of an alternative technology that would offer a greater number of channels for distribution, thus enhancing the number of "voices" (or "ideas") in the marketplace.

The *Cable Communications Policy Act of 1984* was written as an amendment to the *Communications Act of 1934*, and is known as the document that deregulated the cable industry. What has happened since 1984, however, suggests a measurement for the effectivity of deregulation.

In terms of the *structural* goals of deregulation, the number of homes cabled has increased, in part due to the growth of cable franchises awarded, but the actual number of information outlets has not kept pace. As Entman and Wildman (1992, p. 10) have written, the number of multiple system operators (MSOs) that coordinate program development and sharing for cable systems have actually functioned to effect a "further narrowing [of] the gateway" between producers of ideas and information and the public. MSOs save costs by sharing facilities and sources.

*David Easter
and Jarice
Hanson*

The dominance of such efficiency-based arrangements, according to Entman and Wildman, also questions the assumption that deregulation will spur product innovation and introduction. The economic and technical efficiencies derived by producers and users of large networks, with common technical standards, may mitigate against this: "Research has shown that network industries may not be able to switch to new, more effective technologies or benefit from the switch, especially when the new technologies and organizations are incompatible with those they replace." The debate over the introduction of High Definition Television (HDTV) is an example. The disruption caused by the need to switch standards and product could provide a disincentive to an industry that has built its networks and audience around use of a particular technical standard and technology: "In such situations, confidence in the efficiency of a competitive marketplace may be unfounded and government intervention in an otherwise competitive industry may be justified" (p. 10).

In terms of the affordable access goal, the cost of subscriber access has increased significantly. According to the General Accounting Office [GAO] 1991 Survey of Cable Television Rates and Services, from 1986 (when deregulation went into effect) to 1991, rates for the most popular basic cable tier rose 61%; rates for the lowest priced tier increased 56%. Meanwhile, the cost of consumer goods rose only 17.9% during the same 5-year period. Between December 1989 and April 1991, rates for lowest price cable service rose 9%. During the same time period, the average number of channels offered on this tier decreased by one. Said Senator Daniel Inouye: "Consumers are paying more for less." Also, the report found that cable companies are not informing customers about services. Many touted a low-priced tier, but would not inform customers that it existed (Inouye, 1991, p. S11092).

Furthermore, the FCC's June 1991 "effective competition" decision (FCC, 1991) fails to address the problem of rates. It raised the criteria for effective competition by ruling that rate regulation would apply in markets with less than six broadcast signals, up from the prior criteria of three. However, GAO reported that even under this criteria, 80% of subscribers' rates would not be subject to rate regulation.

In terms of content, along with the tendency to control against alternative programming as described earlier, there is a growing commodification of information, a blurring of the lines between news, entertainment, and advertising. *Infotainment* may be the operant word for the form in which an increasing portion of the media-generated information in our society is packaged and disseminated. While this merging of news, advertising, and entertainment may reflect production efficiencies, it does not counter the deregulationist assertion that "innovation" in economic goods leads to innovation in the idea marketplace.

Congress has recently sought to redress what many see as the negative consequences of deregulation through the Cable Television Consumer Protection Act (S. 12, H.R. 1303). Focusing specifically on the need to control skyrocketing rates and the problem of monopolistic practices, this "reregulation" initiative acknowledges that some of the worst fears about the consequences of deregulation have become a reality.

Sponsors of the bill charge that the cable companies have instituted unfair rate increases and lowered standards for customer service and protection.

Also, the companies have engaged in anticompetitive practices against video programmers and competitors, to the point where, as then Senator Albert Gore (D-Tenn.) (1991, p. S590) put it, the MSOs have "life or death" control over new programming services.

The legislation takes several measures to counter these developments. It empowers the FCC to regulate rates for the basic tier of service, which includes the retransmission of television signals, and it provides broadcasters with more power concerning terms of carriage of their signals. It requires the cable companies to deal with other video distributors in a nondiscriminatory way, in terms of prices and conditions of sale of programming. Furthermore, the cable companies cannot discriminate against noncable programmers seeking access, or require these programmers to give them a financial interest as a condition of carriage. Finally, the bill gives the FCC authority to establish rates, terms, and conditions for access to leased access channels, including for billing and collection. This provision is an important corrective to the Cable Act, which, since it allowed the cable companies to set the price and terms of carriage and not to handle billing, rendered leased access "a virtual dead letter" (Aufterheide, 1992, p. 56).

Even though its sponsors touted it as a "modest" and "balanced" attempt to reregulate, the bill faced "stiff challenges from a strong cable lobby and a White House opposed to sterner regulation" (p. 56), serving testimony to the dominance of deregulatory philosophy in the current policy environment. Furthermore, it underscores how far an industry, which in the late 1960s and early 1970s was rallied around by industry officials, policymakers, and grass roots activists alike as a potential "electronic soapbox" (Streeter, 1987) has acceded to commercial logic and control.

Despite this environment, some argue that much stronger "reregulation" measures are required. Aufterheide (1992), for example, suggests that the problem of control over information could be addressed through reconsidering the application of common carrier regulations to the cable industry, something that the Cable Act explicitly prohibited. Similarly regulatory measures concerning horizontal integration and cross-ownership could be considered. As for universal service, a more "basic, basic" tier could be created for low-income subscribers. Finally, there could be a renewed commitment to public access channels, including the creation of access centers and funding for production and distribution facilities. However, thus far, "legislative reform proposals have been virtually silent on access, much less on any as yet untested mechanisms to create new public spaces" (Aufterheide, 1992, p. 60). Generally, given the uphill battle confronting even modest reregulatory proposals, the outlook for renewed consideration of these issues is bleak.

CONCLUSION

The debate over cable reregulation may be indicative of future policy reform analyses and discussions as the impact of industrywide deregulation is gauged.

It is possible, however, that one of the most important reshapings of the industry will occur at the most fundamental level—the licensing process itself. Indeed, the strategic lynchpin of the Fowler FCC's deregulatory project involved the establishment of a system of property rights in telecommunications. To many in the free market camp, privatization of the licensing process, replacing the comparative hearing process with lotteries and auctions, was the necessary precondition for developing a truly market-based communication system. Ultimately, under this scenario, the FCC's regulatory role largely would be reduced to that of "spectrum management," that is, as a resolver of property disputes between frequency owners.

Given that a bipartisan consensus has emerged in Congress to auction off the spectrum to the private sector, such a scenario does not appear as far-fetched as it once did. Potentially, money derived from auctions could be used to improve the telecommunications infrastructure or to fund new and existing programs, services, and technologies, as some members of Congress have proposed. However, the Bush administration and the majority of Democrats who supported the plan favored funneling auction revenues to offset the federal deficit. According to an administration official, the shift to an auction process "promotes spectrum efficiency and provides fiscal relief to the American taxpayers" ("Spectrum Auction," 1991, p. 34). Whatever the merits of providing fiscal relief, consideration of the relationship between such efficiency-based proposals and the enhancement of the public sphere is largely absent from the dialogue. Instead, this discourse reveals that notions concerning communications resources as a "public good" are being eclipsed by economic imperatives, giving credence to Fejes and Schwoch's scenario for the privatization of the information sector.

REFERENCES

Aufterheide, P. (1992). Cable television and the public interest. *Journal of Communication, 42,* 52–65.

Dahlgren, P. (1987). Ideology and information in the public sphere. In J. D. Slack & F. Fejes (Eds.), *The ideology of the information age* (pp. 25–45). Norwood, NJ: Ablex Publishing Corp.

Entman, R. M., & Wildman, S. S. (1992). Reconciling economic and non-economic perspectives on media policy: Transcending the "Marketplace of Ideas." *Journal of Communication, 42,* 5–19.

Evangelist of the airwaves. (1983, November 21). *Time,* p. 58.

Federal Communications Commission. (1991, June 13). *Reexamination of the effective competition standard for the regulation of cable television basic service rates, MM Docket No. 90-4, FCC 90-412, Report and Order and Second Further Notice of Proposed Rulemaking.*

Fejes, F., & Schwoch J. (1987). A competing ideology for the information age: A two-sector model for the new information society. In J. D. Slack & F. Fejes (Eds.), *The ideology of the information age* (pp. 159–169). Norwood, NJ: Ablex Publishing Corp.

Fowler, M. S., & Brenner, D. L. (1988). A marketplace approach to broadcast regulation. *Texas Law Review, 60* (2), 207–257.

Gore, A. (1991, January 14). Remarks. *Congressional Record*, pp. S589-S592. Washington: Government Printing Office.

Habermas, J. (1974). The public sphere. *New German Critique, 3,* 49–55.

Inouye, D. (1991, July 26). Remarks. *Congressional Record*, p. S11092. Washington: Government Printing Office.

Slack, J. D. (1989). Contextualizing technology. In B. Dervin, L. Grossberg, B. J. O'Keefe, & E. Wartella (Eds.), *Rethinking communication* (Vol. 2, pp. 329–345). Newbury Park, CA: Sage.

Spectrum auction pros and cons debated. (1991, October 14). *Broadcasting*, p. 34.

Streeter, T. (1987). The cable fable revisited: Discourse, policy, and the making of cable television. *Critical Studies in Mass Communication, 4,* 174–200.

6.2 ROBERT W. McCHESNEY

Corporate Media and the Threat to Democracy

In reaction to the effects of deregulation, media companies have increasingly merged and undergone changes in ownership. Robert McChesney, an associate professor in the School of Journalism and Mass Communication at the University of Wisconsin–Madison, has written extensively on the impact of deregulation and the increasing globalization of major media firms. He has carefully and painstakingly identified how these regulatory changes in ownership have severely limited democratic practices.

In the following selection from his Open Media Pamphlet Series volume, *Corporate Media and the Threat to Democracy* (Seven Stories Press, 1997), McChesney discusses the corporate media structure that has resulted from deregulation and examines how these ownership changes have affected the practice of journalism. McChesney portrays the culture of the corporate media giants as limiting ideas to those related to selling products. He indicates that increasing commercialism will be the undercurrent of all future media content and that alternative viewpoints or controversial topics are being screened from viewers by zealous corporations that focus on the profit margin above all else. McChesney demonstrates careful scholarship and attention to detail in portraying a future of "nonregulation" in which media content is entirely controlled by the desire of corporations to make a profit and to influence viewers—a frightening vision of the role of media in our society.

As you read this selection, consider whether or not there are alternatives to the scenario that the author provides. How will future research into the area of media and social life be conducted? Will new research paradigms be developed to account for the increasing control exercised by corporate media giants? What role might media play in a world that is increasingly concerned with consumerism?

Key Concept: corporate media content and control

CORPORATE MEDIA CONSOLIDATION

The journalism that emerged in the 20th century is a product well suited to the needs of the dominant media firms and advertisers that profited from the status quo. Yet the system was far from stable. On the one hand, new technologies like radio and television emerged and changed many aspects of media and journalism. On the other hand, the market moved inexorably toward becoming an integrated oligopoly, with a handful of firms dominating all forms of U.S. media, from radio, television, music and film to newspapers, magazines, and book publishing. In the early 1980s, Ben Bagdikian's *The Media Monopoly* concluded that less than 50 firms had come to dominate the entirety of the U.S. media, with the result that journalism was increasingly losing its ability to address the role and nature of corporate power in the U.S. political economy. As Bagdikian put it, the range of debate in U.S. journalism concerning capitalism and corporate power was roughly equivalent to the range of debate in the Soviet media concerning the nature of communism and the activities of the Communist Party. In the decade following the publication of *The Media Monopoly*, as traditional ownership regulations were relaxed, the market continued to consolidate at an even faster rate. By the time of the fourth edition of *The Media Monopoly*, in 1992, Bagdikian calculated that mergers and acquisitions had reduced the number of dominant media firms to two dozen.

Since 1992 there has been an unprecedented wave of mergers and acquisitions among media giants, highlighted by the Time Warner purchase of Turner and the Disney acquisition of Cap Cities/ABC. Fewer than ten colossal vertically integrated media conglomerates now dominate U.S. media. The five largest firms—with annual sales in the $10–25 billion range—are News Corporation, Time Warner, Disney, Viacom, and TCI. These firms are major producers of entertainment and media software and have distribution networks like television networks, cable channels and retail stores. Time Warner, for example, owns music recording studios, film and television production studios, several cable television channels, cable broadcasting systems, amusement parks, the WB television network, book publishing houses, magazine publishing interests, retail stores, motion picture theaters, and much else. In most of the above categories, Time Warner ranks among the top five firms in the world. The next three media firms include NBC (owned by General Electric), Universal (formerly MCA, owned by Seagram), and Sony. All three of these firms are conglomerates with non-media interests, with Sony and GE being huge electronics concerns that at least double the annual sales of any other media firm.

Below this first group there are another dozen or so quite large media firms—usually conglomerates—with annual sales generally in the $2–5 billion range.[1] This list includes Westinghouse (owner of CBS), Gannett, Cox Enterprises, The New York Times, Advance Communications, Comcast, Hearst, Tribune Co., The Washington Post Co., Knight-Ridder, Times-Mirror, DirecTV (owned by General Motors and AT&T), Dow Jones, Reader's Digest, and McGraw-Hill. By the year 2000 it is probable that some of these firms will make deals to get larger or be acquired by other firms seeking to get larger.

The most striking development in the 1990s has been the emergence of a global commercial media market, utilizing new technologies and the global trend toward de-regulation. A global oligopolistic market that covers the spectrum of media is now crystallizing with very high barriers to entry. National markets remain, and they are indispensable for understanding any particular national situation, but they are becoming secondary in importance. The U.S. based firms just named dominate the global media market along with a handful of European-based firms and a few Latin American and Asian operations. By all accounts they will do so for a long time to come.[2] Firms like Disney and Time Warner have seen their non-U.S. revenues climb from around 15 percent in 1990 to 30 percent in 1996. Sometime in the next decade both firms expect to earn a majority of their income outside of the United States. What stimulates much of the creation of a global media market is the growth in commercial advertising worldwide, especially by transnational firms. Advertising tends to be conducted by large firms operating in oligopolistic markets. With the increasing globalization of the world economy, advertising has come to play a crucial role for the few hundred firms that dominate it. From this vantage point it becomes clear, also, how closely linked the U.S. and global media systems are to the market economy.[3]

Media firms have great incentive to merge, acquire, and globalize. It is when the effects of sheer size, conglomeration, and globalization are combined that a sense of the profit potential emerges. When Disney produces a film, for example, it can also guarantee the film showings on pay cable television and commercial network television, it can produce and sell soundtracks based on the film, it can create spin-off television series, it can produce related amusement park rides, CD-roms, books, comics, and merchandise to be sold in Disney retail stores. Moreover, Disney can promote the film and related material incessantly across all its media properties. In this climate, even films that do poorly at the box office can become profitable. Disney's *Hunchback of Notre Dame* (1996) generated a disappointing $99 million at the North American box office. However, according to *Adweek* magazine, it is expected to generate $500 million in profit (not just revenues), after the other revenue streams are taken into account. And films that are hits can become spectacularly successful. Disney's *The Lion King* (1994) earned several hundred million at the box office, yet generated over $1 billion in profit for Disney.[4] Moreover, media conglomerates can and do use the full force of their various media holdings to promote their other holdings. They do so incessantly. In sum, the profit whole for the vertically integrated firm can be significantly greater than the profit potential of the individual parts in isolation. Firms without this cross-selling and cross-promotional potential are simply incapable of competing in the global marketplace.

In establishing new ventures, media firms are likely to participate in joint ventures, whereby they link up—usually through shared ownership—with one or more other media firms on specific media projects. Joint ventures are attractive because they reduce the capital requirements and risk on individual firms and permit the firms to spread their resources more widely. Each of the eight largest U.S. media firms has, on average, joint ventures with four of the other seven giants. They each also have even more ventures with smaller media firms. Beyond joint ventures, there is also overlapping direct ownership of these firms. Seagram, owner of MCA, for example, owns 15 percent of Time Warner and has other media equity holdings.[5] TCI is a major shareholder in Time Warner and has holdings in numerous other media firms.[6] The Capital Group Companies mutual fund, valued at $250 billion, is among the very largest shareholders in TCI, News Corporation, Seagram, Time Warner, Viacom, Disney, Westinghouse, and several other smaller media firms.[7]

Even without joint ventures and cross-ownership, competition in oligopolistic media markets is hardly "competitive" in the economic sense of the term. Reigning oligopolistic markets are dominated by a handful of firms that compete—often quite ferociously within the oligopolistic framework—on a non-price basis and are protected by severe barriers to entry. The "synergies" of recent mergers rest on and enhance monopoly power. No start-up studio, for example, had successfully joined the Hollywood oligopoly in 60 years.[8] Rupert Murdoch of News Corporation poses the rational issue for an oligopolistic firm when pondering how to proceed in the media market: "We can join forces now, or we can kill each other and then join forces."[9]

When one lays the map of joint ventures over the global media marketplace, even the traditional levels of competition associated with oligopolistic markets may be exaggerated. "Nobody can really afford to get mad with their competitors," says TCI chairman John Malone, "because they are partners in one area and competitors in another."[10] *The Wall Street Journal* observes that media "competitors wind up switching between the roles of adversaries, prized customers and key partners."[11] In this sense the U.S. and global media and communication market exhibits tendencies not only of an oligopoly, but of a cartel or at least a "gentleman's club."

CORPORATE MEDIA CULTURE

The corporate media produce some excellent fare, and much that is good, especially in the production of entertainment material in commercially lucrative genres. But in view of the extraordinary resources the corporate media command, the quality is woeful. In the final analysis, this is a thoroughly commercial system with severe limitations for our politics and culture. As George Gerbner puts it, the media giants "have nothing to tell, but plenty to sell." The corporate media are carpet-bombing people with advertising and commercialism, whether they like it or not. Moreover, the present course is one where much of the world's entertainment and journalism will be provided by a handful of enormous firms, with invariably pro-profit and pro-global market political positions on the central issues of our times. The implications for political democracy, by any standard, are troubling.

One need only look at the United States to see where and how journalism factors into the operations of the media giants. By the end of the 1980s, the wheels had come off U.S. journalism. In the new world of conglomerate capitalism the goal of the entire media product was to have a direct positive effect on the firm's earnings statement. The press, and the broadcast media, too, increasingly use surveys to locate the news that would be enjoyed by the affluent market desired by advertisers.[12] This, in itself, seriously compromises a major tenet of journalism: that the news should be determined by the public interest, not by the self-interest of owners or advertisers. It also meant that media firms effectively wrote off the bottom 15–50 percent of U.S. society, depending upon the medium. As newspapers, for example, have become increasingly dependent upon advertising revenues for support, they have become anti-democratic forces in society. When newspapers still received primary support from circulation income, they courted every citizen with the funds necessary to purchase the paper, often a pittance. But now they are reliant on advertisers whose sole concern is access to targeted markets. Hence media managers aggressively court the affluent while the balance of the population is pushed to the side. Indeed, the best journalism being done today is that directed to the business class by *The Wall Street Journal, Business Week,* and the like. We have quality journalism aimed at the affluent and directed to their needs and interests, and schlock journalism for the masses. As Walter Cronkite observes, intense commercial pressures have converted television journalism into "a stew of trivia, soft features and similar tripe."[13]

To do effective journalism is expensive, and corporate managers realize that the surest way to fatten profits is to fire editors and reporters and fill the news hole with inexpensive syndicated material and fluff. The result has been a sharp polarization among journalists, with salaries and benefits climbing for celebrity and privileged journalists at the elite news media while conditions have deteriorated for the balance of the working press. Layoffs among news workers have been widespread in the past decade; one study reveals that there has been a marked decrease in the number of Washington network correspondents alone in that period.[14] With all this unemployment, salaries for non-elite journalists have plummeted, and beginning salaries are so low that young journalists have a difficult time supporting themselves. These developments have contributed to a collapse in the morale of U.S. journalists, a real loss of faith in their enterprise. The past few years have seen several major editors and journalists leave the profession in anger over these trends.[15] James Squires, former editor of the *Chicago Tribune,* argues that the corporate takeover of the media has led to the "death of journalism."[16] And, aside from the pursuit of profit, even business commentators have been struck by how the media conglomerates are willing to censor and distort journalism to suit their corporate interests. Nowhere is this more evident than in the virtual blackout of critical coverage of the operations of the giant media and telecommunication firms, beyond what is produced in the business press and directed at investors.[17]

What is tragic—or absurd—is that the dominant perception of the "free press" still regards the government as the sole possible foe of freedom. That this notion of press freedom has been and is aggressively promoted by the giant media corporations should be no surprise, though that is rarely noted. Imagine if the federal government demanded that newspaper and broadcast journalism staffs be cut in half, that foreign bureaus be closed, and that news be tailored to suit the government's self-interests. There would be an outcry that would make the Alien & Sedition Acts, the Red Scares and Watergate seem like child's play. Yet when corporate America aggressively pursues the exact same policies, scarcely a murmur of dissent can be detected in the political culture.

With fewer journalists, limited budgets, low salaries and lower morale, the balance of power has shifted dramatically to the public relations industry, which seeks to fill the news media with coverage sympathetic to its clients. In the United States today, one expert estimates that there are 20,000 more PR agents than there are journalists.[18] Their job is to offer the news media sophisticated video press releases and press packets to fill the news hole, or contribute to the story that does fill the news hole.

The effects of this PR blitz on journalism can be seen on the two most important issues in U.S. politics in the 1990s: foreign trade and health care. These two issues are unusual because they provided clear public policy debates on the types of all important long-term issues (globalization of the economy and collapse of living standards and economic security) that professional journalism usually avoids. In the case of GATT [General Agreements on Tariffs and Trade] and NAFTA [North American Free Trade Agreement], the large transnational corporations were almost unanimous and aggressive in their support of "free trade." While there was not the same unanimity in the business community regarding health care, the insurance industry had an enormous stake in maintaining control of the health sector. In both cases, these powerful interests were able to neutralize public opinion, even though, initially, based on personal experience, it was against GATT and NAFTA and for a single-payer health care system.

The demise of journalism was readily apparent in this process. In each of these issues, big business mounted sophisticated, multi-million-dollar PR campaigns to obfuscate the issues, confuse the public and, if not weaken the opposition to the business position, at least make it easier for powerful interests to ignore popular opinion. In effect, corporate America has been able to create its own "truth," and our news media seem unwilling or incapable of fulfilling the mission our society so desperately needs it to fill. And this is the likely pattern for the new global commercial journalism of the media giants.

Nor are newspaper and broadcast journalism the only casualties of a corporate-dominated, profit-motivated media system. The corporate takeover of much of U.S. magazine publishing has resulted in increased pressure upon editors to highlight editorial fare that pleases advertisers or that serves the political agenda of the corporate owners. By 1996 magazine editors were calling for a minimal standard to be voluntarily accepted by their corporate overlords that would respect some rudimentary notion of editorial integrity. A similar process is taking place with book publishing. After a wave of mergers and acquisitions, three of the world's four largest media giants now own the three largest global book publishers. At the retail end, U.S. bookselling is becoming highly concentrated into the hands of a few massive chains; nearly one-half of U.S. retail bookselling is accounted for by Barnes & Noble and Borders.[19] This corporatization of publishing has led to a marked shift to the political right in what types of books clear the corporate hurdles, as well as a trend to make books look "like everything else the mass media turn out." Book publishing, which not too long ago played an important role in stimulating public culture and debate, has largely abandoned that function, except to push the ideas of the corporate owners' favored interests. "The drive for profit," writes former Random House book editor Andre Schiffrin, "fits like an iron mask on our cultural output." He concludes that we may well have corporate "purveyors of culture who feel that one idea can fit all."[20]

Corporate concentration and profit-maximization have similarly disastrous effects upon music, radio, television and film. The stakes have been raised for commercial success. *Variety* concluded after a 1996 study of 164 films that "Films with budgets greater than $60 million are more likely to generate profit than cheaper pics."[21] One Hollywood movie producer notes that media mergers accelerate the existing trend toward "greater emphasis on the bottom line, more homogenization of content and less risk taking."[22] The one film genre that has proven least risky and has the greatest upside has been "action" fare. This is encouraged by the rapid rise in non-U.S. sales for Hollywood, such that they are now greater than domestic revenues. Violent fare, requiring less nuance than comedy or drama, is especially popular across markets. As one media executive said, "Kicking butt plays everywhere."[23] The other route for the corporate media giants to lessen risk is to specifically produce films that lend themselves to complementary merchandising of products: The revenues and profits generated here can often be equal or superior to those generated by traditional box-office sales or video rentals.[24] The ultimate result of this marriage of Hollywood and Madison Avenue came with the 1996 release of Time Warner's film *Space Jam*, based upon Nike shoe commercials, starring Bugs Bunny and Michael Jordan and directed by "the country's hottest director of commercials." As *Forbes* magazine puts it, "the real point of the movie is to sell, sell, sell." Time Warner "is looking to hawk up to $1 billion in toys, clothing, books, and sports gear based on the movie characters."[25] The implications for the "art" of filmmaking are evident.

Indeed, the commercialism of the media system permeates every aspect of its being. The volume of advertising has increased rapidly in the United States over the past decade; U.S. television networks now broadcast 6,000 commercials per week, up 50 percent since 1983. As *Business Week* observes, "the buying public has been virtually buried alive in ads." Desperate to be seen and heard, advertisers are turning to new approaches, including "stamping their messages on everything that stands still."[26] To circumvent this commercial blizzard, and the consumer skepticism to traditional advertising, marketers are working to infiltrate entertainment. There are over two dozen consultancies in Los Angeles, for example, just to help link marketers with film and television producers, usually to get the marketer's product "placed" and promoted surreptitiously inside the programming.[27] "The connections between Madison Avenue and Hollywood have grown so elaborate," *Business Week* concludes, "that nothing is off-limits when studios and advertisers sit down to hammer out the marketing campaign."[28] Traditional notions of separation of editorial and commercial interests are weakening. Advertisers play a large and increasing role in determining media content. Media firms solicit the capital and input of advertising firms as they prepare programming. "Networks are happy to cater to advertisers who want a bigger role," one report stated.[29] A U.S. advertising executive expects advertisers everywhere to demand similar arrangements. "This is just a forerunner of what we are going to see as we get to 500 [television] channels. Every client will have their own programming tailored to their own needs, based on their ad campaign."[30]

1. Diane Mermigas, "Still to come: smaller media alliances," *Electronic Media,* February 5, 1996, p. 38.

2. Doug Wilson, *Strategies of the Media Giants* (London: Pearson Professional Ltd., 1996), p. 5.

3. See Edward S. Herman and Robert W. McChesney, *The Global Media: The New Missionaries of Global Capitalism* (London: Cassell, 1997).

4. Marla Matzer, "Contented Kingdoms," *Superbrands '97,* supplement to *Adweek,* October 7, 1996, pp. 30, 33.

5. Bernard Simon, "Seagram to hold on to 15% stake in Time Warner," *The Financial Times,* June 1, 1995, p. 18.

6. Raymond Snoddy, "Master of bits at home in the hub," *Financial Times,* May 28, 1996, p. 17.

7. Catherine E. Celebrezze, "The Man Who Bought the Media," *Extra!,* Vol. 9, No. 2, March–April 1996, pp. 21–22.

8. Ronald Grover, "Plenty of Dreams, Not Enough Work?" *Business Week,* July 22, 1996, p. 65.

9. Paula Dwyer, "Can Rupert Conquer Europe?" *Business Week,* March 25, 1996, p. 169.

10. Raymond Snoddy, "Master of bits at home in the hub," *Financial Times,* May 28, 1996, p. 17.

11. Elizabeth Jensen and Eben Shapiro, "Time Warner's Fight With News Corp. Belies Mutual Dependence," *The Wall Street Journal,* October 28, 1996, p. A1.

12. Alison Carper, "Paint-By-Numbers Journalism: How Reader Surveys and Focus Groups Subvert a Democratic Press," Discussion paper D-19, Joan Shorenstein Center on the Press, Politics and Public Policy, April 1995.

13. Dorothy Rabinowitz, "Cronkite Returns to Airwaves," *The Wall Street Journal,* December 9, 1996, p. A12.

14. Penn Kimball, *Downsizing the News: Network Cutbacks in the Nation's Capital* (Washington, D.C.: Woodrow Wilson Center Press, 1994).

15. See, for example, Mort Rosenblum, *Who Stole the News?* (New York: John Wiley & Sons, 1993); Doug Underwood, *When MBAs Rule the Newsroom: How the Marketers and Managers are Reshaping Today's Media* (New York: Columbia University Press, 1993); John McManus, *Market-Driven Journalism: Let the Citizen Beware!* (Thousand Oaks, Cal.: Sage, 1994); Dennis Mazzocco, *Networks of Power: Corporate TV's Threat to Democracy* (Boston: South End Press, 1994).

16. James Squires, *Read All About It! The Corporate Takeover of America's Newspapers* (New York: Times Books, 1993).

17. Elizabeth Lesly, "Self-Censorship Is Still Censorship," *Business Week,* December 16, 1996, p. 78.

18. See John Stauber and Sheldon Rampton, *Toxic Sludge is Good for You: Lies, Damn Lies and the Public Relations Industry* (Monroe, Maine: Common Courage Press, 1995).

19. Institute for Alternative Journalism, "Media and Democracy: a blueprint for reinvigorating public life in the Information Age," working paper, December 1996, p. 4.

20. Andre Schiffrin, "The Corporatization of Publishing," *The Nation,* June 3, 1996, pp. 29–32.

21. Leonard Klady, "Why mega-flicks click," *Variety,* November 25–December 1, 1996, p. 1.

22. Barbara Maltsby, "The Homogenization of Hollywood," *Media Studies Journal,* 10 (2–3) (Spring/Summer 1996): p. 115.

23. Bill Carter, "Pow! Thwack! Bam! No Dubbing Needed," *The New York Times,* Week in Review section, November 3, 1996, p. 6.

24. Bruce Orwall, "Disney Chases Live-Action Merchandising Hits," *The Wall Street Journal,* November 27, 1996, p. B1.

25. Luisa Kroll, "Entertainomercials," *Forbes,* November 4, 1996, p. 322, 324.

26. Mary Kuntz and Joseph Weber, "The New Hucksterism," *Business Week,* July 1, 1996, pp. 77–84.

27. Michael Schneider, "Brand name-dropping," *Electronic Media,* August 26, 1996, pp. 1, 30.

28. Mary Kuntz and Joseph Weber, "The New Hucksterism," *Business Week,* July 1, 1996, pp. 77–84.

29. Mary Kuntz and Joseph Weber, "The New Hucksterism," *Business Week,* July 1, 1996, p. 82.

30. Sally Goll Beatty, "CNBC Will Air A Show Owned, Vetted by IBM," *The Wall Street Journal,* June 4, 1996, pp. B1, B8.

PART THREE

Media as Popular Art

On the Internet . . .

Sites appropriate to Part Three

The Manchester Institute for Popular Culture, based at
Manchester Metropolitan University, was set up to promote
theoretical and empirical research in the area of contemporary
popular culture, both within the academy and in conjunction
with local, national, and international agencies. It is a
postgraduate research center particularly engaged in
comparative research projects around aspects of production,
consumption, and regulation of popular culture in the city.

```
http://darion.mmu.ac.uk/h&ss/mipc/inst.htm
```

Images is a quarterly online journal that publishes articles
about a broad range of popular culture artifacts and issues,
including movies, television, videos, and other popular visual
arts.

```
http://www.imagesjournal.com/index.html
```

CHAPTER 7 Cultural Products

7.1 DWIGHT MACDONALD

A Theory of Mass Culture

The emergence of mass media has generated many intellectual and popular questions about the impact of media, what "mediation" does to content, and how audiences respond to the content of the mass media. An early approach to investigating all three of these themes came from initial studies of popular culture as phenomena.

When Dwight MacDonald's essay "A Theory of Mass Culture," from which the following selection has been taken, originally appeared in print in 1953, many people were just beginning to come to terms with the idea of mass-produced cultural artifacts. MacDonald's influential article summarized the growing field of popular culture studies as something unique and distinct from the aesthetic standards that had dominated the arts up until that time.

In his article, MacDonald makes a point of differentiating between "mass culture" and "popular culture." Many critics over the years have seized upon the question of whether there is a significant difference between "mass" and "popular" culture at all or whether the terms are synonymous. MacDonald, however, asserts that the twentieth century saw a great change in the way artifacts were produced. In the "mass" production, different categories for analysis emerged.

The phenomena of mass media and mass culture lend themselves to the idea that the products of mass society are homogenized; that is, that the culture blends together a number of influences to make the product more palatable for a larger audience. To make this point, MacDonald examines several aspects of mass culture to delineate the effects of mass production and mass consumption of mass media.

Key Concept: mass culture

*F*or about a century, Western culture has really been two cultures: the traditional kind—let us call it "High Culture"—that is chronicled in the text-books, and a "Mass Culture" manufactured wholesale for the market. In the old art forms, the artisans of Mass Culture have long been at work: in the novel, the line stretches from Eugène Sue to Lloyd C. Douglas; in music, from Offenbach to Tin-Pan Alley; in art from the chromo to Maxfield Parrish and Norman Rockwell; in architecture, from Victorian Gothic to suburban Tudor. Mass Culture has also developed new media of its own, into which the serious artist rarely ventures: radio, the movies, comic books, detective stories, science fiction, television.

It is sometimes called "Popular Culture," but I think "Mass Culture" a more accurate term, since its distinctive mark is that it is solely and directly an article for mass consumption, like chewing gum. A work of High Culture is occasionally popular, after all, though this is increasingly rare. Thus Dickens was even more popular than his contemporary, G. A. Henty, the difference being that he was an artist, communicating his individual vision to other individuals, while Henty was an impersonal manufacturer of an impersonal commodity for the masses.

THE NATURE OF MASS CULTURE

The historical reasons for the growth of Mass Culture since the early 1800's are well known. Political democracy and popular education broke down the old upper-class monopoly of culture. Business enterprise found a profitable market in the cultural demands of the newly awakened masses, and the advance of technology made possible the cheap production of books, periodicals, pictures, music, and furniture, in sufficient quantities to satisfy this market. Modern technology also created new media such as the movies and television which are specially well adapted to mass manufacture and distribution.

The phenomenon is thus peculiar to modern times and differs radically from what was hitherto known as art or culture. It is true that Mass Culture began as, and to some extent still is, a parasitic, a cancerous growth on High Culture. As Clement Greenberg pointed out in "Avant-Garde and *Kitsch*" (*Partisan Review,* Fall, 1939): "The precondition of *kitsch* (a German term for 'Mass Culture') is the availability close at hand of a fully matured cultural tradition, whose discoveries, acquisitions, and perfected self-conscious *kitsch* can take advantage of for its own ends." The connection, however, is not that of the leaf and the branch but rather that of the caterpillar and the leaf. *Kitsch* "mines" High Culture the way improvident frontiersmen mine the soil, extracting its riches and putting nothing back. Also, as *kitsch* develops, it begins to draw on its own past, and some of it evolves so far away from High Culture as to appear quite disconnected from it.

It is also true that Mass Culture is to some extent a continuation of the old Folk Art which until the Industrial Revolution was the culture of the common people, but here, too, the differences are more striking than the similarities. Folk Art grew from below. It was a spontaneous, autochthonous expression of the people, shaped by themselves, pretty much without the benefit of High Culture, to suit their own needs. Mass Culture is imposed from above. It is fabricated by technicians hired by businessmen; its audiences are passive consumers, their participation limited to the choice between buying and not buying. The Lords of *kitsch*, in short, exploit the cultural needs of the masses in order to make a profit and/or to maintain their class rule—in Communist countries, only the second purpose obtains. (It is very different to *satisfy* popular tastes, as Robert Burns' poetry did, and to *exploit* them, as Hollywood does.) Folk Art was the people's own institution, their private little garden walled off from the great formal park of their masters' High Culture. But Mass Culture breaks down the wall, integrating the masses into a debased form of High Culture and thus becoming an instrument of political domination. If one had no other data to go on, the nature of Mass Culture would reveal capitalism to be an exploitative class society and not the harmonious commonwealth it is sometimes alleged to be....

GRESHAM'S LAW IN CULTURE

The separation of Folk Art and High Culture in fairly watertight compartments corresponded to the sharp line once drawn between the common people and the aristocracy. The eruption of the masses onto the political stage has broken down this compartmentation, with disastrous cultural results. Whereas Folk Art had its own special quality, Mass Culture is at best a vulgarized reflection of High Culture. And whereas High Culture could formerly ignore the mob and seek to please only the *cognoscenti*, it must now compete with Mass Culture or be merged into it.

The problem is acute in the United States and not just because a prolific Mass Culture exists here. If there were a clearly defined cultural *élite,* then the masses could have their *kitsch* and the *élite* could have its High Culture, with everybody happy. But the boundary line is blurred. A statistically significant part of the population, I venture to guess, is chronically confronted with a choice between going to the movies or to a concert, between reading Tolstoy or a detective story, between looking at old masters or at a TV show; i.e., the pattern of their cultural lives is "open" to the point of being porous. Good art competes with *kitsch*, serious ideas compete with commercialized formulae—and the advantage lies all on one side. There seems to be a Gresham's Law in cultural as well as monetary circulation: bad stuff drives out the good, since it is more easily understood and enjoyed. It is this facility of access which at once sells *kitsch* on a wide market and also prevents it from achieving quality....

When to this ease of consumption is added *kitsch's* ease of production because of its standardized nature, its prolific growth is easy to understand. It threatens High Culture by its sheer pervasiveness, its brutal, overwhelming *quantity.* The upper classes, who begin by using it to make money from the crude tastes of the masses and to dominate them politically, end by finding their own culture attacked and even threatened with destruction by the instrument they have thoughtlessly employed....

HOMOGENIZED CULTURE

Like nineteenth-century capitalism, Mass Culture is a dynamic, revolutionary force, breaking down the old barriers of class, tradition, taste, and dissolving all cultural distinctions. It mixes and scrambles everything together, producing what might be called homogenized culture, after another American achievement, the homogenization process that distributes the globules of cream evenly throughout the milk instead of allowing them to float separately on top. It thus destroys all values, since value judgments imply discrimination. Mass Culture is very, very democratic: it absolutely refuses to discriminate against, or between, anything or anybody. All is grist to its mill, and all comes out finely ground indeed.

Consider *Life,* a typical homogenized mass-circulation magazine. It appears on the mahogany library tables of the rich, the glass end-tables of the middle-class and the oilcloth-covered kitchen tables of the poor. Its contents are as thoroughly homogenized as its circulation. The same issue will contain a serious exposition of atomic theory alongside a disquisition on Rita Hayworth's love life; photos of starving Korean children picking garbage from the ruins of Pusan and of sleek models wearing adhesive brassieres; an editorial hailing Bertrand Russell on his eightieth birthday ("A GREAT MIND IS STILL ANNOYING AND ADORNING OUR AGE") across from a full-page photo of a housewife arguing with an umpire at a baseball game ("MOM GETS THUMB"); a cover announcing in the same size type "A NEW FOREIGN POLICY, BY JOHN FOSTER DULLES" and "KERIMA: HER MARATHON KISS IS A MOVIE SENSATION"; nine color pages of Renoirs plus a memoir by his son, followed by a full-page picture of a roller-skating horse. The advertisements, of course, provide even more scope for the editor's homogenizing talents, as when a full-page photo of a ragged Bolivian peon grinningly drunk on coca leaves (which Mr. Luce's conscientious reporters tell us he chews to narcotize his chronic hunger pains) appears opposite an ad of a pretty, smiling, well-dressed American mother with her two pretty, smiling, well-dressed children (a boy and a girl, of course—children are always homogenized in American ads) looking raptly at a clown on a TV set ("RCA VICTOR BRINGS YOU A NEW KIND OF TELEVISION—SUPER SETS WITH 'PICTURE POWER' "). The peon would doubtless find the juxtaposition piquant if he could afford a copy of *Life* which, fortunately for the Good Neighbor Policy, he cannot....

ADULTIZED CHILDREN AND INFANTILE ADULTS

The homogenizing effects of *kitsch* also blurs age lines. It would be interesting to know how many adults read the comics. We do know that comic books are by far the favorite reading matter of our soldiers and sailors, that some forty million comic books are sold a month, and that some seventy million people (most of whom must be adults, there just aren't that many kids) are estimated to read the newspaper comic strips every day. We also know that movie Westerns and radio and TV programs such as "The Lone Ranger" and "Captain Video" are by no means enjoyed only by children. On the other hand, children have access to such grown-up media as the movies, radio and TV. (Note that these newer arts are the ones which blur age lines because of the extremely modest demands they make on the audience's cultural equipment; thus there are many children's books but few children's movies.)

This merging of the child and grown-up audience means: (1) infantile regression of the latter, who, unable to cope with the strains and complexities of modern life, escape via *kitsch* (which in turn, confirms and enhances their infantilism); (2) "overstimulation" of the former, who grow up too fast. Or, as Max Horkheimer well puts it: "Development has ceased to exist. The child is grown up as soon as he can walk, and the grown-up in principle always remains the same." Also note (a) our cult of youth, which makes 18-22 the most admired and desired period of life, and (b) the sentimental worship of Mother ("Momism") as if we couldn't bear to grow up and be on our own. Peter Pan might be a better symbol of America than Uncle Sam.

IDOLS OF CONSUMPTION

Too little attention has been paid to the connection of our Mass Culture with the historical evolution of American Society. In *Radio Research, 1942–43* (Paul F. Lazarsfeld, ed.), Leo Lowenthal compared the biographical articles in *Collier's* and *The Saturday Evening Post* for 1901 and 1940–41 and found that in the forty-year interval the proportion of articles about business and professional men and political leaders had declined while those about entertainers had gone up 50 per cent. Furthermore, the 1901 entertainers are mostly serious artists—opera singers, sculptors, pianists, etc.—while those of 1941 are *all* movie stars, baseball players, and such; and even the "serious" heroes in 1941 aren't so very serious after all: the businessmen and politicians are freaks, oddities, not the really powerful leaders as in 1901. The 1901 *Satevepost* heroes he calls "idols of production," those of today "idols of consumption."

Lowenthal notes that the modern *Satevepost* biographee is successful not because of his own personal abilities so much as because he "got the breaks." The whole competitive struggle is presented as a lottery in which a few winners, no more talented or energetic than any one else, drew the lucky tickets. The effect on the mass reader is at once consoling (it might have been me) and deadening to effort, ambition (there are no rules, so why struggle?). It is striking how closely this evolution parallels the country's economic development. Lowenthal observes that the "idols of production" maintained their dominance right through the twenties. The turning point was the 1929 depression when the problem became how to consume goods rather than how to produce them, and also when the arbitrariness and chaos of capitalism was forcefully brought home to the mass man. So he turned to "idols of consumption," or rather these were now offered him by the manufacturers of Mass Culture, and he accepted them. "They seem to lead to a dream world of the masses," observes Lowenthal, "who are no longer capable or willing to conceive of biographies primarily as a means of orientation and education. . . . He, the American mass man, as reflected in his 'idols of consumption' appears no longer as a center of outwardly directed energies and actions on whose work and efficiency might depend mankind's progress. Instead of the 'givers' we are faced with the 'takers'. . . . They seem to stand for a phantasmagoria of world-wide social security —an attitude which asks for no more than to be served with the things needed for reproduction and recreation, an attitude which has lost every primary interest in how to invent, shape, or apply the tools leading to such purposes of mass satisfaction."

SHERLOCK HOLMES TO MIKE HAMMER

The role of science in Mass Culture has similarly changed from the rational and the purposive to the passive, accidental, even the catastrophic. Consider the evolution of the detective story, a genre which can be traced back to the memoirs of Vidocq, the master-detective of the Napoleonic era. Poe, who was peculiarly fascinated by scientific method, wrote the first and still best detective stories: *The Purloined Letter, The Gold Bug, The Mystery of Marie Roget, The Murders in the Rue Morgue.* Conan Doyle created the great folk hero, Sherlock Holmes, like Poe's Dupin a sage whose wizard's wand was scientific deduction (Poe's "ratiocination"). Such stories could only appeal to—in fact, only be *comprehensible* to—an audience accustomed to think in scientific terms: to survey the data, set up a hypothesis, test it by seeing whether it caught the murderer. The very idea of an art genre cast in the form of a problem to be solved by purely intellectual means could only have arisen in a scientific age. This kind of detective fiction, which might be called the "classic" style, is still widely practiced (well by Agatha Christie and John Dickson Carr, badly by the more popular Erle Stanley Gardiner) but of late it has been overshadowed by the rank, noxious growth of works in the "sensational" style. This was inaugurated by Dashiel Hammett (whom André Gide was foolish enough to admire) and has recently been enormously stepped up in voltage by Mickey Spillane, whose six books to date have sold thirteen million copies. The sensationalists use what for the classicists was the point—the uncovering of the criminal—as a mere excuse for the minute description of scenes of bloodshed, brutality, lust, and alcoholism. The cool, astute, subtle Dupin-Holmes is replaced by the crude man of action whose prowess is measured not by intellectual mastery but by his capacity for liquor, women, and mayhem (he can "take it" as well as "dish it out"—Hammett's *The Glass Key* is largely a chronicle of the epic beatings absorbed by the hero before he finally staggers to the solution). Mike Hammer, Spillane's aptly named hero, is such a monumental blunderer that even Dr. Watson would have seen through him. According to Richard W. Johnston (*Life*, June 23, 1952), "Mike has one bizarre and memorable characteristic that sets him apart from all other fictional detectives: sheer incompetence. In the five Hammer cases, 48 people have been killed, and there is reason to believe that if Mike had kept out of the way, 34 of them—all innocent of the original crime—would have survived." A decade ago, the late George Orwell, apropos a "sensationalist" detective story of the time, *No Orchids for Miss Blandish*, showed how the brutalization of this genre mirrors the general degeneration in ethics from nineteenth-century standards. What he would have written had Mickey Spillane's works been then in existence I find it hard to imagine.

FRANKENSTEIN TO HIROSHIMA

The real heirs of the "classic" detective story today, so far as the exploitation of science is concerned, are the writers of science fiction, where the marvels and horrors of the future must always be "scientifically possible"—just as Sherlock Holmes drew on no supernatural powers. This is the approach of the bourgeoisie, who think of science as their familiar instrument. The masses are less confident, more awed in their approach to science, and there are vast lower strata of science fiction where the marvellous is untrammeled by the limits of knowledge. To the masses, science is the modern *arcanum arcanorum*, at once the supreme mystery and the philosopher's stone that explains the mystery. The latter concept appears in comic strips such as "Superman" and in the charlatan-science exploited by "health fakers" and "nature fakers." Taken this way, science gives man mastery over his environment and is beneficent. But science itself is not understood, therefore not mastered, therefore terrifying because of its very power. Taken *this* way, as the supreme mystery, science becomes the stock in trade of the "horror" pulp magazines and comics and movies. It has got to the point, indeed, that if one sees a laboratory in a movie, one shudders, and the white coat of the scientist is as blood-chilling a sight as Count Dracula's black cloak. These "horror" films have apparently an indestructible popularity: *Frankenstein* is still shown, after twenty-one years, and the current revival of *King Kong* is expected to gross over 2 million dollars.

If the scientist's laboratory has acquired in Mass Culture a ghastly atmosphere, is this perhaps not one of those deep popular intuitions? From Frankenstein's laboratory to Maidenek and Hiroshima is not a long journey. Was there a popular suspicion, perhaps only half conscious, that the nineteenth-century trust in science, like the nineteenth-century trust in popular education, was mistaken, that science can as easily be used for antihuman as for prohuman ends, perhaps even more easily? For Mrs. Shelley's Frankenstein, the experimenter who brought disaster by pushing his science too far, is a scientific folk hero older than and still as famous as Mr. Doyle's successful and beneficent Sherlock Holmes.

THE PROBLEM OF THE MASSES

Conservatives such as Ortega y Gasset and T. S. Eliot argue that since "the revolt of the masses" has led to the horrors of totalitarianism (and of California roadside architecture), the only hope is to rebuild the old class walls and bring the masses once more under aristocratic control. They think of the popular as synonymous with cheap and vulgar. Marxian radicals and liberals, on the other hand, see the masses as intrinsically healthy but as the dupes and victims of cultural exploitation by the Lords of *kitsch*—in the style of Rousseau's "noble savage" idea. If only the masses were offered good stuff instead of *kitsch*, how they would eat it up! How the level of Mass Culture would rise! Both these diagnoses seem to me fallacious: they assume that Mass Culture is (in the conservative view) or could be (in the liberal view) an expression of *people*, like Folk Art, whereas actually it is an expression of *masses*, a very different thing.

There are theoretical reasons why Mass Culture is not and can never be any good. I take it as axiomatic that culture can only be produced by and for human beings. But in so far as people are organized (more strictly, disorganized) as masses, they lose their human identity and quality. For the masses are in historical time what a crowd is in space: a large quantity of people unable to express themselves as human beings because they are related to one another neither as individuals nor as members of communities—indeed, they are not related *to each other* at all, but only to something distant, abstract, nonhuman: a football game or bargain sale in the case of a crowd, a system of industrial production, a party or a State in the case of the masses. The mass man is a solitary atom, uniform with and undifferentiated from thousands and millions of other atoms who go to make up "the lonely crowd," as David Riesman well calls American society. A folk or a people, however, is a community, i.e., a group of individuals linked to each other by common interests, work, traditions, values, and sentiments; something like a family, each of whose members has a special place and function as an individual while at the same time sharing the group's interests (family budget), sentiments (family quarrels), and culture (family jokes). The scale is small enough so that it "makes a difference" what the individual does, a first condition for human—as against mass-existence. He is at once more important as an individual than in mass society and at the same time more closely integrated into the community, his creativity nourished by a rich combination of individualism and communalism. (The great culture-bearing *élites* of the past have been communities of this kind.) In contrast, a mass society, like a crowd, is so undifferentiated and loosely structured that its atoms, in so far as human values go, tend to cohere only along the line of the least common denominator; its morality sinks to that of its most brutal and primitive members, its taste to that of the least sensitive and most ignorant. And in addition to everything else, the scale is simply too big, there are just *too many people.*

Yet this collective monstrosity, "the masses," "the public," is taken as a human norm by the scientific and artistic technicians of our Mass Culture. They at once degraded the public by treating it as an object, to be handled with the lack of ceremony and the objectivity of medical students dissecting a corpse, and at the same time flatter it, pander to its level of taste and ideas by taking these as the criterion of reality (in the case of questionnaire-sociologists and other "social scientists") or of art (in the case of the Lords of *kitsch*). When one hears a questionnaire-sociologist talk about how he will "set up" an investigation, one feels he regards people as a herd of dumb animals, as mere congeries of conditioned reflexes, his calculation being which reflex will be stimulated by which question. At the same time, of necessity, he sees the statistical majority as the great Reality, the secret of life he is trying to find out; like the *kitsch* Lords, he is wholly without values, willing to accept any idiocy if it is held by many people. The aristocrat and the democrat both criticize and argue with popular taste, the one with hostility, the other in friendship, for both attitudes proceed from a set of values. This is less degrading to the masses than the "objective" approach of Hollywood and the questionnaire-sociologists, just as it is less degrading to a man to be shouted at in anger than to be quietly assumed to be part of a machine. But the *plebs* have their dialectical revenge: complete indifference to their human *quality* means complete prostration before their statistical *quantity*, so that a movie magnate who cynically "gives the public what it wants"—i.e., assumes it wants trash—sweats with terror if box-office returns drop 10 per cent.

Popular Culture/ Multiculturalism

John G. Cawelti is a professor in the Department of English at the University of Kentucky in Lexington. He has long been regarded as an important critic of popular culture, and he has been an articulate spokesperson for the diverse number of perspectives on popular, or mass, culture.

In the following selection from an article published in the *Journal of Popular Culture* (Summer 1996), Cawelti addresses the characteristics of the popular culture movement, scholarly analyses of the subject, and the recent trend to mix and overlap formerly separate ethnic traditions to form a new dimension in multicultural studies of popular media.

Cawelti's discourse on the evolution of academic work in the area and his recognition of the changes in cultural production demonstrate a need to continually refine and redefine the questions asked of popular culture. The expression of ethnic and gender differences, growing consumerism, and the acknowledgment of class divisions and distinctions have influenced recent studies and have required different scholarly investigations and approaches. While studies in popular culture proliferate, they, like the artifacts and cultures they describe, continually seek to understand new social relationships.

Key Concept: popular culture and multiculturalism

A little over one hundred years ago, Walt Whitman noted that culture is the word of the modern. Not one of his more original statements, since this was the chorus of most major nineteenth century critics from Carlyle to Arnold. Culture, in both its normative and descriptive senses continued to be a dominant concept of western intellectual life right up to the beginning of the second half of the twentieth century. Normatively, the concept of culture was a unifying ideal, centered around a vision of Western civilization as the climax of cultural progress and synthesis. This vision led to a concept of the humanistic curriculum as a pedagogy leading the student to acquire a significant proportion of the artistic and philosophical canon which was thought to define this civilization.

On the other hand, used descriptively by the new disciplines of anthropology, sociology, and social psychology, culture was a concept used to articulate the multiplicity of behaviors created by actual human beings in different places

and times. Ambiguous and confusing as this double meaning of the word could
be in practice, the two senses of culture worked out a complex dialectic with
each other throughout the nineteenth century. Together they expressed an ideal
of human society as "liberal," that is as both broadly tolerant of religious and
cultural diversity and also as dedicated to the idea of progress toward increasing cultural integration and transcendence of the limitations of past cultures.
This ideal was most powerfully symbolized by the idea of America with its
great motto: *e pluribus unum.* Ultimately there developed a dream of a world
civilization which would embody the best that had been thought and said (to
quote one famous thumbnail definition of culture) and eventually synthesize
individual cultural heritages into one grand stream of civilization.

Alas, too often this cultural ideal really meant the imperializing domination of some national culture, whether the American way of life, British
hegemony, Deutsche kultur, or the Communist international; two world wars
and a half-century of other conflicts have made the progress of civilization
seem more like an appointment with Armageddon than the emergence of a
transcendent world culture. Growing doubts about the value or even the possibility of a unified culture have increasingly led critics and scholars to use
the word with qualifying adjectives—popular, working-class, ethnic, folk, high,
low, and middle, global, etc. The word of the post-modern is no longer culture
but hyphen-culture and two of the most significant of these hyphen-culture
constructs are those which concern us today—popular culture and multiculturalism. These two hyphens emerged around the same time historically and
they do indeed share certain central themes, but in the last two decades they
increasingly diverged until they now seem like quite different ideas.

I'm not even going to try to present a clear definition of either popular culture or multiculturalism. There's still a great deal of controversy about
what these two terms designate and I'd rather be understood as making very
tentative feints *toward* a definition. To begin with, popular culture and multiculturalism both claim a more direct relationship with "the people" than elitist or
canonic culture. In the 1960s when these areas were first emerging, both gender
studies and ethnic studies, now seen as aspects of multiculturalism, were often
subsumed under popular culture....

Three main factors were involved in this divergence between popular
culture and the newer concepts of multicultural studies. First of all, scholars developing multicultural approaches naturally wished to concentrate on the materials associated with their particular hyphenated culture—people in women's
studies are mostly concerned with the works of women or with the patterns
of culture affecting women's lives; African Americanists mainly study black
cultural creations; those in ethnic studies focus on the materials of the particular ethnic groups they are interested in, etc. Second, multiculturalists today
seem especially concerned with developing theories and methodologies which
will protect and project the perspectives and the historical experiences of their
particular cultural groups. Thus, in recent years, both African American studies and women's studies have prolifically created theories and analytical approaches which offer a distinctive angle not only on their own materials but
on other aspects of culture as well. Many of these new approaches have been
extremely interesting and have enriched our understanding of all sorts of texts

and cultural patterns. However, these approaches have also been restrictive insofar as they excluded alternate approaches to the material and have resisted synthesis with other modes of analysis. Moreover this theoretical separatism has sometimes led particular groups devoted to multicultural analysis to claim that only members of particular hyphenated cultures could really understand and apply these analytical methods—only women could produce a successful feminist analysis, only African Americans could interpret African American culture, etc. Finally, while several multiculturalists have made important contributions to popular culture, most of them have been mainly interested in constructing their own canons by highlighting the most powerful, complex and aesthetically interesting works of their traditions. . . .

Popular culture studies, on the other hand, have embraced a very wide definition of culture, have resisted any particular set of theories and methodologies, and, above all, have sought to expand or perhaps more accurately, to abandon the notion of a cultural canon altogether. No form or level of cultural activity or text is automatically excluded from its purview. . . .

These characteristics of the popular culture movement—its resistance to clear definitions of its area of study, its rejection of any sort of official theory or methodology, and its hostility to canon formation—have made it widely suspect in some corners of the university and have also been responsible, I think, for some of the contemporary divergence between students of popular culture and exponents of various forms of multiculturalism. It's perhaps not surprising that in seeking academic recognition and support, new disciplines like gender studies, African-American studies and ethnic studies have sometimes out-theorized and out-canonized the traditional disciplines. In addition, while emphasizing the intellectual rigor and scholarly solidity of their work, these new multicultural disciplines have rejected the inclusiveness and vagueness of Popular Culture in order to assert the difference between the hyphen-cultures they are studying and traditional Anglo-American ideas of civilization. The canons they promulgate are made up of substantial new proportions of women and minority writers, and they tend to insist on viewing these writers through the lenses of different methods of analysis and evaluation. Nonetheless, these revised canons are canons, and the way they are used in the educational process often leads to the establishment of new orthodoxies. One need only look at the latest editions of the major anthologies of American literature to see how the growing number of women, Native American, African American and ethnic American writers now included have fallen neatly into their places in a new canon of American culture, validated by new literary histories like the *Columbia History of American Literature* and reduced to formulas by teacher's manuals and Cliff's Notes. Sometimes one wonders whether this is truly a paradise of multiculturalism, or a new orthodoxy of political correctness.

Unfortunately, in this intellectual context, popular culture's insistence on vagueness, inclusiveness, and synthesis is not much help, for it fails to provide an effective framework for studying the cultural situation of most importance today, the complex interplay in modern societies and in the world at large of many different cultural traditions. While it is fascinating to talk in prophetic and McLuhanesque terms of global villages and international popular culture, or, in more negative terms about the corruptions of cultural imperialism and coca-colonization, the actual interplay or dialectic of cultural traditions in modern culture is really very complex. To understand this process more fully is the most challenging and difficult task of students of popular culture, and it will require more sophisticated theories and methods of analysis than we usually deploy today. This is an area where we, as popular culturalists, have a great deal to learn from the new disciplines of multicultural studies.

To open up the discussion of the relationship between popular culture and multiculturalism in what I hope is a slightly new way, I'd like to offer a preliminary sketch of the interplay of popular culture and multicultural traditions in America from the mid-nineteenth century to the present. By 1850 Americans had successfully suppressed and sequestered one alternative to European cultural traditions—that of the Native Americans—and had enslaved and tried to dehumanize the descendents of another—the African. There still remained, particularly in the Northern states, significant enclaves where cultural traditions differing in language, religion, or pattern of behavior continued to pass on their distinctive ways to new generations. Large areas of German and Spanish speakers persisted, and there were many smaller areas where Scandinavian, Dutch, Jewish, and other traditions struggled to survive. In the 1840s a large Irish immigration had brought in people similar in language, but very different in other ways to Anglo-American culture. Later in the nineteenth century there would be waves of immigrants from very different cultural traditions, including Southern and Eastern European and Asian. However, at midcentury, one thing was common to most of these diverse offshoots of European tradition—their "whiteness"—and in the context of a nation deeply obsessed with the relationship of "colored" and white, this factor encouraged the mutual accommodation and assimilation of these diverse groups into a broader concept of white Americanism. From the middle of the nineteenth century to the time of World War I, popular culture increasingly played a significant part in this process of assimilation, a process based essentially on the assertion of Anglo-American or what used to be called WASP dominance or cultural hegemony.

One can easily see how the popular culture of that time fitted into this pattern. As scholars like McLean and Kasson have shown, popular entertainments like vaudeville, theater, and amusement parks enabled members of different ethnic groups to come together, and to socialize in arenas free from the constraints of ethnic traditions. Presumably in such a venue Abie met his Irish Rose and determined to marry her in spite of parental opposition. In addition, positive and negative stereotypes such as those found in the ever-popular racial, ethnic and gender jokes of this period taught hyphenated-Americans the values and mores of Anglo-Americanism and the shortcomings, absurdities, and outright badness of alternative traditions. One learned through popular culture that being an American meant turning away from traditional attitudes and accepting the political and cultural leadership of the Anglo-American middle class....

However, the role of popular culture as the major promoter of assimilation and Anglo-American hegemony, began to change significantly around the time of World War I. In the 1920s—later referred to as the Jazz Age by some—popular culture entered a decisively new phase marked by several changes. For one thing, popular culture became conscious of itself in a new way. In the mid-nineteenth century, the line between what we would today call popular culture and canonic culture was by no means clear. When Hawthorne complained about that damned mob of scribbling women whose work sold better than his did, he thought their novels were bad, but did not think of them as on a different cultural plane than his own. However, as Lawrence Levine and others have shown, the last decade of the nineteenth century and the first decade of the twentieth brought about a major reconfiguration of American culture in response to the rise of a new industrial elite who sought to recreate in America many aspects of the European tradition of high culture. At the same time, the growth of a mass audience and the emergence of new media like the movies, sound recording, and broadcasting, created tremendous new opportunities for entrepreneurs to develop an industrialized popular culture. Out of this emerged the theory of the brows—highbrow, middlebrow and lowbrow as an expression of the sense that American culture was now significantly divided between a high culture with roots in European artistic traditions and a popular culture more responsive to the everyday needs of Americans. The beginning of popular culture studies also resulted from this major shift in the patterns of American culture. Gilbert Seldes' *The Seven Lively Arts* (1924) brilliantly analyzed such major phenomena of the new popular culture as jazz, the comic strip (Krazy Kat) and the silent comedy (Charlie Chaplin) and probably deserves to be called the pioneer of popular culture studies, though he was certainly not alone. Many intellectuals of the tens and twenties were fascinated by the new phenomenon of popular culture and even such highbrows as T. S. Eliot and Edmund Wilson wrote about it. This new configuring of American culture was solidified at the same time that America's traditionally strong and relatively separate ethnic cultures were being rapidly eroded. By the early twentieth century, the use of European languages like German, Italian, and Swedish in homes, newspapers, books, religious services and other places was being discouraged and this process was intensified by World War I, when anti-German feeling swept the country and made the widespread use of languages other than English increasingly suspect. Even the thriving Yiddish culture which had long been a major feature of New York City began to decline. But these ethnic cultures did not simply fade away. Actually, the increasing need of material in the new arena of popular culture created opportunities for talented musicians, actors, writers, dancers, and entrepreneurs emerging out of the ethnic traditions. Everyone has noticed what an important Jewish presence there was in the movies, in popular music and in comedy. This could also be said about the Irish. And it was in the area of popular culture that African Americans for the first time broke out of the walls of segregation and discrimination that had been constructed to reenslave them after the Civil War. Jazz, the blues, spirituals and other musical creations from the rich African American heritage began during the early twentieth century to enter the mainstream of American popular culture.

While the continued production and widespread popularity of racist myths like *The Birth of a Nation* as well as the widespread use of other anti-ethnic and anti-Semitic themes and stereotypes indicated that in many ways the new popular culture would continue to foster white Anglo-American hegemony as it had traditionally done, there were nonetheless increasing signs of change in areas like the movies, radio, and popular music. Popular music showed perhaps the most significant and important changes. The big band era was an extraordinary confluence of musical traditions, black, white and ethnic. Through their gruelling regime of one night stands across the country and their radio broadcasts and records, white bands like Paul Whiteman, Benny Goodman, Glenn Miller, and Artie Shaw and black bands like Duke Ellington, Fletcher Henderson, Louis Armstrong, and Count Basie played widely to both black and white audiences. As they developed, their music became more and more interrelated. An important symbolic moment of this era, almost accidentally preserved for us by the new technologies of radio and sound recording, represents the synthesizing and transforming tendencies within the new popular culture. This was the great 1938 Carnegie Hall Concert of the Benny Goodman orchestra. Getting to Carnegie Hall indicated a new respectability for popular music and symbolized its breaking across the highbrow-lowbrow barrier. Even more significantly this concert involved both white and black musicians and thus openly revealed the mutual influence which had long been part of the development of jazz. Benny Goodman, a Jewish American band leader, whose white musicians were a very diverse ethnic lot, played together with musicians from the Count Basie band, one of the great black aggregations of that era, symbolizing in a highly public fashion the confluence of black and white musical traditions that had so powerfully shaped the development of swing.

One other major cultural shift played a vital role in the development of this new phase of popular culture. Sometime in the later nineteenth century youth became something very different than it had been. Once it had been a brief period of apprenticeship during which young people learned the skills they would practice as adults. By the ages of fifteen or sixteen many young people had virtually become adults. With the rise of public secondary education and of a more affluent middle class in the later nineteenth century, youth became a much more protracted phase of life, adolescence was discovered, and young people were increasingly socialized into the expectation that they would live in a way different from their parents. This created the phenomenon of generational revolt, so characteristic of twentieth century America. The generation which came of age in the twenties exemplified perhaps for the first time the patterns that would become so characteristic of succeeding generations: rebellion against the past; the quest for liberation; experimentation with new mores and patterns of behavior; and a new kind of immersion in popular culture. The impetus of successive younger generations which tended to be increasingly affluent fueled the development of twentieth century popular culture in a new way, particularly emphasizing its transformational aspects and increasingly subverting its role as agent for the traditional Anglo-American hegemony.

Thus, in the period between the wars, popular culture increasingly became the expression of a new cultural synthesis in America which foreshadowed the post World War II trend toward the integration and acceptance of women and minorities into a more complex presence in American culture. The major characteristics of this new phase in popular culture were confluence, synthesis and transformation. Synthesizing media, driven by the profitability of attracting increasingly large audiences, including the newly affluent young people, developed new modes of organization such as Hollywood studios, radio-television networks and publishing syndicates which could produce and distribute material to the largest possible audiences. The content of these media became more responsive to the interests and values of this increasingly diverse audience by developing generic traditions which could be tailored to a great variety of interests as well as creating new genres with a special appeal to such important components of the audience as women and young people. The new media also created many synthesizing images of American culture—the most obvious being those multi-ethnic bomber crews or infantry squads which became so important in movies of World War II—placing the diverse minorities of America in a new unified constellation. This new unity became increasingly different from the Anglo-American hegemony which had played the leading role in the first phase of popular culture. The history of the complex dialectic between new images of multicultural unity and the traditional Anglo-American hegemony is one of the central areas in the history of popular culture that needs to be more fully researched.

When the popular culture movement developed in the late 1960s and early 1970s, it was at first primarily an acknowledgement of popular culture as synthesizer and transformer of American culture. In fact, most of the early leaders of the popular culture movement—like Ray Browne, Russel Nye, Marshall Fishwick and Leslie Fiedler—came out of American studies or American literature. But even as such forums as the *Journal of Popular Culture* and the Popular Culture Association flourished, popular culture, itself, was beginning another fundamental shift. It was during this time that such ideas as multiculturalism, cultural pluralism, and bilingualism began to gain increasing currency. During the 1960s and '70s, multiculturalism was first connected with powerful thrusts toward cultural separatism among African Americans such as the Black Power and Black Arts movements, the rise of black studies programs in the universities, and the growth of the Black Muslim movement and the legend of Malcolm X. There were also numerous other trends toward ethnic separatism such as those described in Michael Novak's *Rise of the Unmeltable Ethnics* (1972). Native Americans, Asian Americans, and Chicanos and other Latinos also sought to revitalize their own cultural traditions, increasingly demanding bilingualism in the public schools. In addition, these forces of cultural fragmentation were contemporaneous with a rapidly developing feminism which made gender separatism an important part of its agenda.

Supporters of civil rights, integration, and equal rights which had dominated ethnic and gender politics since World War II were initially taken aback by the vehemence and force of this separatist reaction. For a time, the idea of cultural pluralism became itself a contested area; did cultural pluralism mean increasing tolerance and acceptance of cultural differences or did it mean separation between different cultures. Throughout this time the popular culture movement retained its openness and hospitality to divergent view, but for many younger scholars devoted to feminism or Black studies or Native American liberation, openness was not what they wanted and they rejected the framework of popular culture to pursue their work in the context of gender studies, ethnic studies, or African American history and culture. At the same time and for somewhat different reasons, various kinds of media studies and cinema studies also increasingly pursued different paths. In this context popular culture lost its claim to universality and synthesis as well as its position in the vanguard of cultural studies.

To an extent, that is still the case at the present time. However, in the last decade or so, another important development has taken place in the shifting dialectic of American culture. During this time there has been a considerable lessening of the separatist impulse and an increasing tendency toward mixing and overlapping of hitherto separate ethnic traditions. Something of the same sort has happened in the area of gender with the development of new concepts of masculinity and the emergence of "queer" studies not so much in opposition to, but in a complex dialectical relationship with feminism. One of the most knowledgeable observers of this new phenomenon, the English scholar A. Robert Lee, describes the contemporary cultural scene in terms of what he calls the "ethnic postmodern," a time "in which the vocabulary is one of hybridity, borderland, margins which have moved to the center, in every way a new order of cultural self-positioning and reference. This, indeed, might be called the ethnic postmodern. It entails not only an extrication out, and beyond, essentialist or one-note identity politics, but a cultural stance . . . which, with uninhibited reflexivity, plays upon, contemplates, actually vaunts, its own imaginative self-mirroring."

Lee's discussion is primarily concerned with avant-garde postmodern writers like Ishmael Reed, Maxine Hong Kingston, and Gerald Vizenor, but much of what he says applies on a different level to contemporary popular culture. With the proliferation of cable, videotape and now internet and cd-rom, new means of production and distribution make possible types of diversity and recombination that would have been unimaginable during the 1950s and 1960s. Correspondingly, there has been a considerable erosion of such unifying structures of the traditional mass media as networks, movie studios, and publishing syndicates. While these changes have also led to huge media consolidations like the Disney-ABC and Time Warner-Turner Broadcasting mergers, these megacorporations are conglomerations of many media enterprises as likely to foster increasing diversity as they are homogeneity and standardization. The popular cultural scene itself seems increasingly attuned to recombinations of traditional heritages, not only in terms of the obvious ways in which new combinations of white, African American and Latino musical traditions are continually creating new popular genres, but where this kind of interplay is spreading to other areas of popular culture like movies and cable television. In addition, contemporary popular culture has become much more responsive to the international scene than ever before. Recombinant lifestyles are becoming more the norm than the exception. Imagine the very model of a modern urban dweller; dressed in cowboy boots and a dashiki, she/he nibbles on sushi while listening to the latest country music. No doubt much of this is superficial and a way of rebelling against the dullness of contemporary corporate culture, but there are signs that the ethnic postmodern has a more profound significance. I was particularly struck a few weeks ago by news reports about a parents' movement which wants the public schools to change the way they record the ethnicity of students in order to register multiple backgrounds. These parents are not satisfied with the standard white, African-American, Native-American,

Latino and Asian categories used by the schools, but have sued to make the schools list their children as African American *and* white *and* Native American, for example. This suggests a basic transformation of attitudes in a culture which, despite its official melting pot ideology, has long been deeply split by racial and ethnic divisions.

In American cultural history popular culture has often expressed the racism, sexism and white protestant ethno-centrism deeply engrained in our history, but it has also been more open to cultural transformations and alternatives than most of our highbrow and middlebrow culture. Even in the later nineteenth and early twentieth centuries when America was dominated by a revitalized racism and a pervasive White Anglo-American cultural hegemony, popular culture, in areas like vaudeville, popular theater and music, and in new media like the movies developed far more multicultural motifs than the literary areas of fiction and poetry which continued to be dominated by white middle-class writers and in which regional and ethnic differences were largely portrayed through the stereotypes of race and ethnicity. Even more avant garde literary movements like naturalism showed relatively little awareness of interest in the burgeoning cultural pluralism of American society until the 1920s, when American critics and intellectuals began tentatively to acknowledge the vitality and significance of the new popular culture.

During the last quarter of a century, a time of bitterness, separatism and neoconservatism in which ethnic and gender groups have increasingly defined themselves *against* the rest of the culture partly in response to the way in which a residual Anglo-American "silent majority" or "Christian conservatism" has tried to reestablish its hegemony, popular culture has continued to subvert such boundaries and cross such frontiers. Ironically, while the continued effect of capitalism on the social and economic level seems to be leading to an increasing class division between rich and poor a capitalist popular culture industry seems to operate more in the direction of undercutting and obfuscating these divisions. It seems to me that this increasingly complex and volatile cultural situation opens up a host of new questions and inquiries for students of popular culture and multiculturalism.

PART FOUR

Critical Theory and Mass Media

On the Internet . . .

Sites appropriate to Part Four

The Centre for Cultural and Media Studies (CCMS) is the South African region's premier graduate research and educational unit in media studies. The staff, research, and publications of the CCMS are internationally renowned and read, and its leading staff members have held visiting professorships in a variety of universities all over the world.

```
http://www.und.ac.za/und/ccms/index.html
```

Other Voices, a peer-reviewed interdisciplinary journal of cultural criticism, is published by an editorial collective at the University of Pennsylvania, College of Arts and Sciences. The journal includes reviews of books and the works of seminal theorists in the field.

```
http://dept.english.upenn.edu/~ov/
```

The Spoon Collective is dedicated to promoting discussion of philosophical and political issues. This site includes discussions of authors and literature.

```
http://lists.village.virginia.edu/
  ~spoons/
```

CHAPTER 8 Mass Media, Power, and Ideology

8.1 HERBERT I. SCHILLER

The Mind Managers

Herbert I. Schiller has had a long and distinguished career as a critical scholar of modern mass media. His work has influenced the field of media studies worldwide. In his many books, including *Mass Communication and American Empire* (A.M. Kelley, 1969) and *Culture, Inc.* (Oxford University Press, 1989), Schiller has systematically investigated the relationship between corporate-owned and controlled mass media and the global expansion of capitalism. Within this larger project, Schiller points to what he sees as a problematic complicity between the mainstream of communication research and the agenda of private corporate and government power. Using a distinction originally made by European social critics, he differentiates between *administrative* researchers (i.e., scholars whose work obscures the connections between mass media and political-economic power) and *critical* researchers.

Schiller argues that critical scholars take the position that mass media institutions are key elements of the modern capitalist world order. He believes that mass media produce both economic profits and the ideology necessary to sustain a world system of exploitative capitalist social relationships. Schiller maintains that it is the job of the critical researcher to untangle the relationships between media and power and to expose the ideology inherent in media content.

In the following selection from his early work *The Mind Managers* (Beacon Press, 1973), Schiller employs the critical perspective to expose the operation of key ideological myths disseminated in the mass media, which act to confuse individuals and to gain their consent to the existing state of power relationships.

Key Concept: manipulation of consciousness

INTRODUCTION

America's media managers create, process, refine, and preside over the circulation of images and information which determine our beliefs and attitudes and, ultimately, our behavior. When they deliberately produce messages that do not correspond to the realities of social existence, the media managers become mind managers. Messages that intentionally create a false sense of reality and produce a consciousness that cannot comprehend or wilfully rejects the actual conditions of life, personal or social, are manipulative messages.

Manipulation of human minds, according to Paulo Freire, "is an instrument of conquest." It is one of the means by which "the dominant elites try to conform the masses to their objectives.[1] By using myths which explain, justify, and sometimes even glamorize the prevailing conditions of existence, manipulators secure popular support for a social order that is not in the majority's long-term real interest. When manipulation is successful, alternative social arrangements remain unconsidered....

The permanent division of the society into two broad categories of "winners" and "losers" arises and persists as a result of the maintenance, recognition, and, indeed, sanctification of the system of private ownership of productive property and the extension of the ownership principle to all other aspects of human existence. The general acceptance of this arrangement for carrying on social activity makes it inevitable that some prosper, consolidate their success, and join the dominant shapers and molders of the community. The others, the majority, work on as mere conformists, the disadvantaged, and the manipulated; they are manipulated especially to continue to participate, if not wholeheartedly, at least positively, in the established routines. The system gives them a return adequate to achieve some marks of economic status, and manipulation leads them to hope that they might turn these routines to greater personal advantage for themselves or their children.

It is not surprising that manipulation, as an instrument of control, should reach its highest development in the United States. In America, more than anywhere else, the favorable conditions we have briefly noted permit a large fraction of the population to escape total suppression and thereby become potential actors in the historical process. Manipulation allows the appearance of active engagement while denying many of the material and *all* of the psychic benefits of genuine involvement....

The means of manipulation are many, but, clearly, control of the informational and ideational apparatus at all levels is essential. This is secured by the operation of a simple rule of the market economy. Ownership and control of the mass media, like all other forms of property, is available to those with capital. Inevitably, radio- and television-station ownership, newspaper and magazine proprietorship, movie-making, and book publishing are largely in the hands of corporate chains and media conglomerates. The apparatus is thus ready to assume an active and dominant role in the manipulative process.

My intention is to identify some of these conditioning forces and to reveal the means by which they conceal their presence, deny their influence, or exercise directional control under auspices that superficially appear benign and/or

natural. The search for these "hidden processes," along with their subtle me-
chanics, should not be mistaken for a more common kind of investigation—the
exposé of clandestine activities. Conspiracy is neither invoked nor considered
in these pages. Though the idea of mind management lends itself easily to such
an approach, the comprehensive conditioning carried on throughout American society today does not require, and actually cannot be understood in, such
terms....

Herbert I.
Schiller

MANIPULATION AND THE
PACKAGED CONSCIOUSNESS

Five Myths That Structure Content

1. The Myth of Individualism and Personal Choice.   Manipulation's greatest triumph, most observable in the United States, is to have taken advantage
of the special historical circumstances of Western development to perpetrate as
truth a definition of freedom cast in individualistic terms. This enables the concept to serve a double function. It protects the ownership of productive private
property while simultaneously offering itself as the guardian of the individual's
well-being, suggesting, if not insisting, that the latter is unattainable without
the existence of the former. Upon this central construct an entire scaffolding of
manipulation is erected. What accounts for the strength of this powerful notion?
     ... The identification of personal choice with human freedom can be seen
arising side-by-side with seventeenth-century individualism, both products of
the emerging market economy.[2]
     For several hundred years individual proprietorship, allied with techno-
logical improvement, increased output and thereby bestowed great importance
on personal independence in the industrial and political processes. The view
that freedom is a personal matter, and that the individual's rights supersede the
group's and provide the basis for social organization, gained credibility with the
rise of material rewards and leisure time. Note, however, that these conditions
were not distributed evenly among all classes of Western society and that they
did not begin to exist in the rest of the world....
     In the newly settled United States, few restraints impeded the imposi-
tion of an individualistic private entrepreneurial system and its accompanying
myths of personal choice and individual freedom. Both enterprise and myth
found a hospitable setting. The growth of the former and consolidation of the
latter were inevitable. How far the process has been carried is evident today in
the easy public acceptance of the giant multinational private corporation as an
example of individual endeavor....
     Privatism in every sphere of life is considered normal. The American life
style, from its most minor detail to its most deeply felt beliefs and practices,
reflects an exclusively self-centered outlook, which is in turn an accurate image
of the structure of the economy itself. The American dream includes a personal

means of transportation, a single-family home, the proprietor-operated business. Such other institutions as a competitive health system are obvious, if not natural, features of the privately organized economy. . . .

Though individual freedom and personal choice are its most powerful mythic defenses, the system of private ownership and production requires and creates additional constructs, along with the techniques to transmit them. These notions either rationalize its existence and promise a great future, or divert attention from its searing inadequacies and conceal the possibilities of new departures for human development. Some of these constructs and techniques are not exclusive to the privatistic industrial order, and can be applied in any social system intent on maintaining its dominion. Other myths, and the means of circulating them, are closely associated with the specific characteristics of this social system.

2. The Myth of Neutrality. For manipulation to be most effective, evidence of its presence should be nonexistent. When the manipulated believe things are the way they are naturally and inevitably, manipulation is successful. In short, manipulation requires a false reality that is a continuous denial of its existence.

It is essential, therefore, that people who are manipulated believe in the neutrality of their key social institutions. They must believe that government, the media, education, and science are beyond the clash of conflicting social interests. Government, and the national government in particular, remains the centerpiece of the neutrality myth. This myth presupposes belief in the basic integrity and nonpartisanship of government in general and of its constituent parts—Congress, the judiciary, and the Presidency. Corruption, deceit, and knavery, when they occur from time to time, are seen to be the result of human weakness. The institutions themselves are beyond reproach. The fundamental soundness of the overall system is assured by the well-designed instrumentalities that comprise the whole.

The Presidency, for instance, is beyond the reach of special interests, according to this mythology. The first and most extreme manipulative use of the Presidency, therefore, is to claim the nonpartisanship of the office, and to seem to withdraw it from clamorous conflict. . . .

The chief executive, though the most important, is but one of many governmental departments that seek to present themselves as neutral agents, embracing no objectives but the general welfare, and serving everyone impartially and disinterestedly. For half a century all the media joined in propagating the myth of the FBI as a nonpolitical and highly effective agency of law enforcement. In fact, the Bureau has been used continuously to intimidate and coerce social critics.

The mass media, too, are supposed to be neutral. Departures from evenhandedness in news reportage are admitted but, the press assure us, result from human error and cannot be interpreted as flaws in the basically sound institutions of information dissemination. That the media (press, periodicals, radio, and television) are almost without exception business enterprises, receiving their revenues from commercial sales of time or space, seems to create no problems for those who defend the objectivity and integrity of the informational services.[3] ...

Science, which more than any other intellectual activity has been integrated into the corporate economy, continues also to insist on its value-free neutrality. Unwilling to consider the implications of the sources of its funding, the directions of its research, the applications of its theories, and the character of the paradigms it creates, science promotes the notion of its insulation from the social forces that affect all other ongoing activities in the nation.

The system of schooling, from the elementary through the university level, is also, according to the manipulators, devoid of deliberate ideological purpose. Still, the product must reflect the teaching: it is astonishing how large a proportion of the graduates at each stage continue, despite all the ballyhoo about the counterculture, to believe in and observe the competitive ethic of business enterprise.

Wherever one looks in the social sphere, neutrality and objectivity are invoked to describe the functioning of value-laden and purposeful activities which lend support to the prevailing institutional system. Essential to the everyday maintenance of the control system is the carefully nurtured myth that no special groups or views have a preponderant influence on the country's important decision-making processes. ...

3. The Myth of Unchanging Human Nature. Human expectations can be the lubricant of social change. When human expectations are low, passivity prevails. There can, of course, be various kinds of images in anyone's mind concerning political, social, economic, and personal realities. The common denominator of all such imagery, however, is the view people have of human nature. What human nature is seen to be ultimately affects the way human beings behave, not because they must act as they do but because they believe they are expected to act that way. ...

It is predictable that in the United States a theory that emphasizes the aggressive side of human behavior and the unchangeability of human nature would find approval, permeate most work and thought, and be circulated widely by the mass media. Certainly, an economy that is built on and rewards private ownership and individual acquisition, and is subject to the personal and social conflicts these arrangement impose, can be expected to be gratified with an explanation that legitimizes its operative principles. How reassuring to consider these conflictful relationships inherent in the human condition rather than imposed by social circumstance! This outlook fits nicely too with the anti-ideological stance the system projects. It induces a "scientific" and "objective" approach to the human condition rigorously measuring human microbehavior in all its depravities, and for the most part ignoring the broader and less measurable social parameters.

Daily TV programming, for example, with its quota of half a dozen murders per hour, is rationalized easily by media controllers as an effort to give the people what they want. Too bad, they shrug, if human nature demands eighteen hours daily of mayhem and slaughter. ...

Fortune finds it cheering, for example, that some American social scientists are again emphasizing "the intractability of human nature" in their explanations of social phenomena. "The orthodox view of environment as the all-important influence on people's behavior," it reports, "is yielding to a new awareness of the role of hereditary factors: enthusiasm for schemes to reform society by remolding men is giving way to a healthy appreciation of the basic intractability of human nature."[4]

The net social effects of the thesis that human nature is at fault are further disorientation, total inability to recognize the causes of malaise—much less to take any steps to overcome it—and, of most consequence, continued adherence to the *status quo*. . . .

It is to prevent social action (and it is immaterial whether the intent is articulated or not) that so much publicity and attention are devoted to every pessimistic appraisal of human potential. If we are doomed forever by our inheritance, there is not much to be done about it. But there is a good reason and a good market for undervaluing human capability. An entrenched social system depends on keeping the popular and, especially, the "enlightened" mind unsure and doubtful about its human prospects. . . .

This does not necessitate ignoring history. On the contrary, endless recitation of what happened in the past accompanies assertions about how much change is occurring under our very noses. But these are invariably *physical* changes—new means of transportation, air conditioning, space rockets, packaged foods. Mind managers dwell on these matters but carefully refrain from considering changes in social relationships or in the institutional structures that undergird the economy.

Every conceivable kind of futuristic device is canvassed and blueprinted. Yet those who will use these wonder items will apparently continue to be married, raise children in suburban homes, work for private companies, vote for a President in a two-party system, and pay a large portion of their incomes for defense, law and order, and superhighways. The world, except for some glamorous surface redecorations, will remain as it is; basic relationships will not change, because they, like human nature, are allegedly unchangeable. As for those parts of the world that have undergone far-reaching social rearrangements, reports of these transformations, if there are any, emphasize the defects, problems, and crises, which are seized upon with relish by domestic consciousness manipulators. . . .

4. The Myth of the Absence of Social Conflict. . . . Consciousness controllers, in their presentation of the domestic scene, deny absolutely the presence of social conflict. On the face of it, this seems an impossible task. After all, violence is "as American as apple pie." Not only in fact but in fantasy: in films, on TV, and over the radio, the daily quota of violent scenarios offered the public is staggering. How is this carnival of conflict reconcilable with the media managers' intent to present an image of social harmony? The contradiction is easily resolved.

As presented by the national message-making apparatus, conflict is almost always an *individual* matter, in its manifestations and in its origin. The social roots of conflict just do not exist for the cultural-informational managers.

True, there are "good guys" and "bad guys," but, except for such ritualized situations as westerns, which are recognized as scenarios of the past, role identification is divorced from significant social categories.

Black, brown, yellow, red, and other ethnic Americans have always fared poorly in the manufactured cultural imagery. Still, these are minorities which all segments of the white population have exploited in varying degrees. As for the great social division in the nation, between worker and owner, with rare exceptions it has been left unexamined. Attention is diverted elsewhere—generally toward the problems of the upward-striving middle segment of the population, that category with which everyone is supposed to identify. . . .

Elite control requires omission or distortion of social reality. Honest examination and discussion of social conflict can only deepen and intensify resistance to social inequity. Economically powerful groups and companies quickly get edgy when attention is called to exploitative practices in which they are engaged. *Variety*'s television editor, Les Brown, described such an incident. Coca-Cola Food Company and the Florida Fruit and Vegetable Association reacted sharply to a TV documentary, "Migrant," which centered on migrant fruit pickers in Florida. Brown wrote that "the miracle of *Migrant* was that it was televised at all." Warnings were sent to NBC not to show the program because it was "biased." Cuts in the film were demanded, and at least one was made. Finally, after the showing, "Coca-Cola shifted all its network billings to CBS and ABC."[5]

On a strictly commercial level, the presentation of social issues creates uneasiness in mass audiences, or so the audience researchers believe. To be safe, to hold onto as large a public as possible, sponsors are always eager to eliminate potentially "controversial" program material.

The entertainments and cultural products that have been most successful in the United States, those that have received the warmest support and publicity from the communications system, are invariably movies, TV programs, books, and mass entertainments (i.e., Disneyland) which may offer more than a fair quota of violence but never take up *social* conflict. . . .

5. The Myth of Media Pluralism. Personal choice exercised in an environment of cultural-information diversity is the image, circulated worldwide, of the condition of life in America. This view is also internalized in the belief structure of a large majority of Americans, which makes them particularly susceptible to thoroughgoing manipulation. It is, therefore, one of the central myths upon which mind management flourishes. Choice and diversity, though separate concepts, are in fact inseparable; choice is unattainable in any real sense without diversity. If real options are nonexistent, choosing is either meaningless or manipulative. It is manipulative when accompanied by the illusion that the choice is meaningful.

Though it cannot be verified, the odds are that the illusion of informational choice is more pervasive in the United States than anywhere else in the world. The illusion is sustained by a willingness, deliberately maintained by information controllers, to mistake *abundance of media* for *diversity of content.* . . .

The fact of the matter is that, except for a rather small and highly selective segment of the population who know what they are looking for and can therefore take advantage of the massive communications flow, most Americans are basically, though unconsciously, trapped in what amounts to a no-choice informational bind. Variety of opinion on foreign and domestic news or, for that matter, local community business, hardly exists in the media. This results essentially from the inherent identity of interests, material and ideological, of property-holders (in this case, the private owners of the communications media), and from the monopolistic character of the communications industry in general.

The limiting effects of monopoly are in need of no explanation, and communications monopolies restrict informational choice wherever they operate. They offer one version of reality—their own. In this category fall most of the nation's newspapers, magazines, and films, which are produced by national or regional communications conglomerates. The number of American cities in which competing newspapers circulate has shrunk to a handful.

While there is a competition of sorts for audiences among the three major TV networks, two conditions determine the limits of the variety presented. Though each network struggles gamely to attract as large an audience as possible, it imitates its two rivals in program format and content. If ABC is successful with a western serial, CBS and NBC will in all likelihood "compete" with "shoot-'em-ups" in the same time slot. Besides, each of the three national networks is part of, or is itself, an enormous communications business, with the drives and motivations of any other profit-seeking enterprise. This means that diversity in the informational-entertainment sector exists only in the sense that there are a number of superficially different versions of the main categories of program. For example, there are several talk shows on late-night TV; there may be half a dozen private-eye, western, or law-and-order TV serials to "choose from" in prime time; there are three network news commentators with different personalities who offer essentially identical information. One can switch the radio dial and get round-the-clock news from one or, at most, two news services; or one can hear Top 40 popular songs played by "competing" disc jockeys.

Though no single program, performer, commentator, or informational bit is necessarily identical to its competitors, *there is no significant qualitative difference.* Just as a supermarket offers six identical soaps in different colors and a drugstore sells a variety of brands of aspirin at different prices, disc jockeys play the same records between personalized advertisements for different commodities. . . .

Yet it is this condition of communicational pluralism, empty as it is of real diversity, which affords great strength to the prevailing system of consciousness-packaging. The multichannel communications flow creates confidence in, and lends credibility to, the notion of free informational choice. Meanwhile, its main effect is to provide continuous reinforcement of the *status quo.* Similar stimuli, emanating from apparently diverse sources, envelop the listener/viewer/reader in a message/image environment that ordinarily seems uncontrolled, relatively free, and quite natural. How could it be otherwise with such an abundance of programs and transmitters? Corporate profit-seeking, the main objective of conglomerated communications, however real and ultimately determining, is an invisible abstraction to the consumers of the cultural images. And one thing is certain: the media do not call their audiences' attention to its existence or its mode of operation....

The fundamental similarity of the informational material and cultural messages that each of the mass media *independently* transmits makes it necessary to view the communications system as a totality. The media are mutually and continuously reinforcing. Since they operate according to commercial rules, rely on advertising, and are tied tightly to the corporate economy, both in their own structure and in their relationships with sponsors, the media constitute an industry, not an aggregation of independent, freewheeling informational entrepreneurs, each offering a highly individualistic product. By need and by design, the images and messages they purvey are, with few exceptions, constructed to achieve similar objectives, which are, simply put, profitability and the affirmation and maintenance of the private-ownership consumer society.

Consequently, research directed at discovering the impact of a single TV program or movie, or even an entire category of stimuli, such as "violence on TV," can often be fruitless. Who can justifiably claim that TV violence is inducing delinquent juvenile behavior when violence is endemic to all mass communications channels? Who can suggest that any single category of programming is producing male chauvinist or racist behavior when stimuli and imagery carrying such sentiments flow unceasingly through all the channels of transmission?

It is generally agreed that television is the most powerful medium; certainly its influence as a purveyor of the system's values cannot be overstated. All the same, television, no matter how powerful, itself depends on the absence of dissonant stimuli in the other media. Each of the informational channels makes its unique contribution, but the result is the same—the consolidation of the *status quo.*

NOTES

1. Paulo Freire, *Pedagogy of the Oppressed* (New York: Herder and Herder, 1971), p. 144.

2. C. B. MacPherson, *The Political Theory of Possessive Individualism* (Oxford: Clarendon Press, 1962).

3. Henry Luce, the founder of *Time, Life, Fortune, Sports Illustrated,* and other mass circulation magazines, knew otherwise. He told his staff at *Time:* "The alleged journalistic objectivity, a claim that a writer presents facts without applying any value judgment to them [is] modern usage—and that is strictly a phony. It is that that I had to renounce and denounce. So when we say the hell with objectivity, that is what we are talking about." W. A. Swanberg, *Luce and His Empire* (New York: Charles Scribner's Sons, 1972), p. 331.

4. "The Social Engineers Retreat Under Fire," *Fortune,* October 1972, p. 3.

5. Les Brown, *Television: The Business Behind The Box* (New York: Harcourt, Brace Jovanovich, 1971), pp. 196–203.

The Media Cartel: Corporate Control of the News

In the following selection from *Unreliable Sources: A Guide to Detecting Bias in News Media* (Carol Publishing Group, 1990), Martin A. Lee and Norman Solomon examine the consequences of corporate ownership of mass media. Their research is part of a larger media "watchdog" project called Fairness and Accuracy in Reporting, or FAIR, of which Lee and Solomon are a part. For FAIR the key issue is that mass media systems are not only run as profit-making ventures but they are also now owned and operated by powerful multinational corporations that have close ties to national governments. Given the propaganda function of the media, the authors believe that corporate media will systematically represent their own interests—i.e., those of their owning corporations—which include ties between the corporate sphere and the state. Lee and Solomon further contend that corporate-state power represents its own interests *not* by informing the public as to the operation of its political-economic power but by disseminating myths that operate to conceal the real function of this power and, thus, to gain public consent to the existing situation.

Lee and Solomon argue that the public must become critical consumers of media messages and learn how to detect systematic bias in favor of corporate-state interests in the mass media. In the following selection, the authors analyze the implications of corporate control of news production in the cases of the merger of Time, Inc. and Warner, Inc., and the General Electric Corporation's acquisition of the NBC television network.

Key Concept: military-industrial-media complex

Do the business priorities of their corporate bosses affect the way journalists cover the news? Consider network news coverage of the 1988 Winter Olympics in Calgary, Canada. All three network news divisions had to decide how much attention the Olympics warranted. NBC devoted a total of 33 minutes of national news coverage to the games, while CBS News provided 17 minutes of coverage. Compare these figures to ABC, which found the Winter Olympics worthy of 47 minutes on its nightly newscasts. Is it merely coincidental that ABC also televised the Winter Olympics and a heavy news focus helped build ratings and profits? Are we to believe that such concerns had no bearing on the "independent news judgment" of ABC producers?

ABC News found the 1988 Summer Olympic Games in Seoul, South Korea, less newsworthy than the winter games. That's because ABC didn't televise the Summer Olympics—NBC did. As it turned out, NBC News considered the summer games and their Korean hosts far more newsworthy than the other networks. NBC's inflated news coverage was geared toward attracting a larger audience—which translated into greater earnings for the network. So much for the hallowed precept that news choices are based solely on the intrinsic importance of a story and are immune to financial considerations.

The truth of the matter is that financial interests play a major role in determining what we see—and don't see—on television. Most of the top network sponsors are powerful multinational corporations. These global mammoths dominate our broadcast and print media far more extensively than most people realize. They exert tremendous leverage over the media industry because they are its principal source of revenue: TV and radio get nearly 100 percent of their income from advertisers, newspapers 75 percent, and magazines about 50 percent....

TIME WARNER TANGO

"It looks like the Rolling Stones are coming here next week," remarked a security guard as he eyed a mob of would-be spectators waiting outside a packed Delaware courthouse. They were there to witness in person the Delaware Supreme Court's historic decision on the fate of Time Inc., target of one of the year's fiercest takeover battles. But only those with special passes were permitted inside on July 24, 1989; the rest had to settle for watching the courtroom drama unfold on Cable News Network. It was the first time ever in Delaware corporate law that TV cameras were allowed in a courtroom.

Even in an era of deregulated merger mania, this corporate tryst was remarkable for the attention it generated. It began in March 1989, when Time and Warner, two communications giants, announced a major stock swap as part of a friendly deal which would have effectively combined the companies, forming the largest—and arguably the most influential—media conglomerate in the world. The business profile of Time Inc., America's biggest magazine ad revenue earner and publisher (*Time, Life, Fortune, People, Sports Illustrated*, etc.), meshed particularly well with Warner, the number-one record and TV production company in the United States. With combined assets somewhere between $25 and $30 billion, they also controlled a major chunk of the cable, motion picture and book markets, including Home Box Office (the nation's largest pay TV channel), Lorimar Studios and the Book-of-the-Month Club.

Such an amalgam of lucrative components gave Time Warner distinct advantages for promoting their products in a multiplicity of media. A magazine article with the company copyright, for example, could be expanded into a Time Warner book. It could serve as the basis for a film made at an in-house studio, which would then be distributed through a movie theater chain owned by the same company. The movie doubtless will be reviewed in widely-read magazines also published by Time Warner, and the soundtrack would be issued on a company record label. To catch a re-run, turn to one of Time Warner's cable channels. "More and more, we will be dealing with closed loops," predicts Ben Bagdikian, as a handful of mega-conglomerates squeeze out others in the field.

The prospect of Time Warner commanding such a dominant position in the news and entertainment universe made executives at Paramount, another media titan, hyperactive with envy. It soon became a three-ring circus, as Paramount leaped into the fray, waving top dollar for Time Inc. stock, which shot up 45 points in a single day. Time was suddenly "in play," as market euphoria carried clusters of media stock skyward, followed by a period of wild fluctuation as rumors swept through Wall Street that other corporate heavyweights, including General Electric, might join the battle for Time.

The well-planned Time Warner merger quickly degenerated into a full-fledged corporate scramble involving investment bankers, blue chip law firms, PR strategists and a fleet of private detectives hired to dig up dirt on the other parties. Time execs rejected Paramount's hostile takeover bid and announced their intention to buy Warner outright. Paramount countered by upping its offer. There was even talk of a reverse takeover—the so-called Pac Man defense—in which Time would turn around and swallow up Paramount. Sensing opportunity amidst all the turmoil, Australian media magnate Rupert Murdoch hovered in the wings, ready to grab any loose assets shed during the scuffle. At stake were commercial empires so vast it staggered the imagination.

While Wall Street movers and shakers were having a field day, those who punched the clock day-in and day-out at Time Inc. grew increasingly nervous. Someone would have to pay for the huge debt amassed by the company, as it sought to stave off Paramount's maneuvers. Given that well-heeled executives and publishers aren't in the habit of volunteering cuts in their seven-figure salaries, it seemed likely that Time's rank-and-file would bear the brunt of the inevitable belt-tightening, layoffs and restructuring that a debt-laden company must undertake.

When the dust finally settled, the Delaware Supreme Court upheld Time's proposed $14 billion buyout of Warner, leaving Paramount to search elsewhere for media industry prey. Most of the press covered the entire ordeal simply as a business story without dwelling on the social and political consequences of such a merger. The main criticisms were voiced by big media execs concerned about facing an even bigger bully on the block. A *New York Times* article, headlined "Time Deal Worrying Competitors," featured comments to that effect by Robert Wright, president of NBC, owned by little ol' GE. Journalists covering the Time Warner merger rarely featured statements by public interest critics warning that mass media concentration in fewer and fewer corporate hands poses a serious threat to pluralism, democratic discourse and the First Amendment....

MILITARY-INDUSTRIAL-MEDIA COMPLEX:
THE CASE OF GENERAL ELECTRIC AND NBC

In January 1961, shortly before he handed over the formal reins of power, President Dwight Eisenhower issued a blunt warning to the American people about the "immense military establishment" whose "total influence—economic, political, even spiritual—is felt in every city, every state house, every office of the federal government." The departing chief added: "We must guard against the acquisition of unwarranted influence ... by the military-industrial complex. The potential for disastrous rise of misplaced power exists and will persist."

General Electric, a financial and industrial behemoth with annual sales topping $50 billion, has long been a key player in the military-industrial complex. Ranked second among U.S. military contractors, GE makes the detonators for every nuclear bomb in America's arsenal. There are few modern weapons systems that GE has not been instrumental in developing. In addition to nuclear and conventional arms, GE manufactures refrigerators, electric motors, medical equipment, plastics, light bulbs and communications satellites. It also owns the Wall Street firm Kidder-Peabody. When it acquired RCA, the parent company of NBC, for $6.28 billion in 1986—at that point the largest non-oil corporate merger in U.S. history—GE added a formidable media component to its worldwide business empire.

The saga of GE—marked by fraud, scandals, labor strife and contempt for the natural environment—illustrates the dangers of misplaced power that Eisenhower spoke about, but which the U.S. media rarely probe at length. Here are a few examples: In 1932, GE initiated a policy of planned obsolescence and cut the life of light bulbs in order to boost sales during the Depression. During World War II, GE was convicted of illegally collaborating with Germany's Krupp company, a linchpin of the Nazi war machine. And in 1961, GE was convicted of price-fixing, bid-rigging and antitrust violations, for which it had to pay a large fine in addition to a $57 million settlement with the U.S. government and other customers. Three GE officials served brief jail terms. But GE's attorney Clark Clifford (chair of the CIA's Foreign Intelligence Advisory Board and a future Defense Secretary) convinced the IRS that the damages GE had to pay for its criminal activities could be written off as a tax-deductible business expense!

With the IRS doling out favors to big business, the pattern of corruption continued. In 1981, GE was found guilty of bribing a Puerto Rican official to obtain a $92 million contract to build a power plant on the island. GE paid no income tax that year, even though its pre-tax earnings were a nifty $2.66 billion; what's more, GE somehow qualified for a $90 million rebate from the IRS. (Is that what they mean by "free enterprise"?) In 1985, GE became the first weapons contractor to be found guilty of defrauding the U.S. government by overcharging on military contracts.

Ronald Reagan: GE Front-Man

GE's well-documented record of deceit should have been grounds for the Justice Department to disqualify the company from acquiring NBC. But GE had friends in high places and the deal went through without a hitch. The fact that Ronald Reagan had previously spent eight years on GE's payroll as the company's chief PR spokesman undoubtedly helped matters. Publicist Edward Langley, who has written on Reagan's GE years, described GE as "a company so obsessed with conservatism that it was not unlike the John Birch Society."

Reagan signed on with GE in 1954, when his acting career was floundering. He hosted and occasionally starred in the long-running *General Electric Theater* series that aired on CBS. Soon Reagan began touring the country at GE's behest, making speeches against communism, labor unions, social security, public housing and, of course, corporate taxes. These GE-sponsored lectures laid the groundwork for Reagan's political career, and the rest, as they say, is history.

A number of Reagan cabinet officials had close relations with GE. William French Smith, Reagan's personal attorney, joined GE's board of directors shortly after leaving the administration. It was during Smith's tenure as U.S. Attorney General in the mid-1980s that the Justice Department modified antitrust regulations, thereby enabling GE to buy NBC.

It wasn't always so easy to pull off this kind of merger. ITT's attempt to acquire ABC in 1966–67 provoked a public outcry; the plan was nixed after the Justice Department found that ITT control "could compromise the independence of ABC's news coverage of political events in countries where ITT has interests." The same logic could have been applied to GE, which operates in 50 foreign countries, but its purchase of NBC in 1986 was hardly debated in Washington or the U.S. media.

NBC is one of GE's most profitable assets, largely due to austerity measures such as reducing the news division staff from 1,400 to 1,000. This was par for the course at a GE-owned company. In less than a decade since John Welsh became GE's CEO in 1981, over a hundred thousand employees were laid off —25 percent of GE's total work force. These cutbacks occurred at a time when the company was earning record profits. Welsh has been nicknamed "Neutron Jack" because, like the neutron bomb, he makes people disappear but leaves the buildings standing.

The Nuts and Bolts of Censorship

How has ownership by GE influenced what we see—or don't see—on NBC News programs? NBC has repeatedly insisted that its relationship to GE does not affect its news coverage. But certain incidents suggest otherwise.

For example, a reference to the General Electric Company was surgically removed from a report on substandard products before it aired on NBC's *Today* show on November 30, 1989. The report focused on a federal investigation of inferior bolts used by GE and other firms in building airplanes, bridges, nuclear missile silos and equipment for the NASA space program. It said that 60 percent of the 200 billion bolts used annually in the U.S. may be faulty. The censored portion of the *Today* show included this passage: "Recently, General Electric engineers discovered they had a big problem. One out of three bolts from one of their major suppliers was bad. Even more alarming, GE accepted the bad bolts without any certification of compliance for eight years."

Peter Karl, the journalist who produced the segment, called NBC's decision to eliminate references to GE "insidious." He cited the "chilling effect" on a network that is "overprotective of a corporate owner."

In March 1987, NBC news broadcast a special documentary, "Nuclear Power: In France It works," which could have passed for an hour-long nuclear power commercial. In an upbeat introduction, NBC anchor Tom Brokaw neglected to state that his corporate patron is America's second-largest nuclear energy vendor, with 39 nuclear power reactors in the U.S., and the third-leading nuclear weapons producer—facts which gave rise to the moniker "Nuclear Broadcasting Company" among disgruntled NBC staff.

Herein lay a fundamental conflict of interest, which Brokaw didn't own up to. Citizens' fear of nuclear technology could cut into GE's profits—and these fears were a key target of this so-called "News Special." An NBC crew toured France as if on a pilgrimage to the atomic land of Oz, off to see the wizardry of safe nuclear power plants. "Looking at a foreign country where nuclear power is a fact of life may restore some reason to the discussion at home," said correspondent Steven Delaney. "In most countries, especially the U.S., emotions drive the nuclear debate and that makes rational dialogue very difficult."

Having sung the praises of the French nuclear industry, NBC News bluffed when discussing what to do with radioactive waste, some of which remains lethal for dozens of centuries or longer: "The French will probably succeed in their disposal plan for the same reasons the rest of their nuclear program works... The French have more faith than we do in the government's competence to manage the nuclear program, and the French government has less tolerance for endless dissent."

Unfortunately, faith and lack of tolerance for dissent will not solve critical nuclear problems, even in France. One month after NBC aired its pro-nuclear broadcast, there were accidents at two French nuclear power installations, injuring seven workers. The *Christian Science Monitor* wrote of a "potentially explosive debate" in France, with polls showing a third of the French public opposing nuclear power. While the accidents were widely discussed in the French media and some U.S. newspapers, NBC TV did not report the story.

A telling sidelight to this incident occurred the following year when NBC's pro-nuke documentary won first prize for science journalism in a competition sponsored by the Westinghouse Foundation, an affiliate of Westinghouse Electric Company. Like GE, Westinghouse is a military-industrial powerhouse with large investments in nuclear power and weapons, as well as in broadcast media. Westinghouse owns Group W Cable and is the second largest radio station operator in the United States.

Westinghouse gave NBC its journalism trophy not long after GE was publicly implicated in yet another major scandal. A member of the Nuclear Regulatory Commission (NRC) resigned, charging that GE had "struck a deal" with the NRC to keep secret the contents of a 1975 GE internal report critical of its faulty nuclear reactor design. The report—which documented problems such as earthquake hazards and radiation dangers for plant workers—prompted suits by three Midwest utility companies which claimed that GE knowingly installed unsafe systems. Ironically, Jim Lawless, the *Cleveland Plain Dealer* reporter who first exposed the GE nuclear cover-up, was yanked from the utilities beat after the parent company of Cleveland's powerful electric utility complained to the *Plain Dealer*'s management about alleged "bias" in coverage by Lawless.

In 1986, New York State officials banned recreational and commercial bass fishing after GE had polluted the Hudson River with 400,000 ponds of carcinogenic PCBs. Moreover, according to EPA's 1989 Superfund list, GE was responsible for 47 toxic waste sites around the country—the most of any firm cited.

Not surprisingly, NBC News staffers haven't shown much zeal for investigating environmental abuse by the company that pays their salaries. Nor have they done much digging into Kidder-Peabody, GE's brokerage subsidiary, which has been implicated in insider trading scandals on Wall Street. And the worldwide consumer boycott of GE products launched by INFACT, a group opposed to nuclear profiteering, hasn't been a hot topic on NBC News either. INFACT's TV commercials, urging consumers not to buy GE products, were banned by NBC and other television broadcasters.

Conflicts of Interest

GE and other military contractors made out like bandits during the Reagan administration, which presided over the largest peacetime military build-up in U.S. history. And bandits is exactly what they are, as the Pentagon procurement scandal, involving dozens of military contractors, amply demonstrates. GE was pegged with a 321-count indictment in November 1988 for trying to defraud the Department of Defense.

Despite such shenanigans, GE continued to receive hefty Defense Department contracts. Star Wars research was a veritable cash cow for GE and other high-tech weapons manufacturers. An article in the *New York Times* business section pointed out that the Star Wars program (and, by implication, GE contracts) could be scuttled if a major arms control agreement were reached or if a Democrat got elected to the White House. Star Wars subsequently became an issue during the 1988 presidential campaign; Bush was for it and Dukakis was against it. Thus NBC's owner had a material interest in the outcome of the election. NBC President Robert Wright donated money to the Bush campaign, as did GE chief "Neutron Jack" Welsh. NBC News employees didn't have to be told that a Dukakis victory—or tough, critical reporting on Star Wars—could cost GE millions of dollars.

Given GE's far-flung, diversified interests, there aren't many subjects that NBC News could cover that would not have a direct or indirect bearing on its corporate parent. Conflicts of interest are unavoidable as long as GE owns NBC. "As a newswriter I'm constantly aware who my boss is," a disaffected NBC News staffer told the media watch group FAIR shortly before he was laid off by the network.

Of course, NBC News doesn't completely ignore embarrassing stories about its owner. That would be too blatant, particularly when other news outlets refer in passing to GE corruption. When GE was indicted for its role in the

1988 Pentagon procurement scandal, *NBC Nightly News* gave a straightforward report—that lasted about ten seconds. There was little follow-up on this scandal by any of the major networks. The corporate zeitgeist doesn't encourage a sustained in-depth investigation of such matters.

It would be an overstatement to say that the topic of GE's ownership is banned entirely from NBC broadcasts. Occasionally, David Letterman will make a few joking references to GE on his late-night show. In that ha-ha context, a bit of lampooning about corporate daddy is permissible. At first glance a concession to openness and self-criticism, such quips may be just the reverse—a kind of inoculation, making light of potential conflicts of interests and ethical quagmires. Like the Fool in a Shakespeare play, Letterman is allowed to utter some jestful references to what's really going on beneath the pretenses. But as for serious examination by NBC News, forget it . . .

Nor are the other major networks in much of a position to cast the first stone. CapCities/ABC and CBS are interlinked with other huge conglomerates that are part of the military-industrial complex. The boards of directors of the Big Three are composed of executives, lawyers, financiers and former government officials who represent the biggest banks and corporations in the U.S., including military and nuclear contractors, oil companies, agribusiness, insurance and utility firms.

So too with leading newspapers and other major media. The *New York Times*, for example, is not only the newspaper of record for the Fortune 500; it is also a member in good standing of that elite club. There are numerous interlocks between the board of directors of the *New York Times* and the nuclear industry, which partially explains why it has been a fanatical supporter of nuclear weapon and atomic power plants.

Among the 14-member *New York Times* corporate board is George B. Munroe, retired chair and CEO of Phelps Dodge, a notorious anti-union company involved in uranium mining. Munroe and other *Times* board member, George Shinn, are also directors of Manufacturers Hanover, a bank that lent money to bail out LILCO, a New York utility, as plans for the Shoreham nuclear power plant fell to widespread citizen opposition. (The *Times* steadfastly backed the Shoreham project in dozens of strident editorials, without letting its readers know of these corporate links.) In addition, *Times* board member William R. Cross is vice chairman of the credit policy committee of Morgan bank, another LILCO creditor. And Marian S. Heiskell, sister of *Times* publisher and CEO Arthur Ochs Sulzberger, sits on the board of Con Edison, another nuclear utility.

Time Warner, the world's biggest media corporation, has so many interlocks with Fortune 500 companies that its board reads like a Who's Who of U.S. business and finance. Directors include representatives from military contractors such as General Dynamics, IBM and AT&T, as well as movers and shakers from Mobile Oil, Atlantic Richfield, Xerox and a number of major international banks. But Time Warner and other mass media won't discuss conflicts of interest inherent in interlocking directorates and how these may affect the selection and presentation of news stories. That subject is strictly taboo.

Blueblood media and their corporate cousins have a vast stake in decisions made by the U.S. government. Through elite policy-shaping groups like the Council on Foreign Relations and the Business Roundtable, they steer the ship of state in what they deem to be a financially advantageous direction. (GE, CapCities, CBS, the *New York Times* and the *Washington Post* all have board members who sit on the Council on Foreign Relations.) They have much to gain from a favorable investment climate in Third World countries and bloated military budgets at home.

This was made explicit by former GE President Charles Wilson, a long-time advocate of a permanent war economy, who worked with the Pentagon's Office of Defense Mobilization during the 1950s. In a speech before the American newspaper Publishers Association, he urged the media to rally behind the government's Cold War crusade. "The free world is in mortal danger. If the people were not convinced of that, it would be impossible for Congress to vote vast sums now being spent to avert that danger," said Wilson. "With the support of public opinion, as marshalled by the press, we are off to a good start... It is our job—yours and mine—to keep our people convinced that the only way to keep disaster away from our shores is to build America's might."

Nowadays, General Electric doesn't need to marshall the press to persuade the masses; it owns the press—or at least a sizable chunk of it. Moreover GE's board of directors interlocks with various media, including the Washington Post Company, Harper & Row (book publishers), and the Gannett Foundation. GE also owns a cable channel (CNBC) and sponsors news programs on other networks, such as ABC's *This Week With David Brinkley*, CNN's *Crossfire*, and the *McLaughlin Group* on PBS. As a communications manager at GE explained, "We insist on a program environment that reinforces our corporate messages."

In what has become standard operating procedure for mega-corporations, GE spends millions of dollars each year sprucing up its image. But behind the catchy PR slogan, "We bring good things to life," lurks a legacy of faulty nuclear reactors, toxic waste dumps, bribery, cheating and cover-up. The chasm between this reality and GE's heroic self-image underscores an essential point: advertising is institutionalized lying, and such lies are tolerated, even encouraged, because they serve the needs of the corporate establishment. Network news is brought to us by sponsors that lie routinely, matter-of-factly, as it were. Under such circumstances how truthful can we expect the news to be?

The Think Tank Scam

In an effort to get the corporate message across and maximize sympathetic public opinion, GE and like-minded business firms fill the coffers of influential conservative think tanks. Representatives from these well-heeled organizations are quoted regularly in the press and they often pose as unbiased "experts" on television news and public affairs shows. In this capacity they directly serve the interests of the corporations which hold their purse strings.

Martin A. Lee and Norman Solomon

The American Enterprise Institute (AEI) runs a highly effective PR operation AEI resident scholars, such as would-be Supreme Court justice Robert Bork and former U.N. ambassador Jeane Kirkpatrick, generate a steady flow of opinion columns on political, social and economic issues that are syndicated in hundreds of news dailies; other AEI associates serve as paid consultants for the three main TV networks. AEI "quotemaster" Norman J. Ornstein claimed to have logged 1,294 calls from 183 news organizations in 1988.

AEI receives financial support from various news media, including the *New York Times,* the Philip L. Graham Fund (*Washington Post*) and Times-Mirror (parent company of the *Los Angeles Times*). Among AEI's favorite whipping boys is Jesse Jackson, whose populist, anti-corporate presidential campaigning undoubtedly annoyed the high-brow business executives from Mobile Oil, Proctor & Gamble, Chase Manhattan, Citibank, Rockwell International and GE who sit on AEI's board of trustees.

GE also supports the Center for Strategic and International Studies (CSIS), an AEI spinoff based in Washington. CSIS functions as a way station for U.S. intelligence operatives as they shuttle back and forth through the revolving door that links the public (or at least as public as spooks can be) and private sectors. Representatives from CSIS and the Rand Corporation, another CIA-linked think tank, frequently appear on TV to comment on terrorism and other "national security" issues. Directors of GE and CBS sit on the Rand Corporation board. During one six-week period, CSIS fellows tallied 650 media "contacts" —TV appearances, opinion columns and quotations in news stories.

The Heritage Foundation, which functioned virtually as a shadow government during much of the Reagan administration, is another media favorite, according to a survey of news sources conducted by the University of Windsor. Burton Yale Pines, formerly a *Time* magazine associate editor and AEI "resident journalist," went on to become vice president of Heritage. GE director Henry H. Henley Jr. is a Heritage board member. Funders include Henley's company —Cluett, Peabody—along with Joseph Coors, the Reader's Digest Foundation (which also finances AEI), Mobil Oil and other major corporations. According to *The Nation* magazine, Heritage also received money on the sly from South Korean intelligence to support its Asian Studies Center.

It's another closed loop: Analysts from think tanks funded by GE and the Fortune 500 elite appear as "independent experts" on TV networks owned and sponsored by the same corporations. When the networks want someone to ratify corporate news and opinion, they turn to a stable of approved think tank specialists. Not surprisingly these well-paid sluggers go to bat for big business and the national security state, confirming biases already deeply-ingrained in U.S. media. Thus we see a lot of "hot spot" coverage on TV that gives the impression that the world is not a safe place for Americans; this unsettling picture is invariably confirmed by the same coterie of pundits who exude a false aura of objectivity as they define security in terms of brute military force rather than a healthy environment workplace safety and a strong, equitable economy. The prevalence of conservative think-tank mavens on TV and in the press is yet another symptom of corporate domination of the mass media.

CHAPTER 9 Advertising, Media, and Society

9.1 STUART EWEN

Captains of Consciousness: Advertising and the Social Roots of the Consumer Culture

Stuart Ewen, whose work represents a critical perspective in media studies, does not regard advertising as a form of market information designed to help consumers make choices in the marketplace. Nor does Ewen regard advertising simply as another cultural industry alongside television, movies, or radio, transmitting its own brand of consumer propaganda. Rather, he believes that advertising is the economic, social, and ideological keystone of modern capitalist societies. In the following selection from his historical analysis of advertising *Captains of Consciousness: Advertising and the Social Roots of the Consumer Culture* (McGraw-Hill, 1976), Ewen shows that advertising rose to solve, at one stroke, a profound double crisis in the United States at the turn of the twentieth century. By socializing the emerging working class to identify themselves primarily as consumers, advertising helped create a demand for goods, which prevented economic stagnation and gave workers imaginary power and freedom associated with products in ads, thereby staving off the threat of working-class conflict. Ewen reveals *how* advertising acted to form this new consciousness; it did not simply deceive the working class as to the nature and benefits of new products but it *mobilized the instincts* and *civilized the self*, both in terms of consuming industrially produced commodities.

Ewen is a professor of history at Hunter College in New York City. He has expanded his critique of the social and historical role of advertising to include the broader issues of commercial imagery and the associated phenomenon of style in contemporary culture in *All Consuming Images: The Politics of Style in Contemporary Culture* (Basic Books, 1988) and *Channels of Desire: Mass Images and the Shaping of American Consciousness,* 2d ed. (University of Minnesota Press, 1992), coauthored with Elizabeth Ewen.

Key Concept: the social production of consumers

"SHORTER HOURS, HIGHER WAGES..."

In 1910, Henry Ford instituted the "line production system" for "maximum production economy" in his Highland Park, Michigan, plant.[1] The innovation, though in many ways unsophisticated, and hardly educated as to its own implications, was the beginning of a momentous transformation in America's capacity to produce. In quantitative terms, the change was staggering. On the 1910 line, the time required to assemble a chassis was twelve hours and twenty-eight minutes. "By spring of 1914, the Highland Park plant was turning out over 1,000 vehicles a day, and the average labor time for assembling a chassis had dropped to one hour and thirty-three minutes."[2]

Mass production was a way of making production more economical. Through his use of the assembly line, Ford was able to utilize "expensive, single-purpose" machinery along with "quickly trained, single-purpose" workmen to make a single-model, inexpensive automobile at a rate which, with increasing sophistication, continued to dwarf not only the production levels of premassified industry, but the output of less refined mass production systems.[3]

By the 1920s, interest in and employment of the industrial potential of mass production extended far beyond the automobile industry. In recognition of such industrial developments, the United States Special Census of 1921 and 1923 offered a study of productive capacity[4] which was one of the first general discussions of its kind.[5] Consumer goods manufacturers were coming to recognize that mass production and mass distribution were "necessary" steps toward survival in a competitive market. Edward Filene, of the Boston department store family, a businessman founder of the consumer union movement, articulated the competitive compulsion of mass production. Competition, said Filene, "will compel us to Fordize American business and industry."

And yet, what Filene and others meant by "Fordizing" American industry transcended the myopic vision of Henry Ford. While Ford stubbornly held to the notion that "the work and the work *alone* controls us,"[7] others in the automobile industry[8] and, (for our purposes) more importantly, ideologues of mass industry outside of the auto industry viewed the strategy of production in far broader social terms. Before mass production, industry had produced for a limited, largely middle- and upper-class market. With a burgeoning productive capacity, industry now required an equivalent increase in potential consumers of its goods. "Scientific production promised to make the conventional notion of the self-reliant producer/consumer anachronistic."[9]

The mechanism of mass production could not function unless markets became more dynamic, growing horizontally (nationally), vertically (into social classes not previously among the consumers) and ideologically. Now men and women had to be habituated to respond to the demands of the productive machinery. The corollary to a freely growing system of goods production was a "systematic, nationwide plan... to endow the masses with more buying power," a freely growing system of consumer production.[10]...

As capitalism became characterized by mass production and the subsequent need for mass distribution, traditional expedients for the real or attempted manipulation of labor were transformed. While the nineteenth-century industrialist coerced labor (both on and off the job) to serve as the "wheelhorse" of industry, modernizing capitalism sought to change "wheelhorse" to "worker" and "worker" to "consumer."[11]

For the workers, the movement toward mass production had severely changed the character of labor. The worker had become a decreasingly "significant" unit of production within the modern manufacturing process. "The man who had been the more or less creative maker of the whole of an article became the tender of a machine that made only one small part of the article."[12] The time required to teach the worker the "adept performance" of his "operation on assembly work" was a matter of a few hours.[13] This development had significant repercussions both in terms of the way in which a laborer viewed his proletarian status and in terms of the manufacturer's need to mass distribute the mountainous fruits of mass production. The two phenomena merged in the redefinition of the proletarian status. While mass production defined labor's work in terms of monotony and rationalized its product to a fragment, some businessmen spoke of "economic freedom" or "industrial democracy"[14] as the blessing promised the worker by modern production methods. Yet the "freedom" and "democracy" offered by mass industry stopped short of a freedom to define the uses or to rearrange the relationships of production....

Not only was this alleged democracy designed to define the modern worker as a smoothly running unit of industrial production, it also tended to define protest and proletarian unrest in terms of the desire to consume, making these profitable as well. By the demand of workers for the right to be better consumers, the aspirations of labor would be profitably coordinated with the aspirations of capital. Such convictions implicitly attempted to divest protest of its anticapitalist content. Modern labor protest should have no basis in class antagonism.[15]

By the twenties, the ideological vanguard of the business community saw the need to endow the masses with what the economic historian Norman Ware has called the money, commodity, and psychic wages (satisfactions) correlative and responsive to the route of industrial capitalism.[16] There was a dramatic movement toward objective conditions which would make mass consumption feasible: higher wages and shorter hours....

The question of shorter hours was also tantamount to offering labor the "chance" to expand the consumer market. And yet, this notion of "chance," like the notions of "industrial democracy" and "economic freedom," were subterfuges in so much as these alleged freedoms and choices meant merely a transformed version of capitalism's incessant need to mold a work force in its own image. "As modern industry... [was] geared to mass production, time out for mass consumption becomes as much a necessity as time in for production."[17] The shortening of hours was seen as a qualitative as well as quantitative change in the worker's life, without significantly altering his relation to power over the uses and means of production.... Shorter hours and higher wages were seen as a first step in a broader offensive against notions of thrift and an attempt to habituate a national population to the exigencies of mass production.... Now priorities demanded that the worker spend his wages and leisure time on the consumer market....

Within the vision of consumption as a "school of freedom," the entry onto the consumer market was described as a "civilizing" experience. "Civilization" was the expanded cultural world which flowed from capitalism's broad capacity to commodify material resources. The experience of civilization was the cultural world this capacity produced.

And yet the "school of freedom" posed various problems. The democratic terminology within which the profitable vision of consumption was posed did not reveal the social and economic realities that threatened that vision. In terms of economic development, the financial growth of industrial corporations averaged 286 percent between 1922 and 1929. Despite wage hikes and relatively shorter hours in some industries,[18] the average manufacturing wage-earner showed a wage increase of only 14 percent during this same period.[19] The discrepancy between purchasing power and the rate of industrial growth was dealt with in part by the significant development of installment selling[20] which grew as an attempt to bolster "inadequate" markets in the economically depressed years of the early twenties.

Despite the initiation of a corporate credit system which offered consumers supplementary money, the growth of the productive system forced many industrial ideologues to realize the continuous need to habituate people psychically to consumption beyond mere changes in the productive order which they inhabited.

MOBILIZING THE INSTINCTS

... Modern advertising must be seen as a direct response to the needs of mass industrial capitalism. Second in procession after the manager of the production line, noted Whiting Williams [personnel director for a steel company and an ideologue of "scientific" management], "came the leader who possessed the ability to develop and direct men's desires and demands in a way to furnish the organized mass sales required for the mass production made possible by the massed dollars."[21] Advertising, as a part of mass distribution within modernizing industries, became a major sector for business investment. Within the automobile industry, initiated by the broad and highly diversified G.M. oligopoly, distribution came to account for about one half of that investment. Among producers of smaller consumer goods, the percentage of capital devoted to product proliferation was often greater.[22] ...

Advertising offered itself as a means of efficiently creating consumers and as a way of homogeneously "controlling the consumption of a product."[23] Although many corporations boasted of having attained national markets without the aid of advertising, the trade journal *Printers' Ink* argued that these "phantom national markets" were actually inefficient, unpredictable and scattered agglomerations of heterogeneous local markets.[24] The significance of the notion of efficiency in the creation of consumers lies in the fact that the modern advertising industry, like the modern manufacturing plant, was an agent of consolidated and multi-leveled commerce. As Ford's assembly line utilized "expensive single-purpose machinery" to produce automobiles inexpensively and at a rate that dwarfed traditional methods, the costly machinery of advertising that Coolidge had described set out to produce consumers, likewise inexpensively and at a rate that dwarfed traditional methods. To create consumers efficiently the advertising industry had to develop universal notions of what makes people respond, going beyond the "horse sense" psychology that had characterized the earlier industry.[25] Such general conceptions of human instinct promised to provide ways of reaching a mass audience via a universal appeal. Considering the task of having to build a mass ad industry to attend to the needs of mass production, the ad men welcomed the work of psychologists in the articulation of these general conceptions.[26] ...

While agreeing that "human nature is more difficult to control than material nature,"[27] ad men spoke in specific terms of "human instincts" which if properly understood could induce people "to buy a given product if it was scientifically presented. If advertising copy appealed to the right instincts, the urge to buy would surely be excited."[28] The utilitarian value of a product or the traditional notion of mechanical quality were no longer sufficient inducements to move merchandise at the necessary rate and volume required by mass production.

Such traditional appeals would not change the disposition of potential markets toward consumption of given products. Instead each product would be offered in isolation, not in terms of the nature of the consumer, but through an argument based on the intrinsic qualities of the item itself.

The advertisers were concerned with effecting a self-conscious change in the psychic economy, which could not come about if they spent all their time talking about a product and none talking about the "reader." Advertising literature, following the advent of mass production methods, increasingly spoke in terms of appeals to instinct. Anticipating later implementation, by 1911, Walter Dill Scott, psychologist/author of *Influencing Men in Business*, noted that "goods offered as means of gaining social prestige make their appeals to one of the most profound of the human instincts."[29] Yet the instinct for "social prestige," as well as others of a broad "constellation"[30] of instincts, was channeled into the terms of the productive system. The use value of "prestige," of "beauty," of "acquisition," of "self-adornment," and of "play" were all placed in the service of advertising's basic purpose—to provide effective mass distribution of products....

Advertising demanded but a momentary participation in the logic of consumption. Yet hopefully that moment would be expanded into a life style by its educational value. A given ad asked not only that an individual buy its product, but that he experience a self-conscious perspective that he had previously been socially and psychically denied. By that perspective, he could ameliorate social and personal frustrations through access to the marketplace.

In light of such notions as [Floyd Henry] Allport's "social self" and other self-objectifying visions of popularity and success,[34] a new cultural logic was projected by advertising beyond the strictly pecuniary one of creating the desire to consume. The social perception was one in which people ameliorated the negative condition of social objectification through consumption—material objectification. The negative condition was portrayed as social failure derived from continual public scrutiny. The positive goal emanated from one's *modern* decision to armor himself against such scrutiny with the accumulated "benefits" of industrial production. Social responsibility and social self-preservation were being correlated to an allegedly existential decision that one made to present a mass-produced public face. Man, traditionally seen as exemplary of God's perfect product, was not hardly viable in comparison with the man-made products of industrial expertise.... Such social production of consumers represented a shift in social and political priorities which has since characterized much of the "life" of American industrial capitalism. The functional goal of national advertising was the creation of desires and habits. In tune with the need for mass distribution that accompanied the development of mass production capabilities, advertising was trying to produce in readers personal needs which would dependently fluctuate with the expanding marketplace....

ADVERTISING: CIVILIZING THE *SELF*

In his sympathetic book on the *History and Development of Advertising*, Frank Presbrey articulated the conception of a predictable, buying, national population in proud and patriotic terms. "To national Advertising," noted Presbrey, "has recently been attributed most of the growth of a national homogeneity in our people, a uniformity of ideas which, despite the mixture of races, is found to be greater here than in European countries whose population is made up almost wholly of people of one race and would seem easier to nationalize in all respects.[32] Presbrey's conception of "national homogeneity" was a translucent reference to what Calvin Coolidge saw as "the enormous capacity for consumption of all kinds of commodities which characterizes our country."[33]

The idea that advertising was producing a homogeneous national character was likened within the trade as a "civilizing influence comparable in its cultural effects to those of other epoch-making developments in history."[34] Yet not all of the conceptions of advertising were expressed in such epic and trans-historical terminology. Sensitive to the political and economic context of such notions as "civilizing," "national homogeneity" and "capacity for consumption," William Allen White bridged the gap between "civilization" and civil society, noting that modern advertising was particularly a formation of advanced capitalist production. Aiming his critique at internal and external "revolutionist" threats to capitalism, White turned contemporary conceptions of revolution to their head. Reasserting the efficacy of the American Revolutionary tradition, he argued that advertising men were the true "revolutionists." Juxtaposing the consumer market to revolution of a socialistic variety, White presented a satirical political strategy to halt the "golden quest" for consumer goods. "I would cut out the advertising and fill the editorial and news pages with material supplied by communists and reds. That would stop buying—distribution of things. It would bring an impasse in civilization, which would immediately begin to decay."[35] Identifying ad men with the integrity and survival of the American heritage, White numbered advertising among our sacred cultural institutions.

Through advertising, then, consumption took on a clearly cultural tone. Within governmental and business rhetoric, consumption assumed an ideological veil of nationalism and democratic lingo. The mass "American type," which defined unity on the bases of common ethnicity, language, class or literature, was ostensibly born out of common desires—mass responses to the demands of capitalist production. Mass industry, requiring a corresponding mass individual, cryptically named him "Civilized American" and implicated his national heritage in the marketplace. By defining himself and his desires in terms of the good of capitalist production, the worker would implicitly accept the foundations of modern industrial life. By transforming the notion of "class" into "mass," business hoped to create an "individual" who could locate his needs and frustrations in terms of the consumption of goods rather than the quality and content of his life (work). . . .

In an attempt to massify men's consumption in step with the requirements of the productive machinery, advertising increasingly offered mass-produced solutions to "instinctive" strivings as well as to the ills of mass society itself. If it was industrial capitalism around which crowded cities were being built and which had spawned much of the danger to health, the frustration, the loneliness and the insecurity of modern industrial life, the advertising of the period denied complicity. Rather, the logic of contemporaneous advertising read, one can free oneself from the ills of modern life by embroiling oneself in the maintenance of that life. A 1924 ad for Pompeian facial products argued that

> unless you are one woman in a thousand, you must use powder and rouge. Modern living has robbed women of much of their natural color . . . taken away the conditions that once gave natural roses in the cheeks.[36]

Within such literature, the term "modern living" was an ahistorical epithet, devoid of the notion "Modern Industrial Society," and teeming with visions of the benefits of civilization which had emerged, one would think, quite apart from the social conditions and relations to which these "benefits" therapeutically addressed themselves. On the printed page, modern living was defined as heated houses, easy transportation, and the conveniences of the household. To the reader it may have meant something considerably different: light-starved housing, industrial pollution, poor nutrition, boredom. In either sense, modern life offered the same sallow skin and called for a solution through consumption. Within such advertisements, business called for a transformation of the critique of bourgeois society to an implicit commitment to that society.

The advertising which attempted to create the dependable mass of consumers required by modern industry often did so by playing upon the fears and frustrations evoked by mass society—offering mass produced visions of individualism by which people could extricate themselves from the mass. The rationale was simple. If a person was unhappy within mass industrial society, advertising was attempting to put that unhappiness to work in the name of that society.

In an attempt to boost mass sales of soap, the Cleanliness Institute, a cryptic front group for the soap and glycerine producers' association, pushed soap as a "Kit for Climbers" (social, no doubt). The illustration was a multitudinous mountain of men, each climbing over one another to reach the summit. At the top of this indistinguishable mass stood one figure, his arms outstretched toward the sun, whose rays spelled out the words "Heart's Desire." The ad cautioned that "in any path of life, that long way to the top is hard enough—so make the going easier with soap and water." In an attempt to build a responsive mass market, the Cleanliness Institute appealed to what they must have known was a major dissatisfaction with the reality of mass life. Their solution was a sort of mass pseudodemassification....

Listerine, whose ads had taken the word *halitosis* out of the inner reaches of the dictionary and placed it on "stage, screen and in the home," offered this anecdote:

> He was conscious that something stood between him and greater business success —between him and greater popularity. Some subtle something he couldn't lay his hands on... Finally, one day, it dawned on him... the truth that his friends had been too delicate to mention.[37]

When a critical understanding of modern production might have helped many to understand what actually stood "between them and greater business success," this ad attempted to focus man's critique against himself—his body had kept him from happiness. Within the world view of a society which was more and more divorcing men from any notion of craft or from any definable sort of product, it was also logical that "you couldn't blame a man for firing an employee with halitosis to hire one without it." The contingency of a man's job was offered a nonviolent, apolitical solution. If man was the victim of himself, the fruits of mass production were his savior. Ads constantly hammered away at everything that was his own—his bodily functions, his self-esteem— and offered something of theirs as a socially more effective substitute.

... Correlative to Allport's vision of "social self," advertising offered the next best thing—*a commodity self*—to people who were unhappy or could be convinced that they were unhappy about their lives. Each portion of the body was to be viewed critically, as a *potential* bauble in a successful assemblage. Woodbury's soap was offered as a perfect treatment for the "newly important face of Smart Today;" another product promised to keep teeth white: "A flashing smile is worth more than a good sized bank account. It wins friends." After she has used Caro Cocoanut Oil Shampoo, a dashing gentleman informs the lady, "I'm crazy about your hair. *It's* the most beautiful of any here tonight." Within the vision offered by such ads, not only were social grace and success attainable: they were also defined through the use of specific products. You don't make friends, your smile "wins" them; your embellished hair, and not you, is beautiful....

During the twenties, civil society was increasingly characterized by mass industrial production. In an attempt to implicate men and women within the efficient process of production, advertising built a vision of culture which bound old notions of Civilization to the new realities of civil society. In what was viewed as their instinctual search for traditional ideals, people were offered a vision of civilized man which was transvaluated in terms of the pecuniary exigencies of society. Within a society that defined real life in terms of the monotonous insecurities of mass production, advertising attempted to create an alternative organization of life which would serve to channel man's desires for self, for social success, for leisure away from himself and his works, and toward a commoditized acceptance of "Civilization."

NOTES

1. Alfred Dupont Chandler, *Giant Enterprise, Ford, General Motors and the Automobile Industry* (1964), p. 29. Chandler is citing the *Federal Trade Commission Report on the Motor Vehicle Industry.*

2. *Ibid.*, p. 26.

3. "... during a period of eighteen years commencing in 1908, Ford Motor Company manufactured and offered for sale only one basic model of passenger automobile.... This was the [black] Model T." See Chandler, pp. 27, 37.

4. Harold Loeb, *National Survey of Potential Product Capacity* (1935), p. 3.

5. This may be seen as a response to a combination of things. Aside from the fact of proliferating mass production methods, the 1921 depression/buyers' strike served as an impetus to this study.

6. Edward A. Filene, *The Way Out: A Forecast of Coming Changes in American Business and Industry* (1924), p. 93.

7. Chandler, p. 143.

8. Notably Alfred P. Sloan of General Motors. Sloan saw productive strategy in broad social terms. His biography, *My Life With General Motors* (1960), gives an account of these early developments.

9. Loeb, p. xv, in regard to "the capacity of the nation to produce goods and services. If full advantage were taken of existing resources, man power, and knowledge... every new invention, every improved method, every advance in management technique will increase the final quantitative estimate." Such a question would be answered by "a running inventory of our approach to perfection rather than a research into existing capacity as determined by production." The survey considered such a potential too open-ended to effect meaningful speculation.

10. Edward A. Filene, *The Consumer's Dollar* (1934), p. 13.

11. Whiting Williams, *What's on the Worker's Mind* (1920), p. 317.

12. Filene, *The Way Out*, pp. 62–63.

13. Williams, *Mainsprings*, p. 51.

14. Filene, *The Way Out*, p. 127.

15. By the 1920s widespread elements of the union movement had accepted such an ideology. Among others, William English Walling of the Labor Progressives dissolved the class struggle in one fell swoop. Virtually paraphrasing the ideologues of scientifically planned capitalism, he felt that "to bring labor to the maximum productivity, the American labor movement believes, requires new organization and policies in the administration of industry." See William Walling, *American Labor and American Democracy* (1926), p. 233.

    Walling Spoke of *labor* and *consumer* as interrelated aspects of the total life of the American worker. His concern for consumer rights reflected the ideology of progressive capital no less than did the writings of Edward Filene, who, although he had one foot in the "consumer category," placed his other on the side of financial power rather than in the monotony of factory life.

16. Norman Ware, *Labor in Modern Industrial Society* (1935), p. 88.

17. Ware, *Labor in Modern Industrial Society*, p. 101.

18. Ware, *Labor in Modern Industrial Society*, p. 95. According to Ware's studies, union manufacturing labor averaged 40–48 hours per week. Nonunion labor in similar industries averaged 50 hours per week, while labor in more traditional areas, mills and shops, worked 48–60 hours per week.

19. *Ibid.* p. 16–17.

20. Robert S. Lynd, "The People as Consumers," *Recent Social Trends in the United States: Report of the President's Research Committee on Social Trends*, Vol. II (1933), p. 862. Such credit buying was initiated primarily in the automobile industry with the General Motors Acceptance Corporation (GMAC).

21. Williams, *What's on the Worker's Mind*, p. 317.

22. "In some lines, such as whiskey and milk, distribution cost is from four to ten times the cost of production." Chandler, p. 157.

23. Editorial, "Senator Borah on Marketing," *P.I.*, CXXIV, No. 5 (August 2, 1923), p. 152.

24. Editorial, "The Phantom of National Distribution," *P.I.*, CXXIV, No. 12 (September 20, 1923), p. 180.

25. Baritz, p. 27.

26. *Ibid.*, p. 26.

27. Walter Dill Scott, *Influencing Men in Business* (originally published 1911; 1928 revised edition enlarged by Delton T. Howard), p. 3.

28. Loren Baritz,, *The Servants of Power* (1960), p. 26.

29. Scott, p. 132.

30. Baritz, p. 26.

31. "Physical or sex attraction... other things being equal, qualities which make one pleasing to look at or to caress render their possessor popular to many and loved by not a few." Floyd Henry Allport, *Social Psychology* (1924), p. 365.

32. Frank Spencer Presbrey, *The History and Development of Advertising* (1929), p. 613.

33. *Ibid.*, p. 622.

34. *Ibid.*, p. 608.

35. *Ibid.*, p. 610.

36. *Ladies' Home Journal* (May 1924), p. 161.

37. *Ibid.*, p. 133.

9.2 DALLAS W. SMYTHE

The Role of the Mass Media and Popular Culture in Defining Development

Dallas W. Smythe (1907–1992) was a critical scholar of mass communication. Concerned about the domination of Canadian culture by the United States, Smythe worked for a time at the Federal Communications Commission (FCC), which oversees the operation of the predominantly commercial mass media in the United States. Over the years, Smythe was commissioned by the Canadian government to study the situation of broadcasting in Canada, which is dominated by the Canadian Broadcasting Corporation (CBC).

The accumulated results of Smythe's work were synthesized in a study of the impact of U.S. commercial media on Canada entitled *Dependency Road: Communications, Capitalism, Consciousness, and Canada* (Ablex, 1981). In the following selection from that book, Smythe focuses on the integral relationship between advertising, media, and audiences. Smythe argues that advertising-supported media systems produce audiences as the commodity through which they make economic profit. TV networks, for example, attract people to watch by offering a regular schedule of programs during prime-time viewing hours. The resulting audiences are sold by the networks to advertisers. Thus, Smythe believes, advertising-supported media are a peculiar form of market; they do not sell cultural goods to people, they sell people to advertisers. Once sold to advertisers, media audiences perform key services for the capitalist economy at large. In fact, Smythe says, audiences are put to work for the capitalist economy in specific ways that are crucial to the reproduction of capitalist social relations.

Key Concept: audience work

*T*he mass media of communications (television, radio, press, magazines, cinema, and books), the related arts (e.g., popular music, comic books), and consumer goods and services (clothing, cosmetics, fast food, etc.) set the daily agenda for the populations of advanced capitalist countries and increasingly for Third World nations. It follows, therefore, that the policy which governs what appears on the daily agenda produced by these institutions has a special role in defining the process of "development" for those populations.

What do I mean by *agenda*? As Ortega y Gasset remarked, "Living is nothing more or less than doing one thing instead of another." Individuals daily live by giving *priorities* to their problems. Whether implicitly or explicitly, they use their time and resources to attend to their problems according to some ordering of these priorities. It is when they act as part of *institutions* that the agenda-setting function becomes a collective rather than an individual process.

Human beings are human because and by means of the relationships or process that links them together. Institutions are social habits—systematic and perpetuated relationships between people. Institutions have specialized agendas for their own actions. Thus, the family is primarily concerned with the nurture of children. Work organizations (factories or farms) are primarily concerned with "production" activities. Military and other security institutions specialize on the use of force to perpetuate a particular class structure's control of people and other resources. The formal educational system is primarily concerned with instructing the next generation in the techniques and values of the dominant social system. Medical institutions are principally concerned with the treatment of illness and accidents. Religious institutions have a special concern with theological and ethical aspects of birth, life, and death.

Each of these institutions also embodies in its actions and propagates the agenda which follows from the ideological theory and practice of the whole social system of which it is a part. Therefore each of these institutions incidentally to its prime purpose states and reinforces priorities in the systemic agendas to which the population gives attention. For example, the military discipline instructs young people in the values of private property and individual subordination to a hierarchy of authority. All these institutions are very old, dating from prehistoric times. As compared with them, the mass media of communications are very young institutions (printing since the late nineteenth century, electronic media since the early twentieth century). What has been distinctive about the capitalist mass media is their *specialized function* of legitimizing and directing the development of the social system. . . .

The real world context for the present dominant institutional structures developed over the past four centuries is that of capitalism. It is a system based on private property in the means of production and consumption and on the appropriation of the surplus product of labor by the owners of capital. It is a worldwide system of interrelated markets for commodities. These markets, through more or less monopolistic prices, determine *what* is to be produced, *how much* is to be produced, *for whom* it is to be produced, and *how* it is to be produced. The answers given through these markets to the *how* question determine the kind, amount, and location of specialization of work and production, as well as the kind, timing, extent, and location of invention and innovation of new products and techniques of productive activity. . . .

Today, the mass media (press, television, radio, magazines, books, cinema) are the central means of forming attitudes, values, and buying behavior —consciousness in action, to put it succinctly. They are the "shock troops" of

Consciousness Industry. It is obvious to all—and is the main concern of liberal and radical critics—that the way the mass media select and present news, portray ethnic groups in the "entertainment," and handle public controversial issues powerfully affects people's behavior.... Here we are concerned to show that the mass media have a more basic influence on our lives and our ideology because they, together with advertisers, take a central part in the process by which the monopoly-capitalist system grows or declines in strength. In the core area, the mass media *produce* audiences and *sell* them to advertisers of consumer goods and services, political candidates, and groups interested in controversial public issues. These audiences *work* to market these things to themselves. *At the same time*, these audiences have their basic human concerns, and part of the *work* they must do is to reproduce their labor power. This work embodies their resistance to the power of Consciousness Industry. That power appears to them through the total mass media *message* (consisting of advertising, entertainment, information, news), through the physical consumer goods, political candidates, and through tangible evidences of social relations problems....

Although the mass media began the *mass* production of information, they are linked through interlocking business organization and a complex of largely managed, i.e., oligopolistic, markets with a much broader base of information production and exchange. The whole complex is Consciousness Industry. Advertising, market research, photography, the commercial application of art to product and container design, the fine arts, teaching machines and related software and educational testing, as well as the formal educational system, are all part of it. The mass media are also linked through corporate ties and intersecting markets with professional and amateur sports, the performing arts, comic books, toys, games, the production and sale of recorded music, hotel, airlines, and a wide variety of consumer goods industries (automobiles, clothing, jewelry, cosmetics, etc.) through "tie-in" contracts and their advertising service to these industries. They are also mutually interdependent with tele-communications operations (point-to-point electronic communications), the computerized storage, transmission, retrieval, and processing of digital information and the industries which produce the equipment for telecommunications and computer operations and which conduce research and development in electronics, physics, and chemistry. The information sector of the United States government and military is at least as large as the civilian telecommunications sector, and both are linked with the mass media by giant corporations. The telecommunications and computer industries dwarf the mass media in terms of revenues and assets and simultaneously generate technical innovations (e.g., television, tele-processing of data) and enlarge their economic and political power by doing so....

The secret of the growth of Consciousness Industry in the past century will be found in (1) the relation of advertising to the news, entertainment, and information material in the mass media: (2) the relations of both the material and advertising to real consumer goods and services, political candidates, and public issues; (3) the relations of advertising and consumer goods and services to the people who consume them; (4) the effective control of people's lives which the monopoly capitalist corporations dominating the foregoing three sets of relationships try to establish and maintain. The capitalist system cultivates the illusion that the three streams of information and things are independent, the advertising merely "supports" or "makes possible" the news, information, and entertainment, which in turn are *separate* from the consumer goods and services we buy. This is untrue. The commercial mass media *are* advertising in their entirety. Advertising messages provide news (that a particular product or sponsor has something "new" to deserve the attention of the audience), entertainment (many television commercials are more entertaining than the programs in which they are imbedded), and information about prices and alleged qualities of the advertised product of the "sponsoring" organization. And both advertising and the "program material" reflect, mystify, and are essential to the sale of goods and services. The program material is produced and distributed in order to attract and hold the attention of the audience so that its members may be counted (by audience survey organizations which then certify the size and character of the audience produced) and sold to the advertiser.

... [R]eaders and audience members of advertising-supported mass media are a commodity produced and sold to advertisers *because they perform a valuable service for the advertisers.* This is why the advertisers buy them. What is the valuable service audiences perform? It is three kinds of work:

1. They market consumer goods and services to themselves.
2. They learn to vote for one candidate (or issue) or another in the political arena.
3. They learn and reaffirm belief in the rightness of their politico-economic system. . . .

Audience power work for Consciousness Industry produces a particular kind of human nature or consciousness, focusing its energies on the consumption of commodities, which [psychoanalyst] Erich Fromm called *homo consumens*—people who live and work to perpetuate the capitalist system built on the commoditization of life. This is not to say that individuals, the family, and other institutions, such as labor unions and the church, are powerless. They resist the pressures of the capitalist system. . . . But for about a century the kind of human nature produced in the core area has, to a large degree, been the product of Consciousness Industry. People with this nature exist primarily to serve the system; the system is *not* under the control, serving them. . . .

The necessity for consumers to buy new products is guaranteed by (1) style changes; (2) quality control in manufacture, not to maximize product life but to produce lives which will end shortly after warranty periods expire so that there is predictable "junking" of products because it would cost more to repair than replace them. And the stylistic features of all consumer goods and services are based on calculated manipulation of public taste so that increasingly consumers pay for images rather than use-values. Having analyzed the American development of science, capital equipment, and production, Professor David Noble of MIT begins his *America by Design*:

Modern Americans confront a world in which everything changes, yet nothing moves. The perpetual rush to novelty that characterizes the modern marketplace, with its escalating promise of technological transcendence, is matched by the persistence of pre-formed patterns of life which promise merely more of the same. Each major scientific advance, while appearing to presage an entirely new society, attests rather to the vigor and resilience of the old order that produced it. Every new, seemingly bold departure ends by following an already familiar path (Noble, 1977, p. xvii).

There are two broad classes of markets in which giant corporations make the "sales effort" which stimulates the realization of surplus that powers the monopoly-capitalist system. First, and most easily recognizable, is the Civilian Sales sector where ordinary civilians buy their consumer goods and services. But it left to depend on this sector alone for its growth, the monopoly-capitalist system would be plunged into ruinous depression. The Military Sales and Welfare sector must be maintained as a giant and increasingly generous "pump primer" in order to compensate for the "leakiness" of the system—the tendency for surplus to be accumulated (or hoarded) by corporations and their direct beneficiaries rather than distributed to workers so that they in turn could buy the consumer goods and services produced. Of course the Military Sales effort also serves to ensure the security of the capitalist system against dissidents and criminals at home and liberation movements in the economic colonies around the world.

... The prime item on the agenda of Consciousness Industry is producing *people* motivated to buy the "new models" of consumer goods and services and motivated to pay the taxes which support the swelling budgets for the Military Sales effort....

In economic terms there are three types of commodities (e.g., wheat), intermediate products (e.g., flour), and end products (e.g., bread). In economic terms, the audiences of the mass media are intermediate products. Like other factors of production, they are consumed in producing, i.e., selling, the end product; their production and use by the advertiser is a marketing cost. The end product of the giant corporations in the consumer goods and services sector is those consumer goods and services. The audiences produced by the mass media are only part of the means to the sale of that end product. But at the larger, systemic level, people, working via audiences to market goods and services to themselves, and their consciousness ultimately are the *systemic* end product: *they* are produced by the system ready to buy consumer goods and to pay taxes and to work in their alienating jobs in order to continue buying tomorrow. The message of the system is a slogan in fine print on a full-page advertisement in the *New York Times*: "Buy something." That way you help keep up the GNP and perhaps keep your job and paycheck so that next time around you will still be able to "buy something."

The media function of producing audiences is not limited to audiences designed to market consumer goods and services. It also includes the production of audiences designed to produce the end product: votes for candidates for political office, and public opinion on "political" matters....

The practice of news management is universal on the part of party candidates, heads of states, government agencies, business corporations, and their organized pressure groups often working through trade associations for the various industries and government intelligence agencies (CIA, etc.). Political parties and candidates advertise heavily in the mass media, and their relation to audiences is the same as that of consumer goods manufacturers. The content of news space in the print media, television, and radio is mostly the result of press releases and publicity-getting events which are staged in order to *make* news. Advertising agency executives have estimated that as much as 85 percent of news is "planted" through the staging of pseudo events (press conferences, publicity stunts, etc.) rather than the result of the initiative of editors and reporters. The objective of political advertising and news management is the same as that of advertisers of consumer goods. It is to produce people who are ready to support a particular policy, rather than some other policy, be it buying brand X rather than brand Y of automobile, or "supporting" one or another political candidate, or supporting employment preference for ethnic minorities or WASPS, or supporting Israel or the Arabs in their long struggle in the Middle East. The mass media thus daily set the agenda of issues and images to which everyone pays some attention. . . .

To be effective, advertising, like the avowedly news, entertainment and information interlarded between the advertisements, must have the same qualities as the ostensibly nonadvertising content: it must catch and hold audience attention and present its message in an entertaining way; that is, it must tell an effective story of some kind. Advertising is storytelling. So also is the news. No matter the claims that news is "objective"; obviously it is not. It has a subjective perspective—determined by stylized customs. Even weather reports on television tell a story about what tomorrow's weather will be. And of course, the so-called entertainment programs on television are stories told in stylized, commoditized ways. TV advertisements cost more than the surrounding program material by a factor of from eight to ten to one per minute of air time. They therefore contain the *concentrated* entertaining and informative qualities which are spread out more thinly in the nonadvertising program content.

A second reason for treating advertising and the surrounding program content as inextricably intermixed is, as alluded to, that the advertisers require that the program content be suited to the advertisements. For example, advertisements for foreign travel in newspapers *must* appear adjacent to the "news stories" of the tourist attractions of visiting Hawaii, or Europe, or if you are in the United States, visiting Canada. And there are very many examples of television programs which reached the air only to be canceled (or never passed the "pilot" stage) not because they were not entertaining, but because they did not produce the particular audience demographics which advertisers demanded. A third reason, which applies particularly to news, is that the great bulk of the news is itself produced by business enterprises, government agencies, and occasionally other institutions (churches, labor unions, and special interest groups, e.g., environmental protection associations)—and hence has the same manipulative intentions as does explicit advertising.

A fourth reason for treating the advertising and nonadvertising content of the mass media as essentially connected with each other is that the business organizations which operate them so consider them. In the early years of the mass media . . . the press in fact generally allowed advertisers to supply directly the news which the latter wished to see published. Only by a long struggle to eliminate the cruder manifestations of such direct dictation have the mass media achieved limited "believability" for the autonomy of the editorial side of the media. (In newspapers the travel and real estate sections still commonly allow advertisers to determine the editorial content.) Edward L. Bernays declared:

> At its 1888 convention, the American Newspaper Publishers Association openly worried about the effects of press agentry.... But there was no real effort to eliminate free publicity until about twenty years later (Bernays, 1952, p. 61).

How different from the nonadvertising content of the mass media which are openly dominated by advertising is the content of other branches of popular cultural industry, such as motion pictures, popular music, paperback books, and comic books? After all, the customers pay for them at the box office or cash register and not indirectly by working for advertisers. From a broad systemic point of view, however, the content of these popular cultural industrial products is *not* different from that in the advertiser-dominated mass media. It is axiomatic in the trade that if a story has what it takes to sell, it matters not whether it first appears in a book, a popular song or musical genre (like rock music), in a movie, or in television-radio. Cross-marketing of nonadvertising material is essential to capitalist popular culture. The Beatles' records dominated radio station programming for a time. "Hit songs" in the juke boxes are takeouts from Hollywood film sound tracks. *Roots,* beginning as a book, was a successful television series. *Peyton Place* was profitable in television, cinema houses, and as a paperback. As the connections noted here are not confined within the media, no matter how broadly defined, but extend to tangible commodity markets.... The point is not merely that these specific cultural commodities were cross-marketed, but that the qualities of form and content which made them successful in one or another branch of cultural industry, whether explicitly advertiser-dominated or not, are deliberately cultivated by *all* branches of cultural industry.

... The mass media screen in the values of the capitalist system and screen out other values—a function which [has been termed] the "hegemonic filter." The agenda set by the mass media is explicitly or implicitly (in much so-called entertainment, e.g., professional sports)—although traditional contradictory elements are included in it—ideologically loaded to support the system. A condensed summary of such values illustrates.

Human nature is portrayed as fixed ("you cannot change human nature"). It is typically and incurably selfish. Therefore, "look out for number one." Let the other fellow take care of himself. In every area, what is private is better than what is public. Private business is clean and efficient. But some people are dishonest and mean and they will be punished by a heroic individual or the efficient military or police forces. Public government is inherently dirty and inefficient, and of course, politics is a dirty business. It follows that prices charged by private business are good because private businessmen "have to meet a payroll" and are efficient. But taxes (which in economic terms are indistinguishable from prices) are bad; and because public officers need not "show a profit," they are inefficient. Private property is virtually sacred. And public planning which would tell private owners what to do with their property is inherently bad. But sometimes bad, miserly landlords should be punished by the community. In fact, that government is best which governs least, leaving everything possible to be provided by the "market." We should be "objective" and respect each other's opinions, unless the others are Communists. In that case they are part of a bad international conspiracy. They are not good Canadians or Americans and ought to be sent back where they came from. . . .

Although its core values are static and rigid, the capitalists system has the necessary flexibility to cope with internal structural conflicts which would otherwise be disruptive. This is a particular virtue of the policy of the mass media which air and coopt such drives. Thus the mass media facilitated the move to the Right which the capitalist system initiated with the Cold War anti-Communist inquisition inaugurated by Richard Nixon and associates in the United States in 1946. And the Black civil rights movement, the anti–Vietnam war movement of the late 1960s and the exposure of the corruption of President Nixon in the Watergate matter were also facilitated by the mass media. Symptomatic of this cooptative capacity of the system was the full-page advertisement in the *New York Times* for a bank. It features a blown-up photograph of Che Guevara and the copy ran about as follows: "We would hire this man if we could. For we are making a revolution in banking." Through this cooptative flexibility, individual and ethnic alienation is kept within tolerable limits for the system. Consciousness Industry *leads* in the cooptation. The distinctive clothing, jewelry, hairstyling, and music of the counterculture of the 1960s was quickly adopted and profitably mass produced and mass marketed. This effectively liquidated its cultural characteristics of "protest" and completed the erosion of potential for structural change or revolution which the young radicals of the 1960s hoped to develop.

The enormous mass of advertisements and other mass media content which bombards the individual in the advanced capitalist state from *all* the mass media has the systemic effect of a barrage of noise which effectively exhausts the time and energies of the population. This is a powerful deterrent to consideration of the possibilities of alternative systems of social relationships. As Robert Merton and Paul Lazarsfeld wrote in 1948, in a scene which did not yet include mass television, the net effect is to "dysfunctionally narcotize" the population:

> For these media not only continue to affirm the *status quo*, but, in the same measure they fail to raise essential questions about the structure of society (Lazarsfeld and Merton, 1949, p. 459).

By attending to the agenda set for them by the mass media, the actions of audiences working for advertisers, narcotizes the population. People are diverted from giving high and continuous priority to the political, economic, and social crises which are marginally on or off the agenda and not dealt with, such as the ecological disasters which the rape of natural resources, environmental pollution, and the threat of extinction of life by nuclear weapons make very real possibilities. . . .

Dallas W.
Smythe

If the role of the mass media and popular culture today is to define development, what do we mean by *development?* Countless United Nations, UNESCO documents and commissions, as well as individual scholars have defined it in terms such as these: Development is the process of creating the conditions for every individual to live in such relations with other human beings and his/her fellow animals and the remainder of the physical environment as will realize the potential of all. It is also the only tenable definition of *peace*. Because we have not yet in the multimillion year evolution of life on this planet approached an awareness of the qualities inherent in that potential, it is impossible now to describe the objective of development more exactly.

Life proceeds through a process of contradictions and the struggles which embody them. The common denominator which runs through these struggles through recorded history to date appears to be the efforts of some social formations to oppress and exploit other social formations (men vs. women, boss vs. workers, rich vs. poor, white vs. nonwhite, for example). The terms *developed* nations, *developing* nations, *underdeveloped* nations have entered our vocabulary within the past 35 years as a result of the struggles focused in international forums such as the United Nations. The concept of development in these terms has been shaped by experience to date. And that experience has been mostly that of the capitalist world order (for the past 400 years at least). It therefore is not surprising that for the greater part of the world's population today, *development* is defined by the capitalist system through the agenda set by its Consciousness Industry, with the communications media as the leading edge of the process. . . .

Regardless of the immediate achievements of capitalist or socialist systems, the rivalry between them reveals for all to see the *processual* nature of development. Now everyone has a real basis to ask questions like these: Who will determine the kind of development which is to be pursued? How? When? Why? And most fundamentally, for whose benefit, i.e., for the benefit of which class of people? The answers given to these questions will describe the *development* any people will experience. In the total power struggle between class interests which *is* the process of development, the peculiar technical forms of power embodied in the mass media where they themselves are developed will play the agenda-setting role in all ideological systems. The mass media, as the specialized institutions created for this purpose, will guide (but not decide in any deterministic fashion) the evolving struggle between contradictory power concentrations within the system. What is *omitted* from the agenda set daily by the mass media for people's attention will hardly shape the strategic level of policy determination for that society. What is generally unconsidered or discontinuously considered cannot enter into mass consciousness.

REFERENCES

Bernays, Edward L. "The Engineering of Consent," *Annuals of the American Academy of Political and Social Science*, Vol. 250, March 1947, pp. 113–120.

Lazarsfeld, P. F., and Merton, R. K. "Mass Communications, Popular Taste, and Orga-
nized Social Action," in Bryson, L., Ed., *The Communication of Ideas.* New York:
Harper & Row, 1948. (Also published in Schramm, W., Ed., *Mass Communications.*
Urbana: University of Illinois Press, 1949.)

Noble, David F. *America by Design: Science, Technology and the Rise of Corporate Capitalism,*
New York: Knopf, 1977.

9.3 SUT JHALLY

Image-Based Culture

Sut Jhally is a professor of communication at the University of Mass-achusetts, Amherst. A scholar in the critical study of mass media, he also directs the Media Education Foundation, located in Northampton, Mass-achusetts, which produces an ongoing series of videotapes that critique key public issues in mass media and popular culture. Perhaps the most widely viewed of these programs is Jhally's *Dreamworlds* (Media Education Foundation, 1990; recently revised and updated as *Dreamworlds II,* 1995), which utilizes the imagery of rock video to criticize the ways in which women are represented and to show the links between these images and real-life violence against women.

Jhally holds that we cannot understand anything coherent about con-temporary mass media and popular culture unless we understand their integral relationship with advertising. His work started with critical analyses of advertising, exemplified by *Social Communication in Advertising,* 2d ed. (Routledge, 1990), coauthored with Canadian communication scholars William Leiss and Stephen Kline, and *Codes of Advertising* (St. Martin's Press, 1987). Jhally has ranged out from this direct critique of advertising to consider questions of race, class, and the media in *Enlightened Racism* (Westview, 1992), coauthored with Justin Lewis, and of the social issues treated in his series of videotapes.

In the following selection from "Image-Based Culture: Advertising and Popular Culture," *The World and I* (July 1990), Jhally shows how the com-mercial imagery of advertising has spread to other areas of popular culture, and he discusses the impact of this on the formation of individual and social identities. Due to the central economic and cultural role of advertising, com-mercial images permeate everyday life. As a result, it is difficult for people to distance themselves enough so that they can critically reflect on the effect of these images on their lives. Furthermore, Jhally argues, since powerful and pleasurable images form the mainstream of popular culture, it is diffi-cult to reject them, even if they are harmful. Jhally concludes that citizens must engage in a *cultural politics of images* to combat the negative effects of advertising.

Key Concept: discourse through and about objects

*B*ecause we live inside the consumer culture, and most of us have done so for most of our lives, it is sometimes difficult to locate the origins of our most cherished values and assumptions. They simply appear to be part of our natural world. It is a useful exercise, therefore, to examine how our culture has come to be defined and shaped in specific ways. . . .

In this context, it is instructive to focus upon that period in our history that marks the transition point in the development of an image-saturated society —the 1920s. In that decade the advertising industry was faced with a curious problem—the need to sell increasing quantities of "nonessential" goods in a competitive marketplace using the potentialities offered by printing and color photography. Whereas the initial period of national advertising (from approximately the 1880s to the 1920s) had focused largely in a celebratory manner on the products themselves and had used text for "reason why" advertising (even if making the most outrageous claims), the 1920s saw the progressive integration of people (via visual representation) into the messages. Interestingly, in this stage we do not see representations of "real" people in advertisements, but rather we see representations of people who "stand for" reigning social values such as family structure, status differentiation, and hierarchical authority.

While this period is instructive from the viewpoint of content, it is equally fascinating from the viewpoint of *form;* for while the possibilities of using visual imagery existed with the development of new technologies, there was no guarantee that the audience was sufficiently literate in visual imagery to properly decode the ever-more complex messages. Thus, the advertising industry had to educate as well as sell, and many of the ads of this period were a fascinating combination where the written (textual) material explained the visual material. The consumer society was literally being taught how to read the commercial messages. By the postwar period the education was complete and the function of written text moved away from explaining the visual and toward a more cryptic form where it appears as a "key" to the visual "puzzle." In the contemporary world, messages about goods are all pervasive—advertising has increasingly filled up the spaces of our daily existence. Our media are dominated by advertising images, public space has been taken over by "information" about products, and most of our sporting and cultural events are accompanied by the name of a corporate sponsor. There is even an attempt to get television commercials into the nations' high schools under the pretense of "free" news programming. As we head toward the twenty-first century, advertising is ubiquitous—it is the air that we breathe as we live our daily lives.

ADVERTISING AND THE GOOD LIFE:
IMAGE AND 'REALITY'

[Advertising is] part of "a discourse through and about objects" because it does not merely tell us about things but of how things are connected to important domains of our lives. Fundamentally, advertising talks to us as individuals and addresses us about how we can become *happy.* The answers it provides are all oriented to the marketplace, through the purchase of goods or services. To understand the system of images that constitutes advertising we need to inquire into the definition of happiness and satisfaction in contemporary social life.

Quality of life surveys that ask people what they are seeking in life—what it is that makes them happy—report quite consistent results. The conditions that people are searching for—what they perceive will make them happy—are things such as having personal autonomy and control of one's life, self-esteem, a happy family life, loving relations, a relaxed, tension-free leisure time, and good friendships. The unifying theme of this list is that these things are not fundamentally connected to goods. It is primarily "social" life and not "material" life that seems to be the locus of perceived happiness. Commodities are only *weakly related* to these sources of satisfaction.[1]

A market society, however, is guided by the principle that satisfaction should be achieved via the marketplace, and through its institutions and structures it orients behavior in that direction. The data from the quality of life studies are not lost on advertisers. If goods themselves are not the locus of perceived happiness, then they need to be connected in some way with those things that are. Thus advertising promotes images of what the audience conceives of as "the good life": Beer can be connected with anything from eroticism to male fraternity to the purity of the old West; food can be tied up with family relations or health; investment advice offers early retirements in tropical settings. The marketplace cannot directly offer the real thing, but it can offer visions of it connected with the purchase of products.

Advertising thus does not work by creating values and attitudes out of nothing but by drawing upon and rechanneling concerns that the target audience (and the culture) already shares....

What are the consequences of such a system of images and goods? Given that the "real" sources of satisfaction cannot be provided by the purchase of commodities (merely the "image" of that source), it should not be surprising that happiness and contentment appear illusory in contemporary society....

It is not simply a matter of being "tricked" by the false blandishments of advertising. The problem is with the institutional structure of a market society that propels definition of satisfaction *through* the commodity/image system. The modern context, then, provides a curious satisfaction experience—one that William Leiss describes as "an ensemble of satisfactions and dissatisfactions" in which the consumption of commodities mediated by the image-system of advertising leads to consumer uncertainty and confusion.[2] The image-system of the marketplace reflects our desires and dreams, yet we have only the pleasure of the images to sustain us in our actual experience with goods.

The commodity image-system thus provides a particular vision of the world—a particular mode of self-validation that is integrally connected with what one *has* rather than what one *is*—a distinction often referred to as one between "having" and "being," with the latter now being defined through the former. As such, it constitutes a way of life that is defined and structured in quite specific political ways. Some commentators have even described advertising as part of a new *religious* system in which people construct their identities through the commodity form, and in which commodities are part of a supernatural magical world where anything is possible with the purchase of a product. The commodity as displayed in advertising plays a mixture of psychological, social, and physical roles in its relations with people. The object world interacts with the human world at the most basic and fundamental of levels, performing seemingly magical feats of enchantment and transformation, bringing instant happiness and gratification, capturing the forces of nature, and acting as a passport to hitherto untraveled domains and group relationships.[3]

In short, the advertising image-system constantly propels us toward things as means to satisfaction. In the sense that every ad says it is better to buy than not to buy, we can best regard advertising as a *propaganda* system for commodities. In the image-system as a whole, happiness lies at the end of a purchase. Moreover, this is not a minor propaganda system—it is all pervasive. It should not surprise us then to discover that the problem that it poses—how to get more things for everyone (as that is the root to happiness)—guides our political debates. The goal of *economic growth* (on which the commodity vision is based) is an unquestioned and sacred proposition of the political culture. As the environmental costs of the strategy of unbridled economic growth become more obvious, it is clear we must, as a society, engage in debate concerning the nature of future economic growth. However, as long as the commodity image-system maintains its ubiquitous presence and influence, the possibilities of opening such a debate are remote. At the very moment we most desperately need to pose new questions within the political culture, the commodity image-system propels us with even greater certainty and persuasion along a path that, unless checked, is destined to end in disaster. . . .

THE SPREAD OF IMAGE-BASED INFLUENCE

While the commodity image-system is primarily about satisfaction, its influence and effect are not limited to that alone. I want to briefly consider four other areas in the contemporary world where the commodity system has its greatest impact. The first is in the area of gender identity. Many commercial messages use images and representations of men and women as central components of their strategy to both get attention and persuade. Of course, they do not use any gender images but images drawn from a narrow and quite concentrated pool. As Erving Goffman has shown, ads draw heavily upon the domain of gender display—not the way that men and women actually behave but the ways in which we think men and women behave.[4] It is because these conventions of gender display are so easily recognized by the audience that they figure so prominently in the image-system. Also, images having to do with gender strike at the core of individual identity; our understanding of ourselves as either male or female (socially defined within this society at this time) is central to our understanding of who we are. What better place to choose than an area of social life that can be communicated at a glance and that reaches into the core of individual identity.

However, we should not confuse these portrayals as true reflections of gender. In advertising, gender (especially for women) is defined almost exclusively along the lines of sexuality. The image-system thus distorts our perceptions and offers little that balances out the stress on sexuality.

If only one or two advertisers used this strategy, then the image-system would not have the present distorted feature. The problem is that the vast majority do so. The iconography of the culture, perhaps more than any previous society, seems to be obsessed with sexuality. The end result is that the commodity is part of an increasingly eroticized world—that we live in a culture that is more and more defined erotically through commodities.

Second, the image-system has spread its influence to the realm of electoral politics. Much has been written (mostly negatively) about the role that television advertising now plays within national electoral politics. The presidency seems most susceptible to "image-politics," as it is the office most reliant on television advertising. The social commentary on politics from this perspective has mostly concerned the manner in which the focus has shifted from discussion of real "issues" to a focus on symbolism and emotionally based imagery.

... The fact that large numbers of people are changing their minds on who to vote for after seeing a thirty-second television commercial says a great deal about the nature of the political culture. It means that politics (for a significant portion of the electorate) is largely conducted on a symbolic realm, and that a notion of politics that is based upon people having a coherent and deep vision of their relationship to the social world is no longer relevant. Politics is not about issues; it is about "feeling good" or "feeling bad" about a candidate—and all it takes to change this is a thirty-second commercial.

The grammar of these images, then, clearly is different to the grammar of verbal or written language. The intrusion of the image-system into the world of electoral politics has meant that the majority of committed voters are held ransom by those who are uncommitted (the undecided or swing votes), and that these groups are influenced differently—and have a different relationship to politics—than those who have an old style view of politics. These huge swings of opinion, based upon information provided by the image-system, suggest that the political culture is incredibly superficial and does not correspond to what we normally think of as "politics."

Third, the commodity image-system is now implicated, due to changes in the way that toys are marketed, in the very structure and experience of children's play. With both children's television programming and commercials oriented around the sale of toys, writers such as Stephen Kline argue that the context within which kids play is now structured around marketing considerations. In consequence, "Children's imaginative play has become the target of marketing strategy, allowing marketers to define the limits of children's imaginations.... Play in fact has become highly ritualized—less an exploration and solidification of personal experiences and developing conceptual schema than a rearticulation of the fantasy world provided by market designers. Imaginative play has shifted one degree closer to mere imitation and assimilation." Further, the segmentation of the child audience in terms of both age and gender has led to a situation where parents find it difficult to play with their children because they do not share the marketing fantasy world that toy advertisers have created and where there is a growing divide between boys and girls at play....

Fourth, the visual image-system has colonized areas of life that were previously largely defined (although not solely) by auditory perception and experience. The 1980s has seen a change in the way that popular music commodities (records, tapes, compact discs) are marketed, with a music video becoming an indispensable component of an overall strategy. These videos are produced as commercials for musical commodities by the advertising industry, using techniques learned from the marketing of products. Viewing these videos, there often seems to be little link between the song and the visual. In the sense that they are commercials for records, there of course does not have to be. Video makers are in the same position as ad makers in terms of trying to get attention for their message and making it visually pleasurable. It is little wonder then that representations involving sexuality figure so prominently (as in the case of regular product advertising). The visuals are chosen for their ability to sell....

SPEED AND FRAGMENTATION: TOWARD A TWENTY-FIRST-CENTURY CONSCIOUSNESS

In addition to issues connected with the colonization of the commodity image-system of other areas of social life (gender socialization, politics, children's play, popular cultural forms) there are also important broader issues connected with its relation to modes of perception and forms of consciousness within contemporary society.

The visual images that dominate public space and public discourse are, in the video age, not static They do not stand still for us to examine and linger over. They are here for a couple of seconds and then they are gone. Television advertising is the epitome of this speed-up. There is nothing mysterious in terms of how it arose. As commercial time slots declined from sixty seconds to thirty seconds (and recently to fifteen seconds and even shorter), advertisers responded by creating a new type of advertising—what is called the "vignette approach"— in which narrative and "reason-why" advertising are subsumed under a rapid succession of life-style images, meticulously timed with music, that directly sell feeling and emotion rather than products....

The speed-up is also a response by advertisers to two other factors: the increasing "clutter" of the commercial environment and the coming of age, in terms of disposable income, of a generation that grew up on television and commercials. The need for a commercial to stand out to a visually sophisticated audience drove the image-system to a greater frenzy of concentrated shorts. Again, sexuality became a key feature of the image-system within this.

The speed-up has two consequences. First, it has the effect of drawing the viewer into the message. One cannot watch these messages casually; they require undivided attention. Intensely pleasurable images, often sexual, are integrated into a flow of images. Watching has to be even more attentive to catch the brief shots of visual pleasure. The space "in between" the good parts can then be filled with other information, so that the commodity being advertised becomes a rich and complex sign.

Second, the speed-up has replaced narrative and rational response with images and emotional response. Speed and fragmentation are not particularly conducive to *thinking*. They induce *feeling*. The speed and fragmentation that characterize the commodity image-system may have a similar effect on the construction of consciousness. In one series of ads for MTV, a teenage boy or girl engages in a continuous monologue of events, characters, feelings, and emotions without any apparent connecting theme. As the video images mirror the fragmentation of thoughts, the ad ends with the plug: "Finally, a channel for the way you *think.*" The generalization of this speed/fragmentation strategy to the entire domain of image culture may in fact mean that this is the form that thought increasingly is taking at the end of the twentieth century.

POLITICAL IMPLICATIONS: EDUCATION IN AN IMAGE-SATURATED SOCIETY

The real question concerning ... [the commodity image-system] has to do with the political implications that one may draw from this kind of approach. Put simply: Is there a problem with this situation, and if so what precisely is it? Further, what solutions may be offered?

... In the history of twentieth-century capitalism the world of substance has been hidden and given a false veil by the world of appearances. People have given up control of the real world and immersed themselves in the ultimately illusory world of appearances. Surface has triumphed over substance.

The question is, how is substance (reality) revealed? Given that our understanding of reality is always socially constructed (that "ideology" is present in any system or situation), visual images are the central mode through which the modern world understands itself. Images are the dominant language of the modern world. We are stuck with them. Further, we have to acknowledge the pleasure that such images provide. This is not simply trickery or manipulation —the pleasure is substantive.

I would focus a cultural politics on two related strategies. First, the struggle to reconstruct the existence and meaning of the world of substance has to take place on the terrain of the image-system....

The second aspect of the strategy centers less on revealing matters of substance (the underlying reality) than on opening up further the analysis of the contemporary image-system, in particular, *democratizing* the image-system. At present the "discourse through and about objects" is profoundly authoritarian —it reflects only a few narrow (mostly corporate) interests. The institutions of the world of substance be engaged to open up the public discourse to new and varied (and dissenting) voices.

The other set of concerns are connected to issues of *literacy* in an image-saturated society.... While we can read the images quite adequately (for the purposes of their creators) we do not know how to *produce* them. Such skills, or knowledge of the process, must be a prerequisite for functional literacy in the contemporary world....

Finally, information about the institutional context of the production and consumption of the image-system should be a prerequisite for literacy in the modern world....

As Noam Chomsky puts it (taking about the media in general) in his book *Necessary Illusions:* "Citizens of the democratic societies should undertake a course of intellectual self-defense to protect themselves from manipulation and control, and to lay the basis for meaningful democracy."[5] Such a course of action will not be easy, for the institutional structure of the image-system will work against it. However, the invigoration of democracy depends upon the struggle being engaged.

NOTES

1. See Fred Hirsch, *Social Limits to Growth* (Cambridge: Harvard University Press, 1976).

2. William Leiss, *The Limits to Satisfaction* (Toronto: Toronto University Press, 1976).

3. See Sut Jhally, *The Codes of Advertising* (New York: St. Martin's Press, 1987) and John Kavanaugh, *Following Christ in a Consumer Society* (New York: Orbis, 1981).

4. Erving Goffman, *Gender Advertisements* (New York: Harper & Row, 1979).

5. Noam Chomsky, *Necessary Illusions: Thought Control in Democratic Societies* (Boston: South End Press), viii.

PART FIVE

Media, Culture, and Society

On the Internet . . .

Sites appropriate to Part Five

The Freedom Forum is a nonpartisan, international foundation dedicated to free press, free speech, and free spirit for all people. The foundation pursues its priorities through conferences, educational activities, publishing, broadcasting, online services, fellowships, partnerships, training, research, and other programs. In addition to news stories related to issues of freedom, this site links to the Freedom Forum's Interactive Museum of News.

```
http://www.freedomforum.org/
```

This site, maintained by the University of Iowa's Department of Communication Studies, links to a number of general resources to several topics in the area of cultural studies.

```
http://www.uiowa.edu/~commstud/resources/
    culturalStudies.html
```

This site contains links to journals, archives, theorists, critics, academic programs, and newsgroups/listservs in many areas of popular culture and cultural studies, both national and international in scope.

```
http://www.mcs.net/~zupko/popcult.htm
```

CHAPTER **10** Mass
Communication as
Cultural Process

10.1 JAMES W. CAREY

A Cultural Approach to Communication

The following selection is from James W. Carey's *Communication as Culture: Essays on Media and Society* (Unwin Hyman, 1989), which is a part of an expanding interdisciplinary field that has come to be called "cultural studies" and whose roots are found within both the United States and Great Britain. Carey, an American communication scholar, argues that any form of communication is not simply about the transmission of information from a "source" (TV network, news journalist, and the like, who produce and transmit messages according to a specific purpose) to a "receiver" (an individual consumer of media messages who is affected one way or another by the message). Rather, he believes that mass communication is a *ritual* process, involving the *shared construction* of the patterns of social behavior, social interaction, and social significance. From this perspective the content of a TV program or a Hollywood film should be regarded as fundamentally similar to that of social rituals, such as the marriage ceremony or the telling of mythical stories.

Carey emphasizes the shared construction of social meaning. The British strand in cultural studies focuses on questions concerning power

237

238

*Chapter 10
Mass
Communication
as Cultural
Process*

and conflict in society. Around the turn of the twentieth century, when the United States was embroiled in the transition from a rural society to an urban, industrial society, many feared that the intimate, interpersonal bonds of small-town society would be overwhelmed by the anonymous forces of the city. There was concern that the new mass media of newspapers, magazines, and radio might exacerbate this tendency by transmitting messages designed to manipulate people's opinions and behaviors from anonymous and powerful sources such as the government or product advertisers. However, there also existed the potential for mass media to draw together otherwise dispersed and isolated urban populations in new forms of community and ritual processes.

In the following selection, Carey argues that the dominance of a transmission view of the mass communication process follows precisely from such concerns about the "massification" of society. He argues that we must recover a working sense of communication as the shared construction of social relationships, not simply as the exercise of power "from above."

Key Concept: ritual view of communication

Two alternative conceptions of communication have been alive in American culture since this term entered common discourse in the nineteenth century. Both definitions derive, as with much in secular culture, from religious origins, though they refer to somewhat different regions of religious experience. We might label these descriptions, if only to provide handy pegs upon which to hang our thought, a transmission view of communication and a ritual view of communication.

The transmission view of communication is the commonest in our culture —perhaps in all industrial culture—and dominates contemporary dictionary entries under the term. It is defined by terms such as "imparting," "sending," "transmitting," or "giving information to others." It is formed from a metaphor of geography or transportation. In the nineteenth century but to a lesser extent today, the movement of goods or people and the movement of information were seen as essentially identical processes and both were described by the common noun "communication." The center of this idea of communication is the transmission of signals or messages over distance for the purpose of control. It is a view of communication that derives from one of the most ancient of human dreams: the desire to increase the speed and effect of messages as they travel in space. From the time upper and lower Egypt were unified under the First Dynasty down through the invention of the telegraph, transportation and communication were inseparably linked. Although messages might be centrally produced and controlled, through monopolization of writing or the rapid production of print, these messages, carried in the hands of a messenger or between the bindings of a book, still had to be distributed, if they were to have their desired effect, by rapid transportation. The telegraph ended the identity but did not destroy the metaphor. Our basic orientation to communication remains grounded, at the deepest roots of our thinking, in the idea of transmission: communication is a process whereby messages are transmitted and distributed in space for the control of distance and people.

I said this view originated in religion, though the foregoing sentences seem more indebted to politics, economics, and technology. Nonetheless, the roots of the transmission view of communication, in our culture at least, lie in essentially religious attitudes. I can illustrate this by a devious though, in detail, inadequate path.

In its modern dress the transmission view of communication arises, as the *Oxford English Dictionary* will attest, at the onset of the age of exploration and discovery. We have been reminded rather too often that the motives behind this vast movement in space were political and mercantilistic. Certainly those motives were present, but their importance should not obscure the equally compelling fact that a major motive behind this movement in space, particularly as evidenced by the Dutch Reformed Church in South Africa or the Puritans in New England, was religious. The desire to escape the boundaries of Europe, to create a new life, to found new communities, to carve a New Jerusalem out of the woods of Massachusetts, were primary motives behind the unprecedented movement of white European civilization over virtually the entire globe. The vast and, for the first time, democratic migration in space was above all an attempt to trade an old world for a new and represented the profound belief that movement in space could be in itself a redemptive act. It is a belief Americans have never quite escaped.

Transportation, particularly when it brought the Christian community of Europe into contact with the heathen community of the Americas, was seen as a form of communication with profoundly religious implications. This movement in space was an attempt to establish and extend the kingdom of God, to create the conditions under which godly understanding might be realized, to produce a heavenly though still terrestrial city.

The moral meaning of transportation, then, was the establishment and extension of God's kingdom on earth. The moral meaning of communication was the same. By the middle of the nineteenth century the telegraph broke the identity of communication and transportation but also led a preacher of the era, Gardner Spring, to exclaim that we were on the "border of a spiritual harvest because thought now travels by steam and magnetic wires" (Miller, 1965: 48). Similarly, in 1848 "James L. Batchelder could declare that the Almighty himself had constructed the railroad for missionary purposes and, as Samuel Morse prophesied with the first telegraphic message, the purpose of the invention was not to spread the price of pork but to ask the question 'What Hath God Wrought?' " (Miller, 1965: 52). This new technology entered American discussions not as a mundane fact but as divinely inspired for the purposes of spreading the Christian message farther and faster, eclipsing time and transcending space, saving the heathen, bringing closer and making more probable the day of salvation.

Soon, as the forces of science and secularization gained ground, the obvious religious metaphors fell away and the technology of communication itself moved to the center of thought. Moreover, the superiority of communication over transportation was assured by the observation of one nineteenth century

240

Chapter 10
Mass
Communication
as Cultural
Process

commentator that the telegraph was important because it involved not the mere "modification of matter but the transmission of thought." Communication was viewed as a process and a technology that would, sometimes for religious purposes, spread, transmit, and disseminate knowledge, ideas, and information farther and faster with the goal of controlling space and people.

There were dissenters, of course, and I have already quoted Thoreau's disenchanted remark on the telegraph. More pessimistically, John C. Calhoun saw the "subjugation of electricity to the mechanical necessities of man . . . (as) the last era in human civilization" (quoted in Miller, 1965: 307). But the dissenters were few, and the transmission view of communication, albeit in increasingly secularized and scientific form, has dominated our thought and culture since that time. Moreover, as can be seen in contemporary popular commentary and even in technical discussions of new communications technology, the historic religious undercurrent has never been eliminated from our thought. From the telegraph to the computer the same sense of profound possibility for moral improvement is present whenever these machines are invoked. And we need not be reminded of the regularity with which improved communication is invoked by an army of teachers, preachers, and columnists as the talisman of all our troubles. More controversially, the same root attitudes, as I can only assert here rather than demonstrate, are at work in most of our scientifically sophisticated views of communication.

The ritual view of communication, though a minor thread in our national thought, is by far the older of those views—old enough in fact for dictionaries to list it under "Archaic." In a ritual definition, communication is linked to terms such as "sharing," "participation," "association," "fellowship," and "the possession of a common faith." This definition exploits the ancient identity and common roots of the terms "commonness," "communion," "community," and "communication." A ritual view of communication is directed not toward the extension of messages in space but toward the maintenance of society in time; not the act of imparting information but the representation of shared beliefs.

If the archetypal case of communication under a transmission view is the extension of messages across geography for the purpose of control, the archetypal case under a ritual view is the sacred ceremony that draws persons together in fellowship and commonality.

The indebtedness of the ritual view of communication to religion is apparent in the name chosen to label it. Moreover, it derives from a view of religion that downplays the role of the sermon, the instruction and admonition, in order to highlight the role of the prayer, the chant, and the ceremony. It sees the original or highest manifestation of communication not in the transmission of intelligent information but in the construction and maintenance of an ordered, meaningful cultural world that can serve as a control and container for human action.

This view has also been shorn of its explicitly religious origins, but it has never completely escaped its metaphoric root. Writers in this tradition often trace their heritage, in part, to Durkheim's *Elementary Forms of Religious Life* and to the argument stated elsewhere that "society substitutes for the world revealed to our senses a different world that is a projection of the ideals created by the community" (1953: 95). This projection of community ideals and their embodiment in material form—dance, plays, architecture, news stories, strings of speech—creates an artificial though nonetheless real symbolic order that operates to provide not information but confirmation, not to alter attitudes or change minds but to represent an underlying order of things, not to perform functions but to manifest an ongoing and fragile social process.

The ritual view of communication has not been a dominant motif in American scholarship. Our thought and work have been glued to a transmission view of communication because this view is congenial with the underlying wellsprings of American culture, sources that feed into our scientific life as well as our common, public understandings. There is an irony in this. We have not explored the ritual view of communication because the concept of culture is such a weak and evanescent notion in American social thought. We understand that other people have culture in the anthropological sense and we regularly record it—often mischievously and patronizing. But when we turn critical attention to American culture the concept dissolves into a residual category useful only when psychological and sociological data are exhausted. We realize that the underprivileged live in a culture of poverty, use the notion of middle-class culture as an epithet, and occasionally applaud our high and generally scientific culture. But the notion of culture is not a hard-edged term of intellectual discourse for domestic purposes. This intellectual aversion to the idea of culture derives in part from our obsessive individualism, which makes psychological life the paramount reality; from our Puritanism, which leads to disdain for the significance of human activity that is not practical and work oriented; and from our isolation of science from culture: science provides culture-free truth whereas culture provides ethnocentric error.

... Perhaps, then, some of the difference between a transmission and a ritual view of communication can be grasped by briefly looking at alternative conceptions of the role of the newspaper in social life.

If one examines a newspaper under a transmission view of communication, one sees the medium as an instrument for disseminating news and knowledge, sometimes *divertissement*, in larger and larger packages over greater distances. Questions arise as to the effects of this on audiences: news as enlightening or obscuring reality, as changing or hardening attitudes, as breeding credibility or doubt. Questions also are raised concerning the functions of news and the newspaper: Does it maintain the integration of society or its maladaption? Does it function or misfunction to maintain stability or promote the instability of personalities? Some such mechanical analysis normally accompanies a "transmission" argument.

A ritual view of communication will focus on a different range of problems in examining a newspaper. It will, for example, view reading a newspaper less as sending or gaining information and more as attending a mass, a situation in which nothing new is learned but in which a particular view of the world is portrayed and confirmed. News reading, and writing, is a ritual act and moreover a dramatic one. What is arrayed before the reader is not pure information but a portrayal of the contending forces in the world. Moreover, as readers make their way through the paper, they engage in a continual shift of roles or of dramatic focus. A story on the monetary crisis salutes them as American patriots fighting those ancient enemies Germany and Japan; a story on the

242

*Chapter 10
Mass
Communication
as Cultural
Process*

meeting of the women's political caucus casts them into the liberation movement as supporter or opponent; a tale of violence on the campus evokes their class antagonisms and resentments. The model here is not that of information acquisition, though such acquisition occurs, but of dramatic action in which the reader joins a world of contending forces as an observer at a play. We do not encounter questions about the effect or functions of messages as such, but the role of presentation and involvement in the structuring of the reader's life and time. We recognize, as with religious rituals, that news changes little and yet is intrinsically satisfying; it performs few functions yet is habitually consumed. Newspapers do not operate as a source of effects or functions but as dramatically satisfying, which is not to say pleasing, presentations of what the world at root is. And it is in this role—that of a text—that a newspaper is seen; like a Balinese cockfight, a Dickens novel, an Elizabethan drama, a student rally, it is a presentation of reality that gives life an overall form, order, and tone.

Moreover, news is a historic reality. It is a form of culture invented by a particular class at a particular point of history—in this case by the middle class largely in the eighteenth century. Like any invented cultural form, news both forms and reflects a particular "hunger for experience," a desire to do away with the epic, heroic, and traditional in favor of the unique, original, novel, new —news. This "hunger" itself has a history grounded in the changing style and fortunes of the middle class and as such does not represent a universal taste or necessarily legitimate form of knowledge (Park, 1955: 71–88) but an invention in historical time, that like most other human inventions, will dissolve when the class that sponsors it and its possibility of having significance for us evaporates.

Under a ritual view, then, news is not information but drama. It does not describe the world but portrays an arena of dramatic forces and action; it exists solely in historical time; and it invites our participation on the basis of our assuming, often vicariously, social roles within it.

Neither of these counterposed views of communication necessarily denies what the other affirms. A ritual view does not exclude the processes of information transmission or attitude change. It merely contends that one cannot understand these processes aright except insofar as they are cast within an essentially ritualistic view of communication and social order. Similarly, even writers indissolubly wedded to the transmission view of communication must include some notion... to attest however tardily to the place of ritual action in social life. Nonetheless, in intellectual matters origins determine endings, and the exact point at which one attempts to unhinge the problem of communication largely determines the path the analysis can follow....

The transmission view of communication has dominated American thought since the 1920s. When I first came into this field I felt that this view of communication, expressed in behavioral and functional terms, was exhausted.

But where does one turn, even provisionally, for the resources with which to get a fresh perspective on communication? For me at least the resources were found by going back to the work of Weber, Durkheim, de Tocqueville, and Huizinga, as well as by utilizing contemporaries such as Kenneth Burke, Hugh Duncan, Adolph Portman, Thomas Kuhn, Peter Berger, and Clifford Geertz. Basically, however, the most viable though still inadequate tradition of social thought on communication comes from those colleagues and descendants of Dewey in the Chicago School: from Mead and Cooley through Robert Park and on to Erving Goffman.

From such sources one can draw a definition of communication of disarming simplicity yet, I think, of some intellectual power and scope: communication is a symbolic process whereby reality is produced, maintained, repaired, and transformed.

Let me attempt to unpack that long first clause emphasizing the symbolic production of reality.

... Both our common sense and scientific realism attest to the fact that there is, first, a real world of objects, events, and processes that we observe. Second, there is language or symbols that name these events in the real world and create more or less adequate descriptions of them. There is reality and then, after the fact, our accounts of it. We insist there is a distinction between reality and fantasy; we insist that our terms stand in relation to this world as shadow and substance. While language often distorts, obfuscates, and confuses our perception of this external world, we rarely dispute this matter-of-fact realism. We peel away semantic layers of terms and meanings to uncover this more substantial domain of existence. Language stands to reality as secondary stands to primary in the old Galilean paradigm from which this view derives.

By the first clause I mean to invert this relationship, not to make any large metaphysical claims but rather, by reordering the relation of communication to reality, to render communication a far more problematic activity than it ordinarily seems.

... Reality is not given, not humanly existent, independent of language and toward which language stands as a pale refraction. Rather, reality is brought into existence, is produced, by communication—by, in short, the construction, apprehension, and utilization of symbolic forms. Reality, while not a mere function of symbolic forms, is produced by terministic systems—or by humans who produce such systems—that focus its existence in specific terms.

Under the sway of realism we ordinarily assume there is an order to existence that the human mind through some faculty may discover and describe. I am suggesting that reality is not there to discover in any significant detail. The world is entropic—that is, not strictly ordered—though its variety is constrained enough that the mind can grasp its outline and implant an order over and within the broad and elastic constraints of nature. To put it colloquially, there are no lines of latitude and longitude in nature, but by overlaying the globe with this particular, though not exclusively correct, symbolic organization, order is imposed on spatial organization and certain, limited human purposes served.

Let us suppose one had to teach a child of six or seven how to get from home to school. The child has driven by the school, which is some six or seven blocks away, so he recognizes it, but he has no idea of the relation between his house and school. The space between these points might as well be, as the saying goes, a trackless desert. What does one do in such a situation?

There are a number of options. One might let the child discover the route by trial and error, correcting him as he goes, in faithful imitation of a con-

244

*Chapter 10
Mass
Communication
as Cultural
Process*

ditioning experiment. One might have the child follow an adult, as I'm told the Apaches do, "imprinting" the route on the child. However, the ordinary method is simply to draw the child a map. By arranging lines, angles, names, squares denoting streets and buildings in a pattern on paper, one transforms vacant space into a featured environment. Although some environments are easier to feature than others—hence trackless desert-space is understood and manageable when it is represented in symbolic form.

The map stands as a representation of an environment capable of clarifying a problematic situation. It is capable of guiding behavior and simultaneously transforming undifferentiated space into configured—that is, known, apprehended, understood—space.

Note also that an environment, any given space, can be mapped in a number of different modes. For example, we might map a particularly important space by producing a poetic or musical description. As in the song that goes, in part; "first you turn it to the left, then you turn it to the right," a space can be mapped by a stream of poetic speech that expresses a spatial essence and that also ensures, by exploiting the mnemonic devices of song and poetry, that the "map" can be retained in memory. By recalling the poem at appropriate moments, space can be effectively configured.

A third means of mapping space is danced ritual. The movements of the dance can parallel appropriate movements through space. By learning the dance the child acquires a representation of the space that on another occasion can guide behavior.

Space can be mapped, then, in different modes—utilizing lines on a page, sounds in air, movements in a dance. All three are symbolic forms, though the symbols differ; visual, oral, and kinesthetic. Moreover, each of the symbolic forms possesses two distinguishing characteristics: displacement and productivity. Like ordinary language, each mode allows one to speak about or represent some thing when the thing in question is not present. This capacity of displacement, of producing a complicated act when the "real" stimulus is not physically present, is another often noted though not fully explored capacity. Second, each of these symbolic forms is productive, for a person in command of the symbols is capable of producing an infinite number of representations on the basis of a finite number of symbolic elements. As with language, so with other symbolic forms: a finite set of words or a finite set of phonemes can produce, through grammatical combination, an infinite set of sentences.

We often argue that a map represents a simplification of or an abstraction from an environment. Not all the features of an environment are modeled, for the purpose of the representation is to express not the possible complexity of things but their simplicity. Space is made manageable by the reduction of information. By doing this, however, different maps bring the same environment alive in different ways; they produce quite different realities. Therefore, to live within the purview of different maps is to live within different realities. Consequently, maps not only constitute the activity known as mapmaking; they constitute nature itself. . . .

This particular miracle we perform daily and hourly—the miracle of producing reality and then living within and under the fact of our own production

—rests upon a particular quality of symbols: their ability to be both representations "of" and "for" reality....

It is no different with a religious ritual. In one mode it represents the nature of human life, its condition and meaning, and in another mode—its "for" mode—it induces the dispositions it pretends merely to portray.

All human activity is such an exercise (can one resist the word "ritual"?) in squaring the circle. We first produce the world by symbolic work and then take up residence in the world we have produced. Alas, there is magic in our self deceptions.

We not only produce reality but we must likewise maintain what we have produced, for there are always new generations coming along for whom our productions are incipiently problematic and for whom reality must be regenerated and made authoritative. Reality must be repaired for it consistently breaks down: people get lost physically and spiritually, experiments fail, evidence counter to the representation is produced, mental derangement sets in—all threats to our models of and for reality that lead to intense repair work. Finally, we must, often with fear and regret, toss away our authoritative representations of reality and begin to build the world anew....

To study communication is to examine the actual social process wherein significant symbolic forms are created, apprehended, and used....

Our attempts to construct, maintain, repair, and transform reality are publicly observable activities that occur in historical time. We create, express, and convey our knowledge of and attitudes toward reality through the construction of a variety of symbol systems: art, science, journalism, religion, common sense, mythology. How do we do this? What are the differences between these forms? What are the historical and comparative variations in them? How do changes in communication technology influence what we can concretely create and apprehend? How do groups in society struggle over the definition of what is real? These are some of the questions, rather too simply put, that communication studies must answer.

Finally, let me emphasize an ironic aspect to the study of communication, a way in which our subject matter doubles back on itself and presents us with a host of ethical problems. One of the activities in which we characteristically engage, as in this essay, is communication about communication itself. However, communication is not some pure phenomenon we can discover; there is no such thing as communication to be revealed in nature through some objective method free from the corruption of culture. We understand communication insofar as we are able to build models or representations of this process. But our models of communication, like all models, have this dual aspect—an "of" aspect and a "for" aspect. In one mode communication models tell us what the process is; in their second mode they produce the behavior they have described. Communication can be modeled in several empirically adequate ways, but these several models have different ethical implications for they produce different forms of social relations....

Models of communication are, then, not merely representations of communication but representations *for* communication: templates that guide, unavailing or not, concrete processes of human interaction, mass and interpersonal. Therefore, to study communication involves examining the construction,

246

*Chapter 10
Mass
Communication
as Cultural
Process*

apprehension, and use of models of communication themselves—their construction in common sense, art, and science, their historically specific creation and use: in encounters between parent and child, advertisers and consumer, welfare worker and supplicant, teacher and student. Behind and within these encounters lie models of human contact and interaction.

Our models of communication, consequently, create what we disingenuously pretend they merely describe. As a result our science is, to use a term of Alvin Gouldner's, a reflexive one. We not only describe behavior; we create a particular corner of culture—culture that determines, in part, the kind of communicative world we inhabit.

... If one tries to examine society as a form of communication, one sees it as a process whereby reality is created, shared, modified, and preserved. When this process becomes opaque, when we lack models of and for reality that make the world apprehensible, when we are unable to describe and share it; when because of a failure in our models of communication we are unable to connect with others, we encounter problems of communication in their most potent form.

10.2 RAYMOND WILLIAMS

The Technology and the Society

The late Raymond Williams was an influential scholar, popular author, and activist in England. Throughout his career, Williams dealt with practical problems dealing with *how* we know *what* we know. Most of his work reminds us that it is important to look at the broad picture of society to understand how the many aspects of daily life affect not only the questions we ask but the way we ask them.

In his book *Television: Technology and Cultural Form* (Schocken Books, 1975), Williams effectively addresses the social impact of television from a number of perspectives, such as how technical development influenced television's use, how the controlling institutions impacted its social acceptance and use, and how critical dimensions were developed in relation to technical development and social use. Williams's approach is indicative of the British cultural studies model, which seeks to examine a number of issues thoroughly, critically, and with a distinctive framework for articulation of results.

Although Williams critiques the applications of the British system of broadcasting in the following selection from *Television,* his theoretical framework could well be applied to the study of other forms of technology within other cultures. In many cases, other people have attempted to replicate his framework, with similarly impressive results.

The following selection not only presents an excellent representation of British cultural studies but it also reminds us that the relationship between media and society is an ongoing process, subject to different constraints in different contexts and at different times.

Key Concept: technological determinism

*I*t is often said that television has altered our world. In the same way, people often speak of a new world, a new society, a new phase of history, being created—'brought about'—by this or that new technology: the steam-engine, the automobile, the atomic bomb. Most of us know what is generally implied when such things are said. But this may be the central difficulty: that we have

247

248

*Chapter 10
Mass
Communication
as Cultural
Process*

got so used to statements of this general kind, in our most ordinary discussions, that we can fail to realise their specific meanings.

For behind all such statements lie some of the most difficult and most unresolved historical and philosophical questions. Yet the questions are not posed by the statements; indeed they are ordinarily masked by them. Thus we often discuss, with animation, this or that 'effect' of television, or the kinds of social behaviour, the cultural and psychological conditions, which television has 'led to', without feeling ourselves obliged to ask whether it is reasonable to describe any technology as a cause, or, if we think of it as a cause, as what kind of cause, and in what relations with other kinds of causes. The most precise and discriminating local study of 'effects' can remain superficial if we have not looked into the notions of cause and effect, as between a technology and a society, a technology and a culture, a technology and a psychology, which underlie our questions and may often determine our answers.

It can of course be said that these fundamental questions are very much too difficult; and that they are indeed difficult is very soon obvious to anyone who tries to follow them through. We could spend our lives trying to answer them, whereas here and now, in a society in which television is important, there is immediate and practical work to be done: surveys to be made, research undertaken; surveys and research, moreover, which we know how to do. It is an appealing position, and it has the advantage, in our kind of society, that it is understood as practical, so that it can then be supported and funded. By contrast, other kinds of questions seem merely theoretical and abstract.

Yet all questions about cause and effect, as between a technology and a society, are intensely practical. Until we have begun to answer them, we really do not know, in any particular case, whether, for example, we are talking about a technology or about the uses of a technology; about necessary institutions or particular and changeable institutions; about a content or about a form. And this is not only a matter of intellectual uncertainty; it is a matter of social practice. If the technology is a cause, we can at best modify or seek to control its effects. Or if the technology, as used, is an effect, to what other kinds of cause, and other kinds of action, should we refer and relate our experience of its uses? These are not abstract questions. They form an increasingly important part of our social and cultural arguments, and they are being decided all the time in real practice, by real and effective decisions.

It is with these problems in mind that I want to try to analyse television as a particular cultural technology, and to look at its development, its institutions, its forms and its effects, in this critical dimension. . . .

THE SOCIAL HISTORY OF TELEVISION AS A TECHNOLOGY

The invention of television was no single event or series of events. It depended on a complex of inventions and developments in electricity, telegraphy, photography and motion pictures, and radio. It can be said to have separated out as a specific technological objective in the period 1875–1890, and then, after a lag, to have developed as a specific technological enterprise from 1920 through to the first public television systems of the 1930s. Yet in each of these stages it depended for parts of its realisation on inventions made with other ends primarily in view.

Until the early nineteenth century, investigations of electricity, which had long been known as a phenomenon, were primarily philosophical: investigations of a puzzling natural effect. The technology associated with these investigations was mainly directed towards isolation and concentration of the effect, for its clearer study. Towards the end of the eighteenth century there began to be applications, characteristically in relation to other known natural effects (lightning conductors). But there is then a key transitional period in a cluster of inventions between 1800 and 1831, ranging from Volta's battery to Faraday's demonstration of electro-magnetic induction, leading quickly to the production of generators. This can be properly traced as a scientific history, but it is significant that the key period of advance coincides with an important stage of the development of industrial production. The advantages of electric power were closely related to new industrial needs: for mobility and transfer in the location of power sources, and for flexible and rapid controllable conversion. The steam engine had been well suited to textiles, and its industries had been based on local siting. A more extensive development, both physically and in the complexity of multiple-part processes, such as engineering, could be attempted with other power sources but could only be fully realised with electricity. There was a very complex interaction between new needs and new inventions, at the level of primary production, of new applied industries (plating) and of new social needs which were themselves related to industrial development (city and house lighting). From 1830 to large-scale generation in the 1880s there was this continuing complex of need and invention and application. . . .

The development of radio, in its significant scientific and technical stages between 1885 and 1911, was at first conceived, within already effective social systems, as an advanced form of telegraphy. Its application as a significantly new social form belongs to the immediate post-war period, in a changed social situation. It is significant that the hiatus in technical television development then also ended. In 1923 Zworykin introduced the electronic television camera tube. Through the early 1920s Baird and Jenkins, separately and competitively, were working on systems using mechanical scanning. From 1925 the rate of progress was qualitatively changed, through important technical advances but also with the example of sound broadcasting systems as a model. The Bell System in 1927 demonstrated wire transmission through a radio link, and the pre-history of the form can be seen to be ending. There was great rivalry between systems—especially those of mechanical and electronic scanning—and there is still great controversy about contributions and priorities. But this is characteristic of the phase in which the development of a technology moves into the stage of a new social form.

What is interesting throughout is that in a number of complex and related fields, these systems of mobility and transfer in production and communication, whether in mechanical and electric transport, or in telegraphy, photography, motion pictures, radio and television, were at once incentives and responses

250

*Chapter 10
Mass
Communication
as Cultural
Process*

within a phase of general social transformation. Though some of the crucial scientific and technical discoveries were made by isolated and unsupported individuals, there was a crucial community of selected emphasis and intention, in a society characterised at its most general levels by a mobility and extension of the scale of organisations: forms of growth which brought with them immediate and longer-term problems of operative communication. In many different countries, and in apparently unconnected ways, such needs were at once isolated and technically defined. It is especially a characteristic of the communications systems that *all were foreseen—not in utopian but in technical ways—before the crucial components of the developed systems had been discovered and refined.* In no way is this a history of communications systems creating a new society or new social conditions. The decisive and earlier transformation of industrial production, and its new social forms, which had grown out of a long history of capital accumulation and working technical improvements, created new needs but also new possibilities, and the communications systems, down to television, were their intrinsic outcome.

THE SOCIAL HISTORY OF THE USES OF TELEVISION TECHNOLOGY

It is never quite true to say that in modern societies, when a social need has been demonstrated, its appropriate technology will be found. This is partly because some real needs, in any particular period, are beyond the scope of existing or foreseeable scientific and technical knowledge. It is even more because the key question, about technological response to a need, is less a question about the need itself than about its place in an existing social formation. A need which corresponds with the priorities of the real decision-making groups will, obviously, more quickly attract the investment of resources and the official permission, approval or encouragement on which a working technology, as distinct from available technical devices, depends. We can see this clearly in the major developments of industrial production and, significantly, in military technology. The social history of communications technology is interestingly different from either of these, and it is important to try to discover what are the real factors of this variation....

The development of the press gives us the evidence for our first major instance. It was at once a response to the development of an extended social, economic and political system and a response to crisis within that system. The centralisation of political power led to a need for messages from that centre along other than official lines. Early newspapers were a combination of that kind of message—political and social information—and the specific messages —classified advertising and general commercial news—of an expanding system of trade. In Britain the development of the press went through its major formative stages in periods of crisis: the Civil War and Commonwealth, when the newspaper form was defined; the Industrial Revolution, when new forms of popular journalism were successively established; the major wars of the twentieth century, when the newspaper became a universal social form. For the transmission of simple orders, a communications system already existed. For the transmission of an ideology, there were specific traditional institutions. But for the transmission of news and background—the whole orienting, predictive and updating process which the fully developed press represented—there was an evident need for a new form, which the largely traditional institutions of church and school could not meet. And to the large extent that the crises of general change provoked both anxiety and controversy, this flexible and competitive form met social needs of a new kind. As the struggle for a share in decision and control became sharper, in campaigns for the vote and then in competition for the vote, the press became not only a new communications system but, centrally, a new social institution. . . .

What can be seen most evidently in the press can be seen also in the development of photography and the motion picture. The photograph is in one sense a popular extension of the portrait, for recognition and for record. But in a period of great mobility, with new separations of families and with internal and external migrations, it became more centrally necessary as a form of maintaining, over distance and through time, certain personal connections. Moreover, in altering relations to the physical world, the photograph as an object became a form of the photography of objects: moments of isolation and stasis within an experienced rush of change; and then, in its technical extension to motion, a means of observing and analysing motion itself, in new ways—a dynamic form in which new kinds of recognition were not only possible but necessary.

Now it is significant that until the period after the First World War, and in some ways until the period after the Second World War, these varying needs of a new kind of society and a new way of life were met by what were seen as specialised means: the press for political and economic information; the photograph for community, family and personal life; the motion picture for curiosity and entertainment; telegraphy and telephony for business information and some important personal messages. It was within this complex of specialised forms that broadcasting arrived.

The consequent difficulty of defining its social uses, and the intense kind of controversy which has ever since surrounded it, can then be more broadly understood. Moreover, the first definitions of broadcasting were made for sound radio. It is significant and perhaps puzzling that the definitions and institutions then created were those within which television developed.

We have now become used to a situation in which broadcasting is a major social institution, about which there is always controversy but which, in its familiar form, seems to have been predestined by the technology. This predestination, however, when closely examined, proves to be no more than a set of particular social decisions, in particular circumstances, which were then so widely if imperfectly ratified that it is now difficult to see them as decisions rather than as (retrospectively) inevitable results.

Thus, if seen only in hindsight, broadcasting can be diagnosed as a new and powerful form of social integration and control. Many of its main uses can be seen as socially, commercially and at times politically manipulative. Moreover, this viewpoint is rationalised by its description as 'mass communication', a phrase used by almost all its agents and advisers as well, curiously, as by most of its radical critics. 'Masses' had been the new nineteenth-century term

252

*Chapter 10
Mass
Communication
as Cultural
Process*

of contempt for what was formerly described as 'the mob'. The physical 'massing' of the urban and industrial revolution underwrote this. A new radical class-consciousness adopted the term to express the material of new social formations: 'mass organisations'. The 'mass meeting' was an observable physical effect. So pervasive was this description that in the twentieth century multiple serial production was called, falsely but significantly, 'mass production': mass now meant large numbers (but within certain assumed social relationships) rather than any physical or social aggregate. Sound radio and television ... were developed for transmission to *individual* homes, though there was nothing in the technology to make this inevitable. But then this new form of social communication—broadcasting—was obscured by its definition as 'mass communication': an abstraction to its most general characteristic, that it went to many people, 'the masses', which obscured the fact that the means chosen was the offer of individual sets, a method much better described by the earlier word 'broadcasting'....

The period of decisive development in sound broadcasting was the 1920s. After the technical advances in sound telegraphy which had been made for military purposes during the war, there was at once an economic opportunity and the need for a new social definition. No nation or manufacturing group held a monopoly of the technical means of broadcasting, and there was a period of intensive litigation followed by cross-licensing of the scattered basic components of successful transmission and reception (the vacuum tube or valve, developed from 1904 to 1913; the feedback circuit, developed from 1912; the neutrodyne and heterodyne circuits, from 1923). Crucially, in the mid-1920s, there was a series of investment-guided technical solutions to the problem of building a small and simple domestic receiver, on which the whole qualitative transformation from wireless telegraphy to broadcasting depended. By the mid-1920s—1923 and 1924 are especially decisive years—this breakthrough had happened in the leading industrial societies: the United States, Britain, Germany and France. By the end of the 1920s the radio industry had become a major sector of industrial production, within a rapid general expansion of the new kinds of machines which were eventually to be called 'consumer durables'. This complex of developments included the motorcycle and motorcar, the box camera and its successors, home electrical appliances, and radio sets. Socially, this complex is characterised by the two apparently paradoxical yet deeply connected tendencies of modern urban industrial living: on the one hand mobility, on the other hand the more apparently self-sufficient family home. The earlier period of public technology, best exemplified by the railways and city lighting, was being replaced by a kind of technology for which no satisfactory name has yet been found: that which served an at once mobile and home-centred way of living: a form of *mobile privatisation*. Broadcasting in its applied form was a social product of this distinctive tendency....

The cheap radio receiver is then a significant index of a general condition and response. It was especially welcomed by all those who had least social opportunities of other kinds; who lacked independent mobility or access to the previously diverse places of entertainment and information. Broadcasting could also come to serve, or seem to serve, as a form of *unified* social intake, at the most general levels. What had been intensively promoted by the radio manufacturing companies thus interlocked with this kind of social need, itself defined within general limits and pressures. In the early stages of radio manufacturing, transmission was conceived before content. By the end of the 1920s the network was there, but still at a low level of content-definition. It was in the 1930s, in the second phase of radio, that most of the significant advances in content were made. The transmission and reception networks created, *as a by-product*, the facilities of primary broadcasting production. But the general social definition of 'content' was already there.

This theoretical model of the general development of broadcasting is necessary to an understanding of the particular development of television. For there were, in the abstract, several different ways in which television as a technical means might have been developed. After a generation of universal domestic television it is not easy to realise this. But it remains true that, after a great deal of intensive research and development, the domestic television set is in a number of ways an inefficient medium of visual broadcasting. Its visual inefficiency by comparison with the cinema is especially striking, whereas in the case of radio there was by the 1930s a highly efficient sound broadcasting receiver, without any real competitors in its own line. Within the limits of the television home-set emphasis it has so far not been possible to make more than minor qualitative improvements. Higher-definition systems, and colour, have still only brought the domestic television set, as a machine, to the standard of a very inferior kind of cinema. Yet most people have adapted to this inferior visual medium, in an unusual kind of preference for an inferior immediate technology, because of the social complex—and especially that of the privatised home—within which broadcasting, as a system, is operative. The cinema had remained at an earlier level of social definition; it was and remains a special kind of theatre, offering specific and discrete works of one general kind. Broadcasting, by contrast, offered a whole social intake: music, news, entertainment, sport. The advantages of this general intake, within the home, much more than outweighed the technical advantages of visual transmission and reception in the cinema, confined as this was to specific and discrete works. While broadcasting was confined to sound, the powerful visual medium of cinema was an immensely popular alternative. But when broadcasting became visual, the option for its social advantages outweighed the immediate technical deficits.

The transition to television broadcasting would have occurred quite generally in the late 1930s and early 1940s, if the war had not intervened. Public television services had begun in Britain in 1936 and in the United States in 1939, but with still very expensive receivers. The full investment in transmission and reception facilities did not occur until the late 1940s and early 1950s, but the growth was thereafter very rapid. The key social tendencies which had led to the definition of broadcasting were by then even more pronounced. There was significantly higher investment in the privatised home, and the social and physical distances between these homes and the decisive political and productive centres of the society had become much greater. Broadcasting, as it had developed in radio, seemed an inevitable model: the central transmitters and the domestic sets.

Television then went through some of the same phases as radio. Essentially, again, the technology of transmission and reception developed before

254

*Chapter 10
Mass
Communication
as Cultural
Process*

the content, and important parts of the content were and have remained by-products of the technology rather than independent enterprises. As late as the introduction of colour, 'colourful' programmes were being devised to persuade people to buy colour sets. In the earliest stages there was the familiar parasitism on existing events: a coronation, a major sporting event, theatres. A comparable parasitism on the cinema was slower to show itself, until the decline of the cinema altered the terms of trade; it is now very widespread, most evidently in the United States. But again, as in radio, the end of the first general decade brought significant independent television production. By the middle and late 1950s, as in radio in the middle and late 1930s, new kinds of programme were being made for television and there were very important advances in the productive use of the medium, including, as again at a comparable stage in radio, some kind of original work.

Yet the complex social and technical definition of broadcasting led to inevitable difficulties, especially in the productive field. What television could do relatively cheaply was to transmit something that was in any case happening or had happened. In news, sport, and some similar areas it could provide a service of transmission at comparatively low cost. But in every kind of new work, which it had to produce, it became a very expensive medium, within the broadcasting model. It was never as expensive as film, but the cinema, as a distributive medium, could directly control its revenues. It was, on the other hand, implicit in broadcasting that given the tunable receiver all programmes could be received without immediate charge. There could have been and can still be a socially financed system of production and distribution within which local and specific charges would be unnecessary; the BBC, based on the licence system for domestic receivers, came nearest to this. But short of monopoly, which still exists in some state-controlled systems, the problems of investment for production, in any broadcasting system, are severe.

Thus within the broadcasting model there was this deep contradiction, of centralised transmission and privatised reception. One economic response was licensing. Another, less direct, was commercial sponsorship and then supportive advertising. But the crisis of production control and financing has been endemic in broadcasting precisely because of the social and technical model that was adopted and that has become so deeply established. The problem is masked, rather than solved, by the fact that as a transmitting technology—its functions largely limited to relay and commentary on other events—some balance could be struck; a limited revenue could finance this limited service. But many of the creative possibilities of television have been frustrated precisely by this apparent solution, and this has far more than local effects on producers and on the balance of programmes. When there has been such heavy investment in a particular model of social communications, there is a restraining complex of financial institutions, of cultural expectations and of specific technical developments, which though it can be seen, superficially, as the effect of a technology is in fact a social complex of a new and central kind.

CHAPTER 11 Cultural Criticism of Mass Media

11.1 STANLEY ARONOWITZ

Working Class Culture in the Electronic Age

Before beginning his career as a scholar and public critic, Stanley Aronowitz was an industrial worker and a union activist. Thus, he brings to his critical scholarship a mix of theory and practice. Today Aronowitz teaches at the Graduate Center of the City University of New York, and he has published numerous books. Throughout his work—both as an academic and as a union activist—Aronowitz has focused on the relationship between culture, education, and the declining fortunes of the working class in modern capitalism. In *False Promises: The Shaping of American Working Class Consciousness* (McGraw-Hill, 1973), he argues that it was not just economic decision making and political policy that caused labor to lose power in the years following World War II. Transformations in education, steady suburbanization, and the spread of mass-mediated culture, primarily through television, shifted working-class consciousness away from awareness of laborers' social and cultural distinctiveness and of their subordinate position in society. In *Education Under Siege* (Bergin & Garvey, 1985), Aronowitz focuses on the social logic of education in the United States.

In "Working Class Culture in the Electronic Age," in Ian Angus and Sut Jhally, eds., *Cultural Politics in Contemporary America* (Routledge, 1989), from which the following selection has been taken, Aronowitz reveals both the ritual nature of working-class culture and the workings of hegemony in the contemporary breakup of that culture. He does this by tracing a key set of historical displacements, which involved the simultaneous movement of workers from closely knit city neighborhoods to the dispersed living patterns of the suburbs and the substitution of mass media images for the cultural institutions of the old neighborhoods, particularly the masculine culture of the local bar.

Key Concept: displacement of working-class culture in mass media representations

*I*ndividual and collective identities are constructed on three articulated sites: the biological, the social, and the cultural. The biologically given characteristics which we bring to every social interaction are often covered over by social relations (such as the family and the school) and the technological sensorium that we call mass or popular culture. In western culture these biological givens assume meaning over which individuals have some control, but are often beyond our powers to reverse. Our race and sex confer boundaries as well as possibilities in various relations, particularly the kind of friends we can make, work we can do, mates that are available to us. Of course, the meanings of race and sex, like those of class, are socially constituted—there is no "inherent" significance to these identities as social signs. However, we are born into these identities, given the social arrangements.

The second crucial site is our interaction with family, school, the workplace, and other conventional institutions such as the Church. These relationships are often conceived as self-determining, that is, free of their biological givens. Obviously, parents and teachers treat boys and girls differently: we might say they enjoy/suffer a different moral development regardless of class membership or race. As many writers have argued, the family remains, perhaps, the crucial site for reproducing sexual differences.

While schools are crucial secondary institutions in reproducing sexual difference, they play a major part in the reproduction of racial difference, the specific forms of which remain to be fully explored. It is enough here to point out that the school is the first place the child experiences as racially segregated, since modernism ended gender segregation. It is in school that the child experiences itself as white or black: needless to say, textbooks make clear to blacks their subordinate status, apart from any overt content. Black images, even when they appear, are tokens of the power of the civil rights movement over the past thirty years, but black history and black culture remain absent, a silence which signifies relations of domination. Of course, there are less subtle signs of difference: the failure of racial integration since the Supreme Court decision outlawing segregation thirty-five years ago is an overwhelming feature of public schooling. White kids learn that they are of a specific race simply by virtue of the absence of blacks in their classrooms. Blacks understand this by parental instruction, but realize that race means subordination by virtue of second-class education, the inferior resources made available to them, and finally come to realize that their individual and collective life chances have been decided long before they enter the workworld (a realization white working-class kids only have by secondary school).

Class representations are largely constructed by mass-mediated culture, especially since the working-class community, like the urban-based mass-production industries that created it, passed into history.... I especially want to trace the *displacement* of representations of the working class in this realm. I will show that there are no longer direct representations of the interactions among workers in American television, but that these have been refracted through the police shows that still (in 1988) dominate prime time.

Mass-media representations can no longer be grouped under institutional socializations which include the family, peer interactions, and schools. The media are *unique* sites precisely because of the specific place of technology in the production of culture.... Louis Althusser's claim that the school is the chief ideological state apparatus may hold for the production of the *symbolic* system, that constellation of signs and codes through which is construed the field of what counts as reliable knowledge.[1] But the mass media construct the *social imaginary*, the place where kids situate themselves in their emotional life, where the future appears as a narration of possibilities....

The electronic media can determine, to some degree, *how* social life is represented (that is, their autonomous field of action consists in modes of representation), but not whether a social category *will* be represented. Therefore, it is literally not possible to totally exclude working-class representations, but is it equally improbable that these representations would remain direct under conditions where the cultural traditions of workers are disappearing or occupying smaller social spaces.

When I worked in the steel mills, the barroom was far more than a place to have a casual beer or to get drunk. It was scene of union politics, the site of convivial relationships that were hard to sustain on the shop floor because of the noise, frequent speedups, and the ever watchful eye of the foreman. Of course we had the john, but only for twenty minutes at a time; as the metal was heating up in furnaces, we often took a break. Sometimes the john substituted for the barroom. Animated arguments took place about baseball, women, or an incident that had just occurred, usually one in which one of our fellow workers was hurt (I remember Felix who caught a hot wire in his leg). But inevitably, the warning buzzer would interrupt our discussions—metal was nearly ready to come out and be drawn into wire.

So, the "gin mill" was the place where our collective identity as a community was forged and reproduced. Even when we had harsh disagreements about things that really mattered (whether we should stop work over a safety grievance or whether Jackie Robinson was a better second baseman than Billy Martin, a tinderbox of an issue in 1960), we knew that the next day we would have to pull together in the hot mill, that our disputes were in the family. We also knew that we had to fight the boss together, not only for the ordinary reasons of better pay and benefits, but for our survival. The mill was a dangerous place and, for most of us, losing a limb meant losing the best paying job we were ever likely to own, for in the union shops of the 1950s and early 1960s, the job was property right. As we used to say, the only reason you could get fired was if you punched the foreman while sober.

Steelwork was definitely male culture. As in Freud's essay on femininity, women were the mysterious "other." We did not know much about them and, apart from the incessant desire that occupied our prurient conversations, they did not enter into our working lives. Women were an obscure object of our desire, but desire also reached out for a secure collective identity....

I went to christenings and confirmations in the area around the place which was located in an industrial suburb. Most of the families were of eastern and southern European backgrounds, not only Italians and Poles (although they were in the majority), but also Czechs, Russians, and Greeks. People lived around the northern New Jersey plants in wood frame one-family houses or in "uppers" (the second and third floors of multiple dwellings). Those of us who were not veterans of the Second World War or the Korean War did not quality for special mortgage deals, so we rented apartments that ate about 25% of our monthly pay. However, a growing minority of my friends were moving to the middle-class suburbs where single-family housing developments were mushrooming, or more graphically, springing up like weeds....

Suburban flight was made feasible by low-interest mortgages, but also by the federal highway program initiated by President Harry Truman and fulfilled by the Eisenhower administration. In earlier years, living fifteen or twenty miles from the plant was simply not an option because the roads were invariably local. Such a round trip could take more than two hours. Now, barring traffic jams, evening- and night-shift workers could make it to work in twenty minutes, and those working days simply left home before rush hour and came back late. For many, being away from the wife and kids presented few, if any, problems; male culture excluded women and the notion that men should share child care was simply unthinkable in most families in those days. Certainly, many workers were left behind—blacks and Hispanics, young workers not yet able to raise a down payment or still unmarried and older workers who had literally failed to recover from the depression wipe-out.

White working-class flight was engendered, in part, by the influx of southern and Caribbean blacks into large northern cities, and also by the failure of federal and state lawmakers to expand the federal housing program beyond the poor.... Racism was not the "cause" of white flight in the sense that individuals who harbored these attitudes decided to move to get away from blacks. Racism is the result of a combination of developments. In addition to the urban housing shortage (where virtually no new one-family moderate income homes were constructed after the war), the era was marked by a precipitous decline in services—schools, hospitals, and amenities such as recreation and child care were in either serious disrepair or overcrowded.

In historical retrospect, the deterioration of the urban regions after the war was federal and corporate policy. By the mid 1960s center-city industrial plants were closing down. In Harrison, the industrial suburb of Newark, General Motors removed its roller bearing plant to the Union county suburb, Kenilworth. General Electric closed its lamp factory in the black section of Newark, and by the end of the decade, no major industrial plant remained in that city. Jersey City and Hoboken suffered similar fates; industrial expansion was still a powerful spur to economic growth, but not in the big cities. Capital and white working-class flight go together with the federal housing and highway programs, and the enthusiasm of local communities to give away the keys to the town to any corporation willing to build a plant, office building, or research facility.

The dispersion of white workers into the suburbs did not immediately destroy working-class communities, although they were considerably weakened by the late 1950s. The gin mill next to the production mill retained its pride of place. Sometimes this function was performed by a bar located in a local union hall or in a fraternal association of, say, Poles or Ukrainians. Typically, a worker would "stop" at the bar after going off shift for an hour or two before going to a home that could be as far as even forty miles away. There, he would play darts, shuffle board, or pool, or sit at the bar and just drink and talk.

Those who worked days arrived home at 7 p.m. (the shift ended at 3 p.m.). After supper, if there were no chores, the family might sit in front of the television set. The television explosion of the 1950s is generally acknowledged to have changed the leisure-time activities of Americans. The simulations that film brought to theater audiences now became daily fare.

Until the early 1960s, a small number of films and TV shows offered direct representations of white workers (usually in a comic or pathetic mode) but the mode of this presentation changed in the next decades. Workers became the object of liberal scorn, portrayed as racist and sexist, and equally important, as politically and socially conservative. Archie Bunker *(All in the Family* [1971–83]) was not only a comic character: he was a moral agent suffused with evil, a direct violation of the code according to which the working class (however scarce its media image) was invariably a hero. In contrast to Marlon Brando's 1954 portrayal *(On the Waterfront)* of a benighted but brave longshoreman who, in the last analysis, comes down for truth and justice, Bunker is a troglodyte, a "hard hat" whose wrath is aimed at the young, the poor, and the blacks.

It was hard for working-class kids to identify with Archie, but he was, as late as the mid-1970s a palpable working-class figure, recognizable by his syntax, his body language, his gruff, semi-articulate speech that parodied the results of working-class culture. As I shall demonstrate, Archie proved to be a rearguard character. After his demise (or, rather, his good fortune in having moved up the social ladder), specifically working-class representations disappear with him. Today, working-class kids may still look forward to getting working-class jobs, but forging a class identity is more difficult than ever. They confront a media complex that consistently denies their existence. However, in what amounts to a grudging acknowledgment that it is really impossible to achieve this result, working-class male identity is *displaced* to other, upwardly mobile occupations (e.g. police, football players, and other sites where conventional masculine roles are ubiquitous)....

Electronically mediated cultural forms play an enlarged role in the formation of cultural identities. Of course, the claim that media are so hegemonic that they exclude the influence of family, peers, and schools appears excessive. But, it would be a serious error to conclude that it is an even match. I claim that electronically mediated cultural forms have the upper hand because they carry the authority of the society that, over the last half century, has displaced pa-triarchial authority. For the discourse of social authority promises what family and friends cannot deliver: a qualitatively better life, consumption on an ex-panded scale, a chance to move beyond the limits of traditional working-class life.

No institution represents the promise of this type of transcendence more than the school, for its curriculum is widely understood as a ticket to class mobility. However, the *content* of that alternative is offered working-class kids by the situation comedies of television, the celluloid dreams of the movies, and especially the advertisements which evoke lifestyles considered worthy of emulation. I argue that the relationship between schooling and media repre-sentations of vocational and cultural aspirations has become symbiotic: to the extent that the curriculum is almost entirely geared to the presumed occupa-tional requirements of modern corporations and the state, the dependence of what counts as education on the collective cultural ideal is almost total. For these occupational requirements, especially in large parts of the service sector, are not so much technical as they are ideological. That is, just as many advertise-ments sell not products but capitalism, so school learning is organized around behaviors required by types of bureaucratic work, as well as the rewards of-fered by consumer society for performance according to established corporate norms. The student is no longer (if *he* ever was) enthusiastic about discover-ing new things to know, much less Truth. Rather, he wants to find out how the real world works, especially what it takes to achieve a certain level of con-sumption. In this, the high school is the major site where the "real" world of work is discovered. The student remembers little or nothing of the content of knowledge (facts of history, how to perform algebraic equations, the story line of *Silas Marner*) but remembers how to succeed in receiving good grades, gain-ing admission to a decent college, or university, and how to curry favor with authorities—teachers, counselors, employers.

Working-class kids often fail to get the message right. As Paul Willis tells us, their rebellion against school authority, manifested as the refusal to inter-nalize the two parts of the curriculum (its manifest "knowledge-based" content and its latent demand for discipline and respect for authority) ensures that they will get working-class jobs rather than make it up the ladder. But, while assembly-line, construction, and other heavy industrial labor was available for school leavers until the 1970s in the US and UK, these options are today fore-closed by the restructured world economy. Parents, especially fathers, can no longer serve as substitute representations of viable occupational alternatives to those imposed by school and the media. Peers may discourage an individ-ual from integrating into the prescribed curricula, but the cultural ideal is now increasingly provided by the media. As this ideal erases working-class repre-sentations so the class sensorium disappears.

... Indeed, if identification is a basis for the forging of a personal iden-tity, school and media consort to persuade, cajole, and, by the absence of rep-resentations, force working-class kids to accept middle-class identities as the only legitimate option available to them. However, it is obvious that many will choose neither to accept this course or, having bought into the aspirations, will "fail" to make the grade. The result for both groups is cultural homelessness. . . .

The stimulation of the unconscious by "imaging" (the term is Teresa di Lauretis's[2]) consists in simulating the dream work so that identities are formed through identification with the gendered characters that appear on the screen. Aural media are also powerful desiring machines, but sound is burdened with an enormous load because images must be produced by the listener. Identification can be fomented but with difficulty. The film form invokes the stark real-life character. Di Lauretis argues that women do not insert themselves into film culture, that they are absent in imagining. They cannot identify with the actual representations of women on the screen, for these women are the objects of male desire—they do not occupy subject positions from which emanates a distinctive female voice. Thus, there is no chance for identification unless women accept the object space to which they have been assigned.

Males identify with characters (protagonists, heroes) who are the subjects of narratives; women are objects of desire/exchange/conflict among males and only assume distinctive character when they occupy male-subject positions from which, in both comedies and drama they must inevitably fall (e.g. the Spencer Tracy/Katherine Hepburn comedies such as *Women of the Year* [1942] and *Desk Set* [1957], and the Joan Crawford soap operas such as *Mildred Pierce* [1945], in which women who speak as male characters find that adopting these personae invites self-destruction). Male workers do find representations in film and television in the 1950s. The characters of Ralph Cramden and Ed Norton in *The Honeymooners* (1951–56; revived 1966–70 as part of *The Jackie Gleason Show)* and Chester Riley in *The Life of Riley* (1949–58) are comically absurd, the situations often artificial and juvenile, but family relationships articulate with the prevalent war between the sexes, the distinctiveness of male culture, the absence of a corresponding women's community.

Ralph Cramden is a bus driver who, like many working-class men, dreams of escaping his routine, relatively low-paid job by entering a constant succession of bound-to-fail business schemes. His driving ambition for wealth and social position is lodged entirely in his (male) imaginary. Ralph's wife Alice can barely disguise contempt for his fantasies and foolish projects—most of which serve not to enhance the opportunity for real social mobility, but Ralph's pathetic efforts to establish his dominance in the home. On the other side is Norton, a sewer worker who harbors neither illusion nor the desire to flee his job. The sewer affords him a considerable measure of autonomy, at least in comparison to factory work or even driving a bus. He enjoys the lack of responsibility his job entails but fervently asserts its dignified character against the constant chidings of his quixotic friend.

As with most television situation comedies, the characters have a cartoon quality: there is no room for complexity in the representations. Additionally, the stripped-down sets evoke 1930s depression decorum rather than the postwar era. The honeymooners have been left behind the white urban exodus; they are transhistorical working-class types. Norton is invariably dressed in a T-shirt and wears his hat indoors. Cramden dons the uniform of a bus driver, signifying the ambiguity of his situation. Clearly he is a wage laborer, but his will is that of a petty official since genuine wealth has been foreclosed to him. Cramden displaces his frustration onto intrafamilial quarrels. His wife's housework never counts as real work—his characteristic posture is that of an inquisitor (what have you been doing all day?). Since she rarely awards him the deference he urgently needs, given his relatively degraded social position, his usual gesture is the verbal threat of violence (against women): "one of these days... pow, right in the kisser." Alice seems bored by his remonstrations, and we, the audience, know that Ralph is simply too henpecked... to follow through.

The Honeymooners retains its large audience after thirty years because it displays the range of class and gender relations. Its class ideology is represented by the absence of the labor process except discursively. The family relations displace the class relations, as Ralph seeks to dominate Alice, who as the real proletarian remains recalcitrant. Here we see the inner core of male fantasies: lacking the power individually to achieve the freedom wealth presumably affords, domination becomes the object of male desire.

Caricature notwithstanding, working-class life demanded representations in the 1950s and early 1960s. By the latter half of the decade, the dispersion of working-class culture made direct representation improbable. . . .

Working-class culture is preeminently urban; it belongs to the industrializing era which, by the late 1960s has passed. Post-industrial culture is already post-modern: it is marked by boundary crossing. As David Halle found, while working-class culture still finds renewal on the shop floor, its residential base is dispersed.[3] In the suburbs of major metropolitan centers, industrial workers mow their lawns alongside professionals, managers, and small business neighbors.

In the 1977–78 season, Archie Bunker, the Queens, New York political and social neanderthal, opened a gin mill. Having pushed himself up into the business-owning small middle class, Archie left his working-class roots behind, not only in his newly found proprietorship, but also in his contacts. In this assimilation, he continued the tendencies of the earlier incarnation of the show; recall, the Bunker family lived in that part of New York that most resembled the suburbs. The only Black family he knew owned and operated a dry cleaning business (the Jeffersons, their *own* TV series beginning in 1975). In other words, he rubbed shoulders with those who had more completely achieved one of the crucial elements of the American dream, a business of one's own. So it is entirely reasonable that Archie should aspire to gaining a toehold in the social ladder. With that, the Archie of *Archie Bunker's Place* (the series' new name, as of 1979) disappears into the middle class.

From the mid-1970s, there simply are no direct representations of working-class males (much less women) in television. Representations are dispersed to beer advertisements (thirty-second images of football players hoisting their favorite brands, jostling each other in timid evocations of the ribbing characteristic of working-class bar culture), and cop shows in which characteristic working-class culture is displaced and recontextualized in the stationhouse, on the streets, and the bars in which cops congregate. These are displacements, so we see only the reminders—conviviality and friendship that is overdetermined by the Police buddy system, the obligatory partnership. It is in these interactions, when the partners of say, *Hill Street Blues* (first aired, 1981), discuss their personal problems or their troubles with the Department, that the old class solidarity bonds are permitted to come to the surface, often against the Captain or even the lieutenants who are a step above the line and possess some authority. We know that the patrolmen (and some patrolwomen) may rise to Sergeant, but are not likely to make Lieutenant, much less Captain. These are not educated men and women. Their bravery entitles them to recognition, not rank. They have their own hangouts, their personal troubles (especially with their love lives). In contrast, officials, whatever their origins, do not congregate in barrooms; they have no sharer of their troubles because they must observe the tacit code of hierarchy.

In recent films, displacement of class to the police continues, but is joined by displacement or sex/gender relations to class as well. Hollywood movies... are marked by a conventional theme in contemporary narrative: the working-class man is powerfully attracted to an upper-class woman, disrupting not only the prohibition of interclass romance, but also the family romance. In these instances, to be working class is identified with masculinity, upper class with femininity....

Someone to Watch Over Me finds a cop of plainly working-class parentage, married to a tough, fiesty working-class woman, who live together with their kids in a modest single-family house in Queens. Archie Bunker's kid has become a cop. The cop is assigned to protect an upper-class woman, ensconced in a Manhattan townhouse. He is assigned the midnight shift and quickly has an affair with her, an event that disrupts his tension-filled but stable home life.... The film reenacts a crucial male working-class fantasy: to dominate a beautiful rich woman, to make the "impossible dream" real.

... The cop is socialized into a conventional honorific position—the centurian—but finds it suffused with mediocrity and, most important of all, marked by repetition and continuity with the anterior generation. What is new is adventure, which can only be fulfilled by sexual indiscretion, "penetration" into the forbidden territory of the upper class. But beside the exotic, for the cop, buried in the routine tasks dictated by a bureaucracy that seems entirely beyond his power to control, sex becomes the power that can propel him out of his own real-life subordination.

It may be that today sex discourse refers to class issues; but it is also true class discourse refers to gender domination. The import of the image of the working class cum cop engaging in sexual relations with a women in an entirely improbable class position is not that American society is somehow democratic —these relationships end in disaster. They are themselves sundered, but more importantly they wreck families, personal lives, and so forth. The significance is otherwise. Class is no barrier when upper-class women are involved. In current representations, the reverse is rarely portrayed. Femininity is not a universal signifier. That privilege is reserved for male culture....

In short, in contrast to the 1950s when a viable working-class culture, connected to powerful large-scale industry, was accorded considerable status in media representations, class has been displaced in two ways: first, to other signifiers of masculinity, and second, to the code violations entailed in sexual relations between working-class or declassed men and upper-class women. In this case, sex/class relations are reversed. Men, despite lower-class roots, achieve class parity with women due to the status conferred upon masculine sexuality and its powers by society.

... [T]he sex/class/power axis in television and movies constitutes a critique of the cultural ideal of consumer society that passes for the 1980s equivalent of the mobility myth. For the entrepreneurial ambition which motored two generations of immigrants in the 20th century has disappeared from view; the remainder is the civil service which has become the far horizon of well-being for a new working class that can no longer count on high-paying factory jobs. The army and the police have replaced industrial labor for working-class men, for whom professional options simply never existed.

Male bonding persists in these contexts, but not the solidarity that is born of mutual recognition among production workers who share a common fate as well as a common existence....

The only vital life consists in dreams of power, the most vivid form of which is male sexuality. Contrasted to earlier direct representations in which sex is virtually absent from discourse, but where class persists, today's movies and television programs code sex, class, and power interchangeably. As with the earlier genre, women do not occupy subject positions: they remain the palpable objects of male desire, and by this precise relation experience class reversal.

NOTES

1. Louis Althusser, "Ideology and Ideological State Apparatuses," in *Lenin and Philosophy* (London: New Left Books, 1971).
2. Teresa Di Lauretis, *Alice Doesn't: Feminism, Semiotics, Cinema* (Bloomington: Indiana University Press, 1984) pp. 37–69.
3. David Halle, *America's Working Men: Work, Home and Politics Among the Blue-collar Property Owners* (Chicago: University of Chicago Press, 1984).

11.2 ROSALIND WILLIAMS

The Dream World of Mass Consumption

In the following selection, originally published in Rosalind Williams's *Dream Worlds* (University of California Press, 1982), Williams describes contemporary concepts of consumption by linking scientific progress and technical determination to the pleasure of spectacle and the growing cultural adoption of merchandising. Her thoughtful critique of the role of expositions, department stores, and cinema sets the stage for twentieth-century electronic culture.

It is sometimes difficult to think that our society ever had different values than it does now, but, as Williams points out, consumer culture grew from a rich combination of artistic, philosophical, and technological convergence. Her essay shows the historical specificity of consumption as a dominant trend in Western culture. Although her examples draw largely from Parisian society in the late nineteenth and early twentieth centuries, similar examples, such as expositions (world's fairs) and the growth of department stores, mail order, and media, can be found in the United States.

The metaphor of a "dream world" of consumption is a powerful image. Often we are unaware of the power of consumer society, or we find it appealing to willingly give ourselves over to a "dream world" of some kind. For example, amusement parks (similar in many ways to expositions) allow us to enter entire environments that ask little of our critical faculties—just that we relax, enjoy, and consume! Perhaps the ultimate "dream worlds" of consumption are Disney World and Disney Land, where one can enter a literal "Magic Kingdom" of fantasy and where consumerism is the quiet, subtle, but ever-present master of the universe!

Williams's historical critique of culture's being increasingly affected by consumerism is a powerful image that provides an important background to understanding contemporary culture and values. As you read the following selection, you may wish to think of other contexts in which consumerism has grown and influenced social values.

Key Concept: consumerism and cultural display

THE SCHOOL OF TROCADÉRO

The arrival of the twentieth century was celebrated in Paris by a universal exposition spread over 500 acres and visited by 50 million people from around the world. The 1900 exposition was the climax of a series of similar events that began with the Crystal Palace exposition in London in 1851 and continued to be held at regular intervals during the second half of the century (in 1855, 1867, 1878, and 1889) in Paris, the undisputed if unofficial capital of European civilization. The purpose of all expositions was, in the popular phrase of the time, to teach a "lesson of things." "Things" meant, for the most part, the recent products of scientific knowledge and technical innovation that were revolutionizing daily life; the "lesson" was the social benefit of this unprecedented material and intellectual progress....

At the 1900 exposition the sensual pleasures of consumption clearly triumphed over the abstract intellectual enjoyment of contemplating the progress of knowledge. This emphasis was evident the moment a visitor entered the grounds through the Monumental Gateway, which, according to one bemused contemporary, consisted of "two pale-blue, pierced minarets and polychrome statues surmounted by oriflammes and adorned with cabochons," terminating in "an immense flamboyant arch" above which, perched on a golden ball, "stood the flying figure of a siren in a tight skirt, the symbolic ship of the City of Paris on her head, throwing back an evening coat of imitation ermine —La Parisienne."[1] Whatever this chic madonna represented, it was certainly not science nor technology. Inside this gateway the sprawling exposition had no orderly arrangement of focal points such as previous ones had possessed. Machines were scattered throughout the grounds next to their products, an indication that tools of production now seemed hopelessly boring apart from the things they made. The vault of the Gallery of Machines had been cut up —desecrated like a "secularized temple," complained one admirer of the 1889 version—and overrun by a display of food products:

> [Instead of] a universal workshop...a festival hall has invaded the center of the structure. The extremities are abandoned to the rustic charms of agriculture and to the fattening joys of eating. No more sharp whistles, trembling, clacking transmission belts; nothing being released except champagne corks.

Despite this confusion or, rather, because of it, thoughtful observers sensed that the 1900 exposition was particularly prophetic, and it was a microcosm of emerging France, a scale model of future Paris, that something rich and strange was happening there which broke decisively with the past and prefigured twentieth-century society. In 1889 and even more in 1900, the expositions attracted a host of journalists of a philosophical bent who provided not only descriptions of the various exhibits but also reflections on their significance. For the most part their sense of the exposition's prophetic value remained poorly articulated. While convinced that the fair revealed the shape of things to come, they were unsure of the contours and were vaguely apprehensive without knowing quite why....

THE SIGNIFICANCE OF THE EXPOSITION

The exposition of 1900 provides a scale model of the consumer revolution. The cultural changes working gradually and diffusely throughout society were there made visible in a concrete and concentrated way. One change was the sheer emphasis on merchandising. Even more striking and disturbing... was the change in how this merchandising was accomplished—by appealing to the fantasies of the consumer. The conjunction of banking and dreaming, of sales pitch and seduction, of publicity and pleasure, is far more unsettling than when each element is taken separately.... Fantasy which openly presents itself as such keeps its integrity and may claim to point to truth beyond everyday experience, what the poet Keats called the "truth of the imagination."...

The 1900 exposition incarnates this new and decisive conjunction between imaginative desires and material ones, between dreams and commerce, between events of collective consciousness and of economic fact. It is obvious how economic goods satisfy physical needs such as those for food and shelter; less evident, but of overwhelming significance in understanding modern society, is how merchandise can fill needs of the imagination. The expression "the dream world of the consumer" refers to this non-material dimension. From earliest history we find indications that the human mind has transcended concerns of physical survival to imagine a finer, richer, more satisfying life. Through most of history, however, only a very few people ever thought of trying to approximate such dreams in daily life. Instead, art and religion provided ways to express these desires. But in the late nineteenth century, commodities that provided an approximation of these age-old longings began to be widely available. Consumer goods, rather than other facets of culture, became focal points for desire. The seemingly contrary activities of hard-headed accounting and dreamy-eyed fantasizing merged as business appealed to consumers by inviting them into a fabulous world of pleasure, comfort, and amusement. This was not at all the future that a conservative nationalist... wished; it was not the vision of a workers' society that socialists wanted; nor did it conform to traditional bourgeois virtues of sobriety and rationality. But welcome or not, the "lesson of things" taught by the make-believe city of the 1900 exposition was that a dream world of the consumer was emerging in real cities outside its gates.

EXOTICISM IN DEPARTMENT STORES

One obvious confirmation of this lesson was the emergence of department stores (in French *grands magasins,* "big" or "great" stores) in Paris. The emergence of these stores in late nineteenth-century France depended on the same growth of prosperity and transformation of merchandising techniques that lay behind the international expositions....

The department store introduced an entirely new set of social interactions to shopping. In exchange for the freedom to browse, meaning the liberty to indulge in dreams without being obligated to buy in fact, the buyer gave up the freedom to participate actively in establishing prices and instead had to accept the price set by the seller. Active verbal interchange between customer and retailer was replaced by the passive, mute response of consumer to things—a striking example of how "the civilizing process" tames aggressions and feelings toward people while encouraging desires and feelings directed toward things. Department stores were organized to inflame these material desires and feelings. Even if the consumer was free not to buy at that time, techniques of merchandising pushed him to want to buy *sometime.* As environments of mass consumption, department stores were, and still are, places where consumers are an audience to be entertained by commodities, where selling is mingled with amusement, where arousal of free-floating desire is as important as immediate purchase of particular items. Other examples of such environments are expositions, trade fairs, amusement parks, and (to cite more contemporary examples) shopping malls and large new airports or even subway stations. The numbed hypnosis induced by these places is a form of sociability as typical of modern mass consumption as the sociability of the salon was typical of prerevolutionary upper-class consumption.

The new social psychology created by environments of mass consumption is a major theme of *Au Bonheur des Dames.* In creating his fictional store Zola did not rely on imagination alone; he filled research notebooks with observations of contemporary department stores before writing his novel. Zola's fictional creation in turn influenced the design of actual stores. He invited his friend, architect Frantz Jourdain, to draw an imaginary plan for Au Bonheur des Dames, and not many years later Jourdain began to collaborate on an ambitious renovation and building program for La Samaritaine, a large department store in the heart of Paris. By 1907, when most of the program was completed, the store closely resembled Zola's descriptions of Au Bonheur des Dames....

The department store dominates the novel.... The counters of the department store present a disconnected assortment of "exhibits," a sort of "universe in a garden" of merchandise. The sheer variety, the assault of dissociated stimuli, is one cause of the numbed fascination of the customers.... It is a style which may without undue flippancy be called the chaotic-exotic. But within one exhibit not chaos but repetition is often employed to numb the spectator even further. When rugs are placed on the ceiling, walls, and floor of the vestibule, when the same item is repeated over and over with minor variations—just as the Andalusian exhibit at the Trocadéro had camels here, camels there, camels everywhere—the sheer accumulation becomes awesome in a way that no single item could be. The same effect is achieved when Mouret fills an entire hall with an ocean of umbrellas, top to bottom, along columns and balustrades and staircases; the umbrellas shed their banality and instead become "large Venetian lanterns, illuminated for some colossal festival," an achievement that makes one shopper exclaim, "It's a fairyland!"[2] ...

THE "AESTHETIC" OF EXOTICISM

...To criticize the chaotic-exotic style as "bad taste," a frequent condemnation even around the turn of the century, misses the point. As a quality of aesthetic judgment, taste does not apply to transient décor whose purpose is "to attract and to hold" the spectator's attention. Why the reliance on fake mahogany, fake bronze, fake marble? Because the purpose of the materials is not to express their own character but to convey a sense of the lavish and foreign. Why the hodgepodge of visual themes? Because the purpose is not to express internal consistency but to bring together anything that expresses distance from the ordinary. Exotic décor is therefore impervious to objections of taste. It is not ladylike but highly seductive. In this aesthetic demi-monde, exotic décor exists as an intermediate form of life between art and commerce. It resembles art, it has recognizable themes and stylistic traits, its commercial purpose is wrapped in elaborate visual trappings; yet it does not participate in traditional artistic goals of creating beauty, harmony, and spiritual significance. This hybrid form is an illusion of art, a "so-called artistic element" posing as the genuine article....

DISTANT VISIONS

For all its innovation in stylistic absurdity, the exotic-chaotic decorative style was traditional in its technology. Its only technical novelty involved the use of increasingly convincing imitation materials to construct "all those domes, balconies, pediments, columns." Nineteenth-century technology developed far more effective ways of creating an illusion of voyage to far-off places, techniques that were dynamic and cinematic rather than static and decorative. They proved so exhilarating and popular that, while occasionally used to publicize products, they more often became products themselves, offered as amusement attractions. At the 1900 exposition twenty-one of the thirty-three major attractions involved a dynamic illusion of voyage. This group of exhibits, like the colonial ones clustered at the Trocadéro, furnished a "lesson of things" in the form of a scale model of a dream world of the consumer.

...Michel Corday (Louis-Léonard Pollet, 1869–1937) assessed the significance of the exhibits providing "Visions Lointaines" ("Distant Visions," or "Views of Faraway Places"). This is the title Corday gave to an article on cinematic exhibits—one of a series he wrote on the exposition—published in the *Revue de Paris*.[3] Corday was well able to appreciate these exhibits from both a technical and a cultural perspective, for he had been educated as an engineer and served with distinction in the army before deciding, at the age of twenty-six, to devote himself to letters. The imprint of Corday's technical training is manifest when he begins by classifying the twenty-one "distant visions" exhibits into five categories, according to the increasing sophistication of the techniques used to convey the illusion of travel: "ensembles in relief," panoramas in which the spectator moves, those in which the panorama itself moves, those in which both move, and moving photographs. One of the more primitive exhibits, an example of the second category, was the World Tour: the tourist walked along the length of an enormous circular canvas representing "without solution of continuity, Spain, Athens, Constantinople, Suez, India, China, and Japan," as natives danced or charmed serpents or served tea before the painted picture of their homeland. The visitor was supposed to have the illusion of touring the world as he strolled by, although Corday hardly found it convincing to have "the Acropolis next-door neighbor to the Golden Horn and the Suez Canal almost bathing the Hindu forests"—the chaotic-exotic style, the universe in a garden, only on canvas! On a somewhat more ingenious level, the Trans-Siberian Panorama placed the spectator in a real railroad car that moved eighty meters from the Russian to the Chinese exhibit while a canvas was unrolled outside the window giving the impression of a journey across Siberia. Three separate machines operated at three different speeds, and their relative motion gave a faithful impression of gazing out a train window. A slight rocking motion was originally planned for the car, but the sponsoring railway company vetoed the idea because it advertised that its trains did not rock....

CINEMATIC VOYAGES

The motion picture is the commercial and technological successor to the "distant visions" exhibits. Between the close of the 1900 exposition and the outbreak of World War I, films became a popular attraction in urban France. In 1907 there were two cinemas in Paris; six years later there were one hundred and sixty, and by 1914 cinema receipts in France were 16 million francs a year.[4] Large, well-financed organizations were established to prepare the décors, costumes, and special effects, to devise the script and hire actors, to shoot the film and edit it, to publicize and distribute the product.

"It is a new, and important, and very modern branch of business," wrote Louis Haugmard in 1913. "This development, extraordinary in its rapidity and extent, this swarming, this 'invasion' of cinematography is a fact which deserves to attract the attention of the casual observer who likes to meditate on things." Haugmard was such an observer. Like Corday, like many other young men in literary circles around the turn of the century, he published a considerable body of creative and critical writings without achieving lasting fame— such is the richness of French letters in that era....

The jumbled chaos of the exposition had been transferred to the silver screen. Haugmard begins his article by remarking upon the way all forms of entertainment—fantastic, sentimental, comic, dramatic, scientific, historical, moralizing—are shown one after the other in the movie house, so that a Western is juxtaposed with a drawing-room comedy, a social documentary with a travelogue, a comic chase sequence with the fall of Troy. "[There is] nothing that cannot be used ... for the confection of a film." Distinctions of significance and even of realism are obliterated when all levels of experience are reduced to the same level of technically ingenious entertainment. Haugmard further suggests that this cinematic syncretism is a result of the need to appeal to a large public with varying tastes. "In fact, the public of cinematographic spectacles is not co-herent. Many 'milieux' are represented there, and all sorts of minds." Because the mass audience is incoherent rather than homogeneous, film programs are also incoherent, for they include something for everyone, just as newspapers and tourist attractions do.

In defining the cinema as a phenomenon of "the people, in the largest meaning of this term," Haugmard agrees with Corday that modern technology widens the horizons of the masses. Not only does film take people to far-off places, "reproduced in their photographic truth, luminous and trembling"; it also allows them to enter hitherto inaccessible reaches of society through "ele-gant and worldly dramas which introduce them to milieux where they cannot otherwise penetrate." Whether the distance is geographic or social, film allows the pleasures of mobility.

Haugmard... condemn[s] these imaginary excursions as childish es-capism. A film advertisement promises "an hour of intense emotion": who could resist this appeal, Haugmard asks? People crave concentrated doses of intense emotion (what Corday called "liquors... which concentrate power and life") to get away from "their sorry and monotonous existence, from which they love to escape." Haugmard notes that moviegoers much prefer fantasies to portrayals of ordinary life:

> "The masses" are like a grown-up child who demands a picture album to leaf through in order to forget his miseries... [T]he "cinema," which is a "circus" for adults, offers to the popular imagination and sensibility, deprived and fatigued, the "beau voyage."

People want to evade reality, not to learn about it. Certainly the technical dexterity of the medium permits convincing reproductions of visual appear-ances, "in their photographic truth, luminous and trembling," but "photo-graphic truth" is not truth. Film can give "the exact reproduction of natural reality" while still being

> a factor of artifice and of falsification.... If it is the realm of fraud, of counterfeit, of trickery, how will a naïve public know how to make the indispensable distinc-tions and the necessary selection, under pain of inevitable misunderstandings and multiple errors?

Just because of its photographic realism, film offers a nearly irresistible temptation not only to inculcate political propaganda but also "to vulgarize, which is to say, to deform" the noblest novels, plays, and poems; " 'to roman-ticize' or falsify" history by giving a partial view; and, on current subjects, "to nourish vanities and launch imitations, for the image excites naïve souls."

Because film speaks in the language of imagery, it is at once emotionally exciting and intellectually deceptive. The rapid succession of "realistic" images captivates the imagination of the viewer without engaging his mind. As an ex-ample, Haugmard describes the way a robbery is portrayed on the screen in a series of scenes of violence, beginning with the hold-up of a delivery van,

even down to the mark of the bullet on the wheel; then the judge is shown
...interrogating the policemen. Imagine the influence on children's minds of the
burglary scenes and the ingenious methods used to throw the pursuers off the
track. The prefect of police in Berlin thought it appropriate to forbid children
under fifteen to enter movie theatres.

Movies excite because they communicate through powerful, concrete, realistic images. They lie because they communicate *only* through images:

> Why does an evening at the movies, however crammed with the most diverse
> films, despite everything leave in the mind an impression of emptiness, of noth-
> ingness?... Hardly is the spectacle over and it is forgotten.
>   It is because only facts are photographed. All the rest is sacrificed, all that
> which is intellectual and interior life, and in the human order, only intelligence
> and soul really count! This exclusive capacity to reproduce only the fact entails
> its consequences. Action, only action, which is rapid and brutal. From this the
> suppression, almost absolute, of all psychology. Cinematography is a notation by
> image, as arithmetic and algebra are notations by figures and letters; now, it is
> convenient to limit as much as possible in the statement or the exposition all that
> which is not the sign itself. It is the triumph of simplification.

These remarks apply most directly to the silent films of that era, but even
when the image is accompanied by a soundtrack its dominance is maintained.
The cinema and its descendant, television, remain positivistic mediums, excluding all that is not fact, visually speaking. By excluding so much, by passing off
simplification as totality, they are... true only partially, and so partially as to
be false. Haugmard points out that movie actors become " 'types,' " which is
to say that their immediately recognizable personal images come to convey a
constellation of values and feelings, down to the child actor who incarnates
" 'Baby.' " In the same way, the images of the exotic—the colorful rug, the belly
dancer, the domed palace—are decorative "types" that incarnate exciting feelings of adventure, romance, and luxury but have little to do with Oriental
reality. The language of imagery is also the language of the dream world of
the consumer....

THE ELECTRICAL FAIRYLAND

By now it is becoming clear how momentous were the effects of nineteenth-
century technological progress in altering the social universe of consumption.
Besides being responsible for an increase in productivity which made possible a rise in real income; besides creating many new products and lowering
the prices of traditional ones; besides all this, technology made possible the
material realization of fantasies which had hitherto existed only in the realm
of imagination. More than any other technological innovation of the late nineteenth century, even more than the development of cinematography, the advent
of electrical power invested everyday life with fabulous qualities. The importance of an electrical power grid in transforming and diversifying production is

obvious, as is its eventual effect in putting a whole new range of goods on the market. What is less appreciated, but what amounts to a cultural revolution, is the way electricity created a fairyland environment, the sense of being, not in a distant place, but in a makebelieve place where obedient genies leap to their master's command, where miracles of speed and motion are wrought by the slightest gesture, where a landscape of glowing pleasure domes and twinkling lights stretches into infinity.

Above all, the advent of large-scale city lighting by electrical power nurtured a collective sense of life in a dream world. In the 1890s nocturnal lighting in urban areas was by no means novel, since gas had been used for this purpose for decades; however, gas illumination was pale and flickering compared to the powerful incandescent and arc lights which began to brighten the night sky in that decade. The expositions provided a preview of the transformation of nighttime Paris from somber semidarkness to a celestial landscape. At the 1878 exposition an electric light at a café near but not actually on the fairgrounds caused a sensation. In 1889 a nightly show of illuminated fountains entranced crowds with a spectacle of falling rainbows, cascading jewels, and flaming liquids, while spotlights placed on the top of the Eiffel Tower swept the darkening sky as the lights of the city were being turned on. At the 1900 exposition electrical lighting was used for the first time on a massive scale, to keep the fair open well into the night. Furthermore, the special lighting effects were stunning. In one of his articles for the *Revue de Paris,* Corday describes the nightly performance:

> A simple touch of the finger on a lever, and a wire as thick as a pencil throws upon the Monumental Gateway ... the brilliance of three thousand incandescent lights which, under uncut gems of colored glass, become the sparkling soul of enormous jewels.
>
> Another touch of the finger: the banks of the Seine and the bridges are lighted with fires whose reflection prolongs the splendor.... The facade of the Palace of Electricity is embraced, a stained-glass window of light, where all these diverse splendors are assembled in apotheosis.[5]

Like the technological marvels already mentioned, this one was at once exploited for commercial purposes. As early as 1873 the writer Villiers de l'Isle-Adam (1838–1889) predicted in a short story, "L'Affichage céleste" (which might be loosely translated as "The Heavenly Billboard"), that the "seeming miracles" of electrical lights could be used to generate "an absolute Publicity" when advertising messages were projected upward to shine among the stars:

> Wouldn't it be something to surprise the Great Bear himself if, suddenly, between his sublime paws, this disturbing message were to appear: *Are corsets necessary, yes or no?* ... What emotion concerning dessert liqueurs ... if one were to perceive, in the south of Regulus, this heart of the Lion, on the very tip of the ear of corn of the Virgin, an Angel holding a flask in hand, while from his mouth comes a small paper on which could be read these words: *My, it's good!*[6]

Thanks to this wonderful invention, concluded Villiers, the "sterile spaces" of heaven could be converted "into truly and fruitfully instructive spectacles.... It is not a question here of feelings. Business is business.... Heaven will finally make something of itself and acquire an intrinsic value." As with so many other writers of that era, Villiers's admiration of technological wonders is tempered by the ironic consideration of the banal commercial ends to which the marvelous means were directed. Unlike the wonders of nature, the wonders of technology could not give rise to unambiguous enthusiasm or unmixed awe, for they were obviously manipulated to arouse consumers' enthusiasm and awe.

The prophetic value of Villiers's story lies less in his descriptions of the physical appearance of the nocturnal sky with its stars obscured by neon lights, than in his forebodings of the moral consequences when commerce seizes all visions, even heavenly ones, to hawk its wares. Villiers's prophecies were borne out by the rapid application of electrical lighting to advertising. As he foresaw, electricity was used to spell out trade names, slogans, and movie titles. Even without being shaped into words, the unrelenting glare of the lights elevated ordinary merchandise to the level of the marvelous. Department-store windows were illuminated with spotlights bounced off mirrors. At the 1900 exposition, wax figurines modeling the latest fashions were displayed in glass cages under brilliant lights, a sight which attracted hordes of female spectators.

When electrical lighting was used to publicize another technical novelty, the automobile, the conjunction attracted mammoth crowds of both sexes. Beginning in 1898, an annual Salon de l'Automobile was held in Paris to introduce the latest models to the public. It was one of the first trade shows; the French were pioneers in advertising the automobiles as well as in developing the product itself. This innovation in merchandising—like the universal expositions the Salon de l'Automobile resembles so closely—claimed the educational function of acquainting the public with recent technological advances, a goal, however, which was strictly subordinate to that of attracting present and future customers. The opening of the 1904 Salon de l'Automobile was attended by 40,000 people (compared to 10,000 who went to the opening of the annual painting salon), and 30,000 came each day for the first week. Each afternoon during the Salon de l'Automobile, the Champs-Élysées was thronged with crowds making their way to the show, which was held in the Grand Palais, an imposing building constructed for the 1900 universal exposition. During the Salon the glass and steel domes of the Grand Palais were illuminated at dusk with 200,000 lights; the top of the building glowed in the gathering darkness like a stupendous lantern. People were enchanted: "a radiant jewel," they raved, "a colossal industrial fairyland," "a fairytale spectacle."[7] ...

Unlike images of far-off places, however, a fairyland cannot be accused of falsity because it never pretends to be a real place. Or can it? Electric lighting covers up unpleasant sights which might be revealed in the cold light of day. The illumination of the Grand Palais disguised the building itself. In the words of one visitor:

> The Grand Palais itself is almost beautiful because you hardly see it anymore: the confused scrap-iron and copperwork... [is] lost in the shadow; the luminous scallop decorations and chandeliers and ... allegories, drowned in the irradiation....

The roof itself, that monstrous skin of a leviathan washed up there on the bank of the river, borrows a sort of beauty from the light which emanates from it.[8]

Through the obscuring glare the same visitor noted that the poles supporting the light fixtures were ridiculously ornamented with nautical motifs and garlands which were coming unstuffed. Others who viewed the décor of the Salon de l'Automobile were appalled when in the daylight they saw booths with doorways plastered to resemble those of Persian mosques, Gothic churches, or Egyptian temples, other booths constructed like bamboo huts hung with Japanese lanterns, and still others rigged with ship's masts complete with ropes, sails, and flags. The visitor quoted above, horrified by this "so-called artistic element" of the Salon, said that the exhibits showed "an incoherent heap of the most laughable imaginings" which the French should be thoroughly ashamed to display to the rest of the world, except that the displays of foreigners were equally ridiculous.[9] But all that junk miraculously disappeared when the lights came on.

Through fantasy, business provides alternatives to itself. If the world of work is unimaginative and dull, then exoticism allows an escape to a dream world. If exotic décor is heavy, unconvincing, and shabby, then another level of deception is furnished by a nightly fairyland spectacle that waves away the exotic with the magic wand of electricity. Robert de La Sizeranne, art critic for the *Revue dex deux mondes*, compared the Salons de l'Automobile to fairytale princesses fought over by "perverse and benevolent powers" so that they were "frightfully ugly all day long [and] at night [became] beauties adorned with dazzling jewels." According to La Sizeranne, this diurnal schizophrenia was being repeated all over Paris. In the day the city displayed "superfluous, ignoble, lamentable ornaments," while at nightfall "these trifling or irritating profiles are melted in a conflagration of apotheosis.... Everything takes on another appearance," the ugly details are lost, and diamonds, rubies, and sapphires spill over the city.[10] Instead of correcting its mistakes, the city buries them under another level of technology. In this respect the whole city is assuming the character of an environment of mass consumption. In the day as well as at night, the illusions of these environments divert attention to merchandise of all kinds and away from other things, like colonialism, class structure, and visual disasters.

How much of the history of consumption is revealed in comparing Mme. de Rambouillet's salon of witty conversation and candlelight with the twentieth-century Salon de l'Automobile, a cacophony of crowds, cars, glass, steel, noise, and light!

NOTES

1. This description is from Paul Morand, *1900 A. D.*, trans. Mrs. Romilly Fedden (New York: William Farquhar Payson, 1931), p. 66....

2. Emile Zola, *Au Bonheur des Dames* (Lausanne: Éditions Rencontre, n.d.), p. [228].

3. Michel Corday, "À l'Exposition.—Visions lointaines," *Revue de Paris* 2 (March 15, 1900): 422–38. Quotations from Corday are from this article unless otherwise noted.

Corday's reports on the exposition are summarized in his book *Comment on a fait l'Exposition* (Paris: E. Flammarion, 1900).

4. Theodore Zeldin, *France 1848–1945*, Vol. II: *Intellect, Taste and Anxiety* (Oxford: Clarendon Press, 1977), in *Oxford History of Modern Europe*, ed. Lord Bullock and Sir William Deakin, p. 389.

5. Michel Corday, "À l'Exposition.—La Force à l'Exposition," *Revue de Paris* 1 (January 15, 1900): 438–39. See his note at the bottom of p. 438 regarding the number of kilowatts involved in this display.

6. In Villiers de l'Isle-Adam, *Oeuvres,* ed. Jacques-Henry Bornecque (n.p.: Le Club Français du Livre, 1957), p. 57. The short story was first published in *La Renaissance littéraire et artistique* (November 30, 1873) and was republished in 1883 as part of Villiers's *Contes Cruels.*

7. Robert de La Sizeranne, "La Beauté des machines, à propos du Salon de l'Automobile," *Revue des deux mondes,* 5th per., 42 (December 1, 1907): 657; Camille Mauclair, "La Décoration lumineuse," *Revue bleue* 8 (November 23, 1907): 656; and Émile Berr, "Une Exposition parisienne.—Le 'Salon' des chauffeurs," *Revue bleue* 11 (December 24, 1904): 829.

8. De Félice, "Le Salon de l'Automobile," pp. 11–12.

9. Ibid.

10. La Sizeranne, "La Beauté," pp. 657–58.

11.3 REEBEE GAROFALO

Definitions, Themes, and Issues

Professor Reebee Garofalo teaches at the University of Massachusetts–Boston. His work on rock music encompasses historical, class, gender, and ethnic interpretations of culture. In the following excerpt from his book *Rockin' Out: Popular Music in the USA* (Allyn & Bacon, 1997), Garafalo examines how each of these categories can be understood by looking at rock 'n' roll as a cultural form. Although his examples are specifically from the evolution of U.S. musical forms, similar considerations can be given to other Western social groups.

It is also interesting to note that the author takes the marketing of musical forms as an important aspect of the evolution of what becomes "acceptable" for the general public. He asserts that marketing and time in history have much to do with the commercial success of musical style, form, and the potential for crossover success.

The following selection shows how music and the recording industry introduce many new ideas to the public. Garofalo rightly states that "popular music always interacts with its social environment." As Garafalo indicates, a number of forces can be examined at any given time to see how popular music both reflects and projects cultural values and ideas to audiences. Although it may be tempting to think of certain audiences as "owning" certain musical forms, the commercial viability of music distribution is also an important factor in critiquing music as a cultural "pulse" of a society. Music may both lead and monitor cultural controversy.

Key Concept: music and the expression of cultural values

INTO THE TWENTIETH CENTURY: POPULAR MUSIC AND MASS CULTURE

In its association with sheet music, Tin Pan Alley can be seen as a descendant of a popular culture that dates back to the invention of the printing press in fifteenth-century Europe.[1] When the music of Tin Pan Alley emerged, popular music was distinguished from both folk music and folk culture on the one hand and classical or art music and high culture on the other. These distinctions are a part of our inheritance that came with European colonization. . . .

Popular culture insinuated itself between folk culture and high culture as a third cultural category, a hybrid that was distinguishable from both but borrowed freely from each as needed. Tin Pan Alley provides an excellent example of these contradictory tendencies. In attempting to cater exclusively to popular (albeit narrow mainstream) tastes, Tin Pan Alley writers consciously sought to construct an alternative to the cultural dominance of European art music. In the process, these writers incorporated influences, however superficially, from [a] wide range of sources including a number of African American genres. At the same, however, these writers often took their cues from classical music and high culture. As late as 1941, for example, the melody of "Tonight We Love," a popular song by Ray Austin and Bobby Worth was lifted virtually note for note from the first movement of Tchaikovsky's *Piano Concerto No. 1*....

The invention of new mass communication technologies—records, radio, film, and eventually, television—inserted yet another distinction into the cultural lexicon, namely the concept of mass culture. The new term indicated cultural dissemination on a scale that increased by orders of magnitude. The question of scale had important implications for qualitative judgments about mass culture. Prior to the advent of mass culture, it was possible to consider popular culture as historically continuous with folk culture, either slowly replacing folk cultures as the next stage of development following the Industrial Revolution or as coexisting with rural or industrial folk cultures in the modern era. When viewed in this way, popular culture, like folk culture, was a culture of the people. With the introduction of the mass media, however, the idea of a continuing historical progression came to an abrupt halt. In the eyes of most observers, the emergence of mass culture was accompanied by a subtle but important shift in orientation from a culture of the people to a culture for the masses. In this deceptively simple change there was a profound transformation of meaning. Mass culture was not seen as the lived culture of an identifiable group of people, which reflected their values and aspirations. It was instead a commodified culture produced by a centralized, corporate culture industry for privatized, passive consumption by an alienated, undifferentiated mass.[2] Thus, although the terms *mass culture* and *popular culture* are often used interchangeably today, most observers tended to distinguish between the two in language that was pejorative and/or politically charged until well into the 1960s....

ROCK 'N' ROLL: THE BIRTH OF A NEW ERA

The straightforward commercialism and mass appeal of rock 'n' roll did not set it apart from other popular music. What made rock 'n' roll different was its urban orientation, focus on youth culture, and appeal to working-class sensibilities, and its relationship to technology and African American musical influences and performance styles. As Charlie Gillett argues in his classic study *The Sound of the City*, rock 'n' roll was the first popular genre to incorporate the relentless pulse and sheer volume of urban life into the music itself. In his words, "Rock and Roll was perhaps the first form of popular culture to celebrate without reservation characteristics of city life that had been among the most criticized."[3]

Here Gillett was referring to urban sounds that were perceived as "brutal and oppressive." It was in this world of droning machines that post-World War II adolescents "staked out their freedom... inspired and reassured by the rock and roll beat."[4]

Gillett's conflation of adolescence and rock 'n' roll highlights the fact that the emergence of the music as a genre coincided with the beginnings of youth culture as a phenomenon. Due to the convergence of a number of social forces in the 1950s, including postwar affluence and a demographic shift in the population toward youth, teenagers became an identifiable consumer group and one that possessed an ample amount of disposable income....

Unlike earlier forms of popular music, rock 'n' roll incorporated the capabilities of advanced technology into the creative process itself. Far from valuing the purity of the live performance, rock 'n' roll records consciously used the technical features of echo, editing, overdubbing, and multitracking to distort the reality of the performance. "Technical processes," as musicologist Peter Wicke has said, "became musical opportunities."[5] The emergence of rock 'n' roll, then, was characterized by a progressively more intimate relationship with the technologies used in its production and dissemination. This relationship continued as rock ventured toward art in the 1960s. Following the release of *Sgt. Pepper,* an album so dependent on studio technology that it couldn't be performed live, rock groups spent untold hours in the studio, experimenting with technological gimmickry, overdubbing and adding special effects, and mixing each cut to perfection. Disco was further immersed in technological wizardry, becoming almost completely a product of the studio. In live performance, the use of feedback and distortion pioneered by Jimi Hendrix has become institutionalized in heavy metal through the use of voltage regulators, special effects boxes, and vocal distortion devices. Rap has pushed the envelope still further, first by using dual turntables as musical instruments, and then by using samplers, sequencers, and programmable drum machines as essential tools of the trade. To the extent that these creative uses of technology have been accepted as artistically valid, they have pushed the very definition of popular music beyond a traditional European conception of music as a pattern of *notes* toward a conception of music as organized *sound.* ...

Analyses of structure, melody, and chord progressions, of course, are not without value. They can offer important insights into the differences existing between popular music and other forms of music, as well as differences among popular genres themselves. Rock 'n' roll and Tin Pan Alley pop, for example, can be distinguished in these terms. However, a surface analysis of these elements alone can not adequately capture the disjuncture that characterized the transition between the two. To get to this level of analysis, it is necessary to examine the full range of cultural practices and performance styles that comprised these respective musical eras. The ascendancy of Tin Pan Alley coincided with the emergence of a number of African American genres, including ragtime, blues, boogie woogie, and jazz. Certain aspects of these African American genres were appropriated by Tin Pan Alley songwriters who were somewhat open to outside influences. From ragtime to swing one can find a hint of syncopation here, a blue note there. But while grassroots blues and jazz lured listeners toward Africa, mainstream pop interpretations of these genres quickly pulled them back to Europe. Tin Pan Alley appropriations were by and large superficial adaptations—what musicologist Charles Hamm has called "a touch of exotic seasoning"[6]—that were incorporated into an aesthetic framework defined by the European tradition....

By all accounts, the eruption of rock 'n' roll entailed a profound shift in cultural values on the part of mainstream youth, a shift away from Euro-American sensibilities and toward African American ones. The most important feature of this shift was an increased emphasis on rhythm. In the words of Christopher Small, "rhythm is to the African musician what harmony is to the European—the central organizing principle of the art.[7] Although in the slave cultures of the Americas, this African tradition was complicated by considerable pressure to adopt European ways of music making (indeed the history of African American music is fraught with this tension), rock 'n' roll is clearly descended from the tradition of organizing musical elements around a recurring rhythmic structure. In its early years, rock 'n' roll was often referred to as the Big Beat. With the ascent of rock 'n' roll, then, this "central organizing principle" came to define mainstream popular music in a way that had never before been the case....

If rock 'n' roll tipped the cultural balance toward an African American aesthetic, it was also a music defined by its hybridity. While Elvis Presley clearly drew on African American performance styles, he was also driven by pop tendencies that were entirely consistent with Tin Pan Alley values. Chuck Berry and Sam Cooke, as well as many doo wop groups, enunciated clearly enough to pass muster with the harshest diction teacher. Indeed, doo wop harmonies and vocal styles defy any attempt to analyze rock 'n' roll solely in terms of race. In short, European cultural standards were never abandoned altogether; rock 'n' roll simply imposed a new cultural formula which favored African American values.

Since the advent of rock 'n' roll, there has been a continuing debate regarding the relative proportions of African American and Euro-American influences in popular music. It was considered a mark of distinction by some critics that many of the San Francisco groups of the late 1960s did not sound like they were emulating African American performance styles. Art rock made its musical statement by looking to classical European influences. The concept of instrumental virtuosity in heavy metal derived from the same source. Punk, which ironically was formed in reaction to the excesses of art rock, stripped the music of whatever African American influences remained. Even disco, in the United States, was marked by the tension between funk and soft soul influences on the one hand and the influence of Eurodisco on the other. Popular music has been re-Africanized in rap, which has concentrated primarily on heavy beats and spoken word rhymes, eschewing melody almost completely. In fact, rap is the only form of U.S. popular music that has become more Afrocentric as it has gained in mainstream acceptance.

MARKETING AND THE POLITICS OF
RACE, LANGUAGE, AND GENDER

If rock 'n' roll represented the triumph of African American culture, it did not automatically follow that African Americans would be the main beneficiaries of the victory. The way in which music actually unfolds as a social practice does not necessarily determine the way in which it reaches the ears of its audience. By the time a creative urge has been fed through the star-making machinery of the culture industry, all the biases of class, race, and gender have been brought to bear on it. Although rock 'n' roll proceeded from an aesthetic impulse that viewed cultural borrowing as both natural and desirable, it developed in a commercial context that was subject to all the foibles and inequities of the larger society. In such a context, the natural process of cultural borrowing can become theft, and artists can be categorized incorrectly or excluded from the marketplace altogether for reasons that have little to do with talent or musical style.

The marketing categories of the music industry have often classified performers as much by race as by musical style. The beginnings of this practice date back to the 1920s, when the music industry organized popular music into three categories: "race" (African American popular music); "hillbilly" (white, working-class rural styles); and "popular" (mainstream pop of the type produced by Tin Pan Alley).[8] Initially, *Billboard*, the leading music industry trade magazine, published popularity charts for only that music classified as "popular" by the industry. However, when *Your Hit Parade*, a radio program based on listener preferences, became one of the most popular programs in the country in 1935, it became apparent that the commercial interests of the industry were not being served by only one chart. Thus, by the end of the decade, *Billboard* had inaugurated a popularity chart for "hillbilly" music and in 1942 added a chart entitled "The Harlem Hit Parade." Three years later, the magazine changed this title to "Race Music." . . .

The term *crossover* refers to that process whereby an artist or a recording from a secondary or specialty marketing category, such as country and western or rhythm and blues (r&b), achieves hit status in the mainstream market. Although recently the term has been used simply to indicate multiple chart listings in any direction, historically it connoted movement from a marginal category to the mainstream. In writing of the golden years of r&b, music historian Arnold Shaw has noted that

> The crossover concept was inherent in R&B from the start. In fact, acceptance by the pop market of an R&B disk (Cecil Gant's "I Wonder") generated the first mushrooming of R&B record companies. While these labels produced disks basically for ghetto consumption, they always hoped that the larger white market might be receptive.[9]

The greater acceptance of African Americans in the mainstream market after World War II not only prompted some changes in music charting practices but also put the industry on the horns of a racial dilemma that has been the subject of heated debate ever since.

As late as 1949, most of the music by African American artists could be found under the heading "Race Music" in record company catalogues. As this music began to cross over to the white market, however, it was decided that a more palatable term was needed. Record companies toyed with labels like ebony and sepia for a while, but these too were obviously distinctions of color, not musical style. Eventually "rhythm and blues" became the accepted term, and from 1949 until 1963 *Billboard* charted the music as such. *Billboard* discontinued its r&b charts from the end of 1963 until the beginning of 1965, presumably because the pop charts were becoming increasingly integrated. During this time, however, the number of African American artists on the pop charts actually declined. Accordingly, the r&b charts were reinstated by the magazine, and in 1969, r&b was replaced with the term "soul". The industry came full circle in 1982 when the soul charts were renamed "black" music. *Billboard* later offered the explanation that " 'soul' was too limited a term to define the diversity of musical styles appearing on the chart, and that 'black' was a better tribute to the music's cultural origins."[10] Ultimately, however, this term was as vulnerable to criticism as the term "race music" had been four decades earlier. Thus in 1990, *Billboard* reinstated the r&b category, explaining that it was "becoming less acceptable to identify music in racial terms."[11] And the beat goes on.

Were it not for this artificial separation of the races, popular music history might read quite differently. When Syd Nathan, the founder of King Records, encouraged his r&b and country and western artists to record different versions of the same songs, he understood intuitively that pieces of music do not automatically have a genre, that they can be interpreted in many idioms. Still, in keeping with prevailing industry practices, he marketed his r&b releases only to black audiences and his country records only to white audiences. While Nathan was not limited in his choice of artists or material, he, like many others, accepted the notion that a separation of the races was "the way things were."

These same prevailing industry practices led Leonard Chess, head of Chess Records, to inform Chuck Berry that his demo of "Ida Red" ("Maybellene") had to be redone because it was too country sounding.[12] In doing so, Chess was telling Berry in no uncertain terms that there was simply no way to market a black man as a country singer. Were it not for that reality, Chuck Berry might well have had a very different career trajectory. R&b artist Jimmy Witherspoon once argued, "Chuck Berry is a country singer. People put everybody in categories, black, white, this. Now if Chuck Berry was white, with the lyrics he writes, he would be the top country star in the world."[13] There have been any number of country versions of Chuck Berry songs, from Hoyt Axton's "Maybellene," Freddy Weller's "Too Much Monkey Business" and "Promised Land," Waylon Jennings' "Brown-Eyed Handsome Man," and Buck Owen's "Johnny B. Goode" to Linda Rondstadt's "Back in the U.S.A.," Emmy Lou Harris' "You Never Can Tell," and Johnny Rivers' "Memphis," but every one has been performed by whites.

Such music marketing practices were briefly challenged when Ray Charles recorded *Modern Sounds in Country and Western Music* (Volume I) and *Modern Sounds in Country and Western Music* (Volume II) for ABC-Paramount in 1962. Through these recordings, Charles proved that an artist does not have to be limited to a single performance style and a song can have more than one genre. He had long felt connections between the blues and country that rendered the rigid separation of markets suspect from a musical point of view. "I really thought that it was somethin' about country music, even as a youngster," Charles once remarked. "Although I was bred in and around the blues, I always... felt the closest music, really, to the blues [was country and western]. They'd make them steel guitars cry and whine, and it really attracted me.[14] ...

The identification of music with race, which has tended to exclude African American artists and others from certain marketing structures in the music industry, makes the task of unearthing an accurate history of U.S. popular music quite difficult and encourages serious underestimates of the degree of cross-cultural collaboration that has taken place. Rockabilly, the country strain of rock 'n' roll in the 1950s, for example, was a legitimate musical movement that integrated blues with country and western styles. It had its own identity, and in singers like Elvis Presley, performers of real originality and talent. While privileged seems far too strong a word to describe the early life circumstances and success of most rockabilly artists, it is impossible to separate their popularity from a racist pattern in which styles pioneered by black artists are popularized, dominated, and even defined by whites as if they were the originators. This pattern is apparent in the history of popular music in the United States, from ragtime to jazz to swing. Rock 'n' roll is neither an exception nor the end of the line. As a result, styles are often described (and defended) in terms which are clearly racial rather than musical.... The late 1960s were marked by endless debates over whether or not whites could sing the blues. The relative absence of African Americans in heavy metal and whites in rap suggest that racial divisions are still powerful determinants in social and cultural relations.

No Hablamos Español: The Language Barrier

Because of this country's history of slavery, there is a tendency to think of racism, whether in the music industry or society as a whole, as a black/white issue. It should be recognized, however, that discriminatory practices have not been limited to African Americans alone. In many ways, the language barrier has proven to be even more intractable than the race barrier. Latin music, for instance, has always been an important influence in U.S. popular music. In the 1950s, there were a series of popular mambos, rumbas, and cha cha chas. Indeed, from Ritchie Valens to Santana to Los Lobos there has always been a strong Chicano presence in rock, and a recognizable Latin influence in dance styles from disco to hip hop. Even so, the number of Top Forty pop hits sung in Spanish in the United States could probably be counted on one hand. "La Bamba" (by Ritchie Valens and Los Lobos) and Santana's "Oye Como Va" readily come to mind, but precious few others. In fact, one could probably tally all of the non-English Top Forty pop hits on two hands. Four versions of "Volare" appeared on the charts as did "Dominique" by the Singing Nun. Kyu Sakamoto's "Sukiyaki" was covered by Taste of Honey during the disco era. While one might quibble about whether to include Ray Barretto's "El Watusi" or Manu Dibango's "Soul Makossa" (both of which are primarily instrumental), the point is clear. Non-English hits in the United States are rare. As a result, artists who might sing in other languages feel compelled to record in English when they approach the U.S. market. In the late 1970s and early 1980s, Spanish balladeer Julio Iglesias, a resident of the United States, was among the best-selling recording artists in the world, but he had never had a hit in this country. The only way he could break into the U.S. market was with two English duets—one with Willie Nelson ("To All the Girls I've Loved Before") and one with Diana Ross ("All of You"), both in 1984. Linda Ronstadt, who achieved U.S. superstardom singing in English, provides an example of this logic in reverse. In 1988, Ronstadt, who is part Mexican, returned to her roots to record *Cancions de mi Padre*. The album never reached the U.S. pop Top Forty, even though it received the 1988 Grammy for Best Mexican/American Performance. Cuban-born Gloria Estefan's Top Ten pop album, *Cuts Both Ways* (1989), included Spanish and English versions of "Don't Wanna Lose You" and "Here We Are," but only the English versions became Top Ten pop hits. The Swedish group ABBA charted fourteen Top Forty hits in the U.S. in the 1970s and 1980s, but all were sung in English. Norway's A-Ha broke into the U.S. market with "Take on Me," a cut with spectacular video animation and sung in English. When French Canadian Celine Dion, a veteran of the Quebec music scene, made a bid for international stardom in 1990, she did so on the basis of her first all-English LP, *Unison*. In 1993, she scored her first number one pop hit in the U.S. with "The Power of Love," which was, of course, sung in English. With the increasing diversity of the U.S. population, this situation is bound to change, but for the moment, language barriers in popular music remain strong.

The Long, Hard Climb: Gender Discrimination

The barriers that women face in the music industry are equally formidable. Historically the images of women in popular songs—from angel and baby to earth mother and sex goddess to bitch and "ho"—have been limiting or belittling, if not flat-out offensive and degrading. Women performers have often been pressured by the industry to assume personas based on these stereotypes. Furthermore, the existence of a double standard regarding intimacy and sexual practices in the United States has made the social dynamics of life on the road more complicated and alienating for women than men. As if these difficulties were not enough, women have had to overcome the obstacles that stand between them and control over the creative processes. Technical processes such as record producing, engineering, mixing, and mastering are still overwhelmingly male-dominated.

While some women were able to achieve a certain status as vocalists in the decades preceding the emergence of rock 'n' roll, no woman ever achieved the status of an Al Jolson, Bing Crosby, or Frank Sinatra, and it was almost never the case that a woman became successful as an instrumentalist. Whatever status could be achieved, disappeared rapidly with the advent of rock 'n' roll. Indeed, rock 'n' roll actually reduced the presence of women in popular music. In the early 1960s, the women who were marketed as folk madonnas were channeled toward softer vocal styles, and were allowed access only to acoustic instruments. This trend continued among the female singer/songwriters of the

1970s, Bonnie Raitt being a notable exception. Even harder rocking women in the 1960s—from the Crystals and the Ronnettes to Grace Slick, Janis Joplin, and Aretha Franklin—were vocalists who never touched the hardware. While there were certain breakthroughs for women when the punk movement rewrote the rules of access, these gains were offset to some degree in the next decade, by the misogyny displayed in rap and heavy metal.

By the late 1980s, women were fairly well represented in most styles (with the exception of heavy metal) and in the early 1990s, they had finally begun to compete on a roughly equal footing with men for lucrative recording contracts. However, as they have achieved greater acceptance in the popular market, they have had to confront an industry infrastructure that is fully owned and operated by men whose ideas about career development frequently push them to conform to male stereotypes of how female performers should act and sound. In other words, like African Americans and other people of color, women performers must confront norms and social practices which limit their development and chances for success.

REGULATING POPULAR MUSIC

Because popular music always interacts with its social environment, it often serves as a lightning rod for the political controversies that invariably accompany change. The Tin Pan Alley pop that dominated the first half of the twentieth century, for example, was marked by a purposeful blandness and a studied inoffensiveness that, in retrospect, makes it difficult to imagine that anything about it, except its saccharine sweetness, could upset anyone. Still, the moral guardians of the early twentieth century felt that even Tin Pan Alley pop was too depraved for mainstream consumption, let alone the jazz that developed concurrently....

Throughout the second half of the twentieth century, popular music has been connected quite explicitly with social change and political controversy. As millions of adults left the intensity of urban life in the 1950s for the new and expansive sprawl called suburbia, rock 'n' roll pulled their offspring back to the sounds of the city. While postwar youth may have found the new sound exciting and engaging, adults found it threatening and loosed criticisms far more damning than Powell's condemnations of Tin Pan Alley pop. Indeed in the late 1950s, a conservative reaction against rock 'n' roll sought to turn back the musical clock by imposing rigid guidelines on radio.

A variation of this same social drama was played out in the 1980s and 1990s, as the custodians of culture became convinced that rap and heavy metal had gone too far and tried to regulate popular music through tactics ranging from a demand for warning labels on sound recordings to outright censorship. In fact, given the pronouncements of a whole range of public figures and elected officials during this period, a compelling case can be made that popular culture—particularly popular music—has become the ideological battlefield upon which struggles for power, values, and identity take place....

1. It should be noted that this discussion concerns cultural development as it occurred in European societies. There are, of course, any number of other societies that developed according to different cultural patterns, but the cultural forms and values of the "New World" were informed by those of the European colonial powers, thus an understanding of cultural development in European societies is relevant to understanding the tensions and complexities of contemporary U.S. culture.

2. This analysis was developed most forcefully by the members of the Frankfurt School, a group of Jewish intellectuals in Germany who were rightly disturbed by Hitler's effective use of the mass media in advancing the cause of fascism in the 1930s and 1940s.

3. Charlie Gillett, *The Sound of the City: The Rise of Rock and Roll* (New York: Outerbridge and Dienstfrey, 1970), i.

4. Ibid.

5. Peter Wicke, *Rock Music: Culture, Aesthetics and Sociology* (Cambridge: Cambridge University Press, 1990), 12.

6. Charles Hamm, *Yesterdays: Popular Song in America* (New York: W. W. Norton, 1983), 358.

7. Christopher Small, *Music of the Common Tongue: Survival and Celebration in Afro-American Music* (New York: Riverrun Press, 1987), 25.

8. The use of the terms "race" and "hillbilly" as marketing categories for music was initiated by producer Ralph Peer. The origin of the terms is explained in detail in the next chapter.

9. Arnold Shaw, *Honkers and Shouters: The Golden Years of Rhythm and Blues* (New York: Collier Books, 1978), 524.

10. "Billboard Adopts 'R&B' As New Name for 2 Charts," *Billboard*, 27 October 1990, 35.

11. Ibid., 6.

12. See Gillett, *The Sound of the City*, 40 and Chapple and Garofalo, *Rock 'n' Roll is Here to Pay*, 39.

13. Shaw, *Honkers and Shouters*, 215.

14. Ben Fong-Torres, "The Rolling Stone Interview: Ray Charles," *Rolling Stone*, 18 January 1973, 18.

CHAPTER 12 # Media, Gender, and Sexual Identity

12.1 MOLLY HASKELL

The Big Lie

Molly Haskell is both a scholar and a critic of popular culture who has written for such periodicals as *Ms., Vogue, Film Comment, The Saturday Review,* and *Mademoiselle.* When her book-length study *From Reverence to Rape: The Treatment of Women in the Movies* (Holt, Rinehart & Winston, 1974) was first published, critics noted the way Haskell systematically developed a chronology of women's portrayals in film from the 1920s through 1973. Haskell wrote this book at a time when the attention of the feminist movement was turning toward culture and focusing on the ways in which stereotyping of women in mass media reinforced the wider subordination of women in society. *From Reverence to Rape* is considered one of the first in-depth critical works on the representation of women in film.

In the following selection from that book, Haskell uses her knowledge of film history and her ability to critically analyze film imagery to reveal the contradictory way in which women have been represented in the movies. On the one hand, cinematic images of women consistently show them in subordinate roles. On the other hand, female characters provide a vehicle for the attainment of power and status. This provides important insight into the ways in which mass media representations can at the same time reflect and challenge wider social relations of gender.

Key Concept: contradictory representations of women in film

*T*he big lie perpetrated on Western society is the idea of women's inferiority, a lie so deeply ingrained in our social behavior that merely to recognize it is to risk unraveling the entire fabric of civilization. [Psychiatrist] Alfred Adler, unique among his professional colleagues as well as among his sex in acknowledging that occasionally women had ambitions similar to men's, called attention to this "mistake"—the notion of women's inferiority and men's superiority —fifty years ago. At about the same time, Virginia Woolf wrote, "Women have served all these centuries as looking glasses possessing the magic and delicious power of reflecting the figure of man at twice its natural size." How ironic that it was in the security of this enlarged image of himself, an image provided by wives or, more often, mothers, that man went forth to fight, conquer, legislate, create. And woman stayed home without so much as "a room of her own," her only "fulfillment" the hope of bearing a son to whom she could pass on the notion of male superiority.

The prejudice against women is no less pernicious because it is based on a fallacy. Indeed, to have sanctioned by law and custom a judgment that goes against our instincts is the cornerstone of bad faith on which monuments of misunderstanding have been erected. We can see that women live longer than men, give birth, and endure pain bravely; yet they are the "weaker sex." They can read and write as well as men—are actually *more* verbal according to aptitude tests. And they are encouraged to pursue advanced education as long as they don't forget their paramount destiny to marry and become mothers, an injunction that effectively dilutes intellectual concentration and discourages ambition. Women are not "real women" unless they marry and bear children, and even those without the inclination are often pressured into motherhood and just as often make a mess of it. The inequity is perpetuated as women transmit their sense of incompleteness to their daughters. But men, too, are victimized by the lie. Secretly they must wonder how they came to be entitled to their sense of superiority if it is to these "inferior" creatures they owe the debt of their existence. And defensively, they may feel "emasculated" by any show of strength or word of criticism from their nominal dependents.

In the movie business we have had an industry dedicated for the most part to reinforcing the lie. As the propaganda arm of the American Dream machine, Hollywood promoted a romantic fantasy of marital roles and conjugal euphoria and chronically ignored the facts and fears arising from an awareness of The End—the winding down of love, change, divorce, depression, mutation, death itself. But like the latent content of any good dream, unconscious elements, often elaborately disguised, came to trouble our sleep and stick pins in our technicolored balloons. The very unwillingness of the narrative to pursue love into marriage (except in the "woman's film," where the degree of rationalization needed to justify the disappointments of marriage made its own subversive comment) betrayed a certain skepticism. Not only did unconscious elements obtrude in the films, but they were part of the very nature of the industry itself.

The anomaly that women are the majority of the human race, half of its brains, half of its procreative power, most of its nurturing power, and yet are its servants and romantic slaves was brought home with peculiar force in the Hollywood film. Through the myths of subjection and sacrifice that were its fictional currency and the machinations of its moguls in the front offices, the film industry maneuvered to keep women in their place; and yet these very myths and this machinery catapulted women into spheres of power beyond the wildest dreams of most of their sex.

This is the contradiction that runs through the history of film, a kink in the machine of sociologists' generalizations: We see the *June Bride* played by Bette Davis surrender her independence at the altar; the actress played by Margaret Sullavan in *The Moon's Our Home* submit to the straitjacket in which Henry Fonda enfolds and symbolically subjugates her; Katharine Hepburn's *Alice Adams* achieve her highest ambitions in the arms of Fred MacMurray; Rosalind Russell as an advertising executive in *Take a Letter, Darling* find happiness in the same arms; Joan Crawford as the head of a trucking firm in *They All Kissed the Bride* go weak in the knees at the sight of the labor leader played by Melvyn Douglas. And yet we remember Bette Davis not as the blushing bride but as the aggressive reporter and sometime-bitch; Margaret Sullavan leading Fonda on a wild-goose chase through the backwoods of Vermont; Katharine Hepburn standing on the "secretarial stairway" to independence; Rosalind Russell giving MacMurray the eye as her prospective secretary; and Joan Crawford looking about as wobbly as the Statue of Liberty.

This tension—between the spirited single girl and the whimpering bride, between the "star" and the "stereotype"—existed for good reason. Audiences for the most part were not interested in seeing, and Hollywood was not interested in sponsoring, a smart, ambitious woman as a popular heroine. A woman who could compete and conceivably win in a man's world would defy emotional gravity, would go against the grain of prevailing notions about the female sex. A woman's intelligence was the equivalent of a man's penis: something to be kept out of sight. Ambition in a woman had either to be deflected into the vicarious drives of her loved ones or to be mocked and belittled. A movie heroine could act on the same power and career drives as a man only if, at the climax, they took second place to the sacred love of a man. Otherwise she forfeited her right to that love.

According to society's accepted role definitions, which films have always reflected in microcosm, the interests of men and women are not only different, but actually opposed. A man is supposedly most himself when he is driving to achieve, to create, to conquer; he is least himself when reflecting or making love. A woman is supposedly most herself in the throes of emotion (the love of man or of children), and least herself, that is, least "womanly," in the pursuit of knowledge or success. The stigma becomes a self-fulfilling prophecy. By defying cultural expectations, by insisting on professional relationships with men who want only to flatter and flirt with her, a woman becomes "unfeminine" and undesirable, she becomes, in short, a monster. This may explain why there is something monstrous in all the great women stars and why we often like the "best friends" better than the heroines, or the actresses who never quite got to the top (Ann Dvorak, Geraldine Fitzgerald, Mary Astor) better than the ones who did (Joan Crawford, Bette Davis, Elizabeth Taylor). The arrogance, the toughness were not merely make-believe. In a woman's "unnatural" climb to success, she *did* have to step on toes, jangle nerves, antagonize men, and run the risk of not being loved.

In no more than one out of a thousand movies was a woman allowed to sacrifice love for career rather than the other way around. Yet, in real life, the stars did it all the time, either by choice or by default—the result of devoting so much time and energy to a career and of achieving such fame that marriage suffered and the home fell apart. Even with allowances made for the general instability of Hollywood, the nature and number of these breakups suggest that no man could stand being overshadowed by a successful wife. The male ego was sacred; the woman's was presumed to be nonexistent. And yet, what was the "star" but a woman supremely driven to survive, a barely clothed ego on display for all the world to see.

The personality of the star, the mere fact of being a star, was as important as the roles they played, and affected the very conception of those roles. In her original literary form —the long-forgotten 1920s novel by Olive Higgins Prouty —Stella Dallas was the prototypical lower-class "woman as martyr." As played by Belle Bennett in Henry King's silent-film version, she is a tasteful and remote figure of pity. But as played front and center, tacky, tactless, and bravura by Barbara Stanwyck in King Vidor's 1937 remake, she is something else again. Stanwyck, in what may be at once the most excruciating and exhilarating performance on film, takes Stella onto a plane where, no longer just Everywoman as victim, she is an outrageous creature who breaks our hearts even as she grates on our nerves. As the boozy, overdressed, social-climbing mother, Stella/Stanwyck ignores the socially accepted "oughts" by which she could keep our—and her daughter's—sympathy; she risks losing both by exposing in egregious detail the seedy and insensitive side of her nature, the unlovable side of her love. Stanwyck brings us to admire something that is both herself and the character; she gives us a Stella that exceeds in stupidity and beauty and daring the temperate limitations of her literary model and all the generalizations about the second sex.

Again, in *Woman of the Year*, screenwriters Ring Lardner, Jr., and Michael Kanin did everything possible to sabotage the career woman played by Katharine Hepburn. In their hands she becomes a Lady Macbeth of overweening ambition with so little of the "milk of human kindness" that she is guilty of criminal negligence toward the child she and her husband Spencer Tracy have adopted. Tracy, by contrast, is a doting father—though never to the neglect of his newspaper work, which seems to say that love and ambition can coexist in a man but not in a woman. Yet, because of the strength of character and integrity Hepburn brought to the screen, and the soft and sensual radiance with which director George Stevens illuminated her (thereby contradicting the screenplay), she transcended the meannesses of the plot without in any way excusing them....

Women have figured more prominently in film than in any other art, industry, or profession (and film is all three) dominated by men. Although few have made it to the seignorial ranks of director and producer, women have succeeded in every other area where size or physical strength was not a factor: as screenwriters, particularly in the twenties and thirties; as editors; as production and costume designers; as critics; and of course, and most especially, as actresses—as the stars who not only invaded our dream lives but began shaping the way we thought about ourselves before we knew enough to close the door. In the roles of love goddesses, mothers, martyrs, spinsters, broads, virgins, vamps, prudes, adventuresses, she-devils, and sex kittens, they embodied stereotypes and, occasionally, transcended them.

Some, like Mae West, Greta Garbo, Katharine Hepburn, and Joan Crawford, were institutions: stars powerful, eccentric, or intimidating enough to choose their projects and determine their own images, for at least some of their careers. Others, like Lillian Gish, Marlene Dietrich, and Monica Vitti were Galateas, molded and magnificently served by their Pygmalions; or, like Marion Davies and Jean Simmons, ruined by their patrons. Having made it as a star on her own, Norma Shearer sustained her career by marrying M-G-M's boy-genius Irving Thalberg. But not all of David Selznick's more tasteful efforts on Jennifer Jones' behalf (*Carrie,* with Laurence Olivier, William Wyler directing; *We Were Strangers,* with John Garfield, John Huston directing) could turn her into a star, probably because women didn't like her. There were actresses like Bette Davis and Ida Lupino who got off on the wrong foot through miscasting or mismanagement, but eventually found themselves. (In the You-Can't-Win department, Davis tells the story of being sent onto the set of the first film of a prop man-turned-director named William Wyler, force-dressed in a low-cut cotton dress that made her feel common, only to have Wyler turn to an assistant and say, "What do you think of these girls who show their chests and think they can get jobs?") There were others—Patricia Neal, Geraldine Fitzgerald, Mary Astor—who were also-rans, actresses of promise who never became stars, but who were as vivid in one or two roles as others were in a lifetime....

And women, in the early and middle ages of film, dominated. It is only recently that men have come to monopolize the popularity polls, the credits, and the romantic spotlight by allocating to themselves not just the traditional male warrior and adventurer roles, but those of the sex object and glamour queen as well. Back in the twenties and thirties, and to a lesser extent the forties, women were at the center. This was amply reflected in the billings, which revealed the shifts in star dynamics from decade to decade. Women were often billed ahead of men, either singly, as in the silents, or as the pivotal member of a team, the dominant form of the thirties. In the forties, because of the shortage of male stars during the war, available leading men were treated as spear-carriers and made to follow women on the marquee.

Far more than men, women were the vessels of men's and women's fantasies and the barometers of changing fashion. Like two-way mirrors linking the immediate past with the immediate future, women in the movies reflected, perpetuated, and in some respects offered innovations on the roles of women in society. Shopgirls copied them, housewives escaped through them. Through the documentary authenticity (new hair styles, fashions in dress, and even fads in physical beauty) that actresses brought to their roles and the familiar, simplified tales in which they played, movie heroines were viscerally immediate and accountable to audiences in a way that the heroines of literature, highbrow or popular, were not. Movie stars, as well as the women they played—Stella Dallas, Mrs. Miniver, Mildred Pierce, Jezebel—were not like the women in print or on canvas. They belonged to us and spoke to each of us personally from what, until the sixties and seventies, was the heart and emotional center of film itself.

Yet, considering the importance of these women in our lives and their centrality to film history, it is astonishing how little attention has been paid them, how little serious analysis, or even tribute, beyond the palpitating prose of the old-time fan-magazine writers or the prying, lively, but no more serious approach of the "new interviewers." At one extreme are the coffee-table picture books, with their two-sentence captions; at the other, film histories that sweep along their predetermined courses, touching on actresses only as they substantiate whatever trends and developments are being promulgated by the author. The political, socially conscious school of criticism (for years the most influential) fathered by the Scots film historian John Grierson, established the line, perfectly consonant with Anglo-American sexual attitudes, that such matters as love, romance, and the loss of virginity were women's concerns and belonged, in a properly demeaned and trivialized fashion, to that untouchable of film categories, the "woman's film." The contempt for the "woman's film" is still a general cultural attitude, not only restricted to critics who mistake "important subjects" for great films (and what could be more important than love anyway?), but conveyed in the snickering response of the supermale, himself a more sophisticated version of the little boy who holds his nose and groans during the hugging and kissing scenes. Critic John Simon describes the dissection of the morality of love and the complex inter-play of feeling and conscience in Eric Rohmer's *Claire's Knee* as "triviality" and the "height of inconsequence." Most men, even in New York art-film audiences, would rather see *The Dirty Dozen, Deliverance, The French Connection,* and *The Godfather* several times apiece than see *Petulia, Sunday, Bloody Sunday,* or *The Touch* once. It is said that many wives got their husbands to go to *A Man and a Woman* for the automobile-racing scenes....

We need more of a sense of film history, and of the context in which films were released and images were formed. Gloria Steinem can write an intelligent and sympathetic article on Marilyn Monroe, and yet miss the satirical point of Howard Hawks' *Gentlemen Prefer Blondes,* which consciously exposes Monroe's ooh-la-la image and the men who collaborate to maintain it. Betty Friedan can write a stolid appraisal of *Husbands* that, like most sociological criticism, takes no account of the film's failures and accomplishments qua film, but sees it only as a convenient substantiation of *The Feminine Mystique.* A soapbox feminist can excoriate Hitchcock in *The New York Times* for the rape in *Frenzy,* ignoring point of view, context, style, the complex interplay of misogyny and sympathy in Hitchcock, and the equally complex interplay of fear and desire by which women respond to the image of rape. Another critic can write a feminist critique of *Last Tango in Paris* as a male fantasy ignoring both the empirical fact that it is largely women, rather than men, who respond to the film, and the more subtle implication that our rearguard fantasies of rape, sadism, submission, liberation, and anonymous sex are as important a key to our emancipation, our self-understanding, as our more advanced and admirable efforts at self-definition. The same critic, offering a plot synopsis to substantiate her claim to the film's sexist point of view, reveals the irrelevancy of this technique, for *Last Tango* is about Brando, is Brando, and our reaction to the film will depend, directly and chemically, on our response to Brando. The plots in five movies may be identical, may all show women degraded and humiliated and chained to stereotype, and we will react differently to each one, depending on the woman, and the director's treatment of her.

Molly Haskell

For despite their impact on cinema, there have been few women in positions of creative authority that would have fostered the development of a woman's point of view. There have been shamefully few women directors (though no fewer, perhaps, than women orchestra conductors or prime ministers or reverends or stage directors), and fewer still in America than in Europe where the unions are less powerfully chauvinistic and the whole structure of filmmaking is looser. In an issue of *Film Comment,* historian Richard Henshaw compiled filmographies of the 150 women known to have directed films. Of the forty-five Americans, no more than five or six names are known to the general public (and of these, several—Lillian Gish, Ida Lupino, Barbara Loden—are known as actresses rather than as directors), and hardly more to film buffs.

The reason, aside from union prejudice, is obvious. Directing—giving orders, mastering not only people but machinery—is a typically masculine, even militaristic, activity. The existence of such a dominant authority figure—and in this respect, the great directors, the *auteurs,* impose their ideas more forcefully than the mere technicians—would seem to present an inherently sexist situation. Decrying such use of power, feminist film critics have hastened to disavow auteurism, but in the next breath they will raise a merely competent director like Ida Lupino to that category, by assuming she has enough artistic control of her projects and enough creative vision to invest her films with a subversive ideology. The attack on auteurism is less theoretical than emotional (and no less valid for that)—an expression of indignation that all the great directors have been men, rather a soundly argued dismissal of these directors and the historical tool (auteurism) that embraces them. For there are certainly subversive elements, obtrusions of a woman's point of view, in the work of men directors, particularly in classical filmmaking, before the twin male cults (director as superstud and superstar) converged to demote women, once again, to chicks, chattels, and pure figures of fantasy.

Hollywood's Mid-1980s Feminist Heroines

Elayne Rapping, a scholar and a critic, has focused much of her work on the representation of gender relations on television and in the movies. In this, she differs from earlier feminist critics who were primarily concerned with stereotypical images of women in mass media and popular culture. Rapping has written book-length scholarly studies, including *The Looking Glass World of Nonfiction TV* (South End, 1987), and she has published numerous articles in *The Nation, The Progressive, The Guardian,* and other journals.

In the following selection from the collection of her critical essays *Media-tions: Forays into the Culture and Gender Wars* (South End Press, 1994), Rapping offers an analysis of TV movies that are aimed at women, partly in response to the critique offered by Susan Faludi in her best-selling book *Backlash: The Undeclared War Against American Women* (Crown Publishers, 1991). In that book, Faludi argues that by the mid- to late-1970s, mass media and popular culture in the United States had responded in positive, but very limited, ways to the issues raised by the feminist movement. For example, more independent female characters populated the movies and TV shows of the time. But through the 1980s, she contends, mass media reflected a broad and powerful backlash against the gains made by feminism. Independent career women were demonized in many Hollywood films, such as *Fatal Attraction.* Faludi argues that through the 1980s there was a return to the image of "happy homemaker" and nurturing mother as the most fulfilling roles for female characters on TV and in the movies.

Rapping responds to Faludi's critique by showing how made-for-TV movies aimed at female viewers have continued to address important women's issues raised by the feminist movement, such as abortion and violence against women. Rapping considers the representation of women on TV a hegemonic process, involving struggles over defining the social world. The producers of TV programs realize that they must attract—not alienate—their audience. However, Rapping does not say that all is well with mass media images of women. She shows how key social antagonisms and conflicts are translated into individual problems and are inevitably resolved, all according to the cultural logic of advertising-supported television, which almost never indicts the social system or leaves its viewers pondering ambiguous or "dark" issues during commercial breaks.

Key Concept: "domesticating" women's social issues

*P*owerful, autonomous women have never been strangers to the Hollywood movie screen. The weak, simpering stereotypes that feminists, since the 1960s, have brought so vividly to our attention—the sex kittens and servants, the Marilyn Monroes and June Allysons—have always had their tougher counterparts.

In fact, as Molly Haskell demonstrated in *From Reverence to Rape: The Treatment of Women in the Movies*, the heroines of the 1930s and 1940s were generally far more active, assertive, and independent than their 1950s and 1960s sisters. Stars like Katharine Hepburn and Rosalind Russell often played women with serious careers who went toe to toe with their male counterparts and in some cases—Irene Dunne as the mayor of the town in *Together Again* or Russell as an advertising executive in *Take a Letter, Darling*—were socially and professionally above their male suitors.

Not that their positions were presented as unproblematic, of course. The conflict between work and love, "femininity" and "ambition," were central themes in all these films. As often as not these women were portrayed as deeply flawed and neurotic, or even, with the coming of *film noir*, downright evil. Joan Crawford, in *Mildred Pierce*, paid dearly for her business success, losing her husband and her children. Those women whose power—realistically enough—was portrayed as sexual rather than social or economic, were, in spite of their attractiveness, often shown as cold-blooded monsters. Joan Bennet in *Scarlet Street*, Barbara Stanwyck in *Double Indemnity*, and Bette Davis in any number of films were typical of Hollywood's underlying fear and hatred of the strong sexual woman.

The reemergence of the strong heroine in the 1970s was not, as is sometimes assumed, a great leap forward, although the "new woman" was presented differently, reflecting the influence of the newly visible women's movement, the changes in family life brought about by feminism, and changes in the economy and women's place in it. The most typical films of the 1950s and 1960s presented women in sexually and socially conservative, "Stand by Your Man" stereotypes. From *The Tender Trap* and *Pillow Talk*, to *Easy Rider* and *Alice's Restaurant*, women were seen as coy, game-playing man-traps or Earth Mothers.

No wonder, then, that the 1970s' preoccupation with "the problems of the modern woman," the breakdown of the traditional family, and the social upheaval caused by changing sex roles seemed progressive. Films such as *Alice Doesn't Live Here Anymore* and *An Unmarried Woman* seemed to—and in certain ways did—point out the very real oppression and diminishment of human capacity suffered by traditionally married women in families. In these films, the end of marriage—foisted upon the heroines by circumstance—was portrayed as liberating, offering the chance for growth, fulfillment, and independence at last. In fact, the futures of these heroines were not as realistic as they were portrayed to be. In both cases, a new, "better" man was a major part of the happy ending. In *An Unmarried Woman*—and this is typical of Hollywood's "women's lib" scenarios—class privilege allows the heroine to escape the most serious consequences of divorce, and the feminization of poverty.

In the later 1970s and early 1980s this genre switched its focus on women to the problems of men. In most "family breakdown" movies of that time, the father and husband suddenly becomes the "hero," the good guy who changes and grows into a responsible, nurturing provider/parent, while the estranged wife is the heavy. In *Kramer vs. Kramer* and *Ordinary People,* for example, it is Dad who "communicates," nurtures, and holds the family together while Mom is selfish, weak, and irresponsible in her emotional or actual abandonment of the family. Even in *Tootsie,* it is a man, impersonating a woman, who is the feminist heroine.

This brief and necessarily sketchy survey of major Hollywood trends in portraying women serves as background against which to understand the crop of mid-1980s films featuring strong independent women. For Hollywood, while responding to real changes in women's status, always has its own agenda, its own axe to grind, in its treatment of these themes. While its messages and images change, and are interestingly contradictory, it is not—with rare exceptions—wholeheartedly or sincerely on women's side. Without feminist interventions, it is Hollywood's style to "keep up with the times" while framing and limiting whatever apparently progressive messages it sends out in order to undercut the real demands and rights of women and to preserve the class- and sex-based power relations upon which our social and economic system is based.

The mid-1980s crop of movies featuring strong, independent women in responsible, successful positions provides an excellent opportunity to look closely at how this is done. The fall of 1985 gave us a remarkable number of releases featuring major stars in just such roles. Unlike any of the trends just described, these films actually took as a given that women were here to stay, in every important area of American public life, and that men, romance, and marriage were not indispensable components of a meaningful female existence. Five of these films—*Sweet Dreams, Jagged Edge, Marie, Agnes of God,* and *Plenty*—provide a nicely varied sample of the structural, stylistic, and dramatic ploys with which Hollywood manages to pay lip service to feminist themes and issues while at the same time seriously, if subtly, undermining those themes and demeaning, in many ways, the image of the "new woman" it seems to present.

That there are five—actually more—major actresses suitable to play strong female roles is itself a tribute to feminism and the women's movement. Jane Fonda, Meryl Streep, Jessica Lange, Glenn Close, and Sissy Spacek make up an impressive group, the likes of which have not been seen since the 1930s and 1940s, with the Crawfords, Davises, Stanwycks, and Bacalls. While the taint of "evil" associated with these women was gone in the 1980s, this new crop of women characters suffered from equally negative, if more subtle flaws, at least from a feminist perspective.

The five films fall into two categories. Three are standard Hollywood formula pieces, while two are more highbrow adaptations from stage dramas. *Marie* is actually closer to the conventions of made-for-TV movies about women than to any theatrical film genre. *Jagged Edge* is a courtroom/mystery thriller and *Sweet Dreams* is a typical Hollywood star biography of country singer Patsy Cline, which traces her path from rags to riches to tragic death. *Agnes of God* and *Plenty,* in contrast, were originally plays.

It is interesting that the women characters themselves, and their respective fates, are in certain ways more positively presented in the less serious offerings.

Jessica Lange's Patsy Cline, for example, is a tough, talented, ambitious woman who knows she's as good as any man in the field, and isn't afraid to push the point. Since the real Cline lived decades ago, some of the characterization in the film is anachronistic in its feminist spirit. "Hell, no," she hoots at the promoter who asks her if she wants to be Kitty Wells, "I wanna be Hank Williams!"

Cline is also, unlike the other heroines considered here, blatantly and aggressively sexual. Unlike the 1940s heroines whose sexuality damned them, she is not a temptress of adventures. She wants a home and kids and loves her husband, played by Ed Harris, to distraction. The film does a good job of dramatizing the tensions that arise within the marriage because of Cline's fame and wealth. In recognizably 1980s fashion, in their relationship the man is ambivalent about the woman's success and power. He falls for her because of her power and talent, but he wavers dangerously between adulation and resentment at what soon becomes his secondary role in the household.

Because *Sweet Dreams* uses the Hollywood star tragedy formula, it avoids dealing with the sexual issues it raises. In fact, while the fine performances of the principals tend to obscure this, it is the slightest and most meaningless of the films. It has no point, really, because it can't decide what the point of Cline's dilemma should be. So it lets life provide an easy out: early death for the heroine. Jessica Lange's performance is masterful and her character intriguing, but we never get below the surface of the character or the issues, and the film remains a clichéd piece of Hollywood fluff about celebrity and its tragic costs.

Marie, on the other hand, does have a point. It too uses a hackneyed formula to get around the real issues of women in society today. It tells the "true story" of Marie Ragghianti, a formerly abused wife and single mother, who gets a meant-to-be token job in the Tennessee governor's office and proceeds to single-handedly and doggedly expose the corruption she discovers in the penal system.

Sissy Spacek plays Marie as a modern-day Dickens heroine. She is sweet, demure, immune to sensual urges, fanatical in her mothering and so honest and determined to "do the right thing" that she quickly becomes a tremendous bore to watch. In one scene illustrating her competence and drive, she ingeniously saves her son's life in a roadstop bathroom. In fact, her single-mindedness in questioning, facing down, and proving herself right against a doctor's erroneous diagnosis of her son's condition is exactly analogous to her behavior at work. There too she refuses to be intimidated or stopped by evil, incompetent, male authority figures. A court finds her innocent of trumped-up charges made up to fire her, and in the process exposes the state's financial hanky-panky.

Formally, this morality tale is dull as dust. In TV-movie manner it plods along from scenes of domestic violence, to the hard work of going to college while raising kids and caring for an invalid mother, to her professional triumphs and troubles. Nothing is unpredictable here. Nothing is emotionally, politically, or psychologically subtle.

The character of Marie was meant, clearly, to be inspirationally feminist. It is, in fact, reactionary, both politically and sexually. Since these movies rarely provide a social or political context for their messages, the audience is left with some implicit but dangerous ideas. For one thing, Marie is a law-and-order girl, after the heart of Ronald Reagan. She acts out all the patriotic, mindless rules about "doing right" and "obeying the law" that the Right so loves. In fact, her efforts, though this is never spelled out, strengthen the penal code and ensure longer sentences and less likelihood of parole for all prisoners.

That "feminism" was used to sell this message is significant, and it fits perfectly with Marie's sexual persona. She is a true Madonna—of the Immaculate Conception, not the Material Girl, variety—of virtue and maternal instinct. Women are working these days, the film tells us, but they aren't slighting their motherly duties or becoming sexually loose because of it. And their work is an extension of their domestic mothering role: to uphold morality and keep things organized and running according to God's will.

Jagged Edge, in which Glenn Close plays an attorney who defends an accused wife-murderer, falls in love with him, wins his case, and finds out he's guilty, is as slick and formulaic as *Marie*, but far more interesting as a film as well as a social statement. It provides a nice example of how Hollywood formulas subvert and co-opt whatever serious, socially threatening issues a film may raise. If Patsy Cline has no real character, and Marie Ragghianti is a modern Little Nell, Glenn Close, as Teddy Barnes, is a real, contradictory woman. She is tough, competent, aggressive, and independent in her work, but she is also emotionally vulnerable and needy, idealistic, and, at times, manipulable. She is a devoted single mother, but her kids are not her whole emotional focus.

She is, then, what early feminist film critics used to cry out for—a "positive role model," but with enough flaws to be credible. In subtle ways, nevertheless, her character—because of her femininity—is portrayed as less capable of succeeding in a man's world than soppy little Sissy Spacek. Most obviously, she is taken in by a cold-blooded sociopathic murderer who happens to be a hunk, with charm to spare. She believes absolutely that he is innocent while her DA opponent, a political cynic and sleaze whose methods are unethical and illegal, sees through the guy immediately.

This film presents a world in which men, and the institutions they rule, are hopelessly corrupt, immoral, and unfeeling. A good woman, no matter how principled and competent, is no match for the devious male minds she must confront. The suggestion that Teddy lets her heart rule her head is obvious. In *Marie*, the Norman Rockwell world buckled easily in the face of Marie's moral authority, while in *Jagged Edge*, a much more believable version of public life, Teddy buckles and can't really play with the big boys.

There are two aspects of the style and setting of this film that further subvert whatever progressive message it might have had. For one thing, all evil is seen to lie solely in political rather than corporate institutions, and in the hearts of individual "bad" men. Teddy, in fact, had worked for the sleazy DA, become disillusioned with criminal law, and moved over to what is presented as "cleaner" corporate work. From a Left perspective, this is definitely a frying-pan/fire decision.

The film's most clever subversion of social implications is the ending. Teddy actually faces down the killer and shoots him in cold blood, before he can kill her. This "solution" is a kind of feminist *Death Wish* ploy. The women in the audience are relieved—Teddy is dramatically returned to stature—but the problem of social evil, and of ruthlessness and violence in powerful men and their institutions, is ignored. Teddy represents many feminist virtues (if we ignore questions of class), but is socially and politically ineffectual precisely because of those virtues. She is left with no emotionally suitable male partners who are on her level intellectually or morally. The solution for Teddy is a retreat from public life, since her integrity and emotional priorities signal weakness, and, implicitly, social eccentricity, at least in the world she inhabits.

In all three films, we see the way Hollywood, at its commercial best, deals with social change and the demands of the relatively powerless. It is easier than one might think to present women as feminist role models and allow them to "be the best you can be," as a popular cosmetic commercial put it, as long as you can contain their strengths and virtues in a form which implicitly subverts their radical thrust. Popular genre forms, by definition, limit the scope and seriousness of subversive challenges to the status quo. The audience expects certain things and not others: it has been trained from childhood to understand these forms. Whether it's a star biography, an uplifting morality tale, or a courtroom thriller, most of the complexities and contradictions of American social and political life are left out.

The legal and governmental worlds of *Jagged Edge* and *Marie* are contained within the limits of the plot, the problem to be solved in a neat 90 minutes or so. No larger questions can arise about, say, the "left" or "right" of Marie's positions, or the political and economic context that produces the kind of corruption and immorality that Teddy Barnes confronts. We are primed to look for clues and happy endings, to find and expunge the bad guys. *Sweet Dreams* similarly flattens and frames the issue of success and celebrity.

Hollywood addresses some of the issues left out of classic pop genres in the stage adaptations. Not surprisingly, the images and fates of the heroines are a lot more depressing, for these films were not necessarily made to be box office blockbusters. They were aimed, primarily, at a different audience—the relatively select group of thinkers and doers who read *The New York Times* rather than *USA Today* and watch the "MacNeil Lehrer News Hour" rather than CNN's "Headline News." Because they were meant to reach the educated "opinion makers," these films took feminism's challenge to established power far more seriously.

Their analyses of the "modern woman" were therefore more mean-spirited and philosophically devastating than the films mentioned above. In fact, both *Agnes of God* and *Plenty* represented a retreat to the Freudian, implicitly woman-hating and -fearing images of the 1940s. But the flaws upon which they focused, and the punishments meted out, were different. Because of the impact of feminism, it was no longer fashionable to portray sexually or socially powerful women as Jezebels or unfeminine victims of penis envy. Instead, they had more demeaning, even pathetic flaws.

In both films, the heroines present real challenges to the legitimacy of powerful institutions and the assumptions and values that sustain them. In both cases, the filmmakers presented a broad, intricate picture of the workings of those institutions, and then proceeded to discredit the heroines' challenges through character assassination.

In *Agnes*, Jane Fonda plays an ultra-rational psychiatrist determined to prove that a delusionary young nun, Sister Agnes (Meg Tilly), who has borne and apparently murdered a child, was raped rather than "visited by the Holy Ghost," which is the feisty Mother Superior's position.

The ideological issues dominate the film. Anne Bancroft's Mother Superior is a woman of the world—she married, had children, and finally turned to the convent as a solace (and escape) from the failures and disappointments of her earlier "normal" life. Fonda's Dr. Livingston, on the other hand, is single, childless, and has left the church because of her emotionally traumatic experiences with religion. The cards are clearly stacked from the start. Bancroft's reasons for turning to religion are seen as valid, since she is now content as she never was in the "world of sorrow" that society had been for her and for the young, emotionally disturbed nun. Agnes, we learn, was abused both mentally and physically as a child.

Dr. Livingston's life is less fulfilling. She is estranged from her mother, has no permanent man, no visible friends or family, and is all business, from her tailored beiges and grays, to her orderly, modern apartment. The church, on the other hand, offers a true community, tradition, culture, and the joy and passion that come with faith.

To see Bancroft and Fonda square off for the young nun's soul is to see Hollywood's dirtiest of dirty pools, where women are concerned. Bancroft, after all, is as tough and hip as Fonda, and more experienced to boot (she even smokes). But the institution she represents is anathema to feminist ideals, for reasons that surely don't need to be explained. Patriarchy, celibacy, retreat from social and political life—these are values that nuns themselves are fighting to change today.

In the end, the church wins and Fonda falters in her convictions. The film ends with a statement from the doctor to the effect that she has been moved and changed by the young nun's (deranged) faith and hopes that there just may be some truth to her religious beliefs, fantastic as they seem. Needless to say, the church in question bears no relation to the progressive church of liberation theology. The conclusion, therefore, must be interpreted as extremely reactionary, both sexually and politically. The "liberated woman" ends up looking very unattractive indeed, while mysticism and blind obedience to institutional authority win the day.

Plenty, which, like *Sweet Dreams,* was set in earlier times but informed by a 1980s sensibility, goes even further than *Agnes* in subverting feminist ideals, and making them, and those who try to live by them, seem seriously flawed and emotionally unstable. This time the setting and themes are political, not religious. Susan Traherne (Meryl Streep) had been a fighter in the French Resistance during World War II. She had loved the adventure and the sense of doing important work for deeply held political principles. Her return to civilian life is a letdown. She goes from job to job—diplomatic service, TV advertising, even office work—and finds them all deadening.

Plenty includes some truly remarkable lines and situations, given its early-1950s setting. Traherne's best friend, for example, is quite eloquent on the matter of male resentment of female friendships. At one point, Traherne enlists a young working-class man to father a child for her, which she will raise alone. At another point, we see her, the lone woman at a meeting, making a suggestion that is ignored, only to be enthusiastically endorsed when a male re-phrases it. Her response is a cynical shrug of the shoulders; she is used to such treatment. Finally, in one of the film's great lines, she tells her friend that she rarely says what she really thinks publicly, in front of the men she knows, "for fear of blowing them out of the room."

This is clearly a woman modern audiences will find familiar. The film, however, sets her up from the start as neurotic. Even in her war scenes she is seen giving in to fear and clinging to a male comrade. While men—heroes at least—never behave this way in war movies, fear is not, certainly, an unusual or abnormal reaction to war.

As the movie progresses, she goes from shaky to thoroughly incompetent. She marries her diplomat husband in a moment of weakness and gratitude after having a "breakdown" when her attempts to become pregnant fail. From there, the film drags us through a series of embarrassing and increasingly hysterical scenes in which she breaks protocol, shocks guests, and at times viciously tirades against British imperialist policies.

When her husband finally castigates her for her "selfishness" and unrealistic fantasies of a better, more meaningful life and world, the audience is meant to feel, "It's about time." He is, after all, a long-suffering, loving, if dull sort, who "deserves" a wife who will help, not hurt his career. The final scenes, which find her in a cheap room, stoned, and reliving the idealism and excitement of her political days, are a damning indictment of what her husband sees as her wasted life.

The film never explains why she does not pursue what at one point seems to be an interest in painting, or why she stays in such an unsuitable marriage. But the unmentioned answer is obvious—this was the 1950s. Because the film and the heroine are so very up-to-date, however, it's hard to remember that. And that is exactly the point of the film's entirely sexist strategy. It takes a woman easily identifiable as a modern-day feminist, a woman of power, drive, and social concerns, and puts her in a setting in which these traits are only interpretable as "crazy."

The 1980s in many ways were a return to 1950s values. The people who have always hated and feared feminism were more influential than ever. It makes sense, then, that this movie, like *Agnes of God*, put forth an image of the "liberated woman" in a contradictory way. On one level, all these films support and accept everything the Women's Movement pushed for in the 1960s and 1970s. On another, more subtle level, however, they are stabs in the back: reactionary attacks on those very ideals. "You've come a long way, Baby," they all seem to say, "Now let's see how you like the bed you've made for yourself."

Hollywood's bed, plush as it looked, was not the one women ordered. Feminism assumes that society itself needs to change in important, democratizing ways. By omitting or distorting every aspect of the larger social world, and its effects on women, Hollywood gives women a message so depressing that it is almost a threat. There is very little in any of these films that would make a young woman envy these heroines. In fact, the Katharine Hepburns and Lauren Bacalls look a lot more enviable in every way. "You've come a long way," indeed.

Out of the Mainstream

The following selection is from "Out of the Mainstream: Sexual Minorities and the Mass Media," which was published in Ellen Seiter et al., eds., *Remote Control: Television, Audiences and Cultural Power* (Routledge, 1989). In this thoughtful essay, Larry Gross, a professor in the Annenberg School for Communications at the University of Pennsylvania, examines the media's treatment of gay and lesbian themes and characters. Although his article predates the televised "coming out" of comedienne Ellen Degeneres's lesbian character on the show *Ellen*, Gross's critique is not only relevant to that landmark event but may cast an understanding of how and why *Ellen* was subsequently cancelled. Even though the "coming out" episode led the ratings and provided a national "coming out" party for many gay men and lesbians, the series suffered when questions of further plot development became controversial for the production company and the television network.

For many years, few academics wrote about homosexuality. Even when they did, it was difficult to get work on issues of gender identity or sexual preference published. The fact that more attention is now being given to homosexuals by the media and that there is a growing (yet still controversial) field of queer studies in schools indicate a cultural change in the United States. The topic still makes many people uncomfortable, but it provides an excellent example of how the media legitimize or distort cultural issues.

Media images and stereotyping have been themes of media research for a long time, but, as Gross points out, gay people have been almost invisible in the media except as victims of violence or ridicule, or as villains. "Normal" behavior, in media and in real life, often reflects the values of the beholder. Gross's article, however, uncovers a number of issues related to how and why any minority group is portrayed in certain ways by the media.

Key Concept: social interpretation of images of homosexuality

*I*n a society dominated by centralized sources of information and imagery, in which economic imperatives and pervasive values promote the search for large, common-denominator audiences, what is the fate of those groups who for one or another reason find themselves outside the mainstream? Briefly, and it is hardly a novel observation, such groups share a common fate of relative invisibility and demeaning stereotypes. But there are differences as well as similarities in the ways various minorities (racial, ethnic, sexual, religious, political) are treated by the mass media. And, given important differences in their life situations, members of such groups experience varying consequences of their mediated images.

In this [selection] I will discuss the general question of minority perspectives applied to the study of mass media content and effects, and I will elaborate in grater detail the situation of sexual minorities (lesbian women and gay men) as members of the mass media audience.

Sexual minorities differ in important ways from the "traditional" racial and ethnic minorities; they are, in an interesting sense, akin to political minorities (so-called radicals and "fringe" groups). In both cases their members typically are self-identified at some point in their lives, usually in adolescence or later, and they are not necessarily easily identifiable by others. These two groups also constitute by their very existence a presumed threat to the "natural" (sexual and/or political) order of things, and thus they are inherently problematic and controversial for the mass media. These characteristics can be seen to affect the way members of such groups are depicted in the media (when they do appear), and also suggest ways to think about the effects of such depictions on the images held by society at large and by members of these minority groups.

Before turning to the discussion of minority audience perspectives, it would be helpful to characterize briefly the role of the mass media, television in particular, in our society.

THE SYSTEM IS THE MESSAGE

First, the economic, political, and social integration of modern industrial society allows few communities or individuals to maintain an independent integrity. We are parts of a Leviathan, like it or not, and its nervous system is telecommunications. Our knowledge of the "wide world" is what this nervous system transmits to us. The mass media provide the chief common ground among the different groups that make up a heterogeneous national community. Never before have all classes and groups (as well as ages) shared so much of the same culture and the same perspectives while having so little to do with their creation.

Second, representation in the mediated "reality" of our mass culture is in itself power; certainly it is the case that non-representation maintains the powerless status of groups that do not possess significant material or political power bases. That is, while the holders of real power—the ruling class—do not require (or seek) mediated visibility, those who are at the bottom of the various power hierarchies will be kept in their places in part through their relative invisibility. This is a form of what Gerbner and I have termed symbolic annihilation.[1] Not all interests or points of view are equal; judgments are made constantly about exclusions and inclusions and these judgments broaden or narrow (mostly narrow) the spectrum of views presented.

Third, when groups or perspectives do attain visibility, the manner of that representation will itself reflect the biases and interests of those elites who define the public agenda. And these elites are (mostly) white, (mostly) middle-aged, (mostly) male, (mostly) middle and upper-middle class, and entirely heterosexual (at least in public).

Fourth, we should not take too seriously the presumed differences between the various categories of media messages—particularly in the case of television. News, drama, quiz shows, sports, and commercials share underlying similarities of theme, emphasis, and value. Even the most widely accepted distinctions (i.e. news vs. fiction programs vs. commercials) are easily blurred. Decisions about which events are newsworthy and about how to present them are heavily influenced by considerations of dramatic form and content (e. g. conflict and resolution) that are drawn from fictional archetypes; and the polished mini-dramas of many commercials reveal a sophisticated mastery of fictional conventions, just as dramatic programs promote a style of consumption and living that is quite in tune with their neighboring commercial messages. More important, the blending of stylistic conventions allows for greater efficacy and mutual support in packaging and diffusing common values.

Fifth, the dominant conventions of our mass media are those of "realism" and psychologically grounded naturalism. Despite a limited degree of reflexivity which occasionally crops up, mainstream film and television are nearly always presented as transparent mediators of reality which can and do show us how people and places look, how institutions operate; in short, the way it is. These depictions of the way things are, and why, are personified through dramatic plots and characterizations which take us behind the scenes to the otherwise inaccessible backstages of individual motivation, organizational performance, and subcultural life.

Normal adult viewers, to be sure, are aware of the fictiveness of media drama: no one calls the police when a character on television is shot. But we may still wonder how often and to what extent viewers suspend their disbelief in the persuasive realism of the fictional worlds of television and film drama. Even the most sophisticated among us can find many components of our "knowledge" of the real world which derive wholly or in part from fictional representations. And, in a society which spans a continent, in a cosmopolitan culture which spans much of the globe, television and film provide the broadest common background of assumptions about what things are, how they work (or should work), and why.

Finally, the contributions of the mass media are likely to be most powerful in cultivating images of groups and phenomena about which there is little first-hand opportunity for learning; particularly when such images are not contradicted by other established beliefs and ideologies. By definition, portrayals of minority groups and "deviants" will be relatively distant from the real lives of a large majority of viewers.

The average American adult spends several hours each day in this television world, children spend even more of their lives immersed in its "fictional reality." As I have already suggested, the mass media, and television foremost among them, have become the primary sources of the common information and images that create and maintain a world view and a value system. In a word, the mass media have become central agents of enculturation. In the Cultural Indicators Project we have used the concept of "cultivation" to describe the influence of television on viewers' conceptions of social reality.[2]

On issue after issue we find that assumptions, beliefs, and values of heavy viewers of television differ systematically from those of light viewers in the same demographic groups. Sometimes these differences appear as overall, main effects, whereby those who watch more television are more likely in all groups —to give what we call "television answers" to our questions. But in many cases the patterns are more complex. We have found that television viewing, not surprisingly, serves as a stable factor differentially integrated into and interacting with different groups' life situations and world views. in our recent work we have isolated a consistent pattern which we have termed "mainstreaming."[3]

The mainstream can be thought of as a relative commonality of outlooks and values that television tends to cultivate in viewers. By mainstreaming we mean the sharing of that commonality among heavy viewers in those demographic groups whose light viewers hold divergent positions. In other words, differences deriving from other factors and social forces—differences that may appear in the responses of light viewers in various groups—may be diminished or even absent when the heavy viewers in these same groups are compared. Overall, television viewing appears to signal a convergence of outlooks rather than absolute, across-the-board increments in all groups.

Choices or Echoes?

The mainstream which we have identified as the embodiment of a dominant ideology, cultivated through the repetition of stable patterns across the illusory boundaries of media and genre, and absorbed by otherwise diverse segments of the population, nevertheless has to contend with the possibility of oppositional perspectives and interpretations. What options and opportunities are available to those groups whose concerns, values and even very existence are belittled, subverted, and denied by the mainstream? Can the power of the mass media's central tendencies be resisted? Can one avoid being swept into the mainstream? The answers to such questions depend in large part on which group or segment we are discussing; while many minorities are similarly ignored or distorted by the mass media, not all have the same options for resistance and the development of alternative channels.

In general the opportunities for organized opposition are greatest when there is a visible and even organized group which can provide solidarity and institutional means for creating and disseminating alternative messages. There are numerous examples of groupings that have sprung up, as it were, along the right bank of the mainstream. Most organized and visible among these are the Christian fundamentalist syndicated television programs. These programs provide their (generally older and less educated) viewers with an array of programs, from news to talk shows to soap operas to church services and sermons, all reflecting perspectives and values that they quite correctly feel are not represented in mainstream, prime-time television or in the movies.[4] As one of Hoover's conservative, religious respondents put it, in discussing network television:

> I think a good deal of it is written by very liberal, immoral people ... Some of the comedies, the weekly things that go on every week, they make extramarital affairs, and sex before marriage an everyday thing like everybody should accept it ... and they present it in a comic situation, a situation that looks like it could be fun and a good deal of these weekly shows I don't like go for that.[5]

The religious sponsoring and producing organizations are not merely engaged in meeting their audiences' previously unmet needs for a symbolic environment in which they feel at home; they are also attempting to translate the (usually exaggerated) numbers of their audiences and their (constantly solicited) financial contributions into a power base from which they can exert pressure to alter the channel of the mainstream and bring it even closer to where they now reside, up on the right bank.

At the moment, and for the foreseeable future in the United States, at least, there is no comparable settlement on the left bank of the mainstream. There are many reasons why the organized left has been unable to match the right's success in harnessing the available resources of media technology. It is not hard to see that some minority perspectives are in fact supportive of the dominant ideology, however much the media's need for massive audiences might sacrifice or offend their interests, while other minority values are truly incompatible with the basic power relationships embodied in that mainstream....

HOMOSEXUALS AND TELEVISION: FEAR AND LOATHING

Close to the heart of our cultural and political system is the pattern of roles associated with sexual identity: our conceptions of masculinity and femininity, of the "normal" and "natural" attributes and responsibility of men and women. And, as with other pillars of our moral order, these definitions of what is normal and natural serve to support the existing social power hierarchy.

The maintenance of the "normal" gender role system requires that children be socialized—and adults retained—within a set of images and expectations which limit and channel their conceptions of what is possible and proper for men and for women. The gender system is supported by the mass media treatment of sexual minorities. Mostly, they are ignored or denied—symbolically annihilated; when they do appear they do so in order to play a supportive role for the natural order and are thus narrowly and negatively stereotyped. Sexual minorities are not, of course, unique in this regard.[6] However, lesbians and gay men are unusually vulnerable to mass media power; even more so than blacks, national minorities, and women. Of all social groups (except perhaps communists), we are probably the least permitted to speak for ourselves in the mass media. We are also the only group (again, except for communists and, currently, Arab "terrorists") whose enemies are generally uninhibited by the consensus of "good taste" which protects most minorities from the more public displays of bigotry.

The reason for this vulnerability lies in large part in our initial isolation and invisibility. The process of identity formation for lesbian women and gay men requires the strength and determination to swim against the stream. A baby is born and immediately classified as male or female, white or black, and is treated as such from that moment, for better or worse. That baby is also defined as heterosexual and treated as such. It is made clear throughout the process of socialization—a process in which the mass media play a major role—that one will grow up, marry, have children and live in nuclear familial bliss, sanctified by religion and licensed by the state. Women are surrounded by other women, people of color by other people of color, etc., and can observe the variety of choices and fates that befall those who are like them. Mass media stereotypes selectively feature and reinforce some of the available roles and images for women, national minorities, people of color, etc.; but they operate under constraints imposed by the audiences' immediate environment.

Lesbians and gay men, conversely, are a self-identifying minority. We are assumed (with few exceptions, and these—the "obviously" effeminate man or masculine woman—may not even be homosexual) to be straight, and are treated as such, until we begin to recognize that we are not what we have been told we are, that we are different But how are we to understand, define, and deal with that difference? Here we generally have little to go on beyond very limited direct experience with those individuals who are close enough to the accepted stereotypes to be labeled publicly as queers, faggots, dykes, etc. And we have the mass media.

The mass media play a major role in this process of social definition, and rarely a positive one. In the absence of adequate information in their immediate environment, most people, gay or straight, have little choice other than to accept the narrow and negative stereotypes they encounter as being representative of gay people. The mass media have rarely presented portrayals which counter or extend the prevalent images. On the contrary, they take advantage of them. Typically, media characterizations use popular stereotypes as a code which they know will be readily understood by the audience, thus further reinforcing the presumption of verisimilitude while remaining "officially" innocent of dealing with a sensitive subject.

But there is more to it than stereotyping. For the most part gay people have been simply invisible in the media. The few exceptions were almost invariably either victims—of violence or ridicule—or villains. As Vito Russo noted recently, "it is not insignificant that out of 32 films with major homosexual characters from 1961 through 1976, 13 feature gays who commit suicide and 18 have the homosexual murdered by another character."[7] Even this minimal and slanted presence, however, seems to be so threatening to the "industry" that gay characterizations and plot elements always come accompanied by pressbook qualifications and backpedaling. In his survey of the treatment of gay people in American film,[8] Russo presents a sample of the predictable distancing that gay themes evoke from directors ("*The Children's Hour* is not about lesbianism, it's about the power of lies to destroy people's lives," William Wyler, 1962; "*Sunday, Bloody Sunday* is not about the sexuality of these people, it's about human loneliness," John Schlesinger, 1972; "*Windows* is not about homosexuality, it's about insanity," Gordon Willis, 1979), and actors ("*The Sergeant is* not about homosexuality, it's about loneliness," Rod Steiger, 1968; *Staircase* is not about homosexuality, it's about loneliness," Rex Harrison, 1971). It is easy to imagine how comforting these explanations must have been to lesbian and gay audience members looking for some reflection of their lives in the media. But it is not only the audiences who appear to require protective distancing from gay characters and themes. We are frequently treated to showbiz gossip intended to convey the heterosexual bona fides of any actor cast in a gay role, as when the actor playing the swish drag queen Albin in the stage version of *La Cage aux Folles* told several interviewers that he had consulted with his wife and children before accepting the role.

The gay liberation movement emerged in the late 1960s in the United States, spurred by the examples of the black and feminist movements. Consequently, media attention to gay people and gay issues increased in the early 1970s, much of it positive (at least in comparison with previous and continuing heterosexist depictions and discussions), culminating (in the sense of greater media attention—in the pre-AIDS era) in 1973, with the decision by the American Psychiatric Association to delete homosexuality from its "official" list of mental diseases. By the middle 1970s, however, a backlash against the successes of the gay movement began to be felt around the country, most visibly in Anita Bryant's successful campaign to repeal a gay rights ordinance in Dade County, Florida, in 1977. Since then the gay movement and its enemies, mostly among the "new right," have been constant antagonists (right-wing fund-raisers acknowledge that anti-homosexual material is their best bet to get money from supporters), and television has often figured in the struggle. But, although the right wing has attacked the networks for what they consider to be overly favorable attention to homosexuals, in fact gay people are usually portrayed and used in news and dramatic media in ways that serve to reinforce rather than challenge the prevailing images.

Kathleen Montgomery observed the efforts of the organized gay movement to improve the ways network programmers handle gay characters and themes. In particular she describes the writing and production of a made-for-television network movie that had a gay-related theme, and involved consultation with representatives of gay organizations. And the result?

> Throughout the process all the decisions affecting the portrayal of gay life were influenced by the constraints which commercial television as a mass medium imposes upon the creation of its content. The fundamental goal of garnering the largest possible audience necessitated that (a) the program be placed in a familiar and successful television genre—the crime-drama; (b) the story focus upon the heterosexual male lead character and his reactions to the gay characters rather

than upon the homosexual characters themselves; and (c) the film avoid any overt display of affection which might be offensive to certain segments of the audience. These requirements served as a filter through which the issue of homosexuality was processed, resulting in a televised picture of gay life designed to be acceptable to the gay community and still palatable to a mass audience.[9]

Acceptability to the gay community, in this case, means that the movie was not an attack on our character and a denial of our basic humanity; it could not be mistaken for an expression of our values or perspectives. But of course they were not aiming at us, either; they were merely trying to avoid arguing with us afterwards. In Vito Russo's words, "mainstream films about homosexuals are not for homosexuals. They address themselves exclusively to the majority."[10] However, there will inevitably be a great many lesbians and gay men in the audience.

The rules of the mass media game have a double impact on gay people: not only do they mostly show us as weak and silly, or evil and corrupt, but they exclude and deny the existence of normal, unexceptional as well as exceptional lesbians and gay men. Hardly ever shown in the media are just plain gay folks, used in roles which do not center on their deviance as a threat to the moral order which must be countered through ridicule or physical violence. Television drama in particular reflects the deliberate use of clichéed casting strategies which preclude such daring innovations.

The stereotypic depiction of lesbians and gay men as abnormal, and the suppression of positive or even "unexceptional" portrayals, serve to maintain and police the boundaries of the moral order. It encourages the majority to stay on their gender-defined reservation, and tries to keep the minority quietly hidden out of sight. For the visible presence of healthy, non-stereotypic lesbians and gay men does pose a serious threat: it undermines the unquestioned normalcy of the status quo, and it opens up the possibility of making choices to people who might never otherwise have considered or understood that such choices could be made.

The situation has only been worsened by the AIDS epidemic. By 1983 nearly all mass media attention to gay men was in the context of AIDS-related stories, and because this coverage seems to have exhausted the media's limited interest in gay people, lesbians became even less visible than before (if possible). AIDS reinvigorated the two major mass media "roles" for gay people: victim and villain. Already treated as an important medical topic, AIDS moved up to the status of "front page" news after Rock Hudson emerged as the most famous person with the disease. At present AIDS stories appear daily in print and broadcast news—often with little or no new or important content and the public image of gay men has been inescapably linked with the specter of plague. Television dramatists have presented the plight of (white, middle-class) gay men with AIDS, but their particular concern is the agony of the families/friends who have to face the awful truth: their son (brother, boyfriend, husband, etc.) is, gasp, gay! But, even with AIDS, not too gay, mind you. In the major network made-for-television movie on AIDS, NBC's *An Early Frost*, a young, rich, white, handsome lawyer is forced out of the closet by AIDS. "We know he is gay because he tells his disbelieving parents so, but his lack of a gay sensibility, politics and sense of community make him one of those homosexuals heterosexuals love."[11]

An Early Frost is thus another example of the pattern discerned by Montgomery: although this time the familiar and successful genre is family—not crime-drama, the focus is still on the heterosexual characters and their reactions. As William Henry notes in a recent overview of television's treatment of gays (or lack of same) during the past fifteen years,

> when TV does deal with gays it typically takes the point of view of straights struggling to understand. The central action is the progress of acceptance—not self-acceptance by the homosexual, but grief-stricken resignation to fate by his straight loved ones, who serve as surrogates for the audience. Homosexuality thus becomes not a fact of life, but a moral issue on which everyone in earshot is expected to voice some vehement opinion. Just as black characters were long expected to talk almost exclusively about being black, and handicapped characters (when seen at all) were expected to talk chiefly about their disabilities, so homosexual characters have been defined almost entirely by their "problem."[12]

Being defined by their "problem," it is no surprise therefore that gay characters have mostly been confined to television's favorite problem-of-the-week genre, the made-for-television movie, with a very occasional one-shot appearance of a gay character on a dramatic series (examples include episodes of *Lou Grant, Medical Center* and *St. Elsewhere*). Continuing gay characters tend to be so subtle as to be readily misunderstood by the innocent (as in the case of Sidney in *Love, Sidney*, whose homosexuality seemed to consist entirely of crying at the movies and having a photo of his dead lover on the mantelpiece), or confused about their sexuality and never seen in an ongoing romantic relationship (as in the case of the off-again on-again Steven Carrington in *Dynasty*, whose lovers have an unfortunate tendency to get killed).

Despite their greater freedom from the competition for massive mainstream audiences—perhaps because of their need to compete for the primary audience of teens and young adults—commercial films are no more welcoming to gay characters than television. In fact, as Vito Russo shows in the revised edition of his 1981 study, *The Celluloid Closet* (1987), recent films are awash with gay villains and victims once more:

> The use of the word faggot has become almost mandatory. Outright slurs that would never be tolerated in reference to any other group of people are commonly used onscreen against homosexuals.... Anti-gay dialogue is most often given to the very characters with whom the audience is supposed to identify.[13]

Films offer their makers a degree of license which isn't available to television producers—an opportunity to use language and depictions of sexuality that go far beyond the limits imposed on television—but as far as gay people are concerned, this mostly serves as a hunting license.

COLONIZATION: THE STRAIGHT GAY

There are several categories of response to the mainstream media's treatment of minorities; among them are internalization, subversion, secession, and resistance. To begin with, as we have already noted, we are all colonized by the majority culture. Those of us who belong to a minority group may nevertheless have absorbed the values of the dominant culture, even if these exclude or diminish us. We are all aware of the privileging of male-identified attributes in our patriarchal culture, and the dominance of the male perspective in the construction of mass-mediated realities. Similarly, the US media offer a white-angled view of the world which is shared with people of color everywhere. In a study of Venezuelan children in which they were asked to describe their heroes, the hero was North American in 86 per cent of the cases and Venezuelan in only 8 per cent; English-speaking in 82 per cent and Spanish-speaking in 15 per cent; white heroes outnumbered black heroes 11 to 1; and heroes were wealthy in 72 per cent of the cases.[14]

Sexual minorities are among the most susceptible to internalizing the dominant culture's values because the process of labelling generally occurs in isolation and because:

> We learn to loathe homosexuality before it becomes necessary to acknowledge our own. ... Never having been offered *positive* attitudes to homosexuality, we inevitably adopt *negative* ones, and it is from these that all our values flow.[15]

Internalization and colonization can also result in the adoption of assimilationist strategies which promise upward (or centerward) mobility, although at the cost of cutting off one's "roots." Gay people by and large know how to "pass"; after all, it's what they have been doing most of their lives. But the security attained is fragile and often illusory, and certainly will not provide support in resisting the inferiorizing pressures of the straight culture they attempt to blend into. And all too often, there really isn't any resistance anyway, as the process of internalization has achieved the desired goal. The Zionist polemicist Ahad Ha-Am drew on a biblical analogy to describe this phenomenon, in his essay on Moses: "Pharaoh is gone, but his work remains; the master has ceased to he master, but the slaves have not ceased to be slaves."[16]

The supposedly liberal and tolerant domain of the media does not necessarily permit homosexuals (or other minorities) to overcome the burdens of self-oppression:

> When it comes to keeping minorities in their place, the entertainment industry continues to divide and conquer. For all the organizing that women have done, for instance, in their attempts to break down the barriers, well-placed women executives say they've received very little mutual support from their equally well-placed peers. The old-boy network rules, and the individual women, gays, blacks, or hispanics who attain some degree of success usually have to camouflage themselves in the trappings of their masters.[17]

Similarly, gay writer Merle Miller recalled that, "as editor of a city newspaper, he indulged in 'queer-baiting' to conceal his own homosexuality."[18] Openly gay actor Michael Kearns speaks of "a gay agent who makes it a habit to tell 'fag jokes' at the close of interviews with new actors. If an actor laughs, he's signed up; if he doesn't, he isn't."[19] Working backstage, it would seem, does not exempt one from falling under the spell of the hegemonic values cultivated and reflected by the media. However, as Raymond Williams has suggested, hegemony "is never either total or exclusive. At any time, forms of alternative or directly oppositional politics and culture exist as significant elements in the society."[20]

NOTES

1. George Gerbner and Larry Gross, "Living with Television," *Journal of Communication* 26, no.2 (1976): 182.

2. George Gerbner, Larry Gross, Michael Morgan, and Nancy Signorielli, "Living with Television: The Dynamics of the Cultivation Process," in Jennings Bryant and Dolf Zillman (eds.) *Perspectives on Media Effects* (Hillsdale, NJ: Lawrence Erlbaum Associates, 1986), pp. 17–40.

3. George Gerbner, Larry Gross, Michael Morgan, and Nancy Signorielli, "The 'Mainstreaming' of America," *Journal of Communication* 30, no. 3 (1980): 10–29; George Gerbner, Larry Gross, Michael Morgan, and Nancy Signorielli, "Charting the Mainstream: Television's Contributions to Political Orientations," *Journal of Communication* 32, no. 2 (1982): 100–27; and Gerbner *et al.*, "Living with Television" (1986).

4. See George Gerbner, Larry Gross, Stewart Hoover, Michael Morgan, Nancy Signorielli, Harry Cotugno, and Robert Wuthnow, *Religion and Television* (University of Pennsylvania: The Annenberg School of Communications, 1984); and Stewart Hoover, "The 700 Club as Religion and as Television," unpublished Ph.D. dissertation, University of Pennsylvania, 1985.

5. Hoover, "The 700 Club," pp. 382f.

6. See Larry Gross, "The Cultivation of Intolerance," in G. Melischek *et al.* (eds.) *Cultural Indicators; An International Symposium* (Vienna: Austrian Academy of Sciences, 1984), pp. 345–63.

7. Vito Russo, "A State of Being," *Film Comment* (April 1986): 32.

8. Vito Russo, *The Celluloid Closet: Homosexuality in the Movies* (New York: Harper & Row, 1981).

9. Kathleen Montgomery, "Gay Activists and the Networks," *Journal of Communication* 31, no. 3 (1981): 49–57.

10. Russo, "A State of Being," p. 32.

11. Andrea Weiss, "From the Margins: New Images of Gays in the Cinema," *Cineaste* (1986): 4–8.

12. William Henry, "That Certain Subject," *Channels* (April 1987): 43f.

13. Russo, *The Celluloid Closet*, p. 251.

14. Antonio Pasquali, "Latin America: Our Image or Theirs?", in *Getting the Message Across* (no editor listed) (Paris: The UNESCO Press, 1975), pp. 62f.

15. Andrew Hodges and David Hutter, *With Downcast Gays: Aspects of Homosexual Self-Oppression* (Toronto: Pink Triangle Press, 1977), p. 4.

16. Ahad Ha-Am (Asher Ginzberg), "Moses," in *Selected Essays of Ahad Ha-Am*, Leon Simon, ed. (New York: Atheneum, 1970), p. 320.

17. Gregg Kilday, "Hollywood's Homosexuals," *Film Comment* (April 1986): 40.

18. Barry Adam, *The Survival of Domination: Inferiorization and Everyday Life* (New York: Elsevier, 1978), p. 89.

19. Samir Hachem, "Inside the Tinseled Closet," *The Advocate*, March 17, 1987, p. 48.

20. Raymond Williams, *Marxism and Literature* (Oxford: Oxford University Press, 1977), p. 111.

CHAPTER 13 Media and Race

13.1 BELL HOOKS

Spike Lee Doing Malcolm X

Bell hooks, the popular writer, speaker, and Distinguished Professor of English at City College in New York, is known for her outspoken approaches to the representation of blacks and women in all forms of cultural criticism. She has often written unfavorably about black filmmaker Spike Lee's portrayal of women in his films. However, in the following selection from her book *Outlaw Culture: Resisting Representations* (Routledge, 1994), hooks addresses Lee's representation of black militant leader Malcolm X. Her thesis is that Lee's treatment of the subject merely reproduces black images for a white audience. This is particularly problematic in hooks's view because Malcolm X so actively promoted and encouraged a "critical black gaze." She addresses important issues that have shaped and continue to shape the film industry, and she criticizes Lee for taking the perspective of a Hollywood insider in developing what should have been an important biography of the influential black leader. Although hooks admires Lee's abilities as a gifted filmmaker, she claims that he focuses too much on (white) stereotypical views of black life. She finds that Lee's representation of Malcolm's life lacks the power of Malcolm's political revolution. Instead, hooks says, Malcolm is portrayed in his final days as a failure rather than as a hero who went to extremes to advance black liberation. In this selection, hooks' critiques the treatment of a biography of a controversial figure, but she does much more than that: she identifies what types of films and treatments of real political figures Hollywood is likely to endorse and how it does so. Her position is not only one of a cultural critic but of a social critic as well.

In addition to *Outlaw Culture* hooks is well known for her books *Yearning: Race, Gender, and Cultural Politics* (South End Press, 1990), *Talking Back: Thinking Feminist, Thinking Black* (South End Press, 1989), *Ain't I a Woman: Black Women and Feminism* (South End Press, 1981), *Black Looks: Race and Representation* (South End Press, 1992).

Key Concept: representation of race in film

*S*hortly after the brutal assassination of Malcolm X, Bayard Rustin predicted that "White America, not the Negro people, will determine Malcolm X's role in history." At the time, this statement seemed ludicrous. White Americans appeared to have no use for Malcolm X, not even a changed Malcolm, no longer fiercely advocating racial separatism. Today, market forces in white supremacist capitalist partriarchy have found a way to use Malcolm X. Where black images are concerned, the field of representation has always been a plantation culture. Malcolm X can be turned into hot commodity, his militant black nationalist, antiimperialist, anticapitalist politics can be diffused and undermined by a process of objectification. Calling attention to the dangers inherent in this marketing trend in his essay "On Malcolm X: His Message and Meaning," Manning Marable warns: "There is a tendency to drain the radical message of a dynamic, living activist into an abstract icon, to replace radical content with pure image." Politically progressive black folks and our allies in struggle recognize that the power of Malcolm X's political thought, the capacity of his work to educate for critical consciousness is threatened when his image and ideas are commodified and sold by conservative market forces that strip the work of all radical and revolutionary content.

Understanding the power of mass media images as forces that can overdetermine how we see ourselves and how we choose to act, Malcolm X admonished black folks: "Never accept images that have been created for you by someone else. It is always better to form the habit of learning how to see things for yourself: then you are in a better position to judge for yourself." Interpreted narrowly, this admonition can be seen as referring only to images of black folks created in the white imagination. More broadly, however, its message is not simply that black folks should interrogate only the images white folks produce while passively consuming images constructed by black folks; it urges us to look with a critical eye at all images. Malcolm X promoted and encouraged the development of a critical black gaze, one that would be able to move beyond passive consumption and be fiercely confronting, challenging, interrogating.

At this cultural moment, this critical militancy aimed at the realm of the visual must be reinvoked in all serious discussions of Spike Lee's film, *Malcolm X*. Celebrated and praised in mainstream media, this joint project by white producers and a black filmmaker, Lee's *Malcolm X* risks receiving no meaningful cultural critique. More often than not, black admirers of Lee and his work, both from the academic front and the street, seek to censor, by discrediting or punishing, any view of the film that is not unequivocally celebratory. Black folks who subject the film to rigorous critique risk being seen as traitors to the race, as petty competitors who do not want to see another black person succeed, or as having personal enmity towards Lee. Filmmaker Marlon Riggs powerfully emphasizes the dangers of such silencing in a recent interview in *Black Film Review*. Calling attention to the example of audience response to Spike Lee (who is often quick to denounce publicly all forms of critique as betrayal or attack), Riggs stresses that we cannot develop a body of black cultural criticism as long as all rigorous critique is censored.

> There's also a crying desire for representation. That's what you see when audiences refuse to allow any critique of artists. I've witnessed this personally. At one forum, Spike Lee was asked several questions by a number of people, myself included, about his representations in his movies. The audience went wild with hysterical outbursts to "shut up," "sit down," "make your own goddam movies," "who are you, this man is doing the best he can, and he is giving us dignified images, he is doing positive work, why should you be criticizing him?" I admit that there is often trashing just for the sake of trashing. But even when it is clear that the critique is trying to empower and trying to heal certain wounds within our communities, there is not any space within our culture to constructively critique. There is an effort simply to shut people up in order to deify these gods, if you will, who have delivered some image of us which seems to affirm our existence in this world. As if they make up for the lack, but, in fact they don't. They can become part of the hegemony.

This is certainly true of Spike Lee. Despite the hype that continues to depict him as an outsider in the white movie industry, someone who is constantly struggling to produce work against the wishes and desires of a white establishment, Lee is an insider. His insider position was made most evident when he was able to use his power to compel Warner to choose him over white director Norman Jewison to make the film. In the business to make money, Warner was probably not moved by Spike's narrow identity politics (his insistence that having a white man directing *Malcolm X* would be "wrong with a capital w!"), but rather by the recognition that his presence as a director would likely draw the biggest crossover audience and thus insure that the movie would be a financial success.

Committed as well to making a film that would be a megasuccess, Spike Lee had to create a work that would address the needs and desires of a consuming audience that is predominantly white. Ironically, to achieve this end his film had to be made in such a way as to be similar to other Hollywood epic dramas, especially fictive biographies; hence there is no visual standpoint or direction in *Malcolm X* that would indicate that a white director could not have made this film. This seems especially tragic since Spike Lee's brilliance as a filmmaker surfaces most when he combines aspects of documentary in fictive dramas, providing us with insights we have never before seen on the screen, representations of blackness and black life that emerge from the privileged standpoint of familiarity. No such familiarity surfaces in *Malcolm X*. The documentary footage seems more like an add-on that aims to provide the radical portrait of a revolutionary Malcolm lacking in the fictive scenes.

To appeal to a crossover audience, Spike Lee had to create a fictive Malcolm that white folks as well as conservative black and other non-white viewers would want to see. His representation of Malcolm has more in common with Steven Spielberg's representation of Mister in the film version of *The Color Purple* than with real-life portraits of Malcolm X. By choosing not to construct the film chronologically, Spike Lee was able to focus on that part of Malcolm's story that would easily fit with Hollywood's traditional stereotypical representations of black life. In her insightful essay on *The Color Purple*, "Blues For Mr. Spielberg," Michele Wallace asserts:

> The fact is there's a gap between what blacks would like to see in movies about themselves and what whites in Hollywood are willing to produce. Instead of serious men and women encountering consequential dilemmas, we're almost always minstrels, more than a little ridiculous; we dance and sing without continuity, as if on the end of a string.

Sadly, these comments could be describing the first half of *Malcolm X*. With prophetic vision, Wallace continues her point, declaring

> I suspect that blacks who wish to make their presence known in American movies will have to seek some middle ground between the stern seriousness of black liberation and the tap dances of Mr. Bojangles and Aunt Jemima.

Clearly, Spike Lee attempts to negotiate this middle ground in *Malcolm X*, but does so unsuccessfully.

The first half of the film constantly moves back and forth from neo-minstrel spectacle to tragic scenes. Yet the predominance of spectacle, of the coon show, whether or not an accurate portrayal of this phase of Malcolm's life, undermines the pathos that the tragic scenes (flashbacks of childhood incidents of racial oppression and discrimination) should, but do not, evoke. At the same time, by emphasizing Malcolm as street hustler, Spike Lee can highlight Malcolm's romantic and sexual involvement with the white woman Sophia, thereby exploiting this culture's voyeuristic obsession with interracial sex. It must be remembered that critics of Lee's project, like Baraka, were concerned that this would be the central focus so as to entertain white audiences; the progression of the film indicates the astuteness of this earlier insight about the direction Lee would take. While his relationship with Sophia was clearly important to Malcolm for many years, it is portrayed with the same shallowness of vision that characterizes Lee's vision of interracial romance between black men and white women in *Jungle Fever*. Unwilling and possibly unable to imagine that any bond between a white woman and a black man could be based on ties other than pathological ones, Lee portrays Malcolm's desire for Sophia as rooted solely in racial competition between white and black men. Yet Malcolm continued to feel affectional bonds for her even as he acquired a radical critique of race, racism, and sexuality.

Without the stellar performance of actor Delroy Lindo playing West Indian Archie, the first half of *Malcolm X* would have been utterly facile. The first character that appears when the film opens is not Malcolm, as audiences anticipate, but a comic Spike in the role of Shorty. Lee's presence in the film intensifies the sense of spectacle. And it seems as though his character is actually competing for attention with Malcolm Little. His comic antics easily upstage the Little character, who appears awkward and stupid. Denzel Washington had been chosen to portray Malcolm before Spike Lee joined the producers at Warner. A box office draw, he never stops being Denzel Washington giving us his version of Malcolm X. Despite his powerful acting, Washington cannot convey the issues around skin color that were so crucial to Malcolm's development of racial consciousness and identity. Lacking Malcolm's stature, and his light hue, Denzel never comes across as a "threatening" physical presence. Washington's real-life persona as everybody's nice guy makes it particularly difficult for him to convey the seriousness and intensity of a black man consumed with rage. By choosing him, white producers were already deciding that Malcolm had to be made to appear less militant, more open, if white audiences were to accept him.

Since so much of the movie depicts Malcolm's days as Detroit Red, the remainder is merely a skeletal, imagistic outline of his later political changes in regard to issues of racial separatism. None of his powerful critiques of capitalism and colonialism are dramatized in this film. Early on in the second part of the film, the prison scenes raise crucial questions about Lee's representation of Malcolm. No explanations have been given as to why Lee chose not to portray Malcolm's brother and sister leading him to Islam, but instead created a fictional older black, male prisoner, Blaines (played by Albert Hall), who is tutor and mentor to Malcolm Little, educating him for critical consciousness, leading him to Islam. This element in the filmic narrative is the kind of distortion and misrepresentation of individual biography that can occur in fictional biographies and that ultimately violates the integrity of the life portrayed. Indeed, throughout the film Malcolm X's character is constructed as being without family, even though some member of his family was always present in his life. By presenting him symbolically as an "orphan" Lee not only erases the complex relations Malcolm had to black women in his life—his mother, his older sister—making it appear that the only important women are sexual partners, he makes it appear that Malcolm is more a lone, heroic figure, and by so doing is able to reinscribe him within a Hollywood tradition of heroism that effaces his deep emotional engagement with family and community. Lee insists, along with white producer Worth, that there is no revisionism in this film, that as Worth puts it, "We're not playing games with making up our opinion of the truth. We're doing *The Autobiography of Malcolm X.*" Yet the absence of any portrayal of significant family members and the insertion of fictional characters who never existed does indeed revise and distort the representation of Malcolm. That misrepresentation is not redeemed by Lee's uses of actual speeches or the placing of them in chronological order. He has boasted that this film will "teach," educate folks about Malcolm. In *By Any Means Necessary*, the book that describes the behind-the-scenes production of the film, Lee asserts: "I want our people to be all fired up for this. To get inspired by it. This is not just some regular bullshit Hollywood movie. This is life and death we're dealing with. This is a mind-set, this is what Black people in America have come through."

To insure that *Malcolm X* would not be a "regular bullshit Hollywood movie," Lee could have insisted on accuracy despite the fictionalized dramatic context. To do so might have meant that he would have had to make sacrifices, relinquishing complete control, allowing more folks to benefit from the project if need be. It might have meant that he would have to face the reality that masses of people, including black folks, will see this film and will never know the true story because they do not read or write, and that misrepresentations of Malcolm's life and work in the film version could permanently distort their understanding.

Knowing that he had to answer to a militant Nation of Islam, Spike Lee was much more careful in the construction of the character of Elijah Muhammad (portrayed by Al Freeman, Jr.), preserving the integrity of his spirit and work. It is sad that the same intensity of care was not given either the Malcolm character or the fictional portrait of his widow Betty Shabazz. Although the real-life Shabazz shared with Spike Lee that she and Malcolm did not argue (no doubt because what was deemed most desirable in a Nation of Islam wife was obedience), the film shows her "reading" him in the same bitchified way that all black female characters talk to their mates in Spike Lee films. Nor was Shabazz as assertive in romantic pursuit of Malcolm as the film depicts. As with the white character Sophia, certain stereotypical sexist images of black women emerge in this film. Women are either virgins or whores, madonnas or prostitutes—and that's Hollywood. Perhaps Spike Lee could not portray Malcolm's sister Ella, because Hollywood has not yet created a space for a politically progressive black woman to be imagined on the screen.

If Lee's version of Malcolm X's life becomes the example all other such films must follow then it will remain equally true that there is no place for black male militant political rage in Hollywood. For it is finally Malcolm's political militance that this film erases. (Largely because it is not the politically revolutionary Malcolm X that Lee identifies with.) Even though Lee reiterates in *By Any Means Necessary* that it was crucial that the film be made by an African American director "and not just any African American director, either, but one to whom the life of Malcolm spoke very directly," the film suggests Lee is primarily fascinated by Malcolm's fierce critique of white racism, and his early obsession with viewing racism as being solely about a masculinist phallocentric struggle for power between white men and black men. It is this aspect of Malcolm's politics that most resembles Lee's, not the critique of racism in conjunction with imperialism and colonialism, and certainly not the critique of capitalism. Given this standpoint it is not surprising that the major filmic moment that seeks to capture any spirit of political resistance shows Malcolm galvanizing men in the Nation of Islam to have a face-off with white men over the issue of police brutality. Malcolm is portrayed in these scenes as a Hitler type leader who rules with an iron, leather-clad fist. Downplaying the righteous resistance to police brutality that was the catalyst for this confrontation, the film makes it appear that it's a "dick thing"—yet another shoot out at the OK Corral—and that's Hollywood. But Hollywood at its best, for this is one of the more powerful scenes in the movie.

The closing scenes of *Malcolm X* highlight Lee's cinematic conflict, his desire to make a black epic drama that would both compete with and yet mirror white Hollywood epics made by white male directors he perceives as great, as well as his longing to preserve and convey the spirit and integrity of Malcolm's life and work. In the finale, viewers are bombarded, overloaded with images: stirring documentary footage, compelling testimony, and then the use of schoolchildren and Nelson Mandela to show that Malcolm's legacy is still important and has global impact. Tragically, by the time the film ends, all knowledge of Malcolm X as militant black revolutionary has been utterly erased, consumed by images. Gone is the icon who represents our struggle for black liberation, for militant resistance, and in its place we are presented with a depoliticized image with no substance or power. In *Heavenly Bodies: Film Stars and Society*, Richard Dyer describes the way in which Hollywood manipulates the black image with the intent to render it powerless.

> The basic strategy of these discourses might be termed deactivation. Black people's qualities could be praised to the skies, but they must not be shown to be effective qualities active in the world. Even when portrayed at their most vivid and vibrant, they must not be shown to do anything, except perhaps to be destructive in a random sort of way.

The Malcolm we see at the end of Spike Lee's film is tragically alone, with only a few followers, suicidal, maybe even losing his mind. The didacticism of this image suggests only that it is foolhardy and naive to think that there can be meaningful political revolution—that truth and justice will prevail. In no way subversive, *Malcolm X* reinscribes the black image within a colonizing framework.

The underlying political conservatism of Lee's film will be ignored by those seduced by the glitter and glamor, the spectacle, the show. Like many other bad Hollywood movies with powerful subject matter, *Malcolm X* touches the hearts and minds of folks who bring their own meaning to the film and connect it with their social experience. That is why young black folks can brag about the way the fictional Malcolm courageously confronts white folks even as young white folks leave the theater pleased and relieved that the Malcolm they see and come to know is such a good guy and not the threatening presence they may have heard about. Spike Lee's focus on Malcolm follows in the wake of a renewed interest in his life and work generated by hip-hop, by progressive contemporary cultural criticism, by political writings, and by various forms of militant activism. These counter-hegemonic voices are a needed opposition to conservative commodifications of Malcolm's life and work.

Just as these forms of commodification freeze and exploit the image of Malcolm X while simultaneously undermining the power of his work to radicalize and educate for critical consciousness, they strip him of iconic status. This gives rise to an increase in cultural attacks, especially in the mainstream mass media that now bombards us with information that seeks to impress on the public consciousness the notion that, ultimately, there is no heroic dimension to Malcolm, his life, or his work. One of the most powerful attacks has been that by white writer Bruce Perry. Even though Malcolm lets any reader know in his autobiography that during his hustling days he committed "unspeakable" acts (the nature of which would be obvious to anyone familiar with the street culture of cons, drugging and sexual hedonism), Perry assumes that his naming of these acts exposes Malcolm as a fraud. This is the height of white supremacist patriarchal arrogance. No doubt Perry's work shocks and surprises many folks who need to believe their icons are saints. But no information Perry reveals (much of which was gleaned from interviews with Malcolm's enemies and detractors) diminishes the power of the political work he did to advance the global liberation of black people and the struggle to end white supremacy.

Perry's work has received a boost in media attention since the opening of Spike Lee's movie and is rapidly acquiring authoritative status. Writing in the *Washington Post*, Perry claims to be moved by the film even as he seizes the moment of public attention to insist that Lee's version of Malcolm "is largely a myth" (the assumption being that his version if "truth"). Magazines such as the *New Yorker,* which rarely focus on black life, have highlighted their anti-Malcolm pieces. The December 1992 issue of *Harper's* has a piece by black scholar Gerald Early ("Their Malcolm, My Problem") which also aims to diminish the power of his life and work. Usually, when black folks are attempting to denounce Malcolm, they gain status in the white press. Unless there is serious critical intervention, Bayard Rustin's dire prediction that nonprogressive white folks will determine how Malcolm is viewed historically may very well come to pass. Those of us who respect and revere Malcolm as teacher, political mentor, and comrade must promote the development of a counter-hegemonic voice in films, talks, and political writings that will centralize and sustain a focus on his political contribution to black liberation struggle, to the global fight for freedom and justice for all.

Spike Lee's filmic fictive biography makes no attempt to depict Malcolm's concern for the collective well-being of black people, a concern that transcended his personal circumstance, his personal history. Yet the film shows no connection between his personal rage at racism and his compassionate devotion to alleviating the sufferings of all black people. Significantly, Spike Lee's *Malcolm X* does not compel audiences to experience emphatically the pain, sorrow, and suffering of black life in white supremacist, patriarchal culture. Nothing in the film conveys an anguish and grief so intense as to overwhelm emotionally. And nothing that would help folks understand the necessity of that rage and resistance. Nothing that would let them see why, after working all day, Malcolm would walk the streets for hours, thinking "about what terrible things have been done to our people here in the United States." While the footage of the brutal beating of Rodney King shown at the beginning of the film is a graphic reminder of "the terrible things," the pathos that this image evokes is quickly displaced by the neominstrel show that entertains and titillates.

As sentimental, romanticized drama, *Malcolm X* seduces by encouraging us to forget the brutal reality that created black rage and militancy. The film does not compel viewers to confront, challenge, and change. It embraces and rewards passive response—inaction. It encourages us to weep, but not to fight.

In his powerful essay "Everybody's Protest Novel," James Baldwin reminds readers that

> sentimentality, the ostentatious parading of excessive and spurious emotion, is the mark of dishonesty, the inability to feel; the wet eyes of the sentimentalist betray his aversion to experience, his fear of life, his arid heart; and it is always, therefore, the signal of secret and violent inhumanity, the mask of cruelty.

As Wallace warns, there is no place in Hollywood movies for the "seriousness of black liberation." Spike Lee's film is no exception. To take liberation seriously we must take seriously the reality of black suffering. Ultimately, it is this reality the film denies.

13.2 MICHAEL ERIC DYSON

The Culture of Hip-Hop

Michael Eric Dyson, a professor at the University of North Carolina, Chapel Hill, is an African American cultural critic who applies many tools of cultural criticism to a wide range of issues concerning African American life, racism, mass media, and popular culture. His work is part of a wider movement of African American critical scholarship, which includes the work of bell hooks (see her *Black Looks: Race and Representation* [South End, 1992]) and Cornel West (see his *Race Matters* [Beacon Press, 1993]).

The following selection is excerpted from an article that originally appeared in *Z Magazine* and is reprinted in *Reflecting Black: African-American Cultural Criticism* (University of Minnesota Press, 1993), a collection of Dyson's critical studies focusing on such pop culture phenomena as Spike Lee's films, Michael Jackson's musical performances, Michael Jordan's status as a sports icon, *The Cosby Show,* and the culture of hip-hop and rap music. Dyson's purpose is not to evaluate these African American cultural forms as "good or bad," or "beautiful or ugly," in relation to the popular culture of white America. In each study Dyson dissects the relationship of African American cultural practices to a social order that has been constructed around changing race relations.

Dyson does not regard the representation of blacks in popular culture as a simple matter of racist stereotyping. The culture of hip-hop—the focus of the following selection—is particularly revealing in this regard because it involves a complex and contradictory response by young African Americans to the structures of racist domination. Dyson argues that most white critical response to hip-hop culture, particularly to what is termed "gansta rap" with its explicit threats of violence against white authority, errs by ignoring this point. Hip-hop offers a field for the symbolic expression of the difficulties of growing up black in the United States. Hip-hop, Dyson suggests, is a hegemonic field of struggle over defining social identities and social relationships —in this case, race relations.

Key Concept: cultural resistance

*F*rom the very beginning of its recent history, hip-hop music—or rap, as it has come to be known—has faced various obstacles. Initially, rap was deemed a passing fad, a playful and ephemeral black cultural form that steamed off the musical energies of urban black teens. As it became obvious that rap was here to stay, a permanent fixture in black ghetto youths' musical landscape, the reactions changed from dismissal to denigration, and rap music came under attack from both black and white quarters. Is rap really as dangerous as many critics argue? Or are there redeeming characteristics to rap music that warrant our critical attention? I will attempt to answer these and other questions as I explore the culture of hip-hop.

Trying to pinpoint the exact origin of rap is a tricky process that depends on when one acknowledges a particular cultural expression or product as rap. Rap can be traced back to the revolutionary verse of Gil Scott-Heron and the Last Poets, to Pigmeat Markham's "Here Come de Judge," and even to Bessie Smith's rapping to a beat in some of her blues. We can also cite ancient African oral traditions as the antecedents to various contemporary African-American cultural practices. In any case, the modern history of rap probably begins in 1979 with the rap song "Rapper's Delight," by the Sugarhill Gang. Although there were other (mostly underground) examples of rap, this record is regarded as the signal barrier breaker, birthing hip-hop and consolidating the infant art form's popularity. This first stage in rap record production was characterized by rappers placing their rhythmic, repetitive speech over well-known (mostly R & B) black music hits. "Rapper's Delight" was rapped over the music to a song made by the popular seventies R & B group Chic, titled "Good Times." Although rap would later enhance its technical virtuosity through instrumentation, drum machines, and "sampling" existing records—thus making it creatively symbiotic—the first stage was benignly parasitic upon existing black music.

As rap grew, it was still limited to mostly inner-city neighborhoods and particularly its place of origin, New York City. Rap artists like Funky 4 Plus 1, Kool Moe Dee, Busy Bee, Afrika Bambaata, Cold Rush Brothers, Kurtis Blow, DJ Kool Hurk, and Grandmaster Melle Mel were experimenting with this developing musical genre. As it evolved, rap began to describe and analyze the social, economic, and political factors that led to its emergence and development: drug addiction, police brutality, teen pregnancy, and various forms of material deprivation. This new development was both expressed and precipitated by Kurtis Blow's "Those Are the Breaks" and by the most influential and important rap song to emerge in rap's early history, "The Message," by Grandmaster Flash and The Furious Five. The picture this song painted of inner-city life for black Americans—the hues of dark social misery and stains of profound urban catastrophe—screeched against the canvas of most suburban sensibilities:

> You'll grow up in the ghetto living second rate / And your eyes will sing a song of deep hate / The places you play and where you stay, / Looks like one great big alleyway / You'll admire all the number book takers / Thugs, pimps, and pushers, and the big money makers / Drivin' big cars, spendin' twenties and tens, And you want to grow up to be just like them / ... It's like a jungle sometimes / It makes me wonder how I keep from goin' under.

"The Message," along with Flash's "New York, New York," pioneered the social awakening of rap into a form combining social protest, musical creation, and cultural expression.

As its fortunes slowly grew, rap was still viewed by the music industry as an epiphenomenal cultural activity that would cease as black youth became bored and moved on to another diversion, as they did with break-dancing and graffiti art. But the successes of the rap group Run-D.M.C. moved rap into a different sphere of artistic expression that signaled its increasing control of its own destiny. Run-D.M.C. is widely recognized as the progenitor of modern rap's creative integration of social commentary, diverse musical elements, and uncompromising cultural identification—an integration that pushed the music into the mainstream and secured its future as an American musical genre with an identifiable tradition. Run-D.M.C.'s stunning commercial and critical success almost single-handedly landed rap in the homes of many black and non-black youths across America by producing the first rap album to be certified gold (five hundred thousand copies sold), the first rap song to be featured on the twenty-four-hour music video channel MTV, and the first rap album (1987's *Raising Hell*) to go triple platinum (3 million copies sold).

On *Raising Hell*, Run-D.M.C. showcased the sophisticated technical virtuosity of its DJ Jam Master Jay—the raw shrieks, scratches, glitches, and language of the street, plus the innovative and ingenious appropriation of hard-rock guitar riffs. In doing this, Run-D.M.C. symbolically and substantively wedded two traditions—the waning subversion of rock music and the rising, incendiary aesthetic of hip-hop music—to produce a provocative musical hybrid of fiery lyricism and potent critique. *Raising Hell* ended with the rap anthem, "Proud to Be Black," intoning its unabashed racial pride:

> Ya know I'm proud to be black ya'll, And that's a fact ya'll / ... Now Harriet Tubman was born a slave, She was a tiny black woman when she was raised / She was livin' to be givin', There's a lot that she gave / There's not a slave in this day and age, I'm proud to be black.

At the same time, rap, propelled by Run-D.M.C.'s epochal success, found an arena in which to concentrate its subversive cultural didacticism aimed at addressing racism, classism, social neglect, and urban pain: the rap concert, where rappers are allowed to engage in ritualistic refusals of censored speech. The rap concert also creates space for cultural resistance and personal agency, loosing the strictures of the tyrannizing surveillance and demoralizing condemnation of mainstream society and encougaging relatively autonomous, often enabling, forms of self-expression and cultural creativity.

However, Run-D.M.C.'s success, which greatly increased the visibility and commercial appeal of rap music through record sales and rap concerts, brought along another charge that has had a negative impact on rap's perception by the general public: the claim that rap expresses and causes violence. Tipper Gore has repeatedly said that rap music appeals to "angry, disillusioned, unloved kids" and that it tells them it is "okay to beat people up." Violent incidents at rap concerts in Los Angeles, Pittsburgh, Cleveland, Atlanta, Cincinnati, and New York City have only reinforced the popular perception that rap is intimately linked to violent social behavior by mostly black and Latino inner-city youth. Countless black parents, too, have had negative reactions to rap, and the black radio and media establishment, although not as vocal as Gore, have voted on her side with their allocation of much less airplay and print coverage to rap than is warranted by its impressive record sales.

Such reactions betray a shallow understanding of rap, which in many cases results from people's unwillingness to listen to rap lyrics, many of which counsel antiviolent and antidrug behavior among the youths who are their avid audience. Many rappers have spoken directly against violence, such as KRS-One in his "Stop the Violence." Another rap record produced by KRS-One in 1989, the top-selling *Self Destruction,* insists that violence predates rap and speaks against escalating black-on-black crime, which erodes the social and communal fabric of already debased black inner cities across America:

> Well, today's topic is self-destruction, It really ain't the rap audience that's buggin' / It's one or two suckers, ignorant brothers, Tryin' to rob and steal from one another / ... 'Cause the way we live is positive. We don't kill our relatives / ... Back in the sixties our brothers and sisters were hanged. How could you gangbang? / I never, ever ran from the Ku Klux Klan, and I shouldn't have to run from a black man, 'Cause that's / Self-destruction, ya headed for self-destruction.

Despite such potent messages, many mainstream blacks and whites persist in categorically negative appraisals of rap, refusing to distinguish between enabling, productive rap messages and the social violence that exists in many inner-city communities and that is often reflected in rap songs. Of course, it is difficult for a culture that is serious about the maintenance of social arrangements, economic conditions, and political choices that create and reproduce poverty, racism, sexism, classism, and violence to display a significant appreciation for musical expressions that contest the existence of such problems in black and Latino communities. Also disappointing is the continued complicity of black radio stations in denying rap its rightful place of prominence on their playlists. The conspiracy of silence and invisibility has affected the black print media, as well. Although rapper M. C. Shan believes that most antirap bias arises from outside the black community, he faults black radio for depriving rap of adequate airplay and laments the fact that "if a white rock 'n' roll magazine like *Rolling Stone* or *Spin* can put a rapper on the cover and *Ebony* and *Jet* won't, that means there's really something wrong."

In this regard, rap music is emblematic of the glacial shift in aesthetic sensibilities between blacks of different generations, and it draws attention to the severe economic barriers that increasingly divide ghetto poor blacks from middle- and upper-middle-class blacks. Rap reflects the intraracial class division that has plagued African-American communities for the last thirty years. The increasing social isolation, economic hardship, political demoralization, and cultural exploitation endured by most ghetto poor communities in the past few decades have given rise to a form of musical expression that captures the terms of ghetto poor existence. I am not suggesting that rap has been limited to the ghetto poor, but only that its major themes and styles continue to be drawn from the conflicts and contradictions of black urban life. One of the later trends in rap music is the development of "pop" rap by groups like JJ Fad, The Fat Boys, DJ Jazzy Jeff and The Fresh Prince, and Tone Loc. DJ Jazzy Jeff and

The Fresh Prince, for example, are two suburbanites from South West Philadelphia and Winfield. (For that matter, members of the most radical rap group, Public Enemy, are suburbanites from Long Island.) DJ Jazzy Jeff and The Fresh Prince's album, *He's the DJ, I'm the Rapper,* sold over 3 million copies, boosted by the enormously successful single "Parents Just Don't Understand." This record, which rapped humorously about various crises associated with being a teen, struck a chord with teenagers across the racial and class spectra, signaling the exploration of rap's populist terrain. The Fresh Prince's present success as the star of his own Quincy Jones–produced television series is further testimony to his popular appeal.

Tone Loc's success also expresses rap's division between "hardcore" (social consciousness and racial pride backed by driving rhythms) and "pop" (exploration of common territory between races and classes, usually devoid of social message). This division, while expressing the commercial expansion of rap, also means that companies and willing radio executives have increasingly chosen pop rap as more acceptable than its more realistic, politically conscious counterpart. (This bias is also evident in the selection of award recipients in the . . . rap category at the annual Grammy Awards.) Tone Loc is an L.A. rapper whose first single, "Wild Thing," sold over 2 million copies, topping *Billboard's* "Hot Singles Chart," the first rap song to achieve this height. Tone Loc's success was sparked by his video's placement in heavy rotation on MTV, which devotes an hour on Saturdays to "Yo! MTV Raps," a show that became so popular that a daily hour segment was added.

The success of such artists as Tone Loc and DJ Jazzy Jeff and The Fresh Prince inevitably raises the specter of mainstream dilution, the threat to every emergent form of cultural production in American society, particularly the fecund musical tradition that comes from black America. For many, this means the sanitizing of rap's expression of urban realities, resulting in sterile hip-hop that, devoid of its original fire, will offend no one. This scenario, of course, is a familiar denouement to the story of most formerly subversive musical genres. Also, MTV's avid acceptance of rap and the staging of rap concerts run by white promoters willing to take a chance on rap artists add further commentary to the sad state of cultural affairs in many black communities: the continued refusal to acknowledge authentic (not to mention desirable) forms of rap artistry ensures rap's existence on the margins of many black communities.

Perhaps the example of another neglected and devalued black musical tradition, the blues, can be helpful for understanding what is occurring among rap, segments of the black community, and mainstream American society. The blues now has a mostly young white audience. Blacks do not largely support the blues through concert patronage or record buying, thus neglecting a musical genre that was once closely identified with devalued and despised people: poor southern agrarian blacks and the northern urban black poor, the first stratum of the developing underclass. The blues functioned for another generation of blacks much as rap functions for young blacks today: as a source of racial identity, permitting forms of boasting and asserting machismo for devalued black men suffering from social degradation, allowing commentary on social and personal conditions in uncensored language, and fostering the ability to transform hurt and anguish into art and commerce. Even in its heyday, however, the blues existed as a secular musical genre over against the religious traditions that saw the blues as "devil's music" and the conservative black cultural perspectives of the blues as barbaric. These feelings, along with the direction of southern agrarian musical energies into a more accessible and populist soul music, ensured the contraction of the economic and cultural basis for expressing life experience in the blues idiom.

Robert Cray's . . . success in mainstreaming the blues perhaps completes the cycle of survival for devalued forms of black music: it originates in a context of anguish and pain and joy and happiness, it expresses those emotions and ideas in a musical language and idiom peculiar to its view of life, it is altered as a result of cultural sensibilities and economic factors, and it undergoes distribution, packaging and consumption for leisurely or cathartic pleasure through concert attendance or record buying. Also, in the process, artists are sometimes removed from the immediate context and original site of their artistic production. Moreover, besides the everyday ways in which the music is used for a variety of entertainment functions, it may occasionally be employed in contexts that undermine its critique of the status quo, and it may be used to legitimize a cultural or social setting that, in negative ways, has partially given rise to its expression.

Interestingly, a new wave of rap artists may be accomplishing this goal, but with foreboding consequences. For example, N.W.A. (Niggaz With Attitudes) reflects the brutal circumstances that define the boundaries within which most ghetto poor black youth in Los Angeles must live. For the most part they —unlike their socially conscientious counterparts Public Enemy, Boogie Down Productions, and Stetsasonic—have no ethical remove from the violence, gangbangin', and drugs in L.A.'s inner city. In their song "——Tha Police," N.W.A. gives a sample of their reality:

> . . . A young nigger got it bad 'cause I'm brown / And not the other color, so police think, / They have the authority to kill a minority / . . . Searchin' my car looking for the product, / Thinkin' every nigger is sellin' narcotic / . . . But don't let it be a black and a white one, / 'Cause they'll slam ya down to the street top, / Black police showin' out for the white cop.

Such expressions of violence certainly reflect the actual life circumstances of many black and Latino youth caught in the desperate cycle of drugs and gangs involved in L.A. ghetto living. N.W.A. celebrates a lethal mix of civil terrorism and personal cynicism. Their attitude is both one answer to, and the logical outcome of, the violence, racism, and oppression in American culture. On the other hand, their vision must be criticized, for the stakes are too high for the luxury of moral neutrality. Having at least partially lived the life they rap about, N.W.A. understands the viciousness of police brutality. However, they must also be challenged to develop an ethical perspective on the drug gangs that duplicate police violence in black-on-black crime. While rappers like N.W.A. perform an invaluable service by rapping in poignant and realistic terms about urban underclass existence, they must be challenged to expand their moral vocabulary and be more sophisticated in their understanding that description alone is insufficient to address the crises of black urban life. . . .

Also problematic is the sexist sentiment that pervades so much of rap music. It is a rampant sexism that continues to mediate the relations within the younger black generation with lamentable intensity. While it is true that rap's sexism is indeed a barometer of the general tenor and mood that mediates black male-female relations, it is not the role of women alone to challenge it. Reproach must flow from women *and* men who are sensitive to the ongoing sexist attitudes and behavior that dominate black male-female relationships....

Fortunately, many of the problems related to rap—particularly with black radio, media, and community acceptance—have only fostered a sense of camaraderie that transcends in crucial ways the fierce competitive streak in rap (which, at its best moments, urges rappers on to creative musical heights). While the "dis" rap... is alive and well, the overall feeling among rap artists that rap must flourish outside the sanctions of traditional means of garnering high visibility or securing record sales has directed a communal energy into the production of their music. The current state of affairs has also precipitated cooperative entrepreneurial activity among young black persons. The rap industry has spawned a number of independent labels, providing young blacks (mostly men) with experience as heads of their own businesses and with exposure as managers of talent, positions that might otherwise be unavailable to them. Until recently, rap flourished, for the most part, outside of the tight artistic and economic constraints imposed by major music corporations. Although many independent companies have struck distribution deals with major labels—such as Atlantic, MCA, Columbia, and Warner Brothers—it has usually been the case, until the late 1980s, that the inexperience of major labels with rap, coupled with their relatively conservative musical tastes, has enabled the independent labels to control their destinies by teaching the major music corporations invaluable lessons about street sales, the necessity of having a fast rate of delivery from the production of a record to its date of distribution, and remaining close to the sensibilities of the street, while experimenting with their marketing approach in ways that reflect the diversification of styles in rap.

Rap expresses the ongoing preoccupation with literacy and orality that has characterized African-American communities since the inception of legally coerced illiteracy during slavery. Rap artists explore grammatical creativity, verbal wizardry, and linguistic innovation in refining the art of oral communication. The rap artist, as Cornel West has indicated, is a bridge figure who combines the two potent traditions in black culture: preaching and music. The rap artist appeals to the rhetorical practices eloquently honed in African-American religious experiences and the cultural potency of black singing/musical traditions to produce an engaging hybrid. They are truly urban griots dispensing social and cultural critique, verbal shamans exorcising the demons of cultural amnesia. The culture of hip-hop has generated a lexicon of life that expresses rap's B-boy/B-girl worldview, a perspective that takes delight in undermining "correct" English usage while celebrating the culturally encoded phrases that communicate in rap's idiom.

Rap has also retrieved historic black ideas, movements, and figures in combating the racial amnesia that threatens to relegate the achievements of the black past to the ash heap of dismemory. Such actions have brought a renewed sense of historical pride to young black minds that provides a solid base for racial self-esteem. Rap music has also focused renewed attention on black nationalist and black radical thought. This revival has been best symbolized by the rap group Public Enemy. Public Enemy announced its black nationalism in embryonic form on their first album, *Yo! Bum Rush the Show,* but their vision sprang forward full-blown in their important *It Takes a Nation of Millions to Hold Us Back.* The album's explicit black nationalist language and cultural sensibilities were joined with a powerful mix of music, beats, screams, noise, and rhythms from the streets. Its message is provocative, even jarring, a précis of the contained chaos and channeled rage that informs the most politically astute rappers. On the cut "Bring the Noise," they intone:

> We got to demonstrate, come on now, they're gonna have to wait / Till we get it right / Radio stations I question their blackness / They call themselves black, but we'll see if they'll play this / Turn it up! Bring the noise!

Public Enemy also speaks of the criminality of prison conditions and how dope dealers fail the black community. Their historical revivalism is noteworthy, for instance, as they rap on "Party for Your Right to Fight":

> Power Equality / And we're out to get it / I know some of you ain't wit' it / This party started right in '66 / With a pro-Black radical mix / Then at the hour of twelve / . . . J. Edgar Hoover, and he coulda' proved to 'ya / He had King and X set up / Also the party with Newton, Cleaver, and Seale / . . . Word from the honorable Elijah Muhummad / Know who you are to be Black / . . . the original Black Asiatic man.

Public Enemy troubled even more sociocultural waters with their Nation of Islam views, saying in "Don't Believe the Hype":

> The follower of Farrakhan / Don't tell me that you understand / Until you hear the man.

Such rap displays the power and pitfalls associated with the revival of earlier forms of black radicalism, nationalism, and cultural expression. The salutary aspect of the historical revival is that it raises consciousness about important figures, movements, and ideas, prompting rappers to express their visions of life in American culture. This renewed historicism permits young blacks to discern links between the past and their own present circumstances, using the past as a fertile source of social reflection, cultural creation, and political resistance.

On the other hand, it has also led to perspectives that do not provide *critical* reflection on the past. Rather, many rappers attempt to duplicate the past without challenging or expanding it. Thus, their historical insight fails to illumine our current cultural problems as powerfully as it might, and the present generation of black youth fails to benefit as fully from the lessons that it so powerfully revives. This is an unfortunate result of the lack of understanding and communication among various segments of the black community, particularly along generational and class lines, problems symbolized in the black community's response to rap. Historical revival cries out for contexts that render the past understandable and usable. This cannot occur if large segments of the black community continue to be segregated from one of the most exciting cultural transformations occurring in contemporary American life: the artistic expression, cultural exploration, political activity, and historic revival of hip-hop artists. . . .

Rap is a form of profound musical, cultural, and social creativity. It expresses the desire of young black people to reclaim their history, reactivate forms of black radicalism, and contest the powers of despair and economic depression that presently besiege the black community. Besides being the most powerful form of black musical expression today, rap projects a style of self into the world that generates forms of cultural resistance and transforms the ugly terrain of ghetto existence into a searing portrait of life as it must be lived by millions of voiceless people. For that reason alone, rap deserves attention and should be taken seriously; and for its productive and healthy moments, it should be promoted as a worthy form of artistic expression and cultural projection and an enabling source of black juvenile and communal solidarity.

Michael Eric
Dyson

PART SIX

Media and Globalization

On the Internet . . .

Sites appropriate to Part Six

The technology page of the Freedom Forum Online offers news stories of international importance and covers a variety of issues, such as freedoms, law, and fairness.

```
http://www.freedomforum.org/technology/
    welcome.asp/
```

At this site, you can find information about the media systems found throughout the world.

```
http://www.yahoo.com/regional/countries/
```

This page by the Voice of the Shuttle is for humanities research and contains links to many other resources. Click on "Media Theory" for the Media Studies page, which is particularly useful for information on international, comparative, and global media issues.

```
http://humanitas.ucsb.edu/shuttle/
    cultural.html
```

CHAPTER 14 Perspectives on Development

14.1 EVERETT M. ROGERS

Communication and Development: The Passing of the Dominant Paradigm

By the time Everett M. Rogers edited *Communication and Development: Critical Perspectives* (Sage Publications, 1976), from which the following selection is taken, modernization had been criticized for the Western bias that it assumed. In the following selection, Rogers critiques modernization, but he also explores many of the emerging pathways to development that were being explored throughout the 1970s. He discusses his work, and that of others, on the use of *diffusion studies* to better understand how new media were adopted within the specific cultural contexts in changing societies.

The following selection effectively summarizes a shift in communication research that saw a revolution in a *paradigm,* or a way of thinking about a problem. Throughout the 1970s the field of development studies began to explore different methods, theories, and approaches toward understanding the role of media in changing societies. Some of those changes were precipitated by a growing tension articulated by people in the Third World and nonaligned nations in the wake of a new world information order.

Rogers is currently a professor in and chair of the Department of Communication and Journalism at the University of New Mexico. He is a prolific writer, and he has published many significant works in the areas of diffusion research, cultural change, and comparative international studies. Some of his books are *The Media Revolution in America and in Western Europe*, coedited with Frances Balle (Ablex, 1985); *Communication Technology: The New Media in Society* (Free Press, 1986); and *A History of Communication Study: A Biographical Approach* (Free Press, 1994).

Key Concept: diffusion and social change

THE DOMINANT PARADIGM
OF DEVELOPMENT[1]

Through the late 1960s, a dominant paradigm ruled intellectual definitions and discussions of development and guided national development programs. This concept of development grew out of certain historical events, such as the Industrial Revolution in Europe and the United States, the colonial experience in Latin America, Africa, and Asia, the quantitative empiricism of North American social science, and capitalistic economic/political philosophy. Implicit in the ruling paradigm were numerous assumptions which were generally thought to be valid, or at least were not widely questioned, until about the 1970s.

Definitions of development centered around the criterion of the rate of economic growth. The level of national development at any given point in time was the gross national product (GNP) or, when divided by the total population in a nation, per capita income. Although there was a certain amount of intellectual discomfort with per capita income as the main index of development, especially among noneconomists, alternative measures and definitions of development had relatively few proponents. . . .

CRITICISMS OF THE DOMINANT
PARADIGM OF DEVELOPMENT

In short, the old paradigm implied that poverty was equivalent to underdevelopment. And the obvious way for less developed countries to develop was for them to become more like the developed countries.[2]

It was less obvious that the industrially advanced nations largely controlled the "rules of the game" of development. That most of the scholars writing about development were Westerners. That balances of payment and monetary exchange rates were largely determined in New York, London, and Washington. And the international technical assistance programs sponsored by the rich nations, unfortunately, made the recipients even more dependent on the donors. These gradual lessons took some time to emerge and to sink into intellectual thought.

*Everett M.
Rogers*

Theoretical writings about modernization in this period after World War II generally followed an "individual-blame" logic and may have been overly narrow and ethnocentric in a cultural sense. Examples are the works of Walt Rostow (1961), Everett Hagen (1962), and David McClelland (1961), all drawing more or less on the earlier writings of Max Weber. The leading theorists were Westerners, and there often was a rather inadequate data base to support their conceptualizations. Portes (1973) criticized this Western and person-blame bias: "There is, I believe, a profoundly ethnocentric undercurrent in characterizations of modern men in underdeveloped countries. An invariably positive description obviously has something to do with similarity of these individuals with the self-images and values of researchers." Many economists insisted that their discipline consisted of a universally valid body of theory, applicable to both. One might ask rhetorically how different economic theory would be if Adam Smith had been Chinese or a Sikh. "Economic theorists, more than other social scientists, have long been disposed to arrive at general propositions and then postulate them as valid for every time, place, and culture" (Myrdal, 1968: 16).

After reviewing the history and nature of the dominant paradigm and contrasting it with the reality of Asian development, Inayatullah (1975, 1976) concludes: "The Western development theory . . . is not an adequate intellectual framework . . . as it suffers from an overemphasis on the role of factors internal to Asian societies as causes of underdevelopment to the exclusion of external factors."

Continuing underdevelopment was attributed to "traditional" ways of thinking and acting of the mass of individuals in developing nations. The route to modernization was to transform the people, to implant new values and beliefs.

The dominant paradigm sought to explain the transition from traditional to modern societies. In the 1950s, the traditional systems were the nations of Latin America, Africa, and Asia. All were relatively poor, with GNPs averaging about one-fifth or less those of the developed nations of Europe and North America. Almost all were former colonies (the African and Asian nations more recently so), and most were still highly dependent on the developed nations for trade, capital, technology, and, in many cases, for their national language, dress, institutions, and other cultural items. It seemed that the developing nations were less able to control their environment and were more likely to be influenced by unexpected perturbations in their surroundings. In these several respects, the developing countries seemed to be somehow "inferior" to the developed nations, but of course with the hoped-for potential of catching up in their overall development. The developed nations of the West were taken as the ideal toward which the developing states should aspire.[3] The development of traditional societies into modern ones was a contemporary intellectual extension of social Darwinian evolution.

Western models of development assumed that the main causes of under-development lay within the underdeveloped nation rather than external to it. The causes were thought to be (1) of an individual-blame nature[4] (peasants were traditional, fatalistic, and generally unresponsive to technological innovation) and/or (2) of a social-structural nature within the nation (for example, a tangled government bureaucracy, a top-heavy land tenure system, and so on). Western intellectual models of development, and Euro-American technical assistance programs based on such models, were less likely to recognize the importance of external constraints on a nation's development: international terms of trade, the economic imperialism of international corporations, and the vulnerability and dependence of the recipients of technical assistance programs. The dominant paradigm put the blame for underdevelopment on the developing nations rather than on the developed countries, or even jointly on both parties.

During the 1950s and 1960s, this assumption of blame-attribution was widely accepted not only in Euro-America, but also by most government leaders and by many social scientists in Latin America, Africa, and Asia. Many of the latter were educated in the United States or Europe, or at least their teachers and professors had been. And the power elites of developing countries were often coopted to the "within-blame" assumption by international technical assistance agencies or by multinational corporations.

International power in the 1950 to 1970 era was concentrated in the hands of the United States, and this helped lead international efforts in the development field to follow a within-blame causal attribution and to reinforce it as an assumption. As the U.S. corner on world power began to crack in the 1970s (at least, in the UN General Assembly), so did faith in the dominant paradigm of development. The "oil blackmail" of Euro-America following the Yom Kippur War in 1973 not only redistributed millions of dollars from developed to certain developing countries, but it dramatically demonstrated that developing countries could redefine the social situation of international finance....

ALTERNATIVE PATHWAYS TO DEVELOPMENT

In the very late 1960s and the 1970s, several world events combined with the intellectual critiques just described and began to crack the prior credibility of the dominant paradigm.

1. The ecological disgust with environmental pollution in the developed nations led to questioning whether they were, after all, such ideal models for development. Pollution problems and overpopulation pressures on available resources helped create doubts about whether unending economic growth was possible or desirable, and whether high technology was the most appropriate engine for development.

2. The world oil crisis demonstrated that certain developing countries could make their own rules of the international game and produced some suddenly rich developing nations. Their escape from national poverty, even though in part at the expense of other developed countries, was a lesson to their neighbors in Latin America, Asia, and Africa. No longer were these nations willing to accept prior assumptions that the causes of underdevelopment were mainly internal.

3. The sudden opening of international relations with the People's Republic of China allowed the rest of the world to learn details of her pathway to development. Here was one of the poorest countries, and the largest, that in two decades had created a miracle of modernization. A public health and family planning system that was envied by the richest nations. Well-fed and clothed citizens. Increasing equality. An enviable status for women. And all this was accomplished with very little foreign assistance and presumably without much capitalistic competition. China, and to a lesser extent Cuba, Tanzania, and Chile (in the early 1970s), suggested that there must be alternatives to the dominant paradigm.

4. Finally, and perhaps most convincing of all, was the discouraging realization that development was not going very well in the developing countries that had closely followed the paradigm. However one might measure development in most of the nations of Latin America, Africa, and Asia in the past 25 years, not much had occurred. Instead, most "development" efforts have brought further stagnation, a greater concentration of income and power, high unemployment, and food shortages in these nations. If these past development programs represented any kind of test of the intellectual paradigm on which they were based, the model has been found rather seriously wanting.

Elements in the New Development

From these events grew the conclusion that *there are many alternative pathways to development.* While their exact combination would be somewhat different in every nation, some of the main elements in this newer conception began to emerge.

1. *The equality of distribution of information, socioeconomic benefits, and so forth.* This new emphasis in development led to the realization that villagers and urban poor should be the priority audience for development programs and, more generally, that the closing of socioeconomic gaps by bringing up the lagging sectors was a priority task in many nations.

2. *Popular participation in self-development planning and execution, usually accompanied by the decentralization of certain of these activities to the village level.* Development came to be less a mere function of what national governments did *to* villagers, although it was recognized that perhaps some government assistance was necessary even in local self-development. An example is the "group planning of births" at the village level in the People's Republic of China, where the villagers decide how many babies they should have each year and who should have them. Another illustration of decentralized development was occurring in Tanzania, where social mobilization activities by the political party,

the army, and by radio listening groups help provide mass motivation for local participation in development activities. As President Julius K. Nyerere stated: "If development is to benefit the people, the people must participate in considering, planning, and implementing their development plans" (in Tanganyika African National Union, 1971). People cannot *be* developed; they can only develop themselves. And this realization was demonstrated not only in communist and socialist nations, but also in such capitalistic settings as Korea and Taiwan.

3. *Self-reliance and independence in development, with an emphasis upon the potential of local resources.* Mao Tse-tung's conception of national self-development in China is an illustration of this viewpoint, including the rejection of foreign aid (after some years of such assistance from Russia), as well as the decentralization of certain types of development to the village level (as mentioned previously). Not only may international and binational technical assistance be rejected, but so too are most external models of development—leading to a viewpoint that every nation, and perhaps each village, may develop in its own way. If this occurs, of course, standardized indexes of the rate of development become inappropriate and largely irrelevant.

4. *Integration of traditional with modern systems, so that modernization is a syncretization of old and new ideas, with the exact mixture somewhat different in each locale.* The integration of Chinese medicine with Western scientific medicine in contemporary China is an example of this approach to development. Acupuncture and antibiotics mix quite well in the people's minds as shown by this experience. Such attempts to overcome the "empty vessels fallacy" remind us that tradition is really yesterday's modernity. Until the 1970s, development thinking implied that traditional institutions would have to be entirely replaced by their modern counterparts. Belatedly, it was recognized that these traditional forms could contribute directly to development. "African countries should not imitate the patterns of development of the industrialized countries, but adopt development patterns suited to African indigenous traditional and cultural patterns" (Omo-Fadaka, 1974).

By the mid-1970s it seemed safe to conclude that the dominant paradigm had "passed," at least as the main model for development in Latin America, Africa, and Asia. Of course, it would still be followed enthusiastically in some nations, but even then with certain important modifications. The Chinese model, or at least particular components, had been (and were being) adopted elsewhere when nations were willing to forego certain advantages of liberal democracy for the tighter government control that they thought to be necessary to maintain nationhood over tribal, religious, or regional factions. While Cambodia, Vietnam, and perhaps Tanzania were influenced by the Chinese route to development, they seem far from very exact replicas. So multiple and varied models of development were not in style.

What Is Development?

Out of the various criticisms of the dominant paradigm of development grew a questioning of the concept of development from one that had centered on materialistic, economic growth to a definition that implied such other valued ends as social advancement, equality, and freedom. These valued qualities should be determined by the people themselves through a widely participatory process.... Development is change toward patterns of society that allow better realization of human values, that allow a society greater control over its environment and over its own political destiny, and that enables its individuals to gain increased control over themselves (Inayatullah, 1967: 101).

We summarize these newer conceptions of development by defining development as *a widely participatory process of social change in a society, intended to bring about both social and material advancement (including greater equality, freedom, and other valued qualities) for the majority of the people through their gaining greater control over their environment* (Rogers, 1975b).[5]

Thus the concept of development has been expanded and made much more flexible, and at the same time more humanitarian, in its implications....

CRITICISMS OF COMMUNICATION IN DEVELOPMENT

By the late 1960s and the 1970s a number of critical evaluations were being made of the mass communication role in development. Some scholars, especially in Latin America, perceived the mass media in their nations as an extension of exploitive relationships with U.S.-based multinational corporations, especially through the advertising of commercial products. Further, questions were asked about the frequent patterns of elite ownership and control of mass media institutions in Latin America and the influence of such ownership on the media content. The 1965–1975 decade saw a rising number of military dictatorships in Latin America, Africa, and Asia, and these governments stressed the media's propaganda role, decreasing the public's trust in mass communication.

Communication researchers also began to question some of their prior assumptions, becoming especially critical of earlier inattention to (1) the content of the mass media, (2) the need for social-structural changes in addition to communication if development were to occur, and (3) the shortcomings of the classical diffusion-of-innovations viewpoint which had become an important explanation of microlevel development.

Inattention to Media Content

[M]ass media exposure on the part of individuals in developing nations [is] highly correlated with their modernization, as expressed by their exhibiting modern attitudes and behavior. This seemed logical because the mass media were thought to carry generally pro-development messages (Rogers with Svenning, 1969).

However, a strange anomaly was encountered. When individuals in developing nations who had adopted an innovation like a weed spray, a new crop variety, or family planning, were asked the sources/channels through which they had learned about the new idea, *the mass media were almost never reported.* Interpersonal channels with peers totally predominated in diffusing the innovation. A possible explanation of this anomaly seemed to lie in the contents of the media messages, which investigation showed seldom to carry specific messages about the innovation (such as what it is, where to obtain it and at what cost, and how to use it), even though there was much content promoting national development in a general sense (such as news of a new highway being constructed, appointment of a new minister of agriculture, and so on). So when the media content was analyzed it was found to contain very little attention to the technological innovations that were diffusing; they spread most frequently through interpersonal communication (1) from government development workers to their clients and (2) among peers in the mass audience....

Need for Structural Change As Well As Communication

Even in the days of the dominant paradigm, it was realized that the contribution of mass communication to development was often limited by the social structure, by the unavailability of resource inputs, and the like. There was much more, of course, to development than just communication and information. But there was at least some hope that by raising the public's aspirations for modernization, pressure was created toward changing some of the limiting factors on development.

By the 1970s, it was becoming apparent that the social-structural restraints on development were often unyielding to the indirect influences of the media or even to more direct intervention. Under these conditions, it was realized that mass communication's role in development might be much more diminished than previously thought. And communication research was designed to determine just how limiting the structure might be on the development effects of mass communication. Illustrative of such researches is Grunig's (1971) investigation among Colombian farmers; he concluded that "communication is a complementary factor to modernization and development ... it can have little effect unless structural changes come first to initiate the development process." Such studies helped to modify the previously enthusiastic statements by communication scholars about the power of the media.

Diffusion of Innovations and Development

One of the most frequent types of communication research in developing nations dealt with the diffusion of innovations.... In such research, an idea perceived as new by the receiver—an innovation—is traced as it spreads through a system (Rogers with Shoemaker, 1971). The innovation is usually a technological idea, and thus one can see that past diffusion research fits well with the dominant paradigm's focus on technology and on its top-down communication to the public.

During the 1960s, there was a tremendous increase in the number of diffusion studies in developing countries; these researches were especially concerned with the spread of agricultural innovations and of family planning methods. In fact, there were about 500 family planning diffusion studies in India alone (Rogers, 1973). Many of them left much to be desired in scientific rigor or in the originality of their design.

A number of criticisms of the assumptions and directions of diffusion research appeared in the 1970s: Marceau (1972), Grunig (1971), Golding (1974), Havens (1972), and Beltrán (1975), as well as the articles by Díaz Bordenave and Röling et al.... These critiques centered on the pro-innovation bias of such research and on the propensity for diffusion to widen the socioeconomic gaps in a rural audience. Out of such frank criticism came a number of modifications in the classical diffusion model and in the research designs utilized (such as more field experiments and network analysis), and these newer approaches are now being tried (Rogers, 1973, 1976).

After a tour of 20 U.S. communication research centers, Nordenstreng (1968) criticized North American scholars for their "hyperscience," which he explains as due to the fact that "American communication research has grown up in an atmosphere of behaviorism and operationalism, which has made it correct in technical methodology but poor in conceptual productivity." This comment on communication research in the United States may also apply to diffusion research. Such inquiry often sided unduly with the source "against" the receiver, perhaps a reflection of the one-way linear model of communication and of the mechanistic/atomistic components approach of much communication research.

NOTES

1. The following section is adapted from Rogers (1975b).
2. Karl Marx in *Das Kapital* stated: "the country that is more developed industrially only shows, to the less developed, the image of its own future." Lerner (1967: 115) stated: "Indeed, the Western model is virtually an inevitable baseline for Asian development planning because there is no *other* model which can serve this purpose." This predominance of the Western paradigm of development was probably correct at the time of Lerner's writing.
3. An assumption criticized by Portes (1973): "Modernity as a consequence of Western structural transformations may have little to do with, or be in fact detrimental to, causes of development in Third world nations."
4. Caplan and Nelson (1973) argue that social scientists are more likely to accept an individual-blame definition of a social problem that they investigate than a system-blame definition. For instance, unemployment and poverty are considered to be due to laziness, not to the unavailability of work and to blocked opportunities.
5. Note how my thinking has changed as to the definition of development in the past seven years: "*Development* is a type of social change in which new ideas are introduced into a social system in order to produce higher per capita incomes and levels of living through more modern production methods and improved social organization" (Rogers with Svenning, 1969).

*Chapter 14
Perspectives on
Development*

BELTRAN S., L. R. (1975) "Research ideologies in conflict." J. of Communication 25: 187–193.

CAPLAN, N. and S. D. NELSON (1973) "On being useful: the nature and consequences of psychological research on social problems." Amer. Psychologist 28: 199–211.

GOLDING, P. (1974) "Media role in national development: critique of a theoretical orthodoxy." J. of Communication 24: 39–53.

GRUNIG, J. E. (1971) "Communication and the economic decision-making processes of Colombian peasants." Econ. Development & Cultural Change 18: 580–597.

HAGEN, E. (1962) On the Theory of Social Change. Urbana: Univ. of Illinois Press.

HAVENS, A. E. (1972) "Methodological issues in the study of development." Sociologia Ruralis 12: 252–272.

INAYATULLAH (1976) "Western, Asian, or global model of development," in W. Schramm and D. Lerner (eds.) Communication and Change in the Developing Countries: Ten Years After. Honolulu: Univ. of Hawaii/East-West Center Press.

____ (1967) "Toward a non-Western model of development," in D. Lerner and W. Schramm (eds.) Communication and Change in the Developing Countries. Honolulu: Univ. of Hawaii/East-West Center Press.

McCLELLAND, D. C. (1961) The Achieving Society. New York: Van Nostrand.

MARCEAU, F. J. (1972) "Communication and development: a reconsideration." Public Opinion Q. 36: 235–245.

MYRDAL, G. (1968) Asian Drama. New York: Pantheon.

NORDENSTRENG, K. (1968) "Communication research in the United States: a critical perspective." Gazette 14: 207–216.

OMO-FADAKA, J. (1974) "Develop your own way." Development Forum 2.

PORTES, A. (1973) "The factorial structure of modernity: empirical replications and a critique." Amer. J. of Sociology 79: 15–44.

ROGERS, E. M. (1976) "Where we are in understanding the diffusion of innovations," in W. Schramm and D. Lerner (eds.) Communication and Change in the Developing Countries: Ten Years After. Honolulu: Univ. of Hawaii/East-West Center Press.

____ (1975b) "The anthropology of modernization and the modernization of anthropology." Reviews in Anthropology 2: 345–358.

____ (1973) Communication Stategies for Family Planning. New York: Free Press.

____ with F. F. SHOEMAKER (1971) Communication of Innovations: A Cross-Cultural Approach. New York: Free Press.

ROGERS, E. M., with L. SVENNING (1969) Modernization Among Peasants: The Impact of Communications. New York: Holt, Rinehart & Winston.

ROSTOW, W. W. (1961) The Stages of Economic Growth. New York: Cambridge Univ. Press.

14.2 J. MARTÍN-BARBERO

The Processes: From Nationalisms to Transnationals

The growth of and interest in comparative international studies in the 1970s witnessed many different approaches toward understanding how the media has influenced national change. In Latin America, for example, the diverse regions, nations, and cultural issues defied one uniform "pathway" to development.

In his book *Communication, Culture, and Hegemony: From the Media to Mediations* (Sage Publications, 1987), Jesus Martín-Barbero carefully investigates the different approaches toward development taken throughout the nations of Latin America. In the following excerpt from that book (which was translated by Elizabeth Fox and Robert A. White), Martín-Barbero describes "unequal" development throughout Latin America. The different histories, economies, politics, and cultural components contributed a different set of conditions amenable to development in each country. Foreign trade, adaptability to foreign-produced technology and media content, and supportive infrastructures in each region of Latin America had much to do with how well the media served the purpose of change.

It is clear from the following selection that there is no one correct path to change and that a number of factors can and will influence development in any country. This selection describes historical conditions for development, but it also focuses on how the media can play both ideological and political roles in social change.

Martín-Barbero is a professor at the University del Valle, Cali, in Colombia, and a former president of the Latin American Association of Communication Research.

Key Concept: development, dependency, and colonization in national development and social change

A DIFFERENCE THAT IS MORE
THAN UNDERDEVELOPMENT

Any reference to a 'Latin America' beyond the original unity imposed by the Spanish conquest and domination lies necessarily in the other 'visible unification' that J.L. Romero speaks of in his study of the region's incorporation into the processes of industrial modernization and international trade.... If it is true that the different Latin American nationalisms took different routes and rates of development, starting in the 1930s, this diversity of patterns, as a whole, began to undergo a profound transformation.

After the 1930s the possibility of 'becoming a nation' in the *modern* sense of this term hinged on establishing a national market, something that, in turn, depended on adjusting to the needs and requirements of the international market. The fact that Latin America's access to modernization was through political-economic dependency revealed its processes of 'unequal development', the basic inequality on which capitalist development rests. This dependency also revealed the contradictions of its 'simultaneous discontinuities' in which Latin America lives and carries out its modernization (Lechner, 1981: 12). These discontinuities occur at three levels: firstly, the processes of becoming a state and a nation are often out of phase with each other so that some states become nations much later and some nations delay a long time in becoming a state; secondly, the 'deviant' way in which the popular classes enter the political system and become part of the process of forming the nation state—more as the result of the general crisis of the system, setting the popular classes in confrontation with the state, than as a product of the autonomous development of their own organizations; and, thirdly, the fact that the mass media play not just an ideological but a *political* role in the incorporation of the masses into the nation....

THE MASS MEDIA IN THE FORMATION
OF NATIONAL CULTURES

... The focus on mediations and social movements has shown the necessity of distinguishing two quite different stages in the introduction of media institutions and the constitution of mass culture in Latin America. In the first stage, which stretches from the 1930s to the end of the 1950s, the efficacy and social significance of the mass media do not lie primarily in the industrial organization and the ideological content, but rather in the way the popular masses have appropriated the mass media and the way the masses have recognized their identity in the mass media. Of course, economics and ideology influence how the media functioned, but to discover the meaning and ideology of economic structure we must go deeper to the conflict which in that historical moment gave structure and dynamism to the social movements, namely, the conflict between the masses and the state and the resolution of this conflict in the nationalist populisms and populist nationalisms.

During this first stage, the decisive role of the mass media was their ability to convey the challenge and the appeal of populism, which transformed the mass into the people and the people into the nation.…

The second stage in the constitution of mass culture in Latin America began after 1960. When the model of import substitution 'reached the limits of its coexistence with the archaic sectors of society' and populism could no longer be sustained without radicalizing the first social reforms, the myth and strategies of *development* with its technocratic solutions and encouragement of a consumer society began to replace the worn out populist policies (Intercom, 1981: 21). At this point, the political function of the media was removed and the economic function took over.…

A Cinema in the Image of the People

Let us begin our analysis of the role of media in the period from 1930 to the late 1950s with that media experience which is the clearest and most easily identifiable expression of Latin American nationalism and mass, popular culture: the cinema of Mexico. According to Edgar Morin, until 1950, film was the backbone of mass culture (1977); and Mexican film performed this function in a special way for the mass culture of Latin America. Film was the centre of gravity of the new culture because

> the Mexican and the Latin American public in general did not experience cinema as a specific artistic or industrial phenomenon. The fundamental reason for the success of film was structural and touched the centre of life. In films this public saw the possibility of experimenting, of adopting new habits and of seeing codes of daily life reiterated and dramatized by the voices they would like to have or hear. They did not go to the movies to dream; they went to learn. Watching the styles and fashions of the actors, the public learned to recognize and transform itself finding solace, comfort and, secretly, exaltation. (Monsiváis, 1976: 446)

… In the process of permitting people to see themselves, film formed them into a national body; not in the sense of giving them a nationality but in the way they experienced being a single nation. Along with all of its mystifications and chauvinistic attitudes, film provided an identity for the urban masses which diminished the impact of cultural conflicts and enabled them for the first time to conceive of the country in their own image. Monsiváis sums up the ambiguity and force of this national image in five verbs: people *recognize* themselves in film with a recognition that is not passive but that *transforms* them; for a people coming from the Revolution this meant to *pacify* and *resign* oneself, but also to secretly *move upwards*. In other words, it was an experience not only of consolation but of revenge.…

Mexican film had three stages of development. Between 1920 and 1940 movies rewrote the popular legends. Pancho Villa was passed through the traditional models and myths of banditry which made cruelty a form of generosity. The Revolution appeared more as a backdrop than a storyline—the heroic death of the rebel, the assault on the rich hacienda, the march of the soldiers—appear again and again as the scene of the film action. The struggle against injustice was transformed from a fight for an ideal into a fight motivated by loyalty to the leader. This melodramatic transformation stripped the Revolution of its political meaning, but did not become reactionary until the second stage, after the 1930s, when the *ranchero* appeared, making *machismo* the expression of a nationalism that by now had become folklore. This was a *machismo* that was no longer a way that the people could understand and confront death but a compensatory mechanism for social inferiority. *Machismo* becomes the 'excess that redeemed the original sin of poverty ... a plaintive cry for recognition' (Monsiváis, 1977: 31–2).

After the 1940s, Mexican films began to diversify their subject matter. We find now the urban comedy in which the neighbourhood replaced the countryside as the place where the old values found refuge and where the personal relations cut off by the city could be re-created....

From the Creole Circus to Radio Theatre

In Latin America the Argentinians became the masters of radio drama....

But the early development of a technical infrastructure in Argentina tells only half the story. It attributes to the medium alone something that must be traced back to a sociocultural process and 'connects' radio with the country's long tradition of popular cultural expressions. In Argentina, the 'literary' country of Latin America *par excellence,* the disdain of writers for radio lasted many years and marked the 'distance between a media filled with possibilities and a cultural structure riddled with surprising paradoxes' (Rivera, 1980b: 383). Radio became the domain of the popular, the realm of the oral....

The true importance of radio theatre in Argentina was its bridging role between the cultural traditions of the people and mass culture. Patricia Terrero views the function of Argentine radio theatre in terms of its continuity, examining 'its proximity to certain expressions of the national, popular imagination and its relationship to mythification, popular beliefs, and the formation of the social and cultural identity of the popular sectors' (1983: 5). Terrero's analysis looks beyond the radio medium itself to the experiences of listeners and the strategies of reception. It means taking into consideration the presence of the audiences in the studios where the radio dramas were transmitted, the provincial road tours of theatre groups presenting summaries of the broadcast dramas, listeners' letters, etc. This approach to analysis of radio brings to the fore once again the relation of the forms of listening to radio and the way people collectively listened to reading which, for so long, was customary in the popular culture. Fernando Ortiz makes this relationship explicit in his study of the evolution from collective reading to radio listening in the tobacco factories (Ortiz, 1947)....

The Argentine radio theatre had several stages of development. In the first stage, dialogue was minimal, and presentations were built around songs, ballads and country music. In a second stage, beginning after 1935, the radio theatre found its own form. The theatrical companies came together, music was used dramatically and as a function of the plot, and the plots used themes from the gaucho tradition or from history. Gaucho literature was represented mainly in the works of González Pulido who collected the legends, verses and stories in a mythology of the outlaw, with their models of social protest and demands. The historical themes, the work of Héctor Pedro Blomberg, were based on archetypal characters among which the *Amores célebres de América Latina*, portraying the lives of the heroines of the independence movement, were especially popular with the public. The production of the radio theatre diversified after the mid-1940s in a way similar to what occurred with Mexican films. Although the gaucho legends continued to be important, two new themes entered the repertoires: detective stories and children's stories, most of which were adaptations. 'Love stories' appeared with enormous popular success. Most of these were produced in Argentina, but they already contain some of the characteristic stereotypes that would be used in the melodramas of the culture industry. An important aspect of this subgenre is that many of the producers were women. Studies carried out with women on the significance of radio theatre for its audience have revealed to what extent the interpretation by the public activates the keys to meaning which connect radio theatre with expressions of culture and elements of popular life. Before becoming Peronism, Argentine populism was a way of plugging mass culture into a wide family of existing expressions of popular culture. How significant it is that Evita became much more than just an actress through her role in a radio theatre company!

The Urban Legitimation of Black Music

'To firmly stabilize a music expression from a popular background as a means of getting control of a language that reconciles a nation horizontally across geography and vertically across classes'. With this phrase Mario de Andrade described the role of music in the nationalizing project of Brazil in the 1930s. Perhaps in no other country of Latin America did music express so strongly the secret link between the integrating 'ethos' and the 'pathos' in the universe of feeling as it did in Brazil. This link made music especially appropriate for populist uses. What happened in Brazil with black music, especially its aberrant, off-course path to social and cultural legitimation, reveals the inability of both intellectual and populist currents of thought to comprehend the web of contradictions and seductions forming the relationship between popular and mass, the urban beginnings of populism.

The path that led Brazilian music from the samba chorus—with this ritual space: the *terreiro de candomblé*—to the radio and to records, passes through a multiplicity of manifestations that can be organized in terms of two historical moments: the social incorporation of the productive physical 'gestural style' of the black people and the cultural legitimation of the musical rhythm that this gesture contained. National populism accompanied and in some ways made possible the passage from one stage to the next. Populism, however, was overwhelmed by a process that was too big for its political framework, that defied both the authoritarian pedantry of the Enlightenment tradition and purist idealism of Romanticism.

At the historical point when political independence was attempting to gather strength by radically changing the economy, slave labour began to be less

productive and less of an economic advantage than free labour. The opening up
of the national market to the whole population broke down the traditional isolation of the plantation, revealing the productivity of the physical gestural style
of the blacks at the social and national level. The conclusion was reached that
if black people produce as much as the immigrant, then let us encourage their
productivity by giving them what they are worth. The physical gesture of the
blacks, however, was not just an external manifestation. The social incorporation of the black gestural style set in motion a process at another level. 'To the
extent that the blacks survived exclusively by physical labour, it was in the "gesture", in the physical manifestation of their humanity, that they imposed their
culture' (Squeff and Wisnik, 1983: 43).

A link, unknown to whites, emerged between the gestures of physical
work and the rhythm of the dance, the symbiosis of work and rhythm that was
the survival strategy of the slave. Black people, using an almost hypnotic ca-
dence, were able to survive backbreaking work; fatigue and effort became less
painful when trapped in a frenetic rhythm. It was an intoxication without al-
cohol but heavy with fantasy and dreams. This does not attempt to reduce all
meaning of the dance to work, but tries to reveal in the 'indecency' of black
gestures and movements not just an 'unabashed' relationship with sex but a
process of work that is at the heart of the dance, in its rhythm. The dialectic of
this double indecency is what truly scandalized 'society'. It did not, however,
prevent this society from accepting the profitable productivity of blacks, but
this acceptance was kept on the economic level. For an acceptance of blacks at
a cultural level, a political crisis would be necessary....

In order to become urban, black music had to cross two ideological barriers. The first of these barriers was the populist concept of culture which insisted
that the only authentically popular culture was that which could be traced back
in its essence and roots, not to the actual historically verified origins, but to
an idealized origin in a rural, peasant context. [See for example, Burke, 1978.]
Because of this illusion, populism could never resolve the contradiction between its romantic notion of the people and the reality of the urban masses
—rootless, politicized, bitterly resentful, with degraded tastes, cosmopolitan—
characteristics and aspirations which populism was somehow supposed to assume as its own. A second quite contrary ideological barrier for black music was
the intellectual tradition of the Enlightenment which identified culture with fine
arts, an art which emphasized its distance and distinction, careful social limits
and discipline to dramatize its difference from the new, undisciplined and un-
classifiable musical manifestations of the city. Popular music could became art
only when it was elevated, distanced from its immediate environment and put
into the form, for example, of a sonata....

The Birth of the Popular Mass Press

... Of all the media the press has the most written history, not only because
it is the oldest, but because it is where those who write about history receive
cultural acknowledgement. The history of the press looks mainly at the 'serious
press'. When it examines the sensationalist press, it does so almost exclusively

in economic terms: the growth of circulation and advertising. According to this type of journalism history, it is impossible to speak of politics, much less of culture, when one is dealing with newspapers that are nothing more than a business and scandal-mongering, exploiting the ignorance and low passions of the masses. In contrast to this concept that denies the sensationalist press any political meaning, another type of historical analysis has begun to introduce questions from the sociology of culture and political science. . . .

A process of political change beginning in the 1920s culminated in 1938 with the formation of the Popular Front and the participation of the parties of the left in the government. During these years the Chilean press changed radically. The workers' press became the left-wing newspapers, and the sensationalist daily papers appeared. The first change was basically a shift in the workers' papers from a purely local setting to an interest in national topics or a presentation of local topics in a national language. This implied at least a potential new group of followers for the left-wing discourse: the mass public. The form of discourse of these newspapers, however, remained within the constraining matrix of the rationalistic Enlightenment, performing a function of popular educational formation and political propaganda. The objectives continued to be the education of the populace—raising their political consciousness—and to represent the interests of the masses in relation to the state. But that representation was limited to those issues that the Marxist left considered political or potentially political. Their concept of politics—and therefore of popular representation—did not include other actors than the working class and employers. Such a political press was concerned only with the conflicts that emerged out of the relationships of production—the clash between labour and capital—and only with the factory and labour union. It was a heroic vision that ignored daily life, personal subjectivity and sexuality as well as the cultural practices of the people such as their story telling, their religious customs and the fund of knowledge of the people. All this was ignored or, worse still, stigmatized as sources of alienation and obstacles in political struggle. . . .

In the United States and Europe the appearance of the sensationalist press is normally 'explained' as a function of the development of printing technology and the competition between the big newspapers. In Latin America, when the sensationalist press is studied, it is to provide a clear example of the penetration of North American models that, by putting profits ahead of any other criteria, have corrupted the region's tradition of serious journalism. . . .

Chile, like many other Latin American countries since the second half of the nineteenth century, has had a great many popular publications which, like the *gacetas* in Argentina (Rivera, 1980a) or the literature of the *cordel* in Brazil (Luyten, 1981), mixed together news, poetry, and popular narratives. In Chile, these were called *liras populares,* and after the First World War they began to gain in news value what they lost in the quality of their poetry. Thus, they began to 'assume the functions of journalism at a historical moment when the experiences of popular culture were on the threshold of mass culture' (Sunkel, 1985: 80). In this prototype of popular journalism, written mainly for oral distribution, that is, to be read, declaimed or sung in public places such as the markets, the railway station or in the street, we find the beginnings of the sensationalist press. Already they have the large headlines calling attention to the main story, the prominent graphics illustrating the story, the melodramatization of a discourse gripped by violence and the macabre, and the exaggerated fascination with the stars of sports and entertainment....

The issue of sensationalism calls attention to traces in the discourse of the press of another cultural matrix, much more symbolic and dramatic, which have their origins in the practices and moulds of popular culture. This matrix does not operate on the basis of concepts and generalizations but expresses itself in images and concrete situations. Rejected by the world of official education and serious politics, it survives in the world of the culture industry, and from this base it continues to exercise a powerful appeal to the popular....

DEVELOPMENTALISM AND TRANSNATIONALIZATION

... What is the role of the mass media in the new phase of Latin American modernization? What changes have occurred in the role media plays in the creation of a mass society and in relation to the masses themselves? ...

A New Meaning of Massification

In contrast to what happened during the period of the populisms, when the 'mass' meant the ambiguous political weight of the masses in the city and their explosive charge of social realism, in the years of developmentalism, mass came to connote exclusively the means for homogenization and control of the masses. Massification was felt even where there were no masses. The media, which formerly were mediators between the state and the masses, between the rural and the urban, between tradition and modernity, increasingly tended to become only a simulation or even the instrument of deactivation of these relationships. Although the media continued to 'mediate', and although simulation was already at the root of their social role, something was beginning to change. It was not an abstract change in the sense that the media became the message. It was a change in the same direction as development, the schizophrenic growth of a society whose reality did not coincide with its demands. Only with such changes in meaning could communication be measured in the quantitative circulation of newspapers and the number of radio and television receivers. Indeed, measurement became the cornerstone of development. The experts of the Organization of American States could proclaim, 'Without communication there is no development.' Now the radio dial became saturated with stations in cities with no running water, and slums sprouted TV aerials. Indeed, the TV aerials were symptomatic of changes that had occurred in the concept of mass.

REFERENCES

Burke, P. (1978) *Popular Culture in Early Modern Europe.* Aldershot: Wildwood.

Intercom (1981) 'Documento básico', in Márquez de Melo, J. (ed.), *Populismo e Comunicaçao*. São Paulo: Cortez.

Lechner, N. (ed.) (1981) *Estado y Política en América Latina*. Mexico: Siglo XXI.

Luyten, J.M. (1981) *A Literatura de Cordel em São Paulo*. São Paulo.

Monsiváis, C. (1976) 'Notas sobre la cultura mexicana en el siglo XX', in *Historia General de México,* vol. IV. Mexico: El Colegio de México.

Monsiváis, C. (1977) *Amor Perdido*. Mexico: Era.

Morin, E. (1977) *O Espirito do Tempo, 2: Necrose*. Rio de Janeiro: Forense Universitária.

Ortiz, F. (1947) *Cuban Counterpoint: Tobacco and Sugar*. New York: Knopf.

Rivera, J.B. (1980a) *El Escritor y la Industria Cultural*. Buenos Aires: CE de AL.

Rivera, J.B. (1980b) *La Forja del Escritor Profesional*. Buenos Aires: CE de AL.

Squeff, E. and Wisnik, J.M. (1983) *O Nacional e o Popular na Cultura Brasileira: Música*. São Paulo: Brasiliense.

Sunkel, G. (1985) *Razón y Pasión en la Prensa Popular*. Santiago: ILET.

Terrero, P. (1983) 'Radioteatro y teleteatro', mimeo. Buenos Aires.

CHAPTER 15

The Homogenization of Culture

15.1 ANTHONY SMITH

Media Globalism in the Age of Consumer Sovereignty

As media corporations merge and ownership takes on a more international scope, it is likely that the content of the media will also change to reflect fewer alternative viewpoints. In the following essay, Anthony Smith, former director of the British Film Institute in London and current president of Magdalen College, Oxford, discusses the impact that concentration of information and entertainment businesses has on Europe's media landscape. The effect of increasing corporate control throughout the world, Smith writes, is an effect of the twentieth century.

While the content of popular culture is changed by these new ownership structures, the relationship between governments and the media also changes. Smith identifies earlier government-media relationships that established regulatory frameworks and boundaries for media. Today, however, he indicates that bureaucratic changes have contributed to some social instability that will undoubtedly affect the political realities of the future. What constitutes "information" may undergo a significant change so that the media support only those ideas that are politically "safe" for the global media owners. This, of course, would lead to a new concept of the "global empire of information."

As you read the following selection from "Media Globalism in the Age of Consumer Sovereignty," *Gannett Center Journal* (Fall 1990), consider whether or not national identity will survive in an age of global media ownership. Might we be on the threshold of global media? If so, what will become of culture in the future? Might there be one overriding global culture that dominates all others? Or will global ownership of the media industries be yet one more option for content in a world that is increasingly tied together by communication technology?

Key Concept: global media and corporate control

The long West European search throughout the 1980s for a cultural counterpart to the continent's movement in politics culminated in 1989 in the publication of an important European Community Green Paper, *Television Without Frontiers*. Its purpose was to allow the national programming of Community members to circulate throughout the Community—in short, "a common market for broadcasters and audiences." The plan was clearly designed to help shift European television towards commercialism and away from its traditional public service nature. Accordingly, a crucial tenet was the effort "to secure the free flow of information, ideas, opinions and cultural activities within the Community."

Yet the Green Paper also called for the creation of a trade barrier to limit American entertainment imports—in the name of national cultural "preservation." To the powerful lobbyists in the Motion Picture Association of America, the Community's talk of quotas was simply a blow at their legitimate commercial interests. To the Europeans, the MPAA appeared just to want to grab a vast new market which might cover for Hollywood's uncontrollable cost spiral while simultaneously turning Europe's 350 million people into cultural vassals of America.

... There is a widely shared European fear that transnationalism in all its forms, even when it issues from the EC offices in Brussels, is inimical to the whole tradition of nationally based broadcasting to national audiences. But the opposition is not primarily nationalist in character; rather, it springs from the same source as the widespread private and public fear of globalization.

In many countries today—including some in Central Europe—information media are passing into the hands of non-residents. The (originally) Australian Rupert Murdoch, for example, now enjoys unchallenged ownership of newspapers in Britain, the United States and elsewhere, not to mention the burgeoning transnational satellite station Sky Television. Whole sections of the entertainment industry, traditionally part of national, city, local, regional, or ethnic political and social life and manners, are passing into the control of managements whose outlook is exclusively global. Is this just a facet of the ending of the nationalist phase in world history? Is the ownership of large enterprises irrelevant to a company's ability to respond to the cultural needs of specific audiences? Indeed, is the oft-expressed anxiety about media internationalization based on a nostalgic, sentimentalized and patronizing view of popular culture?

Such an anxiety is rooted in the belief that the world is losing the logic of indigenousness and therefore a kind of authenticity; that, where our hope was that the media would act as means of reconciliation, they are turning into instruments of homogenization; and that technology will, in the forms it has actually taken, deprive us of a home under the pretense of giving us a larger one.

Globalization—the concentration of a substantial number of the world's information and entertainment businesses into a series of huge international companies—has been under way for over a century. This is especially true of national news agencies (wire services) and magazine firms, which even in the 19th century were starting to shrink into a tiny group, dominated by French, German, British and American firms that divided the world according to the spheres of influence of their respective governments. The anxiety this provoked was a straightforwardly political one; To what extent would those governments influence the shaping of news values or even deliberately manipulate the information that circulated around the globe?

The problem today, just as irreversible, is also more intractable. The worldwide extension of three familiar processes—chain ownership of newspapers, cross-ownership between media, and acquisition of media by ordinary industrial concerns—means that national governments cannot easily enforce even the modest rules some have adopted to regulate or impede these processes (though even free enterprise governments on the whole do not like major newspapers passing into foreign hands: Australia recently foiled Robert Maxwell's attempt to purchase a paper there).

The paradox of the present phase of corporate change is that it is occurring at precisely the moment in technological history when it has become extremely cheap and, in practical terms, easier than it has been for several decades for new firms in all media to enter the market. It costs little to start a radio station, and much less than it did in the 1960s to start a local television station; publishing has been transformed by the arrival of desktop computer equipment; book stores have multiplied throughout the developed world, making it much easier for authors to find their readers. Digitization is similarly transforming video production and recording; through cable it is becoming annually easier, in theory, to acquire whole television channels for specialist services, and it is relatively cheap to reach audiences within a given city or region. Deregulation, espoused by politicians in country after country, should be guaranteeing this great opening of the information and entertainment market. It is the age of consumer sovereignty.

The end of the 20th century ought to be witnessing a transformation of the media industries into hundreds and hundreds of small companies. That anyway is what was predicted at the start of the computer revolution. This was supposed to be the end of "mass" society.

At present we can see—often in the same societies at the same time—a process of Hollywood-style cultural homogenization on the one hand, and on the other a paradoxical determination by governments to encourage new competitive enterprises. To some extent the proliferation is indeed taking place. While the new giants are gobbling up the smaller giants everywhere from Buenos Aires and Hollywood to Paris and Tokyo, an army of small-scale entrepreneurs are also establishing themselves. In France, the talk is of Hersant, Maxwell, Berlusconi—but also of Teletel, of scores of new radio stations, of a new cohort of artisanal filmmakers. But everywhere the talk is of their vulnerability; of rationalization and takeover, of small independents taking over tiny ones or all of them having to take shelter together in the bosom of a Behemoth. In Britain the 400-odd small production companies conjured into existence by Channel Four in the 1980s still, a decade later, have only a tiny number of potential buyers. The new cable and satellite channels are in practice commissioning very little work, the BBC has barely started to honor its commitment to buy from the independent sector, and Channel Four itself will soon be competing for the sale of its own advertising time and may be drawn into the competition for large audiences and cheap production.

The process of globalization also opens up the issue of ethnic and political pluralism. The new ubiquity, via satellite and cable, of television channels originating in America, Britain and perhaps France can only be at the expense of the smaller nations and ethnic groups within them. Of course, the promise always embedded in the new technology was that entrepreneurs within minority audiences would find ways of making commercial channels work within the compass of a small ethnic or national community, but beyond a few vaunted experiments this has yet to occur. Politics, not markets, seems to be the only effective savior of minority cultures.

One cannot adduce audience figures in support of such a contention—rather the reverse. The marketplace gives expression, almost unanswerably, to the needs of *consumers*. But perhaps as *citizens* we hold preferences that our behavior as consumers does not reveal. The simple fact that we cheerfully used to buy ozone-unfriendly hair sprays does not mean that we were freely deciding that we wanted a polluted atmosphere—merely that the consumer choices available were not organized to help us articulate the more collectively beneficial choice.

It has always been the task of the press and broadcasting to act as conduits for the flow of information and debate. Democratic societies could not really exist in the absence of such a facility. But the Western media consist of enterprises that function within a market economy, and markets are prone to concentrations of control and the amalgamation of competing forces for mutual protection. The new climate provides enormous advantages and opportunities for companies that combine previous rival information businesses. Even media institutions that operate from the public sector of market-oriented societies are caught up in the vortex of fresh corporate temptations.

But democracies tend to feel that citizens should be exposed—in reality as well as in high-minded theory—to a multiplicity of sources. Ongoing amalgamation throws this essential pluralism into jeopardy; while it can be argued that the sheer dynamic of the open market compensates by creating new pluralistic openings, it is increasingly possible for people to fail in practice to be exposed to competing views and outlooks. In the new culture of diversity a person has to choose his or her sources of competing intellectual influence rather than to chance upon them willy-nilly.

Today, in the era of privatization and the worldwide scramble for the acquisition and control of media industries, we need to understand more clearly how the industrial giants who control vast areas of the information and entertainment media affect the evolution of national and world cultures. And, even more urgently, we have to inquire whether individual societies should seek to limit or channel the process of global amalgamations in the interest of maintaining fundamental freedoms.

The method by which newspapers are manufactured and distributed, for example, has always had profound implications for what might be called the moral condition of journalism. Newspapers, like all the other, newer media, have always had to balance not only their commercial and intellectual roles but also the overlapping and sometimes conflicting needs of readers and advertisers, proprietors and editors, sources and governments. Press freedom, however essential, has never been absolutely available; at any moment it depends, obviously, upon prevailing constitutional and legal arrangements, and the attitude of the current government—but also on the way that the medium as an enterprise is being managed.

Governments (and other institutions) have always seen the media as potentially rival sources of authority. They have concerned themselves with the nature of the cultural forms (pamphlets, books, Bibles, newspapers, the novel) which emerged from the press and from the other technologies of information and entertainment.

The regulatory systems that were developed to govern modern communication devices derive ultimately from the bureaucracy for licensing and registration which grew up to cope with the newspaper. In electronic systems for delivering information we are witnessing a kind of ultimate extension of periodicity, for in electronic mode the information source is permanently present; we have learned since the arrival of radio and television what had already been suspected in the late 19th century—that information media shape the realities of a society, they interact with the processes of government, and provide the terms of the relationship between governors and governed, even (perhaps especially) in totalitarian societies.

Regulatory systems evolved to police, select, control or otherwise demarcate the boundaries between media; to prevent concentrations of what was deemed to be excessive power; to calculate the consequences of media operations in order to counteract them; to make certain that those in control of specific media command the trust of government; to guarantee forms of economic competition sufficient to prevent the evolution of monopolies. It is this regulatory paraphernalia that has largely drawn the map of the media world today. In the United States, for example, the doctrine of localness governing the franchising of broadcast outlets and the legal limits of the number of local stations in a network, added to the controls on cross-ownership of media and other doctrines governing monopoly, fairness and business practices, have between them created the American broadcasting system as we know it. In turn, the changing of the regulatory systems now taking place in many countries is today bringing about a re-working of all the boundaries on the world's media map.

Each technological transformation has occasioned its own appropriate organizational devices, what one might call its "enterprise formation." The characteristic form of the newspaper of the 18th century was a printing house that took in jobbing work and added books and periodical publications as a way of using its capacity to the full; that, in turn, was determined by the working practices of a highly organized work force divided into minute craft specialties. The newspaper of the 19th century required far more working capital to operate, with its growing teams of correspondents attached to the new technologies of the telegraph, and began progressively to detach itself from the general printing business. It became more technology specific. Newspaper owners remained close to the world of political patronage, their independence being secure only when their readership was sufficient to cover their increasing costs.

The 20th century newspaper has required still larger quantities of capital —but it has found itself through its dependence on advertising deeply implicated in the general market economy. The newspaper since World War I has ceased to be dependent on the economics of the political world, earning its income from its citizen readers, and has become more wholeheartedly an instrument of advertising. The newspaper and the magazine (and broadcasting, too, in some societies) quickly became engines of the 20th-century consumer economy, their information fueling the growth of tastes and fashions, their internal economics greatly influenced by the cycles of trade. Writing in 1922, Walter Lippmann said, "The real problem is that the readers of a newspaper, unaccustomed to paying the cost of news gathering, can be capitalized only by turning them into circulation that can be sold to manufacturers and merchants. And those whom it is most important to capitalize are those who have the most money to spend." Lippmann was noticing, as many others were at the time, the nature of the new tension with which the newspaper editor had to live.

Since the 1920s we have seen the growth of group ownership of newspapers, and the reduction of competition among daily newspapers within given markets. Since the early years of the century there have been repeated dire prophecies of the loss of an essential disinterestedness in journalism as a result of the growth of newspaper combines, and many fitful attempts to stop newspaper proprietors from gobbling one another up. But the process has seemed relentless except where governments have provided financial subsidy and/or vigorous regulation.

The new economic system establishing itself in the media industries throughout the world entails an emphasis on the ownership of information itself rather than just of the mechanically produced forms which information takes. Narrative fiction, for example, plays a part in publishing, in magazines, in cinema and television, and the same work can find a place in all of these media in a world market. Publishers want to be in a position to exploit a work of talent across the whole media landscape; they have come to fear the consequences of being excluded from an audience if they do not have a finger in every kind of media pie. Furthermore, it is becoming easier in technological terms to become involved in a wider range of media. Transnational media empires are thus coming into being to exploit new opportunities and as a protection against possible losses of opportunity. Newspapers, film businesses, radio, television and publishing are passing into the same institutional hands.

In many countries such linkages have long been thought to be a danger to society, and in some cases the law has sought to prevent them. But to turn back the present tide altogether would be to stand in the path of the inevitable —and the commercially necessary. Audiences appear to want the new diversity of information which is the counterpart of the new concentrations in media ownership. A viewer can choose to see a film on video, on cable or satellite or (later) on conventional television, or can read the book instead, possibly published by the same company. The new enabling technologies are arriving as a result of other wider changes in telephony, in electronics, in the exploitation of space. National legal systems are helpless to prevent the arrival of alien television channels from unregulated satellites, and in any case markets are no longer containable inside the inherited national forms. It is impossible to regulate the media and information industries in one way and the markets for apples in another.

Right across the industries of information, whether based on text or image, whether based on paper or cathode ray tube, these unfamiliar contemporary economics now prevail, and politicians and regulators see it as their duty to help, through deregulatory measures, to force margins down and thus serve the consumer. Together with computerization, deregulation is one of the engines of globalization.

The result is that all of the companies concerned are driven towards self-protective merger, scale economy, constant self-reorganization, and a search for the ultimate in rationalized markets. Few really quarrel with the legal, institutional and political motivations behind this activity; however, no one has calculated its moral consequences. It is possible that some will conclude that there aren't any, that information goods are fundamentally the same as others and that we all benefit from the results, whatever they may be, of the enforced efficiencies of deregulation and a more competitive economy.

But this change is also producing consequences that tend to conflict with other socially desirable objectives, among these the maintenance of diverse sources of ownership in the companies that produce our information and entertainment.

So great are the institutional and corporate changes which are flowing from these fundamental shifts in technology and in the prevailing conceptions of communication that it is difficult as yet to discern all of the implications for society. It is hard to see where the fundamental requirements of a society actually lie. We are used to a pattern of newspapers that work in mutual competition and in competition with radio and television. We are used to cinema and television living in a state of mutual tension, and in joint competition with video. We think of newspapers and book publishing as completely different businesses. In particular we have been brought up to see the newspaper as a lightly or entirely unregulated medium and television as highly regulated, with obligations of impartiality imposed because of its powerful political presence, its highly persuasive nature.

However, we are moving into an era in which the distinction between the corporations that own these different entities is impossible to draw. The processes of the new technologies and the pressures generated in the new regulatory environment are suggesting to managers of these enterprises that survival and further growth depend upon mergers and alliances across the political divides. That which nations are powerless to prevent does not of course automatically become desirable; but it does become necessary to ask again what the former prohibitions were intended to protect or secure and to see whether society can achieve the same objective by some easier means.

There has been little research into what one might call the intellectual consequences of media monopoly. In a modern society with its many sources of potential influence upon opinion, does a decline in competition between newspapers, say, really matter? In 1989 the London-based Broadcasting Research Unit carried out a comparative opinion survey of the readers of the three News International-owned British national daily newspapers, the *Times*, the *Sun* and *Today*, with those of other journals. The three papers concerned have all consistently taken a broadly similar editorial line on a number of public issues affecting the future of the media, and thus of great moment to News International itself. All of these papers have supported the abolition of the license fee on which the BBC has traditionally been funded; they have celebrated in banner headlines the launching of the first satellite channels available in Britain; and they have argued that the BBC should be obliged to take advertising. (The continued existence of an adequately funded BBC could mean that a large portion of the British audience at any moment would be watching something other than Rupert Murdoch's Sky TV).

The BRU found that readers of the papers concerned are markedly more likely to be "critical of terrestrial television; to welcome new channels; and to oppose the license fee"—a profile that is not consistent with these papers' readers' political leanings, nor with their demographic profile. The editor of one of the papers agreed that its intention was "to destabilize the set-up" of British television. Should a media enterprise use the influence of one of its parts (and that inflated by multiple title ownership) to pursue the interests of another? The readers, it may be argued, know what they are reading and ought to be able to discount arguments—perfectly legitimately advanced—which they suspect of being tendentious. But can they? Do they? The argument that they may choose no longer pertains in the era of the information of abundance, for a democratic society requires that contradictory opinions should actually reach a large proportion of people, not merely that these opinions are somewhere available. That is the heart of the problem. In the old and familiar media environment, dominated to a great extent by the public sector bodies, the problem was concealed, or perhaps just ignored. We are living through the aftermath of mass society; the new media environment is one in which it is decreasingly likely that entire populations will be subject to the same shared flows of information and participate in the same pool of common allusion. Yet behind the diversities are new homogeneities in information and entertainment a circumstance allied to the emergence of the new media empires and the new generation of media moguls.

Take, for example, the recent wave of transactions that have taken place within the international film industry. In practice there are seven film libraries and film studios that fill the needs of the world cinema market. They are all based in the United States and have been accumulating their stores of movies for up to 70 years.

In the 1980s these studios have discovered that more and more sales income is available outside the United States as a result of the arrival in country after country of the electronic and consumer revolution. VCRs are everywhere. Acquiring a film library is like discovering an overlooked seam in a[n] unused gold mine. But the U.S. domestic market remains the most profitable in the world.

There are, however, five or six countries in the world where there are entrepreneurs who wish now to enter the U.S. film market, and to do so they realize that the easiest route—perhaps the only one—is to acquire one of the existing seven "majors." That is really the constituting principle of globalization—the desire to enter an established media market which is wholly clogged by indigenous occupants, one of which is available for merger or acquisition. That is why companies located thousands of miles apart have suddenly discovered the potential benefits of globalizing, even in cultural industries which have been traditionally bound to a national, local or ethnic remit. The worldwide growth in the demand for entertainment materials has outstripped old constraints and inhibitions. The prospects for future growth are so great as to fuel a constant pressure towards acquisition and consolidation.

In 1988 the U.S. majors earned $1.13 billion in domestic sales. Foreign earnings alone in 1990, however, are likely to equal domestic revenues, even though the latter are still increasing. Those figures help to explain why in 1985 Rupert Murdoch's News Corporation was keen to acquire 20th Century Fox for $575 million and why the Qintex Group of Australia paid even more a few years later for United Artists. Meanwhile the relatively small but then rapidly growing British company, TV South, decided to buy MTM entertainment—a deal that later turned sour. Giancarlo Parretti of Italy bought a controlling interest in the Cannon Group, having already acquired France's Pathé Cinema. The objective of all of these transactions was to expand into a business which was undergoing a rapid upward leap in its overall operations around the world but of which the U.S. market remains the bedrock.

The moving image has not been the only targeted medium, of course. Hachette of France acquired the Grolier Company in 1987, as well as the Diamandis magazine group; Hachette paid $1.2 billion in all, and thereby established a business with an annual sales figure of $4 billion, half of it outside France.

It was the linking of Time and Warner which produced the largest single media enterprise hitherto known anywhere in the world; the merged company had a total sales figure of $8.7 billion. In some ways the merger could be seen, at least from the point of view of Time, which had had an unhappy experience with cable in the 1970s, more as an old-style defensive merger than a new-industry "synergy." At the moment the Time-Warner merger was announced, stock markets rumored bids for Time from Germany's Bertelsmann and Rupert Murdoch's News Corporation. Time was a farraginous mixture of businesses, containing among them book publishing and some cable (including the successful HBO). Warner had added the Lorimar company to its already successful film and television interests, but this, too, was more to ward off predators than out of a deliberate corporate plan.

The Time-Warner marriage set off a wave of fears for the survival of pluralism in the American media. Rupert Murdoch already owned *TV Guide.* Time already owned Little Brown. So would print media, owned by a moving image entrepreneur, still feel free to criticize the latter's product? Was there to be a collapse of proper journalistic standards? Would television news programs transmitted by one of these companies criticize the movies (and books) produced in the same group or deliberately castigate or ignore those produced by a rival group?

Familiar critics of the U.S. news media such as Ben Bagdikian and Joshua Meyrowitz, Todd Gitlin and Nicholas Johnson, have all warned that such consequences are inevitable. "The lords of the global village have their own political agenda," writes Bagdikian. "Together, they exert a homogenizing power over ideas, culture and commerce that affects populations larger than any in history. Neither Caesar, nor Hitler, Franklin Roosevelt nor any Pope, has commanded as much power to shape the information on which so many people depend to make decisions on everything from whom to vote for to what to eat." The dangers are of course precisely those expressed, but as yet there is little evidence that they are real. Indeed, a whole new world of independent companies has emerged in many countries, and these remain outside the newly homogenizing forces, the new global empires of information.

Cultural Imperialism and Cultural Identity

The work of Ali Mohammadi is part of a recent shift in critical scholarship of international communication toward a focus on the construction of national-cultural identities in the former European colonies of Africa, Asia, and the Americas. From this perspective, mass media, along with other cultural forms such as literature, do not operate in any simple or unidirectional way to impose cultural domination. Mass media and popular culture are caught up in conflicts over cultural tradition and national independence. For example, in *The Empire Writes Back* (Routledge, 1989), Bill Ashcroft, Gareth Griffiths, and Helen Tifflin show that writers in postcolonial societies do not simply adopt European literary forms and styles. Rather, they *adapt* them to the complex and contradictory problems of expressing their own cultural situation, in particular the problem of resisting European domination.

In the following selection from "Cultural Imperialism and Cultural Identity," in John Downing, Ali Mohammadi, and Annabelle Sreberny-Mohammadi, eds., *Questioning the Media: A Critical Introduction,* 2d ed. (Sage Publications, 1995), Mohammadi argues that global media today are controlled by a narrow set of powerful economic and political interests and are enmeshed within a new imperialist order. However, in the case of the Iranian revolution, resistance to the U.S.-supported dictatorship of the Shah was fermented through the use of alternative, "small" media: cheaply produced and widely distributed cassette recordings of religious leaders. These recordings helped cultivate a powerful sense of Muslim identity and solidarity among many otherwise diverse segments of the Iranian population, which, according to Mohammadi, played a large part in the overthrow of the Shah's regime.

Mohammadi teaches and conducts his research at Nottingham Trent University in England. He and Annabelle Srebreny-Mohammadi have written more extensively on postcolonialism and the Iranian situation in *Small Media, Big Revolution: Communications, Culture, and the Iranian Revolution* (University of Minnesota Press, 1994).

Key Concept: alternative media and the struggle over cultural identity

INTERNATIONAL POWERS AND NATIONAL CULTURES: AN UNEVEN CONTEXT

One description of the world we live in it "postimperialist." Much of world history from 1945 has centered on the struggles of subjugated peoples to extricate themselves from the European empires of the nineteenth century and to create the newly independent nations of Africa, the Middle East, and Asia. But despite the demise of political imperialism, the economic dominance of the West has meant that many nations of the Third World find themselves still tied in very complex ways to the dynamics of Western industrial societies. Hence these Third World nations find it very difficult to pursue their own definitions of, and paths to, independent development. These new ties are different from the older ties of imperialism. The new kinds of ties are often referred to as ties of *dependency*, and "cultural imperialism" has been analyzed as one major form of dependency. The purpose of this [selection] is to analyze this new cultural imperialism and to show the vitally important role that communications technologies and flows of cultural products have in keeping planetary ties of dependency alive.

This process will be illustrated through a detailed examination of one Third World country, Iran. Although at the turn of the twentieth century the British and the Russians competed for influence in Iran, and the United States played a major role in Iranian affairs, helping to reinstate the shah in 1953, Iran was never directly colonized. Iran tried very deliberately to use communications for a particular development strategy, one strongly supported by the West, but found that the costs were greater than the benefits. This is a case study with powerful implications for other Third World nations and for mainstream —noncritical—communications analysis.

WHAT IS IMPERIALISM?

The essence of imperialism is domination by one nation over another. That relationship might be direct or indirect, and might be based on a mixture of military, political, and economic controls. There have been many different forms of imperial relations throughout world history, from the Greek and Roman empires to the Persian, Moghul, Chinese, Ottoman, and many others. But the forms of empire that have had the greatest impact on our contemporary world are the European, American, and Japanese forms of empire that prevailed through the nineteenth century into the twentieth century. Even European domination went through various stages. There were relationships that were more purely economic or "mercantilist," as in the early Portuguese empire, where the European power essentially extracted the resources it required, whether gold or ivory or slaves, from the dominated territory. Often such relations required military conquest on the outset and a continued military presence to enforce the economic exploitation.

By the end of the nineteenth century, a new form of relation had been developed that was based on the formal conquest, annexation, and administration of territories by the imperial powers. As Hobsbawm (1989) summarizes the process:

> Between 1880 and 1914... most of the world outside Europe and the Americas was formally partitioned into territories under the formal rule or informal political domination of one or the other of a handful of states: mainly Great Britain, France, Germany, Italy, the Netherlands, Belgium, the USA and Japan. (p. 57)

About one-quarter of the globe's land surface was distributed or redistributed among a half dozen states, ushering in the age of imperialism based on colonial rule. This form of direct political and administrative domination helped to create a truly planetary capitalist economy in which economic transactions and flows of goods, capital, and people now penetrated into the most remote regions. The world was fundamentally divided into strong and weak, advanced and backward areas (Hobsbawm, 1989).

There were many different reactions to and consequences of imperialism, both within the "mother" power, such as movements for democracy, for socialism, and for women's rights, and also within the Third World, where revolution —as in Mexico between 1910 and 1920 or in China toward the end of the nineteenth century—or growing anticolonial movements for liberation—as in India —began to develop. Since 1945, the "postwar world" has been defined by these struggles against imperial domination and the success of independence movements in the creation of "new," independent political nations in Africa, Asia, and the Middle East. Thus, for example, India freed itself from the British in 1947, Indonesia liberated itself from the Dutch in 1960, Zaire was freed from Belgian domination in 1960, and Algeria became independent from the French in 1962 (Harris, 1987).

This process of political independence might appear to be the end of the story, but in fact it is only the start of a new global dynamic that we might label the process of *cultural imperialism* or *cultural dependency*. When the colonial powers packed their bags and removed their nationals from administrative positions directly running the government and the economy, that was not the end of their influence. Often they left behind a European language, as the "lingua franca" of the country's new governing classes. They left behind European values and attitudes, including religion, ways of organizing public life, styles of politics, forms of education, and professional training, clothing styles, and many other cultural habits, none of which had existed prior to colonial domination. All of these phenomena continued to have effects long after the formal, direct, political rule of the colonies was ended, and have created a new kind of model of domination called *neocolonialism*. In turn, neocolonialism has sparked new kinds of struggles to eradicate this enduring cultural influence in the Third World. Let us look at the constitution of this Third World and then examine how cultural issues came to be such a central focus in current international politics....

CULTURAL IDENTITY IN THE THIRD WORLD

It was the independence movements in the developing world that made many people aware of the cultural dimensions of colonial domination. Many leaders in the Third World have paid serious and continuing attention to the issue of cultural freedom. For example, one of Gandhi's major concerns while he led India's independence movement was how to create an independent national identity that could unite the Indian people, who were scattered over 750,000 villages and spoke many different languages. Concerned about how to foster national unity in the face of the legacy of British cultural domination, Gandhi once proclaimed:

> I do not want my house to be walled on all sides and my windows to be stuffed. I want the culture of all lands to be blown about my house as freely as possible but I refuse to be blown off my feet by any one of them. (quoted in Hamelink, 1983, p. 26)

In a major echo of Gandhi's concern, at a key 1973 meeting of the heads of states of the nonaligned nations there was a formal joint declaration that the activities of imperialism were not limited to the economic and political domains, but encompassed social and cultural areas as well, imposing a foreign ideological domination on the peoples of developing world. Many Third World nations were becoming aware of the superiority of the advanced world, in communications technologies but also in communications software, the news, entertainment, and other cultural products that the technologies transmitted, and that, as a result, their own national cultures and identities had become threatened (Harris, 1987).

It is not very hard to recognize that the continuance of Western dominance over Third World nations, even after their formal independence, was based partly on advanced technologies, including communication technologies. But it was also based on an ideology, accepted in many parts of the Third World, that there was only one path to economic development, which was to emulate the process of development of Western industrial capitalist societies.

In the 1960s, when certain Third World nations did not appear to be developing economically as fast as they had been expected to, Western analysts began to develop models and theories of development and to explain the "blockages" to development that they thought prevented Third World countries from developing like Western ones....

What was valuable in the traditional culture was defined, effectively, as anything that did not impede the growth of Western capitalist endeavors; what had to change culturally was anything that interfered with this process....

To begin to draw attention to some of these issues, it is instructive to examine a major Middle Eastern nation at the heart of the U.S. and Western oil-related strategy in the region, namely, Iran.... Iran is ... an instructive case study because it was never directly colonized, so an examination of the impact of Western culture in Iran shows vividly how neocolonial subordination and cultural inferiority can be fostered from a distance, without the elaborate machinery of colonial rule.

THE CASE OF IRAN

Iran is located on the southern border of Central Asia and stretches south to the Persian Gulf. It borders Turkey to the northwest and Afghanistan and Pakistan to the east. In 1994 it had a population of more than 60 million. From a geopolitical viewpoint, the strategic location of Iran between East and West is very crucial. Iran's political system up to 1979 was monarchical dictatorship, but then, 2,500 years of kingship were terminated by the Iranian revolution under the leadership of the Ayatollah Khomeini.

Media and Development in Iran

Through a close look at the process of development in Iran we can see a clear pattern of dependent economic development that was centrally based on the export of crude oil and raw materials, with expansion linked to foreign investment. This economic dependence provided the basis for political and military dependence in both technological and human expertise. In the 1970s businessmen from all over the world waited in Tehran hotels to clinch multimillion-dollar deals of all kinds. Slowly, too, the media in Iran tried to convince people of the benefits of modernity and created new needs that consumer durables could satisfy.

Prior to World War II, Iran did not have a national broadcasting system. Iran's first radio transmitter went on the air in 1940. Radio programs were limited to evening broadcasts that consisted of the national anthem, major messages from government, news, and some Persian and Western music. In the early days of radio, loudspeakers and radio receivers were hooked up in various parts of Tehran, the capital, and people were very excited by this unprecedented form of communication. When the national anthem was played, people would rise and stand still. This was one of the first modern symbols of Iranian nationhood, broadcast over electronic media imported from the advanced world. Slowly, radio was used to maintain political control, to spread the ideological rhetoric of modernization, and to prepare Iranians for the neocolonial relationship that would strengthen after World War II.

In 1959, the last shah of Iran was persuaded by an imaginative urban entrepreneur to allow the establishment of commercial television. The entrepreneur was the son of a rich businessman whose wealth was based on importing Pepsi Cola from the United States. This first television station was allowed to operate tax free for five years while it developed commercial television and promoted the expansion of a consumer market, as in the United States. The family who controlled the television monopoly also controlled the importation of most television receivers, prossessing the franchise of RCA products in Iran.

Television became a multiplier of Western and consumption values. These were overtly displayed in advertisements for new consumer products and were also embedded in the depiction of Western lifestyles carried by American films and television series such as *I Love Lucy* and *Bonanza*. Private television supported the monarchy's strategy of capitalist development. After some studies were undertaken, and worried that the Baha'i religious sect was monopolizing television, the shah decided to take over private television and transform it into a government-financed and -operated service. In 1966 National Iranian Television started broadcasting (its first message was from the shah, of course), and among the first test week's programming was the broadcast of the shah's birthday celebration. Soon radio was amalgamated with television to create National Iranian Radio and Television (NIRT). Consumerism was still encouraged through advertising, but, more important, NIRT tried to foster support for the regime through the glorification of the monarchy and support for modernization, maintaining the state ideology. Every royal activity was broadcast, and the glorious history of 2,500 years of Persian monarchy was celebrated wherever possible, but the media also propagated the idea that the shah's major concern was to modernize Iran along the lines of the countries of Western Europe; television nightly news began with images of dams and new buildings, the physical symbols of development.

Radio and television were given substantial government budgets, so that coverage expanded rapidly. From 2 television transmitters in 1966, the number rose to 88 by 1974, and coverage increased from 2.1 million people to 15 million of both urban and rural populations, more than half the country; radio coverage was almost universal (Mohammadi, 1976). By the mid-1970s, NIRT had became the second-largest broadcasting network in Asia, after NHK of Japan. Thus most of the nation was connected through broadcasting, linking small villages with major urban centers and creating a novel national audience.

Yet, at the same time, literacy levels remained low, particularly for women, and there were not enough primary schools to accommodate all children of school age. Publishing and the press were strictly censored, so there was little choice among the dull daily newspapers, which thus had very low circulations. One commentator noted that "if Iran continues on its present path, it will be the first nation in the world to have nationally spread television before a nationally spread press." Thus Iran seemed to leap over the stage of literacy and print development, moving almost directly from a traditional oral culture to an electronic one.

Even a brief glance at Iranian mass media in the mid-1970s would have indicated that the broadcast or published materials were not designed to preserve national culture or to raise the level of public education. Rather, they promoted the alluring manifestation of Western culture, with little consideration of the urgent needs and demands of Iranian society; they did little more than amuse and entertain their audience. One international study made in 1975 revealed that of 11 developing countries studied, NIRT had one of the highest levels of imported television programming, including Western feature films—78% of all television content—and broadcast the lowest proportion of serious programs—only 22% of total broadcast time. Typical imported programs were *Baretta, Star Trek, Marcus Welby, MD, Tarzan*, and the soap opera *Days of Our Lives*. When homemade programs were aired they became extremely popular, but much domestic programming was rather anemic because of actual and self-censorship. The prevailing policy seemed to disregard the cultural implications of importing so much Western media content, which carried Western lifestyles, gender roles, consumption values, and so on. And whereas, for many developing countries, the economic argument that it is much cheaper to buy foreign programming than to produce your own had some justification, NIRT's large budgets did not support such an argument. It seemed to be safer for the regime to allow a lot of Western entertainment to be imported than allow possibly critical homemade programs to appear (Motamed-Nejad, 1976).

The rapid expansion of broadcasting was a central element of the shah's ambitious development project, as he tried to use the communications media to help bring about the change from a traditional to a modern society. But it failed because the modernization process did not go far enough; indeed, the strategy has been described as "pseudo-modernization," a desire for the superficial style of modernity without the deeper structural changes that true development requires. For example, the government, through the mass media, talked about modernization but failed to provide adequate and coherent national health care or education. It spent millions in developing NIRT, but failed to electrify large areas, so many rural people ran their televisions and lighting from small portable generators. It talked about improving working conditions, but would not allow labor unions to operate. It established many universities, but would not allow the free exchange of ideas or free access to written materials. Iranian writers, artists, and broadcasters all had to fit in with the prevailing rhetoric of modernization, and no criticism was allowed. The security system of SAVAK (the shah's secret police) was waiting for any oppositional voices to be raised. Severe political repression thus blocked popular participation and discussion of social needs, the heart of political development.

Those in the educated middle class felt frustrated about the lack of political participation and the lack of cultural freedom, which allowed importation of American television but blocked the production of good, critical, indigenous programs. They felt frustrated as the political concerns of the state interfered in the legal system, the educational system, and the broadcasting system, undermining professional practices and independence. They felt the pinch of rampant inflation in the 1970s, with house and car prices rocketing, and watched as foreign "experts" were favored over Iranians with comparable skills.

The traditional middle classes, particularly the bazaar merchants and the clergy, were threatened by this Westernized mode of development. The economic position of the bazaaris was being undermined by large multinational corporations and agribusiness, and the social authority of the clergy was threatened by secular education and the media. They were also horrified at the effects Western values were having on the fabric of Iranian society. For example, the system of dating and marriage shown in the imported Western programming was totally in contradiction with the Islamic tradition of marriage, in which parents play a very significant role in selecting a suitable spouse and dating of any sort without the presence of a relative is not allowed. Khomeini had been speaking out since the 1940s about the negative impact of Western values, and warned that the media were propaganda vehicles for Western imperialists who were trying to undermine Iran. Some religious authorities publicly denounced watching television, and others declared that having a television was a sinful act. The city of Qum, which is the equivalent of the Vatican for Iranian Shi'ite Muslims, actually banned television during the shah's reign.

From 1976, helped by Jimmy Carter's human rights policy, both the secular opposition and the religious opposition began to use a variety of small media to voice their objections to the regime. Professional groups such as lawyers and writers wrote "open letters" to the shah, demanding an end to regime intervention in the process of law and greater freedom of expression. The religious opposition also began to mobilize, and developed a communications system quite independent from the big media of the state to politicize the people. The leaders used the national network of mosques and bazaars to preach their Islamic identity against the dependent Westernization of the shah. When Khomeini left his isolated place of exile in a small village in Iraq for the outskirts of Paris in 1977, he became the focus of much Western media attention. Also, the religious network transmitted his speeches across the international telephone lines to Tehran, and within hours thousands of audiocassettes of his voice were available on the streets of the capital and were carried to other cities and villages for all to hear—a new international electronic pulpit. In a still very oral culture, where the clergy have great social authority and are used to addressing ordinary people at the mosques, this was very powerful (Sreberny-Mohammadi & Mohammadi, 1994).

A popular movement against the shah began to grow, and when demonstrators were killed through regime violence, the Islamic mourning pattern of the seventh and fortieth days gave the demonstrations a religious rhythm. Gradually, political groups—communist, socialist, nationalist, democratic—banned by the regime resurfaced and countless photocopied leaflets began to circulate, setting out analyses, making political demands, organizing demonstrations. Thus certain small media, particularly audiocassettes and leaflets, were used very effectively in the Iranian popular mobilization.... These small media are interesting because they are so easily reproduced, making it extremely difficult for any regime to block their circulation. When the military tried to maintain order and took over NIRT in November 1978, the personnel went on strike, so for three months radio and television were run by the military while the professionals produced underground newspapers debunking the regime news.

Thus a combination of religious authority and small media mobilized some of the largest demonstrations in recent history, bringing together modern and traditional groups united in hostility to the pattern of Westernized development of the shah, combining a mixture of economic discontents, political frustrations, and cultural concerns into a single slogan, "Down with the shah." In January 1979, the shah left "on holiday," never to return, and in February, the Ayatollah Khomeini established the Islamic Republic of Iran.

CONCLUSION

The communication and development model failed to understand the historically different cultural contexts of Third World societies; as applied to Iran, it served to bring the West into Iranian living rooms and allowed Iranians to compare themselves with Westerners, exacerbating existing economic, political, and cultural frustrations. The model failed to pay attention to political development or less quantifiable aspirations such as equality, justice, freedom, identity, and even happiness. In the context of Iran, the communications and development process seemed to suggest that Western patterns of life and attitudes were the only ones of value, to be imitated by Iranians, and that indigenous Iranian culture had little to offer. The process created not only great gaps of wealth between urban elites and the rural poor but also a deep sense of cultural inferiority, which the clergy effectively used to mobilize people against the regime.

Frantz Fanon (1967) presents a vivid image of the effects of Western cultural products on the people of the Third World:

> Young people have at their disposition leisure occupations designed for the youth of capitalist countries: detective novels, penny-in-the-slot machines, sexy photographs, pornographic literature, films banned to those under sixteen, and above all alcohol. In the West the family circle, the effects of education and the relatively high standard of living of the working classes provide a more or less efficient protection against the harmful action of these pastimes. But in an African country, where mental development is uneven, where the violent collision of two worlds has considerably shaken old traditions and thrown the universe of the perceptions out of focus, the impressionability and sensibility of the young Africans are at the mercy of the various assaults made upon them by the very nature of Western culture. (pp. 157–158)

Although written about a different cultural context, these words could also be applied to Iran. The development strategy in Iran was undermining the very basis of cultural identity and the traditional values of Iranian society. The rapid change from small-scale self-sufficiency to commodity production for the markets, the neglect of channels for political participation, and the blocking of self-expression and indigenous cultural development undermined the harmony and tranquility of cultural life. The process of development, by definition, upsets the pattern of life that went before, but in the West that process went hand in hand with the basic values and cultural patterns of those societies. In Iran, as in much of the developing world, development was replaced by a mimetic Westernization, a copying of the superficial elements of the modern West without the fundamental political and social changes required. Economic dependency, as in the spread of montage industries, which merely assemble consumer technologies developed elsewhere (thus not helping an independent economic sector to grow), was supported by cultural dependency, in which mass media broadcast news and cultural entertainment programs more attuned to the markets of industrial nations or regime needs than the cultural habits of the Iranian people.

Iran is a unique example of a Third World country that implemented the communication and development model to accelerate the process of modernization, and the model failed dramatically. Communications can help people find new norms and harmony in a period of transition, but in the Iranian case, the effect was totally the reverse.

The Iranian experience makes us question the powerful media/powerful effects model of communication. The shah could control all the media, but he could not produce political legitimacy. And Iranians could watch a lot of American programming and still prefer their own values. Thus both the communications and development model—which suggested that media could play such an important, positive, role in economic and political development—*and* the cultural imperialism model—which said that media were carriers of Western values that would swamp Third World cultures—are too one-dimensional, as the Iranian movement has shown.

The rhetoric of revolution included slogans against Westernization, consumerism, and the idea of self-determination, expressed in the slogan of "Not East, nor West, only Islam." The tragedy of Iran is that although cultural identity may be an important appeal against the forces of Westernization, it alone does not guarantee broader progressive social values such as freedom and justice, which were fundamental demands of the popular movement. Also, many felt that their religious identity was their cultural identity, not anticipating the rigid fundamentalism that ensued; currently, many Iranians are concerned that their traditional Iranian culture and its music and dance are being suppressed. Many have been killed or imprisoned, and many others have left Iran. The Islamic Republic has thus bitterly disappointed many hopes, and has inherited many of the old problems that the shah did not solve. Analyzing the global context in which Iranian modernization and then popular resistance took place helps to explain the deep dilemmas of political, economic, and cultural development that confront Third World nations.

REFERENCES

Fannon, F. (1967). *The wretched of the earth.* Middlesex: Penguin.

Hamelink, C. J. (1983). *Finance and information.* Norwood, NJ: Ablex.

Hobsbawm, E. (1989). *Age of empire.* New York: Vintage.

Mohammadi, A. (1976). *Development-support communication and instructional learning centers for rural areas in Iran.* Unpublished doctoral dissertation, Columbia University.

Motamed-Nejad, K. (1976). *Communication and Westernization.* Tehran: College of Mass Communication.

Sreberny-Mohammadi, A., & Mohammadi, A. (1994). *Small media, big revolution: Communications, culture and the Iranian revolution.* Minneapolis: University of Minnesota.

ACKNOWLEDGMENTS

1.1 From Harold D. Lasswell, "The Structure and Function of Communication in Society," in Lyman Bryson, ed., *The Communication of Ideas* (Institute for Religious & Social Studies, 1948), pp. 37–48, 51. Copyright © 1948 by The Louis Finkelstein Institute for Religious and Social Studies–Jewish Theological Seminary of America. Reprinted by permission.

1.2 From Paul F. Lazarsfeld and Robert K. Merton, "Mass Communication, Popular Taste, and Organized Social Action," in William Schramm and Donald F. Roberts, eds., *The Process and Effects of Mass Communication*, rev. ed. (University of Illinois Press, 1977). Copyright © 1977 by The Louis Finkelstein Institute for Religious and Social Studies. Reprinted by permission. Notes omitted.

1.3 From Kurt Lang and Gladys Engel Lang, "The Mass Media and Voting," in Eugene Burdick and Arthur J. Brodbeck, eds., *American Voting Behavior* (Free Press, 1959). Copyright © 1959 by The Free Press. Reprinted by permission of The Free Press, a division of Simon & Schuster.

1.4 From Elihu Katz, "The Two-Step Flow of Communication: An Up-to-Date Report on an Hypothesis," *Public Opinion Quarterly*, vol. 21, no. 1 (Spring 1957), pp. 61–62, 65–77. Copyright © 1957 by University of Chicago Press. Reprinted by permission. Some notes omitted.

1.5 From Jonathan Cohen, "Parasocial Relations and Romantic Attraction: Gender and Dating Status Differences," *Journal of Broadcasting and Electronic Media*, vol. 41 (Fall 1997). Copyright © 1997 by The Broadcast Education Association. Reprinted by permission. Notes and some references omitted.

2.1 From Charles R. Wright, *Mass Communication: A Sociological Perspective*, 3rd ed. (Random House, 1986). Copyright © 1986 by McGraw-Hill Companies. Reprinted by permission of McGraw-Hill.

2.2 From Elihu Katz, Jay G. Blumler, and Michael Gurevitch, "Utilization of Mass Communication by the Individual," in Jay G. Blumler and Elihu Katz, eds., *The Uses of Mass Communications* (Sage Publications, 1974), pp. 19–32. Copyright © 1974 by Sage Publications, Inc. Reprinted by permission.

2.3 From Richard C. Vincent and Michael D. Basil, "College Students' News Gratifications, Media Use, and Current Events Knowledge," *Journal of Broadcasting and Electronic Media*, vol. 41 (Summer 1997). Copyright © 1997 by The Broadcast Education Association. Reprinted by permission.

3.1 From George Gerbner, Larry Gross, Michael Morgan, and Nancy Signorielli, "The 'Mainstreaming' of America: Violence Profile No. 11," *Journal of Communication*, vol. 30, no. 3 (1980), pp. 10–29. Copyright © 1980 by George Gerbner. Reprinted by permission. Some notes omitted.

3.2 From Michael Morgan, "Television and Democracy," in Ian Angus and Sut Jhally, eds., *Cultural Politics in Contemporary America* (Routledge, 1989). Copyright © 1989 by Michael Morgan. Reprinted by permission. Notes omitted.

4.1 From Maxwell E. McCombs and Donald L. Shaw, "The Agenda-Setting Function of Mass Media," *Public Opinion Quarterly*, vol. 36, no. 1 (Spring 1972), pp. 176–182, 184–187. Copyright © 1972 by University of Chicago Press. Reprinted by permission.

4.2 From Kathleen Hall Jamieson, *Packaging the Presidency: A History and Criticism of Presidential Campaign Advertising*, 3rd ed. (Oxford University Press, 1996). Copyright © 1984, 1992, 1996 by Kathleen Hall Jamieson. Reprinted by permission of Oxford University Press, Inc. Notes omitted.

5.1 From Marshall McLuhan, *Understanding Media: The Extensions of Man* (McGraw-Hill, 1964). Copyright © 1964 by Marshall McLuhan; renewed 1980 by Corinne McLuhan. Reprinted by permission of The Canadian Speakers' and Writers' Service Limited, agents for Corinne McLuhan and the Estate of Marshall McLuhan.

5.2 From Neil Postman, *Amusing Ourselves to Death: Public Discourse in the Age of Show Business* (Penguin, 1985), pp. 83–98. Copyright © 1985 by Neil Postman. Reprinted by permission of Viking Penguin, a division of Penguin Putnam, Inc. Notes omitted.

5.3 From Joshua Meyrowitz, *No Sense of Place: The Impact of Electronic Media on Social Behavior* (Oxford University Press, 1985), pp. 131–149, 353. Copyright © 1985 by Joshua Meyrowitz. Reprinted by permission of Oxford University Press, Inc. Some notes and references omitted.

6.1 From David Easter and Jarice Hanson, "Deregulation and the Information Society: Assessing the Marketplace Philosophy," in Jarice Hanson, ed., *Advances in Telematics, vol. 2* (Ablex Publishing, 1994). Copyright © 1994 by Ablex Publishing Corporation. Reprinted by permission.

6.2 Excerpted from Robert W. McChesney, *Corporate Media and the Threat to Democracy* (Seven Stories Press, 1997). Copyright © 1997 by Robert W. McChesney. Reprinted by permission of Seven Stories Press.

7.1 From Dwight MacDonald, "A Theory of Mass Culture," in Bernard Rosenberg and David Manning White, eds., *Mass Culture: The Popular Arts in America* (Free Press, 1957). Originally published in *Diogenes*, no. 3 (Summer 1953). Copyright © 1953 by Intercultural Publications, Inc. Reprinted by permission. Notes omitted.

7.2 From John G. Cawelti, "Popular Culture/Multiculturalism," *Journal of Popular Culture*, vol. 30, no. 1 (Summer 1996). Copyright © 1996 by *Journal of Popular Culture*. Reprinted by permission. Notes and references omitted.

8.1 From Herbert I. Schiller, *The Mind Managers* (Beacon Press, 1973), pp. 1, 3–5, 8–23, 192–193. Copyright © 1973 by Herbert I. Schiller. Reprinted by permission of Beacon Press.

8.2 From Martin A. Lee and Norman Solomon, *Unreliable Sources: A Guide to Detecting Bias in News Media* (Carol Publishing Group, 1990). Copyright © 1990, 1991 by Martin A. Lee and Norman Solomon. Reprinted by permission of Carol Publishing Group. A Lyle Stuart Book.

9.1 From Stuart Ewen, *Captains of Consciousness: Advertising and the Social Roots of the Consumer Culture* (McGraw-Hill, 1976), pp. 23–37, 41–48. Copyright © 1976 by Stuart Ewen. Reprinted by permission.

9.2 From Dallas W. Smythe, *Dependency Road: Communications, Capitalism, Consciousness, and Canada* (Ablex Publishing, 1981). Copyright © 1981 by Dallas W. Smythe. Reprinted by permission of Ablex Publishing Corporation.

9.3 From Sut Jhally, "Image-Based Culture: Advertising and Popular Culture," *The World and I* (July 1990), pp. 507–519. Copyright © by *The World and I*, a publication of The Washington Times Corporation. Reprinted by permission.

10.1 From James W. Carey, *Communication as Culture: Essays on Media and Society* (Unwin Hyman, 1989). Copyright © 1988, 1989, 1992 by Routledge, Inc. Reprinted by permission. Notes omitted.

15.2   From Ali Mohammadi, "Cultural Imperialism and Cultural Identity," in John Downing, Ali Mohammadi, and Annabelle Sreberny-Mohammadi, eds., *Questioning the Media: A Critical Introduction,* 2d ed. (Sage Publications, 1995), pp. 363–377. Copyright © 1995 by Sage Publications, Inc. Reprinted by permission.

Index